SONGS OF GENERATIONS: NEW PEARLS OF YIDDISH SONG

with Yiddish Texts and Music, Parallel Transliterations, Translations, Historical Background, Guitar Chords

Compiled by Eleanor Gordon Mlotek and Joseph Mlotek

Translations by Barnett Zumoff
Zalmen Mlotek, Music Editor
Illustrations by Tsirl Waletzky

Published by the Workmen's Circle
New York, NY

Copyright © by the Workmen's Circle
45 East 33 Street, New York, N. Y. 10016
and by Joseph Mlotek and Eleanor Mlotek

Illustrations copyright © by Tsirl Waletzky

All rights reserved. No part of this
publication may be reproduced without
the prior permission of the publisher.

Library of Congress Catalogue
ISBN 1-877909-65-3

l. Songs, Yiddish. 2. Folksongs, Yiddish.
3. Jewish, Music. I. Mlotek, Eleanor G.
II. Mlotek, Joseph. III. Zumoff, Barnett.
IV. Mlotek, Zalmen. V. Waletzky, Tsirl.
VI. Workmen's Circle.

English Calligraphy by Peggy H. Davis
Yiddish Calligraphy by Chonen Kiel

Music Engraving and Page Composition by Chelsea Music Engraving, Inc.

Printed in U.S.A.

**This book was published
with the aid of a gift from
William Wernick, in loving
memory of his dear wife
Ruth Wernick**

---

and gifts by the following major contributors:

Philip Adelman, New York

Esther Burstein, Brooklyn, New York

Harry and Marilyn Cagin, Cleveland, Ohio

Abraham Fajman, Elizabeth, New Jersey

Sarah Friedman, Detroit, Michigan
in memory of her beloved husband Morris

Noah Lewin, Miami Beach, Florida

Abraham and Isaac Lusky and Families, Charlotte, North Carolina
in memory of their beloved parents Yisroel and Feygl Lusky

Victor Saltsman, Margate, Florida
in memory of his beloved brother Shloyme and sister-in-law Bernice

Shelby Shapiro, Washington, D.C.

Moishe Shiveck, Montreal, Quebec
in memory of his beloved mother Mildred

Arnold Sisk, Hallandale, Florida
in memory of his beloved wife Rose

Sender and Mindelle Wajsman, North Miami Beach, Florida

W.C. Southern Region Cultural Foundation, Florida

Motl and Dr. Emma Zelmanowicz, Bronx, New York

CONTENTS

Preface by Elie Wiesel / vi

Foreword by Dov Noy / vii

Introduction by Compilers / viii

The Performance of
Yiddish Songs by Zalmen Mlotek / xiv

SONGS OF CHILDHOOD

Shteyt in feld a beymele / 2
Shlof, mayn feygele / 4
Nor a mame / 6
Heyda nu, tsurik in kheyder / 8
Oy, vet mikh der rebe shmaysn / 9
A sheyner tog / 11
Ver der ershter vet lakhn / 13
A yingele, a meydele / 16
Mir kumen on / 18

SONGS OF LOVE

Brontshele / 21
Ikh hob dikh lib vi a peysakhdikn rosl / 23
Ikh bin shoyn a meydl in di yorn / 24
Shoyn tsvey-dray yor az mir firn a libe / 26
Ikh zits mir bay mayn arbet un ikh arbet / 28
Di sapozhkelekh / 30
Shoyn haynt dray yor az ikh stradaye / 32
Tsvey taybelekh / 34
Ikh zits mir bay der arbet / 36
Du meydele, du fayns / 37
Nem mir aroys a ber fun vald / 39
Kh'hob gelibt a meydl fun akhtsn yor / 41
Vu bistu geven? / 43
Vos dreystu zikh arum bay mayne fentsterlekh? / 45
Vu iz dos gesele? / 47
Er hot mir tsugezogt / 49
Der kashtnboym / 51
Sorele / 53
In der fintster / 56
In mayn gortn / 57
Es iz nokh faran aza blum / 59

SONGS OF WORK AND HOPE

Eyder ikh leyg zikh shlofn / 62
S'falt a shney / 64
Alef—indikes / 67
Shlof, mayn kind, shlof keseyder / 69
Koyft a tsaytung! / 71
Der kremer / 74
Yidn shmidn / 76
Di svet-shap / 78
Shnel loyfn di reder / 80
Di lena / 83
Barikadn / 84
Di tsukunft / 86
Zingendik / 88
Mayne khaveyrim / 90
Dos naye lid / 93

HUMOROUS SONGS AND SONGS FOR CELEBRATIONS AND PARTIES

Lekhayim! / 95
Khatskele / 97
Lomir onheybn tsu derklern / 97
Funem sheynem vortsl aroys / 102
Tonu rabonen / 104
Hob ikh mir a mantl / 106
Hirsh Dovid / 108
Kol mekadesh shevii / 110
In a shtetele pitshe-poy / 113
Itsik shpitsik / 115
A gut-morgn, Feyge Soshe / 117
Yosl un Sore-Dvoshe / 119
Varnitshkes / 122
Der oytser / 124
Nisim, nisim / 127
Nisim venifloes / 130
Tshiribim / 132

HISTORICAL SONGS

Lid fun Mendl Beylis / 135
Lid fun Leo Frenk / 138
Khurbn titanik / 141
Lid fun kishenever pogrom / 144
Di khasene iz geven in der kazarme / 146
Zishe Breytbard / 147

SONGS OF THE STREET

Vilne / 151
Sore un Rifke / 153
Krokhmalne gas / 156
Der yold iz mikh mekane / 160
Ikh ganve in der nakht / 162
Dos kleyne tsigaynerl / 165
Shpil, gitar / 167

HASSIDIC AND NATIONAL SONGS

Fraytik oyf der nakht / 170
Amol iz geven a yid / 172
Der eybershter iz der mekhutn / 174
Royz, royz / 176
Dos freylekhe khosidl / 177
Tsvey briv tsum lyader rebn / 179
Tsion / 181
In mitn veg shteyt a boym / 183
Shnirele perele, gilderne fon / 185
Tsi kenstu dos land? / 187
Khalutsim gikher / 189
Yidish redt zikh azoy sheyn / 191
Dos lid fun mayn dor / 193

SONGS IN A QUIET AND REFLECTIVE MOOD

Leyg dayn kop / 197
Mit farmakhte oygn / 198
Di beryozkele / 200
Ikh un di velt / 202
Aleyn in veg / 205
Fregt di velt an alte kashe / 205

THE GOLDEN LAND

Lozt arayn! / 209
Tunkl brent a fayer / 212
Vu nemt men parnose? / 214
A grus fun di "trentshes" / 216
Hu-tsa-tsa / 219
Levin mit zayn "flying" mashin / 221
Zumer bay nakht oyf di dekher / 223

SONGS OF THE FORMER SOVIET UNION

Dzhankoye / 227
Kegn gold fun zun / 229
S'iz der step / 230
Mashinen hudyen binen / 231
Dos freylekhe shnayderl / 233
Dem zeydns nigndl / 235
A glezele lekhayim / 238
Shpil zhe mir a lidele in yidish / 240
S'yidishe meydele / 242
Ikh bin a yid! / 244
Am yisroel khay! / 246
Shuldike umshuldike / 248
Antshuldikt! / 250

THEATER SONGS

A yor nokh der khasene / 253
Ze dos kleydl, tateshi / 256
Kh'vil nisht keyn sakh nor a bisele / 258
Blimelekh tsvey / 261
Khave / 265
Vu nemt men a bisele mazl? / 267

SONGS OF THE HOLOCAUST

Her, mayn kind, vi vintn brumen / 271
Shvayg, kindele, shvayg, shvelbele / 273
Lid fun byalistoker geto / 275
Eykho / 277
Habeyt mishomayim ureey / 279
Un a yingele vet zey firn / 283

Selected Bibliography / 285
Index of Titles and First Lines / 287
List of Authors and Composers / 289
Combined Index of *Mir Trogn A Gezang, Pearls of Yiddish Song* and *Songs of Generations* / 291
Yiddish Introduction by the Compilers / 299
Yiddish Foreword by Dov Noy / 300
Yiddish Preface by Elie Wiesel / 301

TRANSLITERATION GUIDE

		As in	Example
Vowels	a	far	far
	e	bed	bet
	i	is	iz
	o	for	dos
	u	full	ful
Diphthongs	ay	why	zay
	ey	they	zey
	oy	boy	boy
Consonants	kh	Bloch	bukh
	sh	fish	fish
	ts	lets	tsu
	y	yes	yo
	zh	measure	azh
	tsh	such	pripetshik

In this volume Yiddish orthography and transliteration follow the rules formulated by the YIVO Institute for Jewish Research

Preface by Elie Wiesel

Yiddish songs pass like eternal prayers from generation to generation, from the heart to the mind, from the mind to the soul.

Transmitted this way, they bring solace to weary old men and dreamy children—and not only solace, but also delight and love.

Who was the first to sing our song?

The beloved mother who wanted to put the child to sleep?

Or the wanderer who in the hours of dusk longed to illumine his dream with rays of yesteryear?

Perhaps even the Hassid who with his melody at the *Sholosh Sudes* (third meal) sought to restrain the Sabbath with all his might?

Say "Yiddish Song" and you remember your childhood years.

Say "Yiddish Song" and you feel like singing along with the nostalgic songs like *"Oyfn pripetshik," "Rozhinkes mit mandlen," "Motele,"* and indeed Mordechai Gebirtig's *"Es brent, oy, briderlekh, es brent!"*

Religious ecstatic melodies, soulful songs, workers' songs: It is a garden with many trees, a book with various chapters, a palace with numerous rooms.

From whence does my love for the Yiddish song stem? It is older than my love for music. It is like a treasure in which you find the strings of a timeless violin.

The Yiddish song is the celebration of the Yiddish language—and its obstinate determination to vanquish despair and resignation.

Foreword by Dov Noy

The first two anthologies by Eleanor Chana and Joseph Mlotek—*Mir Trogn A Gezang* (first edition—1972) and *Pearls of Yiddish Song* (1988) occupy the top position among the Yiddish folksong collections and anthologies that were published in the post-war years.

Testimony thereof is the number of editions published and copies sold. Quantity may not always be the criterion of quality. Clearly, the new generation of Yiddish singers and lovers of Yiddish folksong and Yiddish folk music is different from those of prewar generations. Participants in Yiddish song groups and klezmer camps have for the most part received academic training and are not interested only in singing together and even then, not only in the words and melodies. They are also interested in the history of the song, its origin, its diffusion, its variants and parallels, its sources and influences. In Yiddish esthetic literature we have not been accustomed to such a scholarly approach, but the investigative interest of the compilers is apparent in their selections and publications and this unquestionably is a power of attraction for contemporary students who were raised methodologically, on intellectual curiosity.

The 125 songs of the new, third volume complement the earlier collections. They likewise represent both songs whose names of authors have been forgotten and songs whose authors are well known but which have endured by a process of folklorization, which quite frequently altered the words and music of the song, although the base, the frame, remained. In the Jewish tradition the "third time" creates a *"khazoke"*—the right of tenure, a concept which derives from the Hebrew word *"khazak"*—strong. Indeed, the third anthology *strengthens* its two older sisters.

It seems to me that the chief reason for the Mloteks' success lies foremost in the fact that the compilers have managed to unite in their anthologies and in their activities as a whole, two tendencies which generally confront each other. The synthesis unites the love of the singing people, with whom there is a constant contact, together with the love of song, as an expression of Jewish folk creativity. The two loves are closely linked by the Mlotek team and both also occupy in this respect a single and unique place in the history of our press, folklore study and ethnomusicology.

Since 1970, for more than a generation, Chana and Yosl Mlotek have been producing a column in the Forward entitled "Pearls of Yiddish Poetry," whose principal section is devoted to the reader and is actually called "Songs that Readers Recall." Thanks to this constant contact, the readers often become part of the process of searching and research. A selection of the materials printed in the first year and a half of this column's existence was published in Tel Aviv in 1974 under the same title and demonstrates abundantly that such joint work between researchers (the Mloteks actually used this pseudonym—"A. Researcher") and readers is possible and can contribute much to song biographies.

Therefore the compilers merit our appreciation for their complementary anthology. Let us wish them long and healthy years of creativity and of reciprocal contacts with a growing audience of readers, singers, researchers.

INTRODUCTION BY THE COMPILERS

This new anthology comprises songs that were either never printed before or appeared in rare and inaccessible publications—sometimes in different versions and without proper sources. It is the seventh song and poem anthology which the compilers have produced, either singly or together* and no songs have been repeated from any of their previous songbooks. Needless to say, there are still many hundreds of songs waiting to be brought back to life and to the attention of singers and music lovers, and hopefully they will be on our future agenda.

Most of the songs in this book were submitted by readers of our column *"Perl fun der yidisher poezye"* (Pearls of Yiddish Poetry) in the Yiddish newspaper *Der Forverts* (The Forward), initiated in October, 1970.

During these twenty-five years, thousands of songs were collected in correspondence and on cassettes from readers throughout the world, and they represent a veritable national Yiddish song archive. In the course of years the interest, inquiries, contributions and enthusiasm of our readers have kept our own interest unflagging and have reinforced our dedication to this effort. In recent years our participants have also been augmented by new readers from the former Soviet Russia, who receive our newspaper there or from newly-arrived immigrants in this country and Israel.

CONTENTS

The anthology comprises all the former categories of our previous publications and more. Like our previous books, in addition to folksongs, it includes songs by popular folk poets like Mordecai Gebirtig (1877–1942), Nokhem Sternheim (1879–1942), Mark Warshawsky (1840–1907), Abraham Goldfaden (1840–1908). There are also songs by important modern poets including Y. L. Peretz (1852–1915), Abraham Reisen (1875–1953), Abraham Liessin (1882–1938), Moishe Broderson (1890–1956), Itsik Manger (1901–1969), H. Leivick (1888–1962), Chaim N. Bialik (1873–1934) and Wolf Younin (1908–1984). Composers range from David Beigelman (1887–1944), Henech Kon (1898–1972) and Yankl Troupianski (1909–1944) in Poland to Michel Gelbart (1889–1966), Maurice Rauch (1910–1994), Jacob Schaefer (1888–1936), Lazar Weiner (1897–1982) in this country, with contemporary composers like Lev Kogan, Eli Rubinstein, Emil Gorovets, Josh Waletzky and others also represented.

We have added a new category of *Songs of the Former Soviet Russia* where we incorporate songs, whose texts originated in that country, some of which were also sung in other parts of the world. Along with the popular song *"Dzhankoye"* of farmers in the Crimea, we present *"S'yidishe meydele"* (The Jewish Girl), a song that expresses an anti-Semitic encounter and also alludes to the newly-acquired Soviet Jewish custom of painting eggs on Passover. The poet Itsik Fefer's affirmation of his Jewishness *"Ikh bin a yid!"* (I Am a Jew!), which had lain dormant or had been suppressed by the government is presented as well as two of the "Forbidden Songs" which were sung clandestinely in the 1960's: *"Antshuldikt!"* (Forgive Me!) and *"Shuldike umshuldike"* (The Guilty Who Were Innocent).

In the section *Historical Songs,* tragic chapters of Jewish history are brought to life in lyrical form: the pogrom in Kishineff in 1903, when American Jews who heard the appeal "Give shrouds for the dead, bread for the living!" generously collected and sent relief to the victims; Mendel Beilis, who was accused of murdering a Christian child in

---

* The previous six are *Mir Trogn A Gezang / Favorite Yiddish Songs* (1972, 1977, 1982, 1985, 1987, 1988), *Perl Fun Der Yidisher Poezye* (Pearls of Yiddish Poetry, a poetry anthology issued in Israel, 1974), *Pearls of Yiddish Song / Perl Fun Yidishn Lid* (1988, 1992); *We Are Here: 40 Songs of the Holocaust / Mir Zaynen Do* (1983); *25 Geto-Lider* (1969) and *Yomtevdike Teg* (Songbook for the Jewish Holidays, 1977, 1985)—the last three compiled with Malke Gottlieb.

Russia in 1911, and Jews and non-Jews throughout the world, shocked by the horrifying blood-libel, were galvanized into organizing massive protest demonstrations. We bring the song about Leo Frank who was accused of a similar libel in America and, after his sentence of death by hanging was commuted to life imprisonment, a mob of inflamed anti-Semites kidnapped and lynched him in 1915. In this section we also publish a lament over the sinking of the Titanic in 1912*, a song about a new recruit in the Czarist army and a ballad about the legendary Jewish strong man in Poland, Zishe Breitbard, who performed feats of strength in the grandest arenas and circuses of the world.

Other former categories have been retained. *Songs of Childhood* includes lullabies, songs about *kheyder* (religious school) and popular songs of children at play in Poland in the 1930's. *Love Songs* range from our oldest vintage Yiddish folksongs to modern poetic renditions of Zishe Landau (1889–1937), Chaim Nachmen Bialik, Nokhem Sternheim. The folksongs express the sad, heartfelt feelings of parting and separation, obstacles to marriage like the absence of *nadan* (dowry) and *yikhes* (family pedigree). One song *"Er hot mikh tsugezogt"* (He Promised Me) retains lines from one of the earliest extant manuscripts of Yiddish songs of the 16th century. In the section of *Work and Hope,* songs by the worker poets Morris Rosenfeld (1862–1923), David Edelshtat (1866–1892), Morris Winchevsky (1856–1923), Abraham Reisen and Abraham Liessin co-mingle with the simple mode of folksongs. Here are echoed the themes of hope of peace and end to misery and exploitation. The joking alphabet song contrasting the rich and poor that is sung to the traditional *Akdomos* motif alleviates to some degree the plaints of the seamstress and factory worker.

In *Songs of Celebration and Humor* we hear how generations rollicked to the merry-making riddle songs at weddings as well as to parodies, humorous flirtatious duets, interspersed with Russian expressions, and recitals of miracles. *National and Hassidic Songs* treat familiar subjects like the hope of Zion with the paraphrase "May I forget my right hand if I forget thee," the advent of the Messiah who will bring rejoicing and the pilgrimage to Palestine, the allegorical marriage between the Torah and the people of Israel, the yearning for the *Shkhine* (the Divine Presence), the celebration of the Sabbath and the departure of the *Khalutsim* (the new colonists) for Palestine. Some themes expressing love for Zion are also found in songs like *"Ikh breng aykh a grus fun di trentshes"* (I Bring You Greetings from the Trenches) and *"Kh'vil nit keyn sakh nor a bisele"* (I Don't Want Much—Just a Little). In this section are also songs about Yiddish and the songs of our generation.

Amol iz geven (Once a World Existed) and *Songs of the Streets* focus on some of the lively, seedier elements of society. Lyrical *Songs in a Quiet and Reflective Mood* by Itsik Manger, H. Leivick, David Einhorn (1886–1973) and Abraham Reisen, which follow, include a humanitarian yearning to comfort the troubled world and an old philosophical query which cannot be expressed nor answered with words.

In the *Songs of America,* the Golden Land, strains are introduced of the tribulations of immigrants, the appeal to America to open its doors, the striving for a livelihood during the depression; the bitter fate of the *agune* (deserted wife) who was left behind in Europe. Happier moments of American immigrant life are heard in songs like *"Hu-tsa-tsa,"* where Prohibition is circumvented, and *"Zumer bay nakht oyf di dekher"* (Summer Nights on the Rooftops), where a modicum of rest and relaxation could be enjoyed. This section is followed by a few songs that were popular in the Yiddish theater.

The anthology closes with a selection of songs that deal with the Holocaust: a lullaby in which a mother worries that her child may reveal their existence to the enemy, which will bring about their death; the separation of mother and child at Treblinka; the worker's plight in a village near Bialystok, the pleas to God for help and salvation. The

---

* Another lament was published in our previous songbook *Pearls of Yiddish Song.*

last song by H. Leivick *"Un a yingele vet zey firn"* (And a Child Shall Lead Them) was sung at a ghetto memorial in Paris and we felt belonged here as well.

PROVENANCE

Most of the songs appeared in our column *"Perl fun der yidisher poezye."* A few songs were transcribed by the compilers from the following recordings: *"Lozt arayn!"* (Let Us Come In!) from Aaron Lebedeff; *"Itsik shpitsik"* from Perele and Dora Mager on the record *Poems and Songs by Itzik Manger; "Mit farmakhte oygn"* (With Closed Eyes) from Chava Alberstein; *"Krokhmalne-gas"* (Krochmalna Street) from Ben Zion Wittler; *"Leyg dayn kop"* (Lay Your Head) from Mischa Alexandrovich; *"Nisim, nisim"* (Miracles) from Menashe Oppenheim. *"Antshuldikt!"* (Forgive Me!) and *"Shuldike umshuldike"* (The Innocent Who Were Found Guilty) from David Eshet.

The following songs the compilers collected: *"Yosl un Sore Dvoshe," "Der oytser"* (The Treasure), *"Ikh ganve in der nakht"* (I Steal at Night), *"Ikh zits mir bay der arbet"* (I Sit at My Work), the music of *"Der kashtnboym"* (The Chestnut Tree) and *"Dos lid fun mayn dor"* (The Song of My Generation) from Mina Bern, New York; the words of the latter from Sylvia Younin; *"Dos kleyne tsigaynerl"* (The Little Gypsy) from Mascha Benya Matz, Forest Hills, N. Y.; *"Sorele"* and *"Kol mekadesh shevii"* (All Who Keep the Sabbath Holy) from Aaron Feiner, Toronto; *"Sore un Rifke"* and *"Mayne khaveyrim"* (My Comrades) from Sara Rosenfeld and Chana Gonshar, Montreal; *"Di khasene iz geven in der kazarme"* (The Wedding Took Place in the Barracks) from Emil Gorovets, New York; *"In a shtetele pitshepoy"* (In the Town of Pitshepoy) from the late Moishe Kligsberg, New York. Two songs *"Shnirele perele"* (String of Pearls) and *"Di sapozhkelekh"* (The Little Boots) we learned at the Klezkamp Yiddish Folk Arts Program. *"Ikh hob dikh lib vi a peysakhdikn rosl"* (I Love You Like a Passover Broth) and *"Tonu rabonen"* (Our Great Teachers Spoke) were the contributions of the compiler who sang these songs in Poland.

A WORD ABOUT PREVIOUS FOLKSONG COLLECTORS

As in the anthologies *Mir Trogn A Gezang* and *Pearls of Yiddish Song,* we have pointed to the adaptations, additions and variations the songs underwent during their lifetime and posthumous recall. The cited printed sources indicate the collectors and scholars who were involved in the history of folksong collection from its genesis. Among the early names are those of Saul Ginzburg (1866–1940) and Peysakh Marek (1862–1920), two young Russian Jewish historians who pioneered in publishing the texts of 376 Yiddish folksongs in St. Petersburg in 1901. Their volume was reissued with translations and editorial comments by Dov Noy in 1991. The great Yiddish writer Y. L. Peretz, one of the first collectors of Yiddish folksongs in Poland aroused the interest and comprehension of this type of oral folklore among the literati of Warsaw. Y. L. Cahan (1881–1937) was one of the first to gather and publish a large collection of Yiddish songs with music in this country in 1912, to research their historical and geographic origins and influences. His collections and studies were reissued by the YIVO Institute for Jewish Research under the editorship of Max Weinreich in 1952 and 1957. Other notable collectors were members of the St. Petersburg Society for Jewish Folk Music and musicians such as Joel Engel (1868–1927) and Sussman Kisselgof (1876–1939) who participated in the S. Ansky Ethnographic Expedition, 1912–1914; Noyekh Prilutsky (1882–1941), a prolific collector of religious, holiday songs and ballads, who was tortured to death by the Nazis; Menakhem Kipnis (1878–1942), whose important collection of folksongs was reissued in Buenos Aires in 1949. His extensive collections and those of the eminent folklore collector Shmuel Lehman (1886–1941) of

Warsaw were destroyed during the Holocaust. The young promising YIVO collector and scholar Shmuel Zanvl Pipe (1907–1943) also perished in the Holocaust. His collection, research paper, correspondence, reports of his work in the *Aspirantur* (Research Training Program) of the YIVO in Vilna were issued by Dov and Meir Noy in 1971. Moishe Beregovski (1892–1961) and Z. Skuditski were preeminent ethnomusicologists of Soviet Russia whose collection and scholarly work in the field of folklore were "rewarded" by their government by arrest and deportation to a concentration camp. A number of Beregovski's collections and essays were reissued and edited by Mark Slobin in 1982, and his other books will soon also appear in translation. Other distinguished collectors include Leo Winz, Pinkhes Graubard, A. Z. Idelsohn, A. Litvin.

After World War II, the collection and scholarship of Ruth Rubin, Wolf Younin, Dov and Meir Noy, Robert Rothstein, Mark Slobin, Barbara Kirshenblatt-Gimblett and others compensated in some degree (if one can compensate) for the loss of their forebears. Ben Stonehill, an amateur collector, taped hundreds of songs of the survivors of the D.P. camps who came to this country in 1948. Gila Flam collected songs of the Lodz Ghetto which formed the basis of her book *Singing for Survival* in 1992. Shoshana Kalich presented an in-depth selection of 25 Holocaust songs in her book *Yes, We Sang!* in 1985. A 4-volume *Anthology of Yiddish Folksongs* under the editorship of Aharon Vinkovetzky, Abba Kovner and Sinai Leichter was published in Israel in 1983–1987 and a Yiddish-Russian-English anthology edited by M. Goldin and I. Zemtsovsky in St. Petersburg in 1994.

ADAPTATIONS OF SONGS

Songs were borrowed and passed through transformations and adaptations, an indication of their continuing vitality and spirit. *"Royz, royz"* (Rose) is an example of how a Hassidic song about the Divine Presence was transformed from a Hungarian secular one. *"Yidn shmidn"* (Jews Are Forging) became a song about the *"Bin"* (Bees—a children's scout organization of Vilna). *"Khatskele"* was altered to accommodate the Legionnaires going to Palestine. *"Nisim venifloes"* (Miracles and Marvels) was transformed into a children's song about a rabbit. *"Hirsh Dovid"* was converted to a song about learning to dance after retirement to Miami. *"A yingele, a meydele"* (A Little Boy, a Little Girl) evolved from a song about the Jewish clergy: *"Der rebele, der gabele"* (The Rabbi, the Trustee). Two songs are translations of popular Russian songs—which is another component of Yiddish song: *"Aleyn in veg"* (Alone on the Road) from *"Vikhazhu odin ya na dorogu"* and *"Shpil gitar"* (Play Guitar) from *"Chto mnie gore."*

Melodies were contrafacted. *"Alef—indikes"* (A is for Turkeys) was contrafacted, as mentioned, from the traditional *"Akdomos"* motive. The melody in the song of Mendel Beilis was adopted from Mark Warshavsky's song *"Vi halt ikh dos oys?"* (How Do I Bear It?). Although *"Sore un Rifke"* has an original melody, it was also sung to *"Der rebe hot geheysn freylekh zayn"* (The Rabbi Bade Us Be Merry).

The following songs are presented with two melodies: *"Shnel loyfn di reder"* (The Wheels Turn Quickly) by David Edelshtat as rendered by Jacob Schaefer and Lazar Weiner; *"Di shvet-shap"* (The Sweatshop) by Morris Rosenfeld has two anonymous melodies; likewise the song *"S'falt a shney"* (A Snow Is Falling). Of *"Dem zeydns nign"* (Grandfather's Melody) by Shike Driz we have published the melodies by S. Berezovsky and Josh Waletzky and of *"Ikh un di Velt"* (I and the World) the melodies by Maurice Rauch and Sidor Belarsky.

A few songs are also pieces of the klezmer repertoire. The first part of *"Shpil zhe mir a lidele in yidish"* (Play Me a Song in Yiddish) was played as *"Yismekhu bemalkhuskho;" "A yor nokh mayn khasene"* (A Year after My Wedding) appeared in a dance version. *"Vu bistu geven?"* (Where Were You?) is part of the Troika dance.

SONGS ADAPTED DURING THE HOLOCAUST

A number of songs were sung and paraphrased during the darkest history of our people, adding to our folk creation another dimension of significance and awesomeness and connection with the people in their torment. The questions and replies in the love song *"Brontshele"* were directed at the hunger in the Lodz Ghetto and fear of the eldest of the Judenrat, Chaim Rumkowski. *"Tsvey taybelekh"* (Two Doves) with its execrable curses will ever remain a symbol of the heroism of Liuba Levitska of the Vilna Ghetto, who continued to sing the song despite her unbearable torture. The words of *"Di svetshap"* (The Sweatshop) were adapted to refer to work in the factories in the Lodz Ghetto. *"Dos naye lid"* (The New Song) with its message of ultimate peace was sung by the children in the Vilna Ghetto. The placename *"Pitshepoy"* the children of the internment camp in Drancy, France, gave to the imaginary, mysterious place they were going to, which turned out to be Auschwitz. *"Tshiribim"* was transformed into a song about the relief work of the Joint Distribution Committee in the ghetto. Other songs that were sung and adapted during the Holocaust are: *"S'falt a shney"* (A Snow Is Falling), *"Zumer bay nakht oyf di dekher"* (Summer Nights on the Rooftops), *"Vu nemt men parnose?"* (How Can I Make a Living?), *"Vilne,"* *"Dzhankoye,"* *"Shpil zhe mir a lidele oyf yidish"* (Play Me a Song in Yiddish). Two songs in the Lodz Ghetto were contrafacted from a revue song of the underworld *"Ikh ganve in der nakht"* (I Steal at Night). The melody of the ghetto song *"Rifkele di shabesdike"* (Rifkele the Sabbath Widow) derives from the Soviet Yiddish song *"Kegn gold fun zun"* (Toward the Golden Sunrise).

***

It has been a source of gratification to frequently hear the "Pearls" of our previous anthologies presented by so many new and young and talented artists. They are requested at the Music Archive of the YIVO Institute for Jewish Research. They are heard at Yiddish festivals, sometimes in conjunction with popular klezmer concerts throughout the land and in other countries. At a recent Workmen's Circle festival, the New York All Star Klezmer Extravaganza on July 12, 1995, at Damrosch Park, in which the great artist Itzak Perlman took part, songs like *"Der rebe Elimeylekh"* and *"Un mir zaynen ale brider"* (And We Are All Brothers) were enthusiastically played and sung by six klezmer ensembles* and the audience on both sides of the stage in an intermingling of generations singing Yiddish songs—which was an inspiration for the title of this book. We hope that this new anthology will continue to provide repertory and encourage new treatments by the growing number of creative musicians in the field of Yiddish music.

***

We are happy that our children Zalmen and Debby, Mark-Moish and Audrey and their offspring—Lee Brian-Leyzer Benyomin, Avram Yitskhok-Isaac, Marissa Beth-Bashe Malke and Elisha Mendel—share with us the pleasure of hearing and singing these songs. Our Zalmen and Moish, their families and our sisters Malke Gottlieb and Sara Rosenfeld have been our support throughout the entire process of bringing the book to fruition. We hope that many others will enjoy listening to and playing and cherishing this song treasure for a long time to come.

***

And now it's our pleasure to express our acknowledgment and thanks to a few individuals who have helped realize this publication:

We are honored that Elie Wiesel has let his voice be heard among the voices of our

---

* The Lipovsky/Mlotek/Warschauer Trio, Kapelye, Andy Statman, Brave Old World, Klezmer Conservatory Band and The Klezmatics

people and poets in the Preface. We are grateful to the eminent folklorist Professor Dov Noy for his Foreword. We thank Dr. Barnett Zumoff for his insightful translations of the songs, making the words and feelings more meaningful for our readers. We owe a debt of thanks to Zalmen Mlotek, for his guide on performance styles, for his chordal arrangements and for serving as our musical editor and consultant in every stage of the work. We acknowledge the cover design by Tsirl Waletzky, the calligraphy of Peggy Davis and Chonen Kiel.

We thank Dr. Chava Lapin for helping with the proof reading of the texts; Robert Kaplan for his support and encouragement, Stephen Dowling for production, design, and composition, and Ira Karlick for his guidance. We also thank Elena Leikind, Nachum Lerner, Pearl Krupit and Herbert Lazarus for their help with the manuscript, and Robert Sherwin of Chelsea Music Engraving for the music engraving and typesetting. We are grateful for the assistance from the Workmen's Circle–Arbeter Ring, the Forward, the YIVO Institute for Jewish Research and the Jacob T. Zukerman Culture Fund.

William Wernick of Boston, Mass. deserves our sincere gratitude for helping this publication see the bright light of day—in memory of his wife Ruth. Other major contributors are inscribed elsewhere with thanks for their musical and cultural *mitzvah*.

We are honored that Theodore Bikel, Professor Shikl Joshua Fishman, Bel Kaufman, Professor Barbara Kirshenblatt Gimblett, Professor David Roskes and Professor Mark Slobin have given our work their esteemed *hekhsher*. May newer generations continue to enjoy the riches of our cultural heritage.

—*Joseph and Eleanor Chana Mlotek*

The Performance of Yiddish Songs
by Zalmen Mlotek, Music Editor

Just as there is no definitive way of performing any piece of music, the same situation applies to Yiddish music. There are performers of Yiddish music who opt to sing this material *a capella.* There are others who will sing it accompanied, ranging from a single guitar to larger musical ensembles. The klezmer revival has brought the Yiddish repertoire to broader audiences and to an increasing number of performers, some of whom have little knowledge or experience with the wide range of this material.

I had the privilege of growing up in a home where this music was not only listened to, but constantly performed. Musical soirees took place in my home during my childhood with the major Yiddish song interpreters of their generation. Evenings with artists like Sidor Belarsky, Mascha Benya, Ben Bonus, Mina Bern, Ruth Rubin translated into vivid musical memories for me with strong, specific musical guidelines. I was also present at my father's musical gatherings in our home with his childhood friends from Warsaw, where folk and street songs were recalled with relish. In my home, moreover, my grandfather loved to sing the older songs of Abraham Goldfaden, Eliakum Zunser, Velvel Zbarzher, Berl Broder and the songs of the early Yiddish theater. I often attended concerts and theatrical performances during my childhood and youth—I was present at the choral recitals of Lazar Weiner, Samuel Bugatch, Vladimir Heifetz and others, stood at an early age behind Sholom Secunda as he conducted a special benefit performance of Goldfaden's "Shulamis."

I had the opportunity to experience the broad spectrum of Yiddish music and found myself in a position to serve as a link between the old, traditional, and newer generations. In the Yiddish summer camps, Hemshekh and Boiberik I regularly directed and taught hundreds of children Yiddish songs which I put in a contemporary musical context that they could relate to, growing up in the 60s and 70s.

It has been my experience with performing Yiddish music that this material is so rich that it can withstand divergent approaches and treatments. The composer Stefan Wolpe once said "When using the folklore material for creative purposes the composer strives to reveal and to remould in a novel fashion the traits which nobody but himself is able to detect in it. Such creative interpretation of the age-old "national" material may be compared to the type of variation which expands the original features of a musical subject by presenting them in different perspectives, as it were. It thus preserves and transforms the subject at the very same time."*

It would be beneficial for newcomers to this material to be aware of a few basic points.

The most obvious point is to know the meaning of the words that are sung in order to be able to communicate them as naturally as possible. I don't only mean a word-for-word literal translation. The text may contain idioms and specific phrases; it may reflect a lifestyle, observances, like the Sabbath or holidays. Thus Point One: the performer should be conversant with the text and implications of the song.

Point Two: I suggest that in order to really comprehend a song, one must learn about the life and work of the author and composer. Beethoven's sonatas and symphonies take on a whole other dimension when performed by musicians who have studied his life.

Similarly, a new dimension is acquired, for instance, in knowing about the Polish-Yiddish folk poet Mordecai Gebirtig (b.1877—perished in the Cracow Ghetto in 1942), whose two new books in Italian and Hebrew translations will soon be published. His songs, like the one in this anthology *"Ver der ershter vet lakhn"* (Who Will Be the First

---

* The Jewish Music Forum, December 1946 and 1947.

to Laugh) were sung throughout the Yiddish-speaking world. They are simple, folklike, with a gentle and wry humor, and should be approached with simplicity in the arrangement which is given to them. Piano arrangements of some songs were made later. All we have of Gebirtig's songs are the melody lines. No piano parts or chords were ever found. His song written in 1938 *"Es brent, brider, es brent"* (Our Town Is Burning, Brothers) which forecast the destruction of the Jewish world, the "shtetl," has been treated to a variety of interpretations, from the simple, to a stark, tragic, dissonant cry of anguish. In this instance there are and had to be extreme differences in interpreting the writing of the same poet.

The singer's task, on the eve of the 21st century, when most of the audiences will be deficient in their knowledge of Yiddish, is a different one from that of singers who performed for audiences in the 1940's through the '70s. The audiences that came those years to hear Yiddish music were fluent in Yiddish and were familiar with the songs and ambiences of their authors and composers.

Point Three: Singers interested in the performance of Yiddish music today should be familiar with the varieties of song types: Holocaust songs as distinct from traditional folk, popular, theater, operatic, art, Hassidic, semi-liturgical, mixed-language songs.

Point Four: Arrangements of songs today might contain more complex arrangements with inner voices, syncopated rhythms and discordant harmonies, reflecting contemporary musical styles.

In some cases of repetitive or concatenated-chained strophes or strophic songs, modulations of certain verses might be a device, when used to highlight the text and the intent of the songs, like *"Brontshele," "Lomir Onheybn Tsu Derklern,"* or *"Fun Dem Sheynem Vortsl Aroys"* in this book.

There may be an addition of two or more polyphonic voices. Repetitive melodic phrases can likewise be rendered in a variety of ways—with embellishments, dynamic shading, like in the songs, *"Di Sapozhkelekh," "Amol Iz Geven A Yid," "Shnirele, Perele Gilderne Fon."*

A blending of two songs may also be an interesting way of dramatizing an effect, like the songs *"S'falt A Shney"* with *"Shnel Loyfn di Reder;" "Khalutsim Gikher"* with *"In Mitn Veg Shteyt A Boym."*

I have often been asked for new piano arrangements of Yiddish songs. My own settings of songs, written or arranged for shows or concerts, offer new treatments, polyphonic parts, new rhythmic styles which are always guided by the individual performer's interpretation of the song as well as my close personal connection to the text. The role of the accompanist on the piano or other instrument is to enhance the performance of the vocalist, to complement the musical thoughts of the composer and the writer. Hopefully, additional contemporary piano arrangements will one day be forthcoming.

ZISE KINDER-YORN...
SONGS OF CHILDHOOD

‎זיסע קינדער-יארן...

SHTEYT IN FELD A BEYMELE

שטייט אין פֿעלד אַ ביימעלע

In the Meadow Stands a Little Tree

Words by Y. L. Peretz (1852–1915) with music by Michel Gelbart (1889–1966). Published in *Mir zingen*, 1951. The poem is one of a cycle of children's poems that Peretz wrote for orphans in Warsaw after World War I. The song was sung in the Yiddish schools in Europe and this country. According to Israeli musicologist Issachar Fater, the poem was set to music by composers Eliyohu Hirshin, Lazar Weiner, Bernardo Feuer, Bluma Mushkes-Saubel, in addition to Moses Milner and Joel Engel. Saul Beresovsky also arranged an anonymous tune for chorus.

Shteyt in feld a beymele,
Hot es grine tsvaygelekh;
Zitst deroyf a feygele,
Makht es tsu di eygelekh.

Oyf di grine tsvaygelekh,
Vakst a goldn epele,
Makh tsu, mayn kind, di eygelekh,
A brokhe oyf dayn kepele.

Oyf di grine tsvaygelekh,
Shlofn shoyn di feygelekh,
Di mame zingt zey: a - a - a. . .
Es iz a shtile nakht, a - a. . .

שטייט אין פֿעלד אַ ביימעלע,
האָט עס גרינע צווײַגעלעך;
זיצט דערויף אַ פֿייגעלע,
מאַכט עס צו די אייגעלעך.

אויף די גרינע צווײַגעלעך,
וואַקסט אַ גאָלדן עפעלע,
מאַך צו, מײַן קינד, די אייגעלעך,
אַ ברכה אויף דײַן קעפּעלע.

אויף די גרינע צווײַגעלעך,
שלאָפֿן שוין די פֿייגעלעך,
די מאַמע זינגט זיי: אַ-אַ-אַ. . .
עס איז אַ שטילע נאַכט, אַ-אַ. . .

In the meadow stands a little tree, it has green branches. On one sits a little bird and closes its little eyes.

On the green branches there grows a golden apple. Close your eyes, my child, a blessing on your head.

On the green branches the birds are already asleep. Their mother sings to them: ah-ah-ah; it's a quiet night, ah-ah.

SHLOF, MAYN FEYGELE

שלאָף, מײַן פֿייגעלע

Sleep, My Little One

Words by Abraham Goldfaden (1840–1908). The lullaby, originally beginning with the words "Shlof in freydn" (Sleep in Joy), was published in Goldfaden's second collection of Yiddish poems *Di yidene* in Odessa, 1872, entitled "Shlof, mayn kind" (Sleep, My Child). It was reprinted in *Di yidishe bine* in 1897, and in 1901 was included as an anonymous folksong in the compilation of S. Ginzburg and P. Marek. The melody derives from the Russian song "Spi mladenets moy prekrasnie" by M. Lermontov. According to musicologist-composer Dr. Jack Gottlieb, George Gershwin based his song "My One and Only" on this melody.

Shlof, mayn feygele,	שלאָף, מײַן פֿייגעלע,
Makh tsu dayn eygele,	מאַך צו דײַן אייגעלע,
Shlof, mayn kind, shlof!	שלאָף, מײַן קינד, שלאָף!
Makh tsu dayn eygele,	מאַך צו דײַן אייגעלע,
Mayn tayer feygele,	מײַן טײַער פֿייגעלע,
Shlof, mayn kind, shlof!	שלאָף, מײַן קינד, שלאָף!
A malakh a giter*	אַ מלאך אַ גיטער (גוטער)
Zol zayn dayn hiter	זאָל זײַן דײַן היטער
Fun haynt biz morgn fri!	פֿון הײַנט ביז מאָרגן פֿרי!
Mit zayn fligele	מיט זײַן פֿליגעלע
Iber dayn vigele	איבער דײַן וויגעלע
Dekt er shtil dikh tsi!**	דעקט ער שטיל דיך צי! (צו)
Shlof in freydn,	שלאָף אין פֿריידן,
Veys fun keyn leydn,	ווייס פֿון קיין ליידן,
Shlof, mayn tayer kind!	שלאָף, מײַן טײַער קינד!
Shlof in freydn,	שלאָף אין פֿריידן,
Veys fun keyn leydn,	ווייס פֿון קיין ליידן,
Shlof zikh oys gezint!***	שלאָף זיך אויס געזינט! (געזונט)

---

* guter
** tsu
*** gezunt

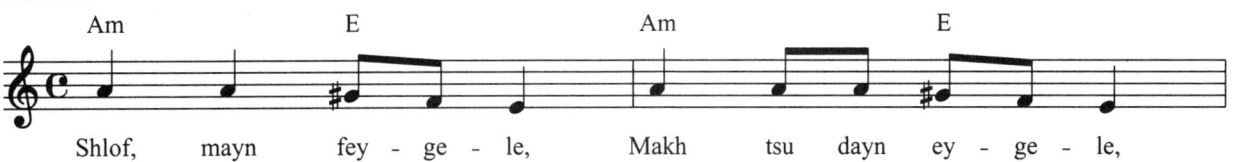

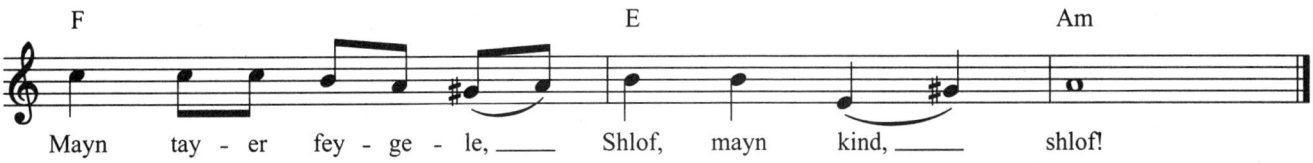

Sleep, my little one, close your little eyes. Sleep, my child, sleep! Close your little eyes, my dear little one. Sleep, my child, sleep!

May a good angel be your guardian from now till tomorrow morning. With his wings spread over your cradle, he'll quietly protect you.

Sleep in peace, may no suffering befall you. Sleep, my dear child! Sleep in peace, may no suffering befall you. Sleep and be well!

NOR A MAME

נאָר אַ מאַמע

Only a Mother

Words by David Einhorn (1886–1873); composer unknown. Published by A. Bulkin and L. Efron in 1917 under the title "Alye lyule." Composer Israel Gladstein, who wrote a different melody, has been credited erroneously with having composed this one. The song was sung by Khaytshe Lerman (nee Banet) in the pre-World War II film *Mir kumen on* (We Are Coming) about the children in the Medem Sanitarium in Miedzeszyn, Poland. The lullaby was repeated a few years ago on a videotape produced in Melbourne, Australia, where it was sung by Khavele Gavenda, the granddaughter of the singer in the original film. A superimposed clip showing both grandmother and granddaughter singing the song is a touching moment in the videotape.

Ay-li, lyu-li, ay-li, lyu-li,	אײַ-לי, ליו-לי, אײַ-לי, ליו-לי,
Shlof, mayn tayerer, in ru.	שלאָף, מײַן טײַערער, אין רו.
Voyl iz dem vos hot a mamen	וווֹיל איז דעם וואָס האָט אַ מאַמען
Un a vigele dertsu,	און אַ וויגעלע דערצו,
Ay-li, lyu-lyu, lyu.	אײַ-לי-ליו-ליו, ליו.
Altsding ken men nokh gefinen,	אַלצדינג קען מען נאָך געפֿינען,
Altsding krigt men nokh far gelt.	אַלצדינג קריגט מען נאָך פֿאַר געלט.
Nor a mame zi iz eyne -	נאָר אַ מאַמע, זי איז איינע -
Mer nit eyne oyf der velt.	מער ניט איינע אויף דער וועלט.
Ay-li, lyu-li-lyu.	אײַ-לי, ליו-לי-ליו.
Shlof, mayn tayerer, mayn liber,	שלאָף, מײַן טײַערער, מײַן ליבער,
Makh di oygn tsu un ru.	מאַך די אויגן צו און רו.
Gut iz dem vos hot a mamen	גוט איז דעם וואָס האָט אַ מאַמען
Un a vigele dertsu.	און אַ וויגעלע דערצו.
Ay-li, lyu-li-lyu.	אײַ-לי, ליו-לי-ליו.
Dos iz dokh a gots matone,	דאָס איז דאָך אַ גאָטס מתּנה,
Vemen es iz nor bashert;	וועמען עס איז נאָר באַשערט;
Vey iz dem vos hot keyn mamen	ווײ איז דעם, וואָס האָט קיין מאַמען
Oyf der groyser, vister erd. . .	אויף דער גרויסער, וויסטער ערד. . .
Ay-li, lyu-li-lyu!	אײַ-לי, ליו-לי-ליו!
Ay-li, lyu-li, ay-li, lyu-li,	אײַ-לי, ליו-לי, אײַ-לי, ליו-לי,
Vi der tsar zol zayn nit groys,	ווי דער צער זאָל זײַן ניט גרויס,
Tomed ken men im farvign	תּמיד קען מען אים פֿאַרוויגן
In der mames shoys.	אין דער מאַמעס שויס.
Ay-li, lyu-li-lyu!	אײַ-לי, ליו-לי-ליו!
Ay-li, lyu-li, ay-li, lyu-li,	אײַ-לי, ליו-לי, אײַ-לי, ליו-לי,
Vi di zind zol zayn nit shver,	ווי די זינד זאָל זײַן ניט שווער,
Opvashn vet tomed kenen	אָפּוואַשן וועט תּמיד קענען
Zi-der mames reyne trer.	זי - דער מאַמעס ריינע טרער.
Ay-li, lyu-li-lyu!	אײַ-לי, ליו-לי-ליו!

Moderato

Ay-li, lyu-li, ay-li, lyu-li, sleep, my dear one, in peace. Happy is he who has a mother, and a little cradle as well. Ay-li, lyu-li-lyu.

Anything can still be found; you can still get anything for money. But a mother—she is one—there's just one in all the world. Ay-li, lyu-li-lyu.

Sleep, my dear one, my beloved, close your eyes and rest. Happy is he who has a mother and a little cradle too. Ay-li, lyu-li-lyu.

For that is a gift from God to whomever is fated to receive it. Woe to him who has no mother in the wide and empty world. Ay-li, lyu-li-lyu.

However great your sorrow, it can always be rocked away in your mother's lap. However great your sins, they can always be washed away by your mother's pure tears. Ay-li, lyu-li-lyu.

HEYDA, NU, TSURIK IN KHEYDER

היידאַ, נו, צוריק אין חדר

Here We Go Now, Back to Kheyder

Words by H. Roisenblatt (1878–1956) with music by Isaac Pirozhnikoff (1859–1933). Previously published by Samuel Bugatch in 1951.

Heyda, nu, tsurik in kheyder,	היידאַ, נו, צוריק אין חדר,
Un genumen zikh geshmak	און גענומען זיך געשמאַק
Tsu dem limed, tsu dem altn,	צו דעם לימוד, צו דעם אַלטן,
Mit a nusakh, mit a knak.	מיט אַ נוסח, מיט אַ קנאַק.
Tsi hot ir, kinder, nit fargesn	צי האָט איר, קינדער, ניט פֿאַרגעסן
Un a likhtl mitgebrakht,	און אַ ליכטל מיטגעבראַכט,
Itster zaynen kleyn di teg shoyn,	איצטער זײַנען קליין די טעג שוין,
Lernen, lernt men bay nakht.	לערנען, לערנט מען בײַ נאַכט.
Lernt, kinderlekh, di toyre,	לערנט, קינדערלעך, די תּורה,
Ire soydes tif un groys;	אירע סודות טיף און גרויס,
Lernt, lernt, libe kinder,	לערנט, לערנט, ליבע קינדער,
Biz dos likhtele geyt oys.	ביז דאָס ליכטעלע גייט אויס.

Here we go now, back to kheyder, and back with enthusiasm to our ancient studies, with melody and vigor.

Have you not forgotten, children, and have you brought a candle with you? The days are getting short now, and we must study at night.

Study children, the Torah, its secrets great and deep; study, study, dear children, till the candle sputters out.

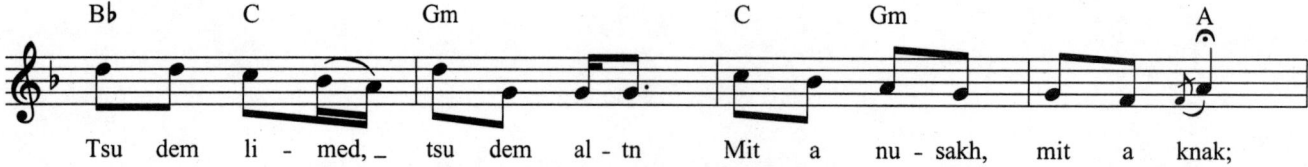

OY, VET MIKH DER REBE SHMAYSN   אוי, וועט מיך דער רבי שמײַסן

Oh, Will the Teacher Whip Me

    The words appear in the 1897 compilation *Di yidishe bine* with Jacob Gordin credited as author, from his play *Der shvartser yid* or *Meyer Yosefovitch*. It was later published by J. and J. Kammen with other words by Mordkhele Chemerinsky. The version presented here is based on the song published in Sarah Schack-Ethel Cohen's songbook (1924) and reprinted in the Soviet compilation of M. Beregovski-Itsik Fefer (1938). In the latter, the word "peyelekh" (little earlocks) was changed to "bekelekh" (cheeks) to conform to the Soviet policy of eliminating religious allusions.
    The song was also printed in Lodz, n.d. entitled Yankev Kalich's *Yankele*, as a folksong adapted by Kalich and sung by Molly Picon. There the song includes six days, from Sunday to Friday. It was published in Hebrew as "Yom alef lo halahti el haheder" in *Songs of Israel* edited by Seymour Silbermintz (1949).

Zuntik bin ikh nit geven in kheyder,	זונטיק בין איך ניט געווען אין חדר,
Vayl zuntik hob ikh faynt,	ווײַל זונטיק האָב איך פֿײַנט
Ven di zun shaynt,	ווען די זון שײַנט
Tsu geyn in fintstern kheyder	צו גיין אין פֿינצטערן חדר
Un kvetshn di bank keseyder.	און קוועטשן די באַנק כּסדר.
Ikh bin gelofn biz ikh bin gevorn mid	איך בין געלאָפֿן ביז איך בין געוואָרן מיד
Un ikh hob gezungen Yankeles lid:	און איך האָב געזונגען יאַנקעלעס ליד:
Oy, vet mikh der rebe shmaysn,	אוי, וועט מיך דער רבי שמײַסן,
Mayn hoyt vet er mir oyf shtiker tseraysn!	מײַן הויט וועט ער מיר אויף שטיקער צערײַסן!
Vayhi erev vayhi voyker	ויהי ערבֿ ויהי בוקר
Yoym ekhod.	יום אחד.
Montik bin ikh nit geven in kheyder,	מאָנטיק בין איך ניט געווען אין חדר,
Vayl montik iz di tsig	ווײַל מאָנטיק איז די ציג
Poshet gevorn klig,*	פּשוט געוואָרן קליג, (קלוג)
Zi hot ibergerisn di shtrik	זי האָט איבערגעריסן די שטריק
Un iz ariber oyf yener zayt brik.	און איז אַריבער אויף יענער זײַט בריק.
Ale zaynen gelofn khapn di tsig,	אַלע זײַנען געלאָפֿן כאַפּן די ציג,
Un ikh hob gezungen Yankeles lid:	און איך האָב געזונגען יאַנקעלעס ליד:
Oy, vet mikh der rebe shmaysn,	אוי, וועט מיך דער רבי שמײַסן,
Mayne peyelekh vet er mir oysraysn!	מײַנע פּאהלעך וועט ער מיר אויסרײַסן!
Vayhi erev vayhi voyker	ויהי ערבֿ ויהי בוקר
Yoym sheni.	יום שני.
Dinstik bin ikh nit geven in kheyder,	דינסטיק בין איך ניט געווען אין חדר,
Vayl dinstik hob ikh nit fargesn	ווײַל דינסטיק האָב איך ניט פֿאַרגעסן
Az ikh hob gehat nit gegesn.	אַז איך האָב געהאַט ניט געגעסן.
Der tate iz arumgelofn, vi a vilder yid,	דער טאַטע איז אַרומגעלאָפֿן ווי אַ ווילדער ייִד,
Di mame iz gegangen layen broyt,	די מאַמע איז געגאַנגען לײַען ברויט,
Un ikh bin gelofn biz ikh bin gevorn mid,	און איך בין געלאָפֿן ביז איך בין געוואָרן מיד,
Un ikh hob gezungen Yankeles lid:	און איך האָב געזונגען יאַנקעלעס ליד:

---

* klug

Oy, vet mikh der rebe shmaysn,
Mayn hoyt vet er mir oyf shtiker tseraysn!
Vayhi erev vayhi voyker
Yoym shlishi.

אוי, וועט מיך דער רבי שמײַסן,
מײַן הויט וועט ער מיר אויף שטיקער צערײַסן!
ויהי ערב ויהי בֹקר
יום שלישי.

Sunday I was not in kheyder because Sunday, when the sun shines, I hate to go to the dark kheyder and constantly sit and study. I ran till I got tired, and I sang Yankele's song. Oh, will the teacher whip me! He'll tear the skin right off me! And it was evening and it was morning—the first day.

Monday I was not in kheyder because Monday the goat got smart. She tore her rope and ran across to the other side of the bridge. Everyone ran to catch the goat, and I sang Yankele's song. Oh, will the teacher whip me! He'll tear my sidecurls off. And it was evening and it was morning—the second day.

Tuesday I was not in kheyder because Tuesday I remembered that I hadn't eaten. My father ran around like a wild man. My mother ran to borrow some bread, and I ran till I got tired, and I sang Yankele's song. Oh, will the teacher whip me! He'll tear the skin right off me. And it was evening and it was morning—the third day.

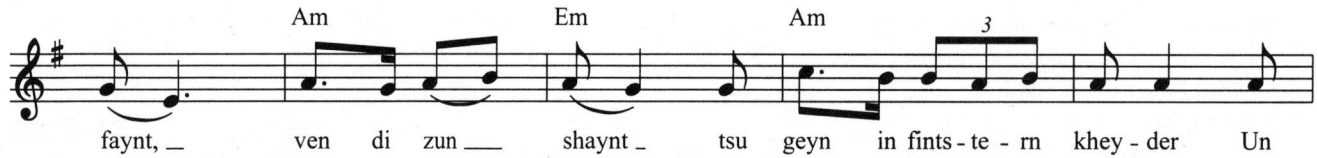

A SHEYNER TOG
א שיינער טאָג

A Beautiful Day

Words by Jacob Adler (1873–1973), composer unknown. The text was published in Abrasha Vayner's collection *Undzer gezang* (Warsaw, 1930) with the title "Zikhroynes" (Memories). The words and music were printed in the *Undzer gezang* collection of 1947. According to compiler Joseph Mlotek and friends, it was popular in Poland in the 1930s. H. Ritterband also set the poem to music.

A sheyner tog, a frilings tog,	אַ שיינער טאָג, אַ פֿרילינגס טאָג,
Vakht oyf in mayn zikorn,	וואַכט אויף אין מײַן זיכּרון,
A sheyner tog, a goldener,	אַ שיינער טאָג, אַ גאָלדענער,
Fun mayne kinder-yorn.	פֿון מײַנע קינדער-יאָרן.
Ikh shtif in undzer gertele,	איך שטיף אין אונדזער גערטעלע,
Di vaynshl-beymer blien,	די וויינשל-ביימער בליִען,
Es flamen mayne bekelekh,	עס פֿלאַמען מײַנע בעקעלעך,
Di eygelekh, zay glien.	די אייגעלעך, זיי גליִען.
Es zogt mir on di mameshi,	עס זאָגט מיר אָן די מאַמעשי,
Ikh zol zikh nisht fargesn,	איך זאָל זיך נישט פֿאַרגעסן,
Vi nor di zun vet untergeyn,	ווי נאָר די זון וועט אונטערגיין,
Dan zol ikh kumen esn.	דאַן זאָל איך קומען עסן.
Der tate hert zikh ayn un kvelt,	דער טאַטע הערט זיך אײַן און קוועלט,
Un git derbay a shmeykhl,	און גיט דערבײַ אַ שמייכל,
Un zogt mir on: Leman-hashem,	און זאָגט מיר אָן: - למען השם,
Farkrikh nisht vayt tsum taykhl!	פֿאַרקריך נישט ווײַט צום טײַכל!

Moderato

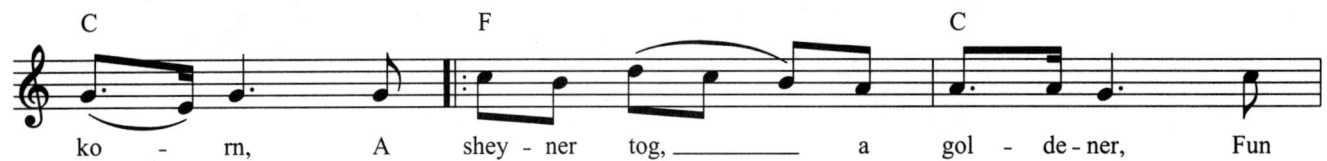

A beautiful day, a day in spring, awakens in my memory; a beautiful day, a golden day, from my childhood years.

I'm playing in our little garden, the cherry trees are blooming. My cheeks are flaming red, and my eyes are shining.

My dearest mother tells me not to forget that as soon as the sun sets, I should come in and eat.

My father listens and swells with pride, and smiles a little smile, and says to me: For heaven's sake, don't go wandering down to the creek!

VER DER ERSHTER VET LAKHN   ווער דער ערשטער וועט לאַכן

Who Will Be the First to Laugh

Words and music by Mordecai Gebirtig, popular folk poet (1877—killed by the Nazis in the Cracow Ghetto, 1942). Published in the author's collection, 1936. The song was sung in English in the musical *Those Were the Days* by Zalmen Mlotek and Moishe Rosenfeld, 1991–1992. In her book *Singing for Survival* Gila Flam writes that the song was popular in the Lodz Ghetto Revue Theater, where her informants believed that it was an original ghetto composition.

- Kh'vel zikher, Avreml, der ershter nisht lakhn,	כ׳וועל זיכער, אָוורעמל, דער ערשטער נישט לאַכן,
Ikh vet zikh, megst vi nokh zikh vitslen,	איך וועט זיך, מעגסט ווי נאָך זיך וויצלען,
Kh'vel nemen in zinen mir troyerike zakhn,	כ׳וועל נעמען אין זינען מיר טרויעריקע זאַכן,
Nu, megstu afile mikh kitslen.	נו, מעגסטו אַפילו מיך קיצלען.
- Vest lakhn, ikh vet zikh,	- וועסט לאַכן, איך וועט זיך,
Vest, Shloymele, shoyn lakhn,	וועסט, שלמהלע, שוין לאַכן,
Ikh hob a mitl gor a voyle zakh:	איך האָב אַ מיטל גאָר אַ ווילע זאַך:
Megst hobn zikh in zinen	מעגסט האָבן זיך אין זינען
Di troyerikste zakhn,	די טרויעריקסטע זאַכן,
Vet muzn zayn bay dir der ershter lakh.	וועט מוזן זיין ביי דיר דער ערשטער לאַך.
- Dos ershte, Avreml, nem ikh mir in zinen	– דאָס ערשטע, אָוורעמל, נעם איך מיר אין זינען
Mayn oremen tatn dem shvakhn,	מיין אָרעמען טאַטן דעם שוואַכן,
Vos zukht arum arbet un ken nisht gefinen,	וואָס זוכט אַרום אַרבעט און קען נישט געפינען,
Nu, vet zikh mir glustn tsu lakhn?	נו, וועט זיך מיר גלוסטן צו לאַכן?
- Vest lakhn, ikh vet zikh,	– וועסט לאַכן, איך וועט זיך,
Vest, Shloymele, farshpiln,	וועסט, שלמהלע, פֿאַרשפילן,
Ikh hob a mitl gor a voyle zakh:	איך האָב אַ מיטל גאָר אַ ווילע זאַך:
Kh'vel myauken vi a ketsl	כ׳וועל מיאָוקען ווי אַ קעצל
Un vi a hintl biln,	און ווי אַ הינטל בילן,
Vet muzn zayn bay dir der ershter lakh.	וועט מוזן זיין ביי דיר דער ערשטער לאַך.
Ikh vel zikh dermonen,	– איך וועל זיך, דערמאָנען,
Kh'hob nekhtn in kheyder	כ׳האָב נעכטן אין חדר
Di sedre vos geyt haynt fargesn,	די סדרה וואָס גייט היינט פֿאַרגעסן,
Der rebe, er vil nor kh'zol lernen keseyder,	דער רבי, ער וויל נאָר כ׳זאָל לערנען כסדר,
Er veyst nisht vi mir vilt zikh esn.	ער ווייסט נישט ווי מיר ווילט זיך עסן.
- Vest lakhn, ikh vet zikh,	– וועסט לאַכן, איך וועט זיך,
Vest nisht zayn aza shlekhter,	וועסט נישט זיין אַזאַ שלעכטער,
Kh'shtel ayn a knepl, kh'shtel akegn fir,	כ׳שטעל אײן אַ קנעפל, כ׳שטעל אַקעגן פֿיר,
Vest haltn zikh di zaytn	וועסט האַלטן זיך די זײַטן
Un kaykhn fun gelekhter,	און קײַכן פֿון געלעכטער,
Derzeendik vos ikh hob do bay mir.	דערזעענדיק וואָס איך האָב דאָ ביי מיר.

- Un kh'vel zikh dermanen dem rebns tsornik ponem,
Ven r'hot mikh genumen farhern,
Nokh hob ikh fun kantshik fil bloe simonim,
Geveynt fun yisurim mit trern.

- Vest lakhn, vest lakhn,
Aher gib shoyn dos knepl,
Ze, Shloymele, vos ikh hob do far dir!
A zemele mit puter,
Un hering a fayn kepl,
Anu, zog, Shloymele, ver vet lakhn frier?

A zemele mit puter
Un hering a fayn kepl,
Kh'vel morgn vider vetn zikh mit dir.

– אוּן כ׳װעל זיך דערמאַנען דעם רבינס צאָרניק פּנים,
װען ר׳האָט מיך גענומען פֿאַרהערן,
נאָך האָב איך פֿון קאַנטשיק פֿיל בלאָע סימנים,
געװײנט פֿון יסורים מיט טרערן.

– װעסט לאַכן, װעסט לאַכן,
אַהער גיב שוין דאָס קנעפּל,
זע, שלמהלע, װאָס איך האָב דאָ פֿאַר דיר!
אַ זעמעלע מיט פּוטער,
און הערינג אַ פֿײַן קעפּל,
אַנו, זאָג, שלמהלע, װער װעט לאַכן פֿריִער?

אַ זעמעלע מיט פּוטער,
און הערינג אַ פֿײַן קנעפּל,
כ׳װעל מאָרגן װידער װעטן זיך מיט דיר.

I, Avreml, will certainly not be the first to laugh, I bet you, no matter what jokes you tell. I'll think of sad things, you can even tickle me.

You'll laugh, I bet you, you'll surely laugh, Shloymele. I have a way, a very clever way. Even if you think about the saddest things, you'll have to be the first to laugh.

First of all, Avreml, I'll think about my poor weak father who keeps looking for work and can't find any. Well? Will I feel like laughing?

You'll laugh, I bet you, you'll lose the bet, Shloymele. I have a way, a very clever way. I'll meow like a cat and howl like a dog, and you'll have to be the first to laugh.

Let me remind you that yesterday, in kheyder, I forgot the passage for the day. The rabbi only wants me to study all the time—he doesn't know how hungry I am.

You'll laugh, I bet you. You won't be that mean. Bet a button, I'll bet four. You'll hold your sides and gasp with laughter when you see what I have here with me.

And I'll remember the rabbi's angry face when he started to quiz me. I'm still black and blue from his whip, and I cried bitter tears.

You'll laugh, you'll laugh, give me the button already. See, Shloymele, what I have here for you! A roll and butter and a fine herring head! Well, what do you say, Shloymele? Who will laugh first?

A roll and butter and a fine herring head? I'll bet you again tomorrow!

A YINGELE, A MEYDELE

א ייִנגעלע, אַ מיידעלע

A Little Boy, a Little Girl

Published by A. Bulkin and L. Efron in 1917. Adapted from a folksong about the Jewish clergy: "Der rebele, der gabele, / Der khazndl, der shamesl / Gants kley-koydesh geyt dokh tantsn" (The rabbi, the trustee, the cantor, the sexton—the whole clergy is going dancing) published by Sussman Kisselgof in 1911. The Bulkin-Efron version has the rabbi joining the dance. In the adaptation that Joseph Mlotek brings in his textbook *Yidishe kinder*, alef, 1971, it is the mother who is going to dance.

A yingele, a meydele,
A meydele, a yingele,
Lomir ale geyn tantsn.

Lomir ale tantsn geyn,
Di mame aleyn geyt oykh tantsn.

A yingele, a meydele. . .

Der tate aleyn geyt oykh tantsn. . .

Di bobe aleyn geyt oykh tantsn. . .

Der zeyde aleyn geyt oykh tantsn. . .

Di gantse mishpokhe geyt tantsn.

אַ ייִנגעלע, אַ מיידעלע,
אַ מיידעלע, אַ ייִנגעלע,
לאָמיר אַלע גיין טאַנצן.

לאָמיר אַלע טאַנצן גיין,
די מאַמע אַליין גייט אויך טאַנצן.

אַ ייִנגעלע, אַ מיידעלע. . .

דער טאַטע אַליין גייט אויך טאַנצן. . .

די באָבע אַליין גייט אויך טאַנצן. . .

דער זיידע אַליין גייט אויך טאַנצן. . .

די גאַנצע משפּחה גייט טאַנצן.

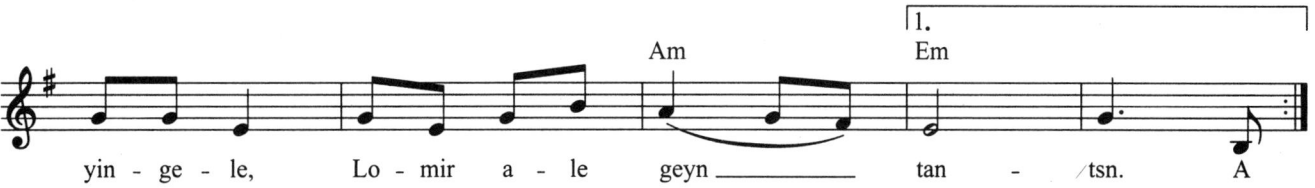

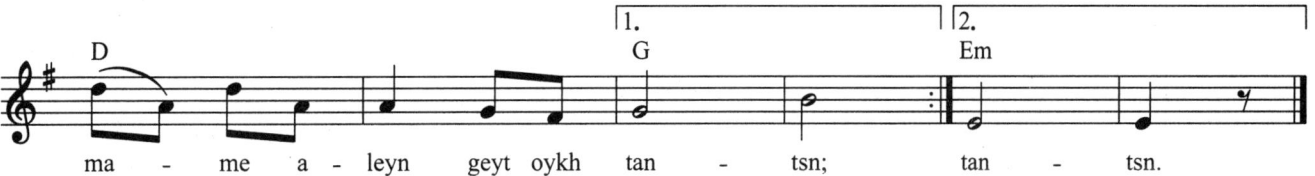

A little boy, a little girl—a little girl, a little boy. Let's all go dancing. Let's all go dancing. Even mother's going dancing. Even father's going dancing. Even grandmother's going dancing. Even grandfather's going dancing. The whole family's going dancing.

MIR KUMEN ON
מיר קומען אָן

We Are Coming

Words by Nokhem Yud (1888–1966) with music by Yankl Troupianski, popular composer and music teacher of the Yiddish schools in Warsaw and Vilna (1909—killed by the Nazis in 1944). The song was published in *Undzer gezang*, 1947. It was the musical theme of the pre-World War II film *Mir kumen on* about the Medem Sanitarium in Miedzeszyn, Poland. Camp Hemshekh, New York, used this song as its anthem in the '60s and '70s. Another melody to the poem by Vladimir Heifetz was published in *Gezang un kamf,* no. 5, 1937.

A yomtev makht oyf ale merk,
Un fayern tsindt on oyf berg!
Mir kumen—shturems on a tsam,
Fun land tsu land, fun yam tsu yam.

Refrain:
Mir kumen on, mir kumen on!
Mir kumen on, mir kumen on!
Un fest un zikher undzer trot!
Mir kumen on fun dorf un shtot.
Mit hunger-fayern in blik,
Mit hertser oysgebenkt nokh glik!
Mir kumen on, mir kumen on!

Mir geyen ale fest un greyt
Vi likhtik flakert undzer freyd;
Mir shlogn fayer oys fun shteyn
Un ver s'iz yung—muz mit undz geyn!

אַ יום-טובֿ מאַכט אויף אַלע מערק,
און פֿײַערן צינדט אָן אויף בערג!
מיר קומען - שטורעמס אָן אַ צאַם,
פֿון לאַנד צו לאַנד, פֿון ים צו ים.

רעפֿרײן
מיר קומען אָן, מיר קומען אָן!
מיר קומען אָן, מיר קומען אָן!
און פֿעסט און זיכער אונדזער טראָט!
מיר קומען אָן פֿון דאָרף און שטאָט.
מיט הונגער-פֿײַערן אין בליק,
מיט הערצער אויסגעבענקט נאָך גליק!
מיר קומען אָן, מיר קומען אָן!

מיר גייען אַלע פֿעסט און גרייט
ווי ליכטיק פֿלאַקערט אונדזער פֿרייד;
מיר שלאָגן פֿײַער אויס פֿון שטיין
און ווער ס'איז יונג - מוז מיט אונדז גיין!

Declare a holiday in all the markets, and light fires on the mountains!

We are coming—storms without end, from land to land, from sea to sea.

We are coming, we are coming, and our step is firm and sure. We are coming from village and city with the fires of hunger in our gaze, with hearts longing for happiness. We are coming, we are coming!

We're all walking firm and ready—How brightly our joy flares up.

We strike fire from stones, and whoever is young must walk with us.

KH'HOB GELIBT A MEYDL
SONGS OF LOVE

כ'האָב געליבט אַ מיידל

BRONTSHELE

בראָנטשעלע

Brontshele

Folksong. Variant text published by S. Ginzburg and P. Marek in 1901; text and music published by Platon Brounoff in 1911 and Y. L. Cahan in 1912. This version was published by Menakhem Kipnis in 1918. The song motif of the young man requesting permission to enter his lady love's house was traced to the 16th century by folklorist Y. L. Cahan (see Cahan, *Shtudyes*). German and Czech parallels are cited by Cahan, 1912.

On the YIVO recording *Folksongs in the East European Jewish Tradition*, from the repertoire of Mariam Niremberg (1986), produced by Barbara Kirshenblatt-Gimblett, a drunken cardsharp is calling on Rifkele and threatens to poison himself if she won't let him in: "Kh'hob moyre far dayn mamen. / Rifkele, efn mir / Anit vel ikh zikh farsamen." In other songs of this type the girls' names are variously Nekhamele, Brayndele, Khaye-Sorele, Shifkele, Rokhele.

S. Lehman published a variant in *Arbet un frayheyt*, 1921 (48) of a prisoner who says he will keep knocking on the iron door until he will be freed. Motl Zelmanowicz submitted a parody that was sung in the Jewish Labor Bund in Poland in the '20s.

Two parodies that were sung in the Lodz Ghetto were cited by Gila Flam. In one "Ver klapt do azoy shpet bay nakht? / Es klapt der geto hinger" (Who knocks so late at night? It is the Ghetto hunger), the plea is to "Open the provision store, it will make it easier." The girl here fears "dem altn" (The Eldest of the Judenrat of the Ghetto Chaim Rumkowski).

Ver klapt dos azoy shpet bay nakht?	ווער קלאַפּט דאָס אַזוי שפּעט בײַ נאַכט?
Yankele Volyantshik?	יאַנקעלע וואָליאַנטשיק?
Efn, efn, Brontshele,	עפֿן, עפֿן, בראָנטשעלע,
Ikh bin dayn kokhantshik!	איך בין דײַן קאָכאַנטשיק!
Vi kon ikh dir den efenen,	ווי קאָן איך דיר דען עפֿענען,
Kh'hob moyre far mayn mamen.	כ'האָב מורא פֿאַר מײַן מאַמען.
Efn, efn, Brontshele,	עפֿן, עפֿן, בראָנטשעלע,
Kh'vel zikh gornisht zamen!	כ'וועל זיך גאָרנישט זאַמען!
Vi kon ikh dir den efenen,	ווי קאָן איך דיר דען עפֿענען,
Kh'hob moyre far dem tatn.	כ'האָב מורא פֿאַר דעם טאַטן.
Efn, efn, Brontshele,	עפֿן, עפֿן, בראָנטשעלע,
S'vet dir gornisht shatn	ס'וועט דיר גאָרנישט שאַטן
Vi kon ikh dir den efenen,	ווי קאָן איך דיר דען עפֿענען,
Kh'hob moyre far mayn shvester.	כ'האָב מורא פֿאַר מײַן שוועסטער.
Efn, efn, Brontshele,	עפֿן, עפֿן, בראָנטשעלע,
S'vet zayn far dir beser!	ס'וועט זײַן פֿאַר דיר בעסער!
Vi kon ikh dir den efenen,	ווי קאָן איך דיר דען עפֿענען,
Kh'hob moyre far mayn bruder.	כ'האָב מורא פֿאַר מײַן ברודער.
Efn, efn, Brontshele,	עפֿן, עפֿן, בראָנטשעלע,
Makh nisht keyn geruder.	מאַך נישט קיין גערודער.
Vi kon ikh dir den efenen,	ווי קאָן איך דיר דען עפֿענען,
Kh'hob moyre far mayn feter.	כ'האָב מורא פֿאַר מײַן פֿעטער!
Efn, efn, Brontshele,	עפֿן, עפֿן, בראָנטשעלע,
Kh'vel nisht kumen shpeter.	כ'וועל ניט קומען שפּעטער.
Vi kon ikh dir den efenen,	ווי קאָן איך דיר דען עפֿענען,
Kh'hob moyre far mayn mumen.	כ'האָב מורא פֿאַר מײַן מומען.
Efn, efn, Brontshele,	עפֿן, עפֿן, בראָנטשעלע,
Anit vel ikh mer nisht kumen...	אַניט וועל איך מער נישט קומען...

Moderato

Ver klapt dos a - zoy shpet bay nakht?

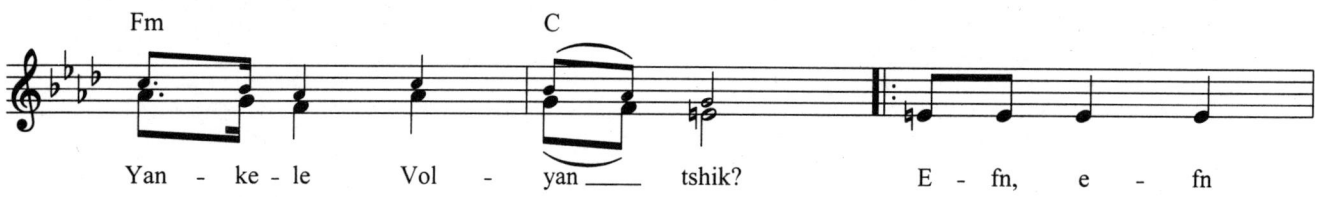
Yan - ke - le Vol - yan tshik? E - fn, e - fn

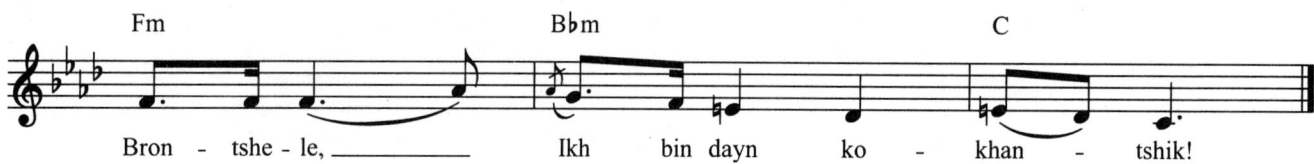
Bron - tshe - le, Ikh bin dayn ko - khan - tshik!

Who's that knocking so late at night? Yankele Volyantshik? - Open up, open up, Brontshele, it's your sweetheart

How can I open the door for you? I'm afraid of my mother. - Open up, open up, Brontshele, I won't stay very long.

How can I open the door for you? I'm afraid of my father. - Open up, open up, Brontshele, I won't do you any harm.

How can I open the door for you? I'm afraid of my sister. - Open up, open up, Brontshele, it will be the better for you.

How can I open the door for you? I'm afraid of my brother. - Open up, open up, Brontshele, don't make a fuss.

How can I open the door for you? I'm afraid of my uncle. - Open up, open up, Brontshele, I won't come back later.

How can I open the door for you? I'm afraid of my aunt.—Open up, open up, Brontshele. If you don't, I won't come back anymore.

IKH HOB DIKH LIB VI A PEYSAKHDIKN ROSL

איך האָב דיך ליב ווי אַ פּסחדיקן ראָסל

I Love You Like a Passover Broth

Folksong in the form of a letter. Sung by compiler Joseph Mlotek, who heard it at a summer camp in Warsaw from Isaac Giterman, director of the Joint Distribution Committee in Poland, in the 1930s. A different melody was published by Schack and Cohen, 1924. The *Tsaytshrift*. . . II-III (1927–1928) has the following text: "Ikh hob dikh lib Vi yontevdikn kigl / Un ale meydlekh / Zaynen ba mir migl / Fun mir, fun mir / Fun mir dayn khosn Idl" (I love you like holiday kugel, all other girls disgust me. From me, your bridegroom Yidl).

Ikh hob dikh lib vi a peysakhdikn rosl,
Du bist dokh take sheyn un fayn;
Ale meydelekh zaynen akegn dir posl.
Fun mir, dayn khosn Yosl.

In droysn geyt a zaverukhe mit a regn.
In shtub iz fintster, nas un kalt.
Mayn harts tut zikh in mir varfn vi a shmate.
Fun mir, dayn kale Zlate.

איך האָב דיך ליב ווי אַ פּסחדיקן ראָסל,
דו ביסט דאָך טאַקע שיין און פֿײַן;
אַלע מיידעלעך זענען אַקעגן דיר פּסול.
פֿון מיר, דײַן חתן יאָסל.

אין דרויסן גייט אַ זאַווערוכע מיט אַ רעגן,
אין שטוב איז פֿינצטער, נאַס און קאַלט;
מײַן האַרץ טוט זיך אין מיר וואַרפֿן ווי אַ שמאַטע.
פֿון מיר, דײַן כּלה זלאַטע.

Oh, I love you like a Passover broth, you're really beautiful and fine. All the other girls fade by comparison. From me, your bridegroom, Yosl.

Outside there's a drenching rain. In the house it's dark, wet and cold. My heart is jumping around inside me, like a dust rag. From me, your bride, Zlate.

IKH BIN SHOYN A MEYDL IN DI YORN　　　איך בין שוין אַ מיידל אין די יאָרן

I'm Not Such a Young Girl Anymore

Folksong that speaks of the two main obstacles to a girl's getting married: *nadan* (dowry) and *yikhes* (family pedigree). Published by M. Kipnis in 1918. In another collection of M. Kipnis', *Populerste lider fun Zeligfeld un Kipnis*, n.d., a third stanza was added by poet Peysakh Kaplan which begins: "Du host mir tsugezogt nemen, / Tsi hostu in mir genart?" (You promised to wed me. Were you disappointed in me?) Folk singer Isa Kremer included an additional stanza in her *Album* with a thinly disguised curse: "Un efsher hostu shoyn an andere, / A shenere un besere fun mir / Zol ir got gebn fir yor libe / Un aza sof vi bay mir" (And perhaps you have another girl, prettier and better than me. Let God give her four years of a love affair with such an outcome as mine). This feeling of anger is also echoed in a stanza that the compilers collected from Sorelle Skolnick, St. James, N. Y. (originally from Mozyr, Minsk province): "Un efsher gefelt dir Khane-Sore beser, / Vayl ir nadn iz greser; / To gey zhe mir fun danen am shnelstn avek, / Un zol es nemen an ek" (And perhaps you like Khane Sore more because her dowry is larger. So go away from me quickly and let it be over and done with!)

Ikh bin shoyn a meydl in di yorn,
Vos hostu mir dem kop fardreyt?
Ikh volt shoyn lang a kale gevorn
Un efsher take khasene gehat.

Un efsher geyt dir, ketsele, in nadn?
Di mame vet farkoyfn di shtib. . . *
Mir veln beyde khasene hobn,
Vayl ikh hob dikh lib!

Un efsher vilstu visn mayn yikhes?
Der zeyde iz gevezn a rov;
Lomir beyde khasene hobn,
Un zol shoyn nemen a sof!

איך בין שוין אַ מיידל אין די יאָרן,
וואָס האָסטו מיר דעם קאָפּ פֿאַרדרייט?
איך וואָלט שוין לאַנג אַ כּלה געוואָרן
און אפֿשר טאַקע חתונה געהאַט.

און אפֿשר גייט דיר, קעצעלע, אין נדן?
די מאַמע וועט פֿאַרקויפֿן די שטיב; (שטוב)
מיר וועלן ביידע חתונה האָבן,
ווײַל איך האָב דיך ליב!

און אפֿשר ווילסטו וויסן מײַן ייִחוס? -
דער זיידע איז געווען אַ רבֿ;
לאָמיר זשע ביידע חתונה האָבן,
און זאָל שוין נעמען אַ סוף!

---

*shtub

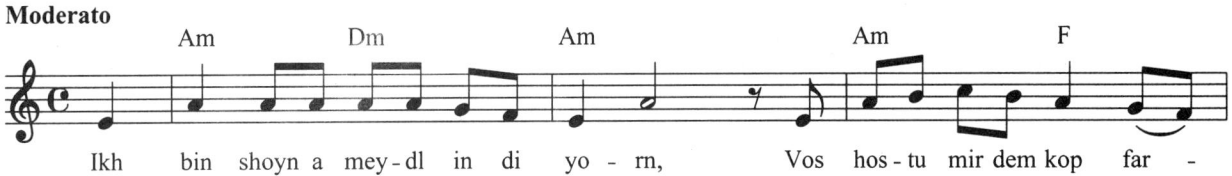

I'm not such a young girl anymore, why have you gotten me all mixed up? I would have become a bride long ago, and perhaps even gotten married.

Perhaps, love, you're concerned about a dowry? My mother will sell our house. The two of us will get married, because I love you.

And perhaps you want to know my pedigree? My grandfather was a rabbi! Let the two of us get married, and let there be an end to all this alreday!

SHOYN TSVEY-DRAY YOR AZ MIR FIRN A LIBE

שוין צוויי-דרײַ יאָר אַז מיר פֿירן אַ ליבע

It's Two or Three Years Now That We've Been Courting

Folksong recorded by Israeli singer Shimen Osevitsky and transcribed by compiler. Published in the YIVO journal *Yidisher folklor*, no. 2 (June, 1955). The record retains the dialect of the singer of the town Grajewo (Grayeve): "wibe" instead of "libe" (love affair). This is one of numerous folksongs in which jilted lovers vent their anger and frustrations in curses. (see: "Er hot mir tsugezogt," "Tsvey taybelekh," "Vos dreystu zikh arum bay mayne fentsterlekh" in this book, and "Tsu keyn libe tor men zikh nit mishn" in *Mir trogn a gezang*.) In most cases the addresser is a woman. This song is one of the exceptions in which a man is levelling the curse.

Shoyn tsvey-dray yor az mir firn a libe,
Fun undzer libe ken shoyn gornisht vern;
Haynt iz undzer libe geshlosn gevorn
Azoy vi a feygele in di nest.*

A feygele in di nest tut dokh flien
Tsu brengen ire kinderlekh esn;
Ikh on dir un du on mir
Kenen mir zikh beyde nisht fargesn.

Di podruges ire ale tsuzamen shteyen fun der vaytn
Un nemen fun mir di nekome;
Sheydn sheyd ikh zikh mit dir
Azoy vi a guf mit der neshome.

Zi hot mir gekoyft a zeyger
Mit tsvey goldene vayzer;
Ikh hob ir gekoyft a sametene torbe,
Zi zol kenen arumgeyn iber di hayzer.

Iber di hayzer zol zi arumgeyn
Un keyner zol ir nisht gebn;
Farsholtn zol vern ire yunge yorn,
Vi zi hot mir farvist mayn lebn.

Zi hot mir gekoyft a podarek,
Der podarekl hengt bay mir oyfn vant,
Un vi es kumt mir on der tog fun mayn
Harts-klemenish,**
Nem ikh ir karte in der hant.

Ir karte in der hant tu ikh haltn
Un reydn ken ikh nisht mit ir;
Oy, mentshn, ver es hot nor aza libe gefirt,
Dem iz khoyshekh un brokhedik vi mir.

---

* The singer pronounces the word "nyest."
** The first time the word is "dosade."

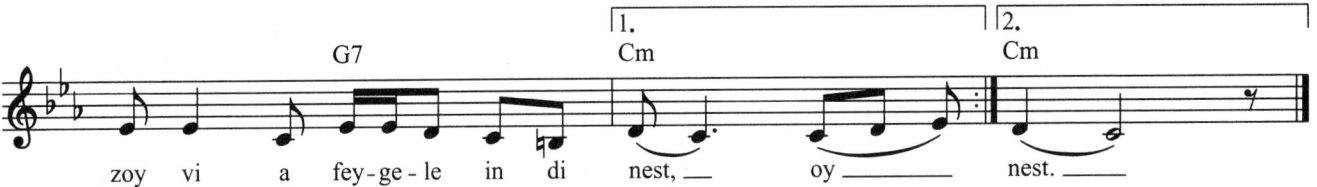

It's two or three years that we've been courting, nothing can come of our love anymore. Today our love is locked up like a little bird in its nest.

For a bird in the nest must fly, after all, to bring its young ones food. I without you and you without me—neither of us can forget the other.

Her friends all stand in the distance and take revenge on me. I separate myself from you like a body from its soul.

She bought me a clock with two golden hands; I bought her a velvet sack so she could go begging from house to house.

May she go from house to house, and may no one give her anything. Cursed be her youthful years, as she made my life empty.

She bought me a present—the little photograph hangs on my wall. And on days when I feel the heartbreak, I take her photograph in my hand.

I hold her photograph in my hand, and cannot speak to her. Oh, people, anyone who has had a love like mine, suffers darkness and anguish like me.

IKH ZITS MIR BAY DER ARBET UN IKH ARBET

איך זיץ מיר בײַ דער אַרבעט און איך אַרבעט

I Sit at My Workbench and Work

Folksong, text published in *Tsaytshrift. . .* II-III (1927–1928); a longer text with music was published in the *Filologishe shriftn fun YIVO*, V (1938). The song was part of a tailors' scene entitled "A shnayderish gezang," written and performed by Ben Bonus. There it was sung by his wife, actress-singer Mina Bern, who submitted it to the compilers.

Ikh zits mir bay der arbet un ikh arbet,
Un fun mayne tsores veyst dokh keyner nit;
Nor eyn padruge flegt mir shtendik zogn:
Vos zhe geystu oys azoy vi a likht?

Di balaboste flegt mir shtendik zogn:
Narish meydl, loz zikh in im nit arayn;
Gib a kuk, vos fun dir iz gevorn,
Az m'firt dikh shoyn in bolnitse arayn.

Di mame, zi flegt mir shtendik zogn:
Vos zhe geystu oys azoy vi a lekht*?
Tsi den ken ikh dir, mameshi, dertseyln,
Kh'hob zikh ayngelibt in a yingele,
un s'iz mir shlekht.

Kh'hob zikh ayngelibt in a yingele biz tsum shtarbn;
Di tshakhotke, mame, hot er mir ongemakht.
Kh'hob zikh ayngelibt in a yingele biz tsum shtarbn
Un tsum ende hot er zikh fun mir oysgelakht.

איך זיץ מיר בײַ דער אַרבעט און איך אַרבעט,
און פֿון מײַנע צרות ווייסט דאָך קיינער ניט;
נאָר איין פּאָדרוגע פֿלעגט מיר שטענדיק זאָגן:
וואָס זשע גייסטו אויס אַזוי ווי אַ ליכט?

די בעל-הביתטע פֿלעגט מיר שטענדיק זאָגן:
נאַריש מיידל, לאָז זיך אין אים ניט אַרײַן;
גיב אַ קוק, וואָס פֿון דיר איז געוואָרן,
אַז מ׳פֿירט דיך שוין אין באָלניצע אַרײַן.

די מאַמע, זי פֿלעגט מיר שטענדיק זאָגן:
וואָס זשע גייסטו אויס אַזוי ווי אַ לעכט? (ליכט)
צי דען קען איך דיר, מאַמעשי, דערציילן,
כ׳האָב זיך אײַנגעליבט אין אַ ייִנגעלע,
און ס׳איז מיר שלעכט.

כ׳האָב זיך אײַנגעליבט אין אַ ייִנגעלע ביז צום שטאַרבן,
די טשאַכאָטקע, מאַמע, האָט ער מיר אָנגעמאַכט.
כ׳האָב זיך אײַנגעליבט אין אַ ייִנגעלע ביז צום שטאַרבן
און צום ענדע האָט ער זיך פֿון מיר אויסגעלאַכט.

---

* likht

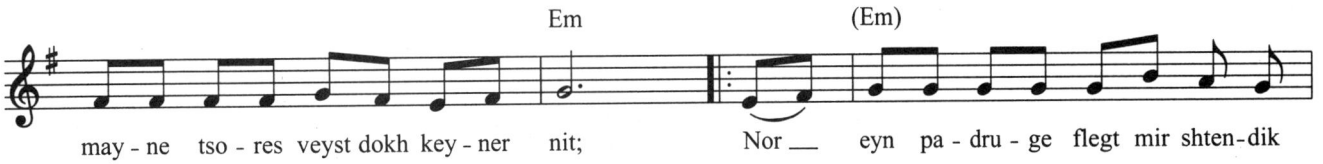

I sit at my workbench and work, and no one knows of my woes. But one of my friends always said to me: Why do you look so bad?

The shop mistress always used to say to me: Foolish girl, don't get involved with him. Just see what has become of you—You're ready to be taken to the hospital.

My mother always used to say to me: Why is your life going out like a candle? Could I explain it to you, dearest mother? I've fallen in love with a boy and I'm feeling bad.

I've fallen desperately in love with a boy. He's given me consumption, mother. I've fallen desperately in love with a boy, and in the end, he made a laughing stock of me.

DI SAPOZHKELEKH דִי סאַפּאָזשקעלעך

Little Boots

Folksong collected by Michael Alpert from the Russian emigre Bronya Sakina (born in Olvanisk, southern Ukraine) and popularized at the Klezkamp Folk Arts Program in 1985. Certain lines have parallels in other folksongs, like *Oy, Abram:* "Ikh on dir un du on mir, / Vi a klyamke on a tir" (I without you and you without me are like a doorknob without a door); and *Zog nor du sheyn meydele:* "Abi mit dir in eynem zayn" (As long as I can be together with you). The song was sung by Eleanor Reissa in the Broadway show *Those Were the Days*. It was made popular by Adrienne Cooper and Joanne Borts.

Farkoyfn di sapozhkelekh	פֿאַרקויפֿן די סאַפּאָזשקעלעך,
Un forn oyf di droshkelekh,	און פֿאָרן אויף די דראָשקעלעך,
Abi mit dir in eynem tsu zayn.	אַבי מיט דיר אין איינעם צו זײַן.
Oy, ikh on dir un du on mir	אוי, איך אָן דיר און דו אָן מיר
Vi a klyamke on a tir,	ווי אַ קליאַמקע אָן אַ טיר,
Ketsele, feygele mayn.	קעצעלע, פֿייגעלע מײַן.
Oy, forn oyf di vokzalekhlekh	אוי, פֿאָרן אויף די וואָקזאַלעכלעך
Un farkoyfn fremde shalekhlekh,	און פֿאַרקויפֿן פֿרעמדע שאַלעכלעך,
Abi mit dir in eynem tsu zayn.	אַבי מיט דיר אין איינעם צו זײַן.
Oy, ikh on dir un du on mir	אוי, איך אָן דיר און דו אָן מיר
Vi a klyamke on a tir.	ווי אַ קליאַמקע אָן אַ טיר,
Ketsele, feygele mayn.	קעצעלע, פֿייגעלע מײַן.
Oy, esn on a tishele,	אוי, עסן אָן אַ טישעלע,
Un shlofn on a kishele,	און שלאָפֿן אָן אַ קישעלע,
Abi mit dir in eynem tsu zayn.	אַבי מיט דיר אין איינעם צו זײַן,
Oy, ikh on dir un du on mir	אוי, איך אָן דיר און דו אָן מיר
Vi a klyamke on a tir,	ווי אַ קליאַמקע אָן אַ טיר,
Ketsele, feygele mayn.	קעצעלע, פֿייגעלע מײַן.
Oy, shlofn oyf di vokzalekhlekh	אוי, שלאָפֿן אויף די וואָקזאַלעכלעך
Un vashn fremde polekhlekh...	און וואַשן פֿרעמדע פּאָלעכלעך...
Abi mit dir in eynem tsu zayn.	אַבי מיט דיר אין איינעם צו זײַן.
Oy, ikh on dir un du on mir	אוי, איך אָן דיר און דו אָן מיר
Vi a klyamke on a tir,	ווי אַ קליאַמקע אָן אַ טיר,
Ketsele, feygele mayn.	קעצעלע, פֿייגעלע מײַן.

I'll sell my boots and ride on wagons, just so I can be together with you.

Oh, I without you and you without me are like a doorknob without a door. My kitten, my little bird.

Oh, I'll go to railroad stations and sell scarves to strangers, just so I can be together with you.

Oh, I'll eat without a table and sleep without a pillow, just so I can be together with you.

Oh, I'll sleep in railroad stations and wash the floors of strangers, just so I can be together with you.

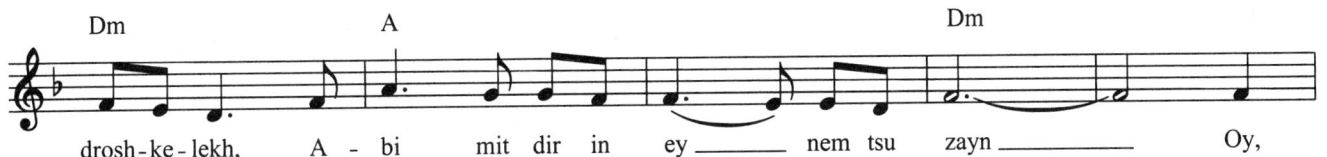

SHOYN HAYNT DRAY YOR AZ IKH STRADAYE

שוין הײַנט דרײַ יאָר אַז איך סטראַדאַיע

It's Three Years Today that I'm Suffering

Folksong published in the YIVO journal *Yidisher folklor*, no. 2 (June 1955). Collected from Charles Leikin, Bronx, N. Y. Several variants were previously published by S. Ginzburg and P. Marek, 1901, Platon Brounoff, 1911, Y. L. Cahan, 1912, and others. The song was one of 50 that Y. L. Peretz collected and had ready for publication in 1896. It was also sung as an underworld song (see S. Lehman, 1928).

Shoyn haynt dray yor az ikh stradaye
Un tsu dir kumen ken ikh nit;
Oy, in mayn hartsn brent a helish fayer,
Un keyner leshn ken dos nit.

שוין הײַנט דרײַ יאָר אַז איך סטראַדאַיע
און צו דיר קומען קען איך ניט;
אוי, אין מײַן הארצן ברענט אַ העליש פֿײַער,
און קיינער לעשן קען דאָס ניט.

Ikh farshelt dem tog fun mayn geboyrn,
Ikh shelt un shelt nokh atsind;
Halevay volt mikh mayn mame geven farloyrn
Beshas ikh bin gevezn a kleyn kind.

איך פֿאַרשעלט דעם טאָג פֿון מײַן געבוירן,
איך שעלט און שעלט נאָך אַצינד;
הלוואַי וואָלט מיך מײַן מאַמע געווען פֿאַרלוירן
בשעת איך בין געוועזן אַ קליין קינד.

Un mayn veytog vert mir gre-ve-ve-veser [greser]
Az ikh ze dikh mit a tsveytn geyn;
Shtekhn volt ikh zikh mit a me-ve-ve-ser [meser]
Kedey mayne oygn zoln dos nit zen.

און מײַן ווייטאָג ווערט מיר גרע-ווע-ווע-וועסער (גרעסער)
אַז איך זע דיך מיט אַ צווייטן גיין;
שטעכן וואָלט איך זיך מיט אַ מע-ווע-ווע-סער (מעסער)
כּדי מײַנע אויגן זאָלן דאָס ניט זען.

Nor zolst nit denken, tayere, az es vet dir gerotn,
Az ikh vel lign azoy yung in dr'erd,
Noykem zayn vet zikh in dir mayn shotn,
Az du zolst nisht hobn bay keynem keyn vert.

נאָר זאָלסט ניט דענקען, טײַערע, אַז עס וועט דיר געראָטן,
אַז איך וועל ליגן אַזוי יונג אין דר'ערד,
נוקם זײַן וועט זיך אין דיר מײַן שאָטן,
אַז דו זאָלסט נישט האָבן בײַ קיינעם קיין ווערט.

Nor eyn zakh, lyube, vel ikh dikh betn,
Az me vet mikh durkhtrogn durkh der tir,
Tsvey-dray trit, oy, zolstu nokh mir gebn
Az laytn zoln zogn s'iz durkh dir.

נאָר איין זאַך, ליובע, וועל איך דיך בעטן,
אַז מע וועט מיך דורכטראָגן דורך דער טיר,
צוויי-דרײַ טריט, אוי, זאָלסטו נאָך מיר געבן
אַז לײַטן זאָלן זאָגן ס'איז דורך דיר.

It's three years today that I'm suffering, and cannot come to you. Oh, in my heart there burns a hellish fire, and no one can extinguish it.

I curse the day that I was born, I curse and curse till now. Would that my mother had lost me when I was a little child!

And my pain gets greater when I see you with someone else. I would rather have stabbed myself with a knife, so my eyes would not see that.

But don't think, dearest that you will succeed if I go so early into my grave. My shadow will avenge me, so you will be worthless to anyone.

But one thing, love, I want to ask of you: When they carry me through the door, take two or three steps after me, so people will say it's because of you.

TSVEY TAYBELEKH צוויי טײַבעלעך

Two Little Doves

Folksong, published by Y. L. Cahan in 1912, was in the repertoire of the folk and opera singer Liuba Levitska of the Vilna Ghetto. Liuba sang this song during a concert that took place after the murder of 1,500 Jews in the Vilna Ghetto in January 1942. Poet Abraham Sutzkever writes (*Vilner geto* 1941–1944): "It is impossible to forget that concert… The mood in the hall was like a memorial service…" Shoshana Kalisch and Ruth Rubin both describe the role the song played in the heroic life and death of Liuba Levitska who was tortured to death by the Nazis. Kalisch writes that legends arose about Levitska's death, one of which recounted that on the drive from Vilna to Ponary, when she was led to the bodies on which she was to die, Liuba kept on singing this song.

Tsvey taybelekh zenen ibern vaser gefloygn,   צוויי טײַבעלעך זענען איבערן וואַסער געפֿלויגן,
In di piskelekh hobn zey zikh gekisht (gekusht),   אין די פּיסקעלעך האָבן זיי זיך געקישט (געקושט),
Farsholtn zol vern nor yener mentsh,   פֿאַרשאָלטן זאָל ווערן נאָר יענער מענטש,
Vos hot zikh in undzer libe arayngemisht!   וואָס האָט זיך אין אונדזער ליבע אַרײַנגעמישט!

Un az du vest kumen in a fremder shtot, lyubelyu,   און אַז דו וועסט קומען אין אַ פֿרעמדער שטאָט, ליובעליו,
Mayne reyd zolstu badenken;   מײַנע רייד זאָלסטו באַדענקען;
Un az du vest kumen iber a vaser, lyubelyu,   און אַז דו וועסט קומען איבער אַ וואַסער, ליובעליו,
Far tsores zolstu zikh nisht dertrenken.   פֿאַר צרות זאָלסטו זיך נישט דערטרענקען.

Un az du vest kumen in a vayter shtot, lyubelyu,   און אַז דו וועסט קומען אין אַ ווײַטער שטאָט, ליובעליו,
Mayne reyd zolstu bakenen;   מײַנע רייד זאָלסטו באַקענען;
Un az du vest kumen iber a fayer, lyubelyu,   און אַז דו וועסט קומען איבער אַ פֿײַער, ליובעליו,
Far tsores zolstu zikh nit farbrenen.   פֿאַר צרות זאָלסטו זיך ניט פֿאַרברענען.

Tsvey taybelekh zenen ibern vaser gefloygn   צוויי טײַבעלעך זענען איבערן וואַסער געפֿלויגן
Mit di fligelekh azoy tseshpreyt;   מיט די פֿליגעלעך אַזוי צעשפּרייט;
Keyn gutn sof zol der mentsh nit hobn,   קיין גוטן סוף זאָל דער מענטש ניט האָבן,
Vos hot undz fun der libe azoy gikh tsesheydt!   וואָס האָט אונדז פֿון דער ליבע אַזוי זיך צעשיידט!

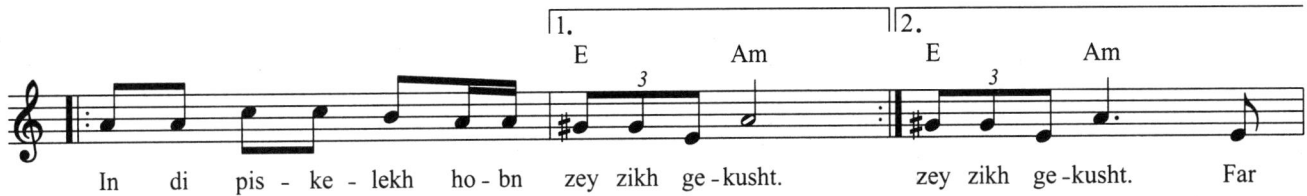
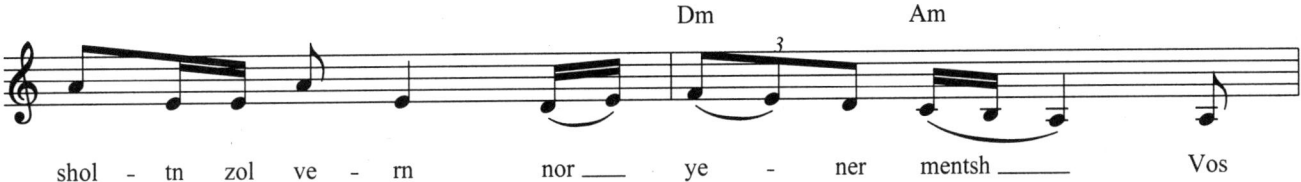
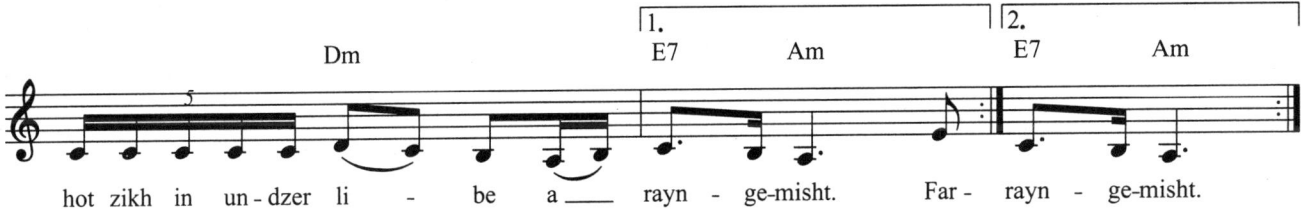

Two little doves flew over the ocean; they kissed each other's beaks. Cursed be that man who interfered in our love!

And when you come to a strange city, love, remember my words; and when you fly over an ocean, love, don't drown because of your woes. And when you come to a distant city, love, remember my words; and when you fly over a fire, love, don't burn yourself up because of your woes.

Two little doves flew over the ocean with their wings spread wide out so. May that man come to no good end who so quickly separated us from our love.

IKH ZITS MIR BAY DER ARBET　　　　　　　　　　איך זיץ מיר בײַ דער אַרבעט

I Sit at My Work

Folksong in the repertory of singer Ben Bonus, submitted by his wife, actress Mina Bern. In the song collection *Al haahava* by Mendel Singer and Moshe Bik, with translations by Shimshon Meltser (1951), which folklorist Ruth Rubin gave the compilers, two verses of the song appear. Ruth Rubin and the compilers were greatly enamored of the melody. A variant of the text was published by Y. L. Cahan in 1927–28 (no. 24 in his *Collected Works*).

Ikh zits mir bay der arbet,　　　　　　　איך זיץ מיר בײַ דער אַרבעט,
Tut mir vey der rukn,　　　　　　　　　טוט מיר ווײ דער רוקן,
Mayne oygn tuen mir shoyn vey　　　　מײַנע אויגן טוען מיר שוין ווײ
Oyf mayn zis-lebn aroystsukukn.　　　　אויף מײַן זיס-לעבן אַרויסצוקוקן.

Kum mit mir shpatsirn　　　　　　　　קום מיט מיר שפּאַצירן
In dem grinem vald,　　　　　　　　　אין דעם גרינעם וואַלד,
Oy-vey, dushe mayne,　　　　　　　　אוי-ווײ דושע מײַנע,
S'iz mir azoy kalt.　　　　　　　　　　ס'איז מיר אַזוי קאַלט.

Ikh heyb ir ayntsutulyen　　　　　　　איך הײב איר אײַנצוטוליען
Un ayntsuhiln,　　　　　　　　　　　און אײַנצוהילן,
Oy-vey, dushe mayne,　　　　　　　　אוי-ווײ דושע מײַנע,
Shver a libe tsu shpiln.　　　　　　　שווער אַ ליבע צו שפּילן.

I sit at my work and my back aches. My eyes begin to hurt from looking so hard for my sweet love.

Come walking with me in the green forest.

Oh, my love, I am so cold. I begin to enfold and embrace her. Oh, my love, it is hard to have a love affair.

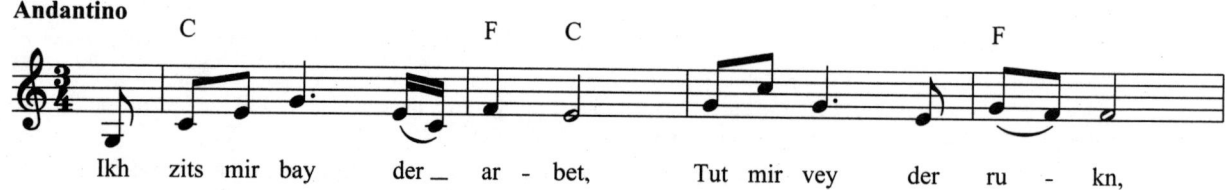

DU MEYDELE, DU FAYNS

דו מיידעלע, דו פֿײַנס

You Fine Little Girl

A variant of the text of this riddle song appeared in the S. Ginzburg-P. Marek collection of 1901; text and melody were published in *Ost und West,* 1905. This song type of the contest between a maiden and young man is a popular international ballad theme—the oldest type mentioned in the Child Collection of Anglo-Scottish Balladry (Child I). A few of the Yiddish riddles were compared to the English type by compiler in her paper "International Motifs in the Yiddish Ballad" (1964). The German parallels were cited by Alfred Landau in 1903. The Yiddish song contains a Jewish motif in two replies, which is absent from other European parallels—that the "Torah is deeper than the spring" and "Mikve-vaser (the water of the ritual bath house) is without a fish." One version (*Mir zingen, Paris,* 1948) combines the riddles of this song with those of the popular song "Tum-balalayke." In *The Jewish Songster,* 1929, the song is translated into Hebrew as "Yaldoh yaldosi."

Du meydele, du fayns,
Du meydele, du sheyns,
Kh'vel dikh epes fregn
A retenish a kleyns:
Vos iz hekher fun a hoyz?
Vos iz flinker fun a moyz?

Du narisher bokher,
Du narisher trop,
Du host nit keyn seykhl
In dayn kop;
Der roykh iz hekher fun a hoyz,
Di kats iz flinker fun a moyz.

Du meydele, du fayns,
Du meydele, du sheyns,
Kh'vel dikh epes fregn
A retenish a kleyns:
Vos flit on fligl?
Un vos iz gemoyert on tsigl?

Du narisher bokher,
Du narisher trop,
Du host nit keyn seykhl
In dayn kop;
Shney flit dokh on fligl,
Der frost iz gemoyert on tsigl.

דו מיידעלע, דו פֿײַנס,
דו מיידעלע, דו שײנס,
כ'וועל דיך עפּעס פֿרעגן
אַ רעטעניש אַ קלײנס:
וואָס איז העכער פֿון אַ הויז?
וואָס איז פֿלינקער פֿון אַ מויז?

דו נאַרישער בחור,
דו נאַרישער טראָפּ,
דו האָסט ניט קיין שׂכל
אין דײַן קאָפּ;
דער רויך איז העכער פֿון אַ הויז,
די קאַץ איז פֿלינקער פֿון אַ מויז.

די מיידעלע, דו פֿײַנס,
דו מיידעלע, דו שײנס,
כ'וועל דיך עפּעס פֿרעגן
אַ רעטעניש אַ קלײנס:
וואָס פֿליט אָן פֿליגל?
און וואָס איז געמויערט אָן ציגל?

דו נאַרישער בחור,
דו נאַרישער טראָפּ,
דו האָסט ניט קיין שׂכל
אין דײַן קאָפּ;
שניי פֿליט דאָך אָן פֿליגל,
דער פֿראָסט איז געמויערט אָן ציגל?

Du meydele, du fayns,
Du maydele, du sheyns,
Kh'vel dikh epes fregn
A retenish a kleyns:
Vos iz royter fun a flam?
Un vos iz getrayer fun a man?

Du, narisher bokher,
Du, narisher trop,
Du host nit keyn seykhl
In dayn kop;
Di fan iz royter fun a flam,
Un a tate iz getrayer fun a man.

דו מײדעלע, דו פֿײַנס,
דו מײדעלע, דו שײנס,
כ'װעל דיך עפּעס פֿרעגן
אַ רעטעניש אַ קלײנס:
װאָס איז רױטער פֿון אַ פֿלאַם?
און װאָס איז געטרײַער פֿון אַ מאַן?

דו נאַרישער בחור,
דו נאַרישער טראָפּ,
דו האָסט ניט קײן שׂכל
אין דײַן קאָפּ;
די פֿאַן איז רױטער פֿון אַ פֿלאַם,
און אַ טאַטע איז געטרײַער פֿון אַ מאַן.

- You fine girl, you pretty girl, I'll ask you a question, a little riddle: What is higher than a house? What is quicker than a mouse?

- You foolish young man, you silly fool, you have no sense in your head. Chimney smoke is higher than a house. A cat is quicker than a mouse.

- You fine girl, you pretty girl, I'll ask you a question, a little riddle: What flies without wings? And what makes walls without bricks?

- You foolish young man, you silly fool—you have no sense in your head. Snow can fly without wings, and frost makes walls without bricks.

- You fine girl, you pretty girl, I'll ask you a question, a little riddle: What is redder than a fire, and what is more faithful than a husband?

- You foolish young man, you silly fool—you have no sense in your head. A frying pan is redder than a fire, and a father is more faithful than a husband.

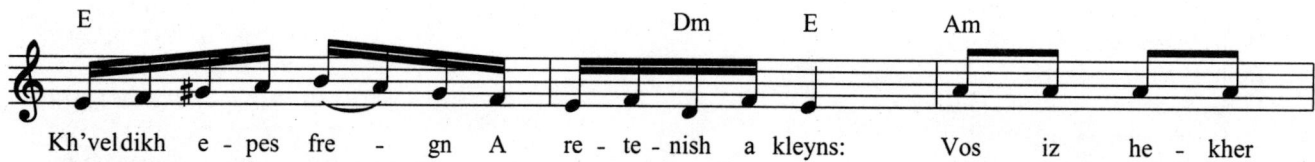

NEM MIR AROYS A BER FUN VALD   נעם מיר ארויס אַ בער פֿון װאַלד

Catch Me a Bear from the Forest

    Folksong of the exchange of impossible tasks. A fragment was published by S. Ginzburg and P. Marek in 1901; music and text were published by Y. L. Cahan in 1912. In the versions of the song there are about four different endings: "Ikh bin klug un du bist oykh nit narish (or: du keyn nar), / Un lomir beyde shvaygn" (I am clever and you aren't foolish either (or you are not a fool), and let's both be silent): in Y. L. Cahan, N. Prilutsky, II; "Ikh bin a nar, un du a greserer / Lomir beyde shvaygn" (I'm a fool and you're a bigger one, so let's be silent): in Moishe Beregovski, 1962; "Bist dokh a kluge, un ikh keyn nar— / To lomir beyde blaybn" (You are smart, and I'm no fool, so let's remain [together]): in Ruth Rubin, *Treasury;* "Zol zhe dikh der tayvl hoyln / Un ikh zol dir nisht kenen" (May the Devil take you and I not know you): in N. Prilutsky, II.

    The song is one of the oldest international ballad themes. In Child 2, it appears as a contest in the ballad of an elfin knight, a demon who tries to seduce the maid and carry her off. By countering his tasks with those of equal difficulty she escapes his trap. This song is one of eleven included by compiler in her paper "International Motifs in the Yiddish Ballad." One Yiddish version of Prilutsky has the impossible task of counting the tears that orphans weep. A Jewish motif is introduced when one of the tasks proposed is to count all the candles that burn on the holy Sabbath.

- Nem mir aroys a ber fun vald Un lern im oys shraybn— Oto dentsmol, un oto dentsmol, Vel ikh dayne blaybn.	‏-נעם מיר אַרויס אַ בער פֿון װאַלד און לערן אים אױס שרײַבן- אָטאָ דענצמאָלט און אָטאָ דענצמאָלט װעל איך דײַנע בלײַבן.
- Ikh vel dir aroysnemen a ber fun vald, Un ikh vel im oyslernen shraybn, Hob zhe mir zibn kinder, Un zolst a meydl blaybn.	‏-איך װעל דיר אַרױסנעמען אַ בער פֿון װאַלד, און איך װעל אים אױסלערנען שרײַבן, האָב זשע מיר זיבן קינדער, און זאָלסט אַ מײדל בלײַבן.
- Ikh vel dir hobn zibn kinder Un a meydl blaybn, Makh zhe mir a vigele On holts un on getsaygn.	‏-איך װעל דיר האָבן זיבן קינדער און אַ מײדל בלײַבן, מאַך זשע מיר אַ װיגעלע אָן האָלץ און אָן געצײַגן.
- Ikh vel dir makhn a vigele On holts un on getsaygn, Ney zhe mir oys zibn hemder On nodlen un on zaydn.	‏-איך װעל דיר מאַכן אַ װיגעלע אָן האָלץ און אָן געצײַגן, נײ זשע מיר אױס זיבן העמדער אָן נאָדלען און אָן זײַדן.
- Ikh vel dir oysneyen zibn hemder On nodlen un on zaydn, Khap zhe mir oys ale fish fun yam, S'zol keyn eyne nit blaybn.	‏-איך װעל דיר אױסנײַען זיבן העמדער אָן נאָדלען און אָן זײַדן, כאַפּ זשע מיר אױס אַלע פֿיש פֿון ים, ס'זאָל קײן אײנע ניט בלײַבן.

- Kh'vel dir oyskhapn ale fish fun yam,
S'zol keyn eyne nit blaybn,
Pregl op zibn fishelekh,
Zey zoln lebedik blaybn.

- Ikh vel dir oppreglen zibn fishelekh,
Zey zoln lebedik blaybn,
Makh zhe mir a leyterl,
S'zol tsum himl shtaygn.

- Ikh vel dir makhn a leyterl
S'zol tsum himl shtaygn,
Ikh bin a nar, un du a greserer,
Lomir beyde shvaygn.

– כ'וועל דיר אויסכאַפּן אַלע פֿיש פֿון ים,
ס'זאָל קיין איינע ניט בלײַבן,
פּרעגל אָפּ זיבן פֿישעלעך,
זיי זאָלן לעבעדיק בלײַבן.

– איך וועל דיר אָפּפּרעגלען זיבן פֿישעלעך,
זיי זאָלן לעבעדיק בלײַבן,
מאַך זשע מיר אַ לייטערל,
ס'זאָל צום הימל שטײַגן.

– איך וועל דיר מאַכן אַ לייטערל
ס'זאָל צום הימל שטײַגן,
איך בין אַ נאַר, און דו אַ גרעסערער,
לאָמיר ביידע שווײַגן.

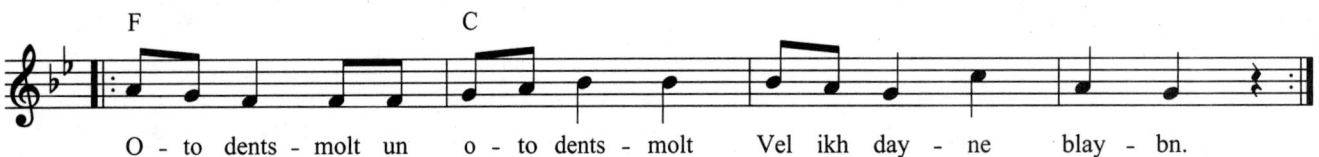

Catch me a bear from the forest and teach him to write. Only then and only then will I be yours.

I will catch you a bear from the forest and teach him to write. Have seven children and remain a virgin.

I'll have seven children for you and remain a virgin, Make me a cradle without wood and without tools.

I'll make a cradle without wood and tools. Sew me seven shirts without needles and thread.

I'll sew you seven shirts without needles and without thread. Catch me all the fish in the ocean so not a single one remains.

I'll catch you all the fish in the ocean so not a single one remains.

Fry me seven little fish and have tham stay alive.

I'll fry you seven little fish and have them stay alive. Make me a ladder that will reach the sky.

I'll make you a ladder that will reach the sky. I'm a fool and you're a bigger one, so let's both be still.

KH'HOB GELIBT A MEYDL FUN AKHTSN YOR

כ'האָב געליבט אַ מיידל פֿון אַכצן יאָר

I Loved a Girl of Eighteen

Folksong collected from Mascha Benya Matz. Published in the YIVO folklore journal, *Yidisher folklor* (vol. I, no. 3, March, 1962). Compiler included this song in: "International Motifs in the Yiddish Ballad." The appearance of the "telegram" is obviously indicative of more recent vintage; words like "knabe" and "dizer" suggest German provenance; "potshtolyontshikl" suggests Slavic.

Kh'hob gelibt a meydl fun akhtsn yor,	כ'האָב געליבט אַ מיידל פֿון אַכצן יאָר,
Un libn lib ikh ir shoyn tsvey-dray yor.	און ליבן ליב איך איר שוין צוויי-דרײַ יאָר.
Kh'hob gevelt visn tsi zi hot mikh lib,	כ'האָב געוועלט וויסן צי זי האָט מיך ליב,
Bin ikh avekgeforn fun mayn shtib (shtub).	בין איך אַוועקגעפֿאָרן פֿון מײַן שטיב (שטוב).
Un vi ikh bin fun mayn shtib avekgeforn	און ווי איך בין פֿון מײַן שטיב אַוועקגעפֿאָרן,
Iz mayn gelibte krank gevorn.	איז מײַן געליבטע קראַנק געוואָרן.
Tsvelf a zeyger bay der nakht,	צוועלף אַ זייגער בײַ דער נאַכט,
Der potshtolyontshikl a telegrame gebrakht.	דער פּאָטשטאָליאַנטשיקל אַ טעלעגראַמע געבראַכט.
Gesheftn gebroset, farmegn farlorn,	געשעפֿטן געבראַסעט, פֿאַרמעגן פֿאַרלאָרן,
Tsu mayn gelibter bin ikh geforn.	צו מײַן געליבטער בין איך געפֿאָרן.
- Gut morgn, gut morgn, mayn sheyner parsheyn, (parshoyn)	– גוט-מאָרגן, גוט-מאָרגן, מײַן שיינער פּאַרשיין, (פּאַרשוין)
Vos tustu lign in betele aleyn?	וואָס טוסטו ליגן אין בעטעלע אַליין?
- Gut yor, gut yor, mayn sheyner knabe,	– גוט-יאָר, גוט-יאָר, מײַן שיינער קנאַבע,
Ot dize betele iz mayn begrabe.	אָט דיזע בעטעלע איז מײַן בעגראַבע.
S'hot nit gedoyert keyn eyn frimorgn,	ס'האָט ניט געדויערט קיין איין פֿרימאָרגן,
Der sheyner knabe iz oykh geshtorbn.	דער שיינער קנאַבע איז אויך געשטאָרבן.
In shtot iz gevorn a yomer, a klog,	אין שטאָט איז געוואָרן אַ יאָמער, אַ קלאָג,
Oy, tsvey gelibte in eyn tog.	אוי, צוויי געליבטע אין איין טאָג.

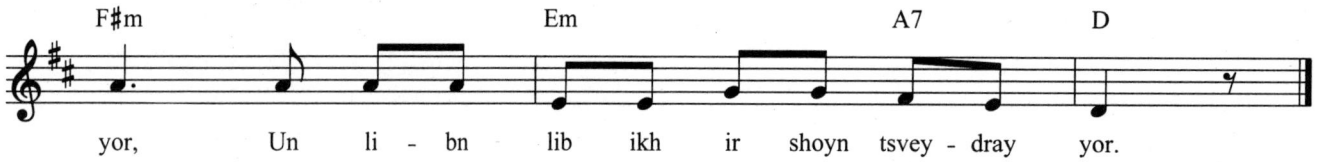

I loved a girl of eighteen; and I loved her for two, three years. I wanted to know whether she loved me, so I traveled away from my house.

And as soon as I went away from my house, my beloved grew ill. Twelve o'clock at night the postman brought me a telegram. My business thrown away, my fortune lost, I rushed to my beloved.

Good morning, good morning, my lovely maiden, why are you lying in the bed alone? - Good morning, good morning, my handsome youth, this little bed will be my grave.

It didn't even take one day, and the handsome youth died too. In the town there was weeping and wailing: Oh, two lovers in one day!

VU BISTU GEVEN?

ווּ ביסטו געוועןִ?

Where Were You?

Folksong published by M. Kipnis in 1925, which he collected from the poet Z. Segalovitsh. Chaim Tauber set his song "Motl der opreyter" to this melody. It also appears in the popular Jewish dance "The Troika."

Vu bistu geven,
Az gelt iz geven
Un der nadn iz gelegn oyfn tish?
Haynt bistu do,
Az keyn gelt iz nishto
Un dos lebn iz gevorn azoy mis.

Vu bistu geven,
Az yugnt iz geven
Un dos lebn iz geven tsuker zis?
Haynt bistu do,
Az di hor zaynen gro
Un dos lebn iz gevorn azoy mis.

Vu bistu geven
Az yugnt iz geven,
Dos harts hot mit libe gebrent?
Haynt bistu do
Az der kop iz shoyn gro
Un es tsitern bay mir shoyn di hent.

ווּ ביסטו געווען
אַז געלט איז געווען
און דער נדן איז געלעגן אויפֿן טיש?
הײַנט ביסטו דאָ,
אַז קיין געלט איז נישטאָ
און דאָס לעבן איז געוואָרן אַזוי מיאוס.

ווּ ביסטו געווען
אַז יוגנט איז געווען
און דאָס לעבן איז געווען צוקער־זיס?
הײַנט ביסטו דאָ,
אַז די האָר זײַנען גראָ,
און דאָס לעבן איז געוואָרן אַזוי מיאוס.

ווּ ביסטו געווען
אַז יוגנט איז געווען,
דאָס האַרץ האָט מיט ליבע געברענט?
הײַנט ביסטו דאָ
אַז דער קאָפּ איז שוין גראָ
און עס ציטערן בײַ מיר שוין די הענט.

Where were you when there was money and the dowry lay on the table? Today you are here, when my money is gone and life has become so grim.

Where were you when we were young and life was sweet as sugar? Today you are here and my hair is gray and life is grim.

Where were you when we were young and my heart burned with love? Today you are here and my hair is already gray and my hands tremble.

Moderato

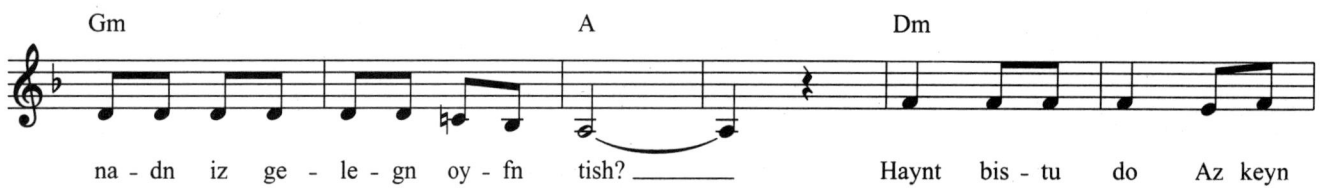

VOS DREYSTU ZIKH ARUM BAY MAYNE FENTSTERLEKH?

וואָס דרייסטו זיך ארום בײַ מײַנע פֿענצטערלעך?

Why Are You Hanging Around Near My Windows?

Popular folksong sung by compiler in pre-World War II, Poland. Published in the second choral collection of I. Gershteyn, Vilna, 1939, in the arrangement of Elye Teitelbaum. Melodic and textual variants were published by Y. L. Cahan and M. Kipnis in 1912 and 1918 respectively.

Vos dreystu zikh arum bay mayne fentsterlekh?
Meynst ikh vel aroysgeyn tsu dir.
Tsi bin ikh den di shenste fun di meydelekh?
Tsi hostu nit keyn shenere fun mir?

Makh mir nisht keyn falshe komplimentelekh,
Zog mir nisht az du host mikh take lib;
Az brenen zolt ir ale vi di lempelekh —
Mayn gelibter punkt azoy vi ir.

וואָס דרייסטו זיך ארום בײַ מײַנע פֿענצטערלעך?
מיינסט, איך וועל אַרויסגיין צו דיר.
צי בין איך דען די שענסטע פֿון די מיידעלעך?
צי האָסטו ניט קיין שענערע פֿון מיר?

מאַך מיר נישט קיין פֿאַלשע קאָמפּלימענטעלעך,
זאָג מיר נישט, אַז דו האָסט מיך טאַקע ליב;
אַז ברענען זאָלט איר אַלע ווי די לעמפּעלעך –
מײַן געליבטער פּונקט אַזוי ווי איר.

Why do you hang around near my windows? Do you think I'll come out to you? Am I, then, the prettiest of all girls? Don't you have any that are prettier than I?

Don't pay me false compliments. Don't tell me that you really love me.

May all of you burn like lamps! My beloved as well as you!

VU IZ DOS GESELE?

ווּ איז דאָס געסעלע?

Where is the Street?

Folksong; the text of one stanza was published in 1912 by Y. L. Cahan. The Ukrainian equivalent, beginning with "Gdye eto ulitsa" was published by Z. Skuditski in 1936. Dov Noy and Meir Noy bring the first stanza in Yiddish, Hebrew and Russian. It also appears in another folksong "Du zolst nit geyn mit keyn andere meydelekh" (You Shouldn't Go With Any Other Girls). The second stanza of the present text was transcribed by the compilers from a recording of Jan Peerce. A related theme is in the song "Fargangene yorn" by Leyb Ayzn in Leye Bloch-Lederer's collection *Di shenste geklibene yidishe lider:* "Ikh ze nokh dem shtetl, ikh ze nokh di shil / Ikh ze nokh dem taykhl vi oykh di vaser-mil / Ikh ze nokh mayn libste fun vayt ergets dort / Zi kumt mir in kholem un redt nit keyn vort" (I still see the town, I still see the synagogue, I still see the brook and the mill. I still see my beloved in the distance. She silently comes to me in my dream.) Actress Mina Bern sang the song in the musical *Those Were the Days*.

Vu iz dos gesele, vu iz di shtib (shtub)?	ווּ איז דאָס געסעלע, ווּ איז די שטיב (שטוב)?
Vu iz dos meydele, vemen kh'hob lib?	ווּ איז דאָס מיידעלע, וועמען כ'האָב ליב?
Ot iz dos gesele, ot iz di shtib,	אָט איז דאָס געסעלע, אָט איז די שטיב,
Ot iz dos meydele, vemen kh'hob lib.	אָט איז דאָס מיידעלע, וועמען כ'האָב ליב.
Vu iz dos taykhele, vu iz di mil?	ווּ איז דאָס טײַכעלע, ווּ איז די מיל?
Vu iz dos derfele, vu iz di shil?	ווּ איז דאָס דערפֿעלע, ווּ איז די שיל?
Ot iz dos taykhele, ot iz di mil,	אָט איז דאָס טײַכעלע, אָט איז די מיל,
Ot iz dos derfele, ot iz di shil.	אָט איז דאָס דערפֿעלע, אָט איז די שיל.
Arayn in di shtiber, mayn veytog iz groys,	אַרײַן אין די שטיבער, מײַן וויײטאָג איז גרויס,
Alts iz geblibn a kholem nor bloyz,	אַלץ איז געבליבן אַ חלום נאָר בלויז,
Nishto mer dos gesele, nishto mer di shtib,	נישטאָ מער דאָס געסעלע, נישטאָ מער די שטיב,
Nishto mer dos meydele vemen kh'hob lib.	נישטאָ מער דאָס מיידעלע וועמען כ'האָב ליב.

Moderato

Where is the street and where is the house? Where is the girl that I loved? Here is the street and here is the house. Here is the girl that I loved.

Where is the creek and where is the mill? Where is the village and where is the synagogue? Here is the creek and here is the mill. Here is the village and here is the synagogue.

I went into the house and how great my pain—all that remained is but a dream. There is no more street and there is no more house. There is no more girl that I loved.

ER HOT MIR TSUGEZOGT   ער האָט מיר צוגעזאָגט

He Promised Me

    Folksong. Text published by S. Ginzburg and P. Marek in 1901; text and music published by Joel Engel in 1909. The song combines the lullaby with the theme of an unhappy love affair. The lines beginning with "Es iz nishto keyn epl" (There is no apple. . .) are found in a song in one of the oldest Yiddish manuscript song collections of Isaac Wallich of the 16th century (Neubauer Catalogue of the Bodleian Library, 2420: no. 20): "Es ist kein apfel so rosenrot / es stecket ein wurm d(e)rin, / es ist kein maidlein so hofisch und fein, / es furt einen falschen sin." (There is no apple, no matter how red, that a worm is not found in it; there is no maiden so elegant and fine, that has no falsehood in mind). (Quoted in Y. L. Cahan, *Shtudyes*, and M. Beregovski, 1962.)

Er hot mir tsugezogt, er hot mir tsugezogt,   ער האָט מיר צוגעזאָגט, ער האָט מיר צוגעזאָגט,
Er hot mir tsugezogt tsu nemen;   ער האָט מיר צוגעזאָגט צו נעמען;
Er geyt avek tsu an ander meydl,   ער גייט אַוועק צו אַן אַנדער מיידל,
Tut mayn harts klemen.   טוט מײַן האַרץ קלעמען.

Refrain: רעפֿרײן:
Shlof, mayn kind, shlof,   שלאָף מײַן קינד, שלאָף,
In dayn tayern shlof!   אין דײַן טײַערן שלאָף!
Ven got vet im batsoln   ווען גאָט וועט אים באַצאָלן
Far der falsher libe,   פֿאַר דער פֿאַלשער ליבע,
Dos vet zayn zayn shtrof!   דאָס וועט זײַן זײַן שטראָף!

S'iz gor nito keyn epele,   ס'איז גאָר ניטאָ קיין עפּעלע,
Vos zol nit zayn keyn vorem in drinen;   וואָס זאָל ניט זײַן קיין וואָרעם אין דרינען;
S'iz gor nito keyn mansperzon,   ס'איז גאָר ניטאָ קיין מאַנספּערזאָן,
Vos zol nit hobn keyn falshn zinen.   וואָס זאָל ניט האָבן קיין פֿאַלשן זינען.

Ikh hob zikh geneyt a kleydele   איך האָב זיך גענייט אַ קליידעלע
Fun finf arshin di breyt;   פֿון פֿינף אַרשין די ברייט;
Keyn guts un keyn hob zoln zey nit hobn   קיין גוטס און קיין האָב זאָלן זיי ניט האָבן,
Di vos hobn undzer libe funandergesheydt.   די, וואָס האָבן אונדזער ליבע פֿונאַנדערגעשיידט.

Adagio non molto

He promised me, he promised me, he promised to marry me. Now he goes to another girl, and my heart is breaking.

Sleep, my child, sleep in your sweet slumber. When God repays him for his false love, that will be his punishment.

There is no apple that has no worm inside. There is no man that isn't false of heart.

I sewed myself a dress, five yards wide. May they have no joy—those who tore our love asunder.

DER KASHTNBOYM

דער קאַשטנבױם

The Chestnut Tree

Words by Yitskhok Perlov (1911–1980); music by Lola Folman (1908–1979). The song was submitted by Hershl Altman, Bronx, N. Y. who heard Lola Folman sing it in the DP Camp Ziegenheim, Germany, in 1945. At that time, he writes, she was touring with her husband, Yitskhok Perlov, to bring comfort to the survivors. In this country the song was popularized by actress Mina Bern, who submitted the melody.

A mame hot a tekhterl, A tekhterl gehat, Sheyne blonde herelekh Hot dos kind gehat. Zi zitst un neyt a kleydele, Zi zitst un neyt un troymt, Dos epele, dos epele Falt nisht vayt fun boym.	אַ מאַמע האָט אַ טעכטערל, אַ טעכטערל געהאַט, שײנע בלאָנדע הערעלעך האָט דאָס קינד געהאַט. זי זיצט און נייט אַ קליידעלע, זי זיצט און נייט און טרוימט, דאָס עפעלע, דאָס עפעלע, פֿאַלט נישט ווײַט פֿון בוים.
Es tsien zikh di yorelekh, Dos lebn geyt zayn gang, Dos tekhterl dervaksn shoyn — Zi iz oykh sheyn un shlank. Di mame, tsvey un fertsik yor, Iz nokh yung un toyg; Dos tekhterl shoyn zekhtsn yor Un hot shoyn fil derfolg.	עס ציִען זיך די יאָרעלעך, דאָס לעבן גייט זײַן גאַנג, דאָס טעכטערל דערװאַקסן שוין – זי איז אויך שיין און שלאַנק. די מאַמע, צוויי און פֿערציק יאָר, איז נאָך יונג און טויג; דאָס טעכטערל שוין זעכצן יאָר און האָט שוין פֿיל דערפֿאָלג.
Es dreyen zikh bokhurimlekh In droysn bay ir hoyz, Zingen sheyne lidelekh Un rufn ir aroys: - Kum aroys, mayn libinke, Vu s'blit der kashtnboym, Ikh bin dayn un du bist mayn Un nor fun dir ikh troym.	עס דרייען זיך בחורימלעך אין דרויסן בײַ איר הויז, זינגען שיינע לידעלעך און רופֿן איר אַרויס: – קום אַרויס, מײַן ליבינקע, װוּ ס׳בליט דער קאַשטנבוים, איך בין דײַן און דו ביסט מײַן און נאָר פֿון דיר איך טרוים.
Di mame meynt dos ruft men ir, Zi loyft tsum shpigl vi a hoz; Dos tekhterl farroytlt zikh Un lozt arop di noz, - Kinder muzn shlofn geyn, In droysn voyen hint, - Mame, kh'bin nisht shleferik, Kh'bin nisht mer keyn kind.	די מאַמע מיינט דאָס רופֿט מען איר, זי לויפֿט צום שפּיגל ווי אַ האָז; דאָס טעכטערל פֿאַררויטלט זיך און לאָזט אַראָפּ די נאָז, – קינדער מוזן שלאָפֿן גיין, אין דרויסן ווויען הינט, – מאַמע, כ׳בין נישט שלעפֿעריק, כ׳בין נישט מער קיין קינד.

Di mame geyt in shlofshtub arayn
Un leygt zikh glaykh in bet,
Hert zi vi der kashtnboym
Klapt in shoyb un redt:
- Ikh hob a mol far dir geblit
Ven du bist yung geven,
Haynt bli ikh far dayn tekhterl,
Vayl zi iz yung un sheyn.

די מאַמע גייט אין שלאָפֿשטוב אַרײַן
און לייגט זיך גלײַך אין בעט,
הערט זי ווי דער קאַשטנבוים
קלאַפּט אין שויב און רעדט:
– איך האָב אַ מאָל פֿאַר דיר געבליט
ווען דו ביסט יונג געווען,
הײַנט בלי איך פֿאַר דײַן טעכטערל,
ווײַל זי איז יונג און שיין.

A mother had a little daughter, a little daughter had she. Beautiful blond hair had the child. She sits and sews a little dress, she sits and sews and dreams: The apple falls not far from the tree.

The years go by, life goes its way. The little daughter is grown up now. She's both beautiful and slender. The mother, forty-two years old, is still young and fit. The daughter is now sixteen years and already has much success.

Young men hang around her, outside, near her house. They sing pretty little songs and call her to come out: Come out, my darling, where the chestnut blooms - I am young and you are mine, and I dream of none but you.

The mother thinks they're calling her. She runs like a rabbit to her mirror. The daughter blushes and hangs her head. - Children must go to sleep, dogs are howling outside. - Mother, I'm not sleepy and I'm no longer a child.

The mother goes into her bedroom, and promptly goes to bed. She hears the chestnut tree rapping on the window pane and saying: - Once upon a time I bloomed for you, when you were young; now I bloom for your daughter, for she is young and fair.

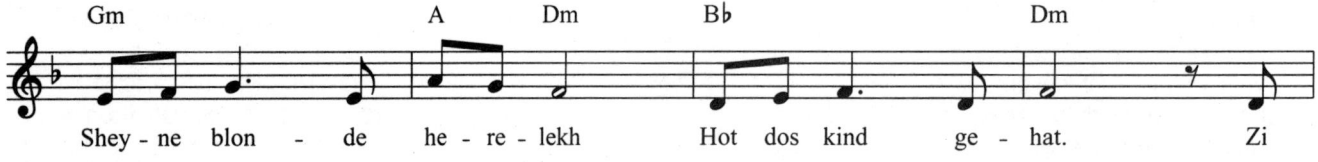

SORELE

שרהלע

Sorele

Words and music by Galician Yiddish folk poet Nokhem Sternheim (1879—killed by the Nazis in 1942), author of popular Yiddish songs like "Hobn mir a nigndl," "Fraytik oyf der nakht," and "Tayere Malkele." The song was in the repertoire of singer Diana Blumenfeld. Aaron Feiner, Toronto, sent us a recording of his version which we are printing here. Other variants were submitted by Sara Rosenfeld, Chana Gonshar and Chaika Spigel, Montreal.

In dem shmoln gesele,	אין דעם שמאָלן געסעלע,
Bay a vaser-fesele,	בײַ אַ וואַסער-פֿעסעלע,
Shteyt a meydl, dortn shteyt;	שטייט אַ מיידל, דאָרטן שטייט;
Es dreyt zikh dort a bokherl,	עס דרייט זיך דאָרט אַ בחורל,
A bagartlt zokherl,	אַ באַגאַרטלט זכרל,
Krayzlt zikh di peyelekh un dreyt.	קרייזלט זיך די פּאהלעך און דרייט.
Er halt in hant a g'morele	ער האַלט אין האַנט אַ גמראלע
Un trakhtn, trakht fun Sorele,	און טראַכטן, טראַכט פֿון שרהלע,
Tsi zi hot im shoyn do gezen.	צי זי האָט אים שוין דאָ געזען.
Er varft a blik tsum fesele,	ער וואַרפֿט אַ בליק צום פֿעסעלע,
Un tsitert oyf in gesele,	און ציטערעט אויף אין געסעלע,
Tsi s'hot im keyner dortn nisht gezen. . .	צי ס'האָט אים קיינער דאָרטן נישט געזען. . .
Sorele, Sorele, Sorele. . .	שרהלע, שרהלע, שרהלע. . .
Vos iz dos far a koyekh, far a kraft?	וואָס איז דאָס פֿאַר אַ כוח, פֿאַר אַ קראַפֿט?
Sorele, Sorele, Sorele,	שרהלע, שרהלע, שרהלע,
Ikh kholem nor fun dir tog un nakht.	איך חלום נאָר פֿון דיר טאָג און נאַכט.
Ir tate iz a shnayderl	איר טאַטע איז אַ שנײַדערל
In dem shmoln kheyderl,	אין דעם שמאָלן חדרל,
Zitst bay a tishele un neyt.	זיצט בײַ אַ טישעלע און נייט.
Nisht vayt fun shnayders hayzele	נישט ווײַט פֿון שנײַדערס הײַזעלע
Gefint zikh dem rebns klayzele,	געפֿינט זיך דעם רבינס קלײַזעלע,
Dreyt zikh dort dos meydele, zikh dreyt.	דרייט זיך דאָרט דאָס מיידעלע, זיך דרייט.
In dem shmoln gesele,	אין דעם שמאָלן געסעלע,
In der vaser-fesele,	אין דער וואַסער-פֿעסעלע,
Shpiglt zikh dos meydele un trakht	שפּיגלט זיך דאָס מיידעלע און טראַכט
Fun dem rebns bokherl	פֿון דעם רבינס בחורל
Mit peyelekh dem zokherl	מיט פּאהלעך דעם זכרל
Vos hot tsu ir geshmeykhlt un gelakht.	וואָס האָט צו איר געשמייכלט און געלאַכט.
Shloymele, Shloymele, Shloymele. . .	שלמהלע, שלמהלע, שלמהלע. . .
Vos iz es far a koyekh, far a makht?	וואָס איז עס פֿאַר אַ כוח, פֿאַר אַ מאַכט?
Shloymele, Shloymele, Shloymele,	שלמהלע, שלמהלע, שלמהלע,
Ikh kholem vegn dir tog un nakht.	איך חלום וועגן דיר טאָג און נאַכט.

Dos shnayderl Reb Urele
Farknasn vil zayn Surele
Nor keyn mezumen hot er nit,
Farzetst er di kapotkelekh
Nemendik di zlotkelekh
Un er fort mit ir tsu a gutn yid.

Zitst zikh dort a tsadikl,
Reb Shloymele in spodikl,
Pidyoynes nemt er shoyn a lange tsayt.
Tsitert oyf der rebenyu,
Ven er nemt dem shnayders pidyen tsu
Farkholemt un er murmlt shtilerheyt. . .

- S'iz dokh Sorele, Sorele, Sorele,
Vos iz es far a koyekh, far a makht?
- Shloymele, Shloymele, Shloymele,
Ikh kholem vegn dir tog un nakht.

דאָס שנײַדערל ר׳ אורעלע
פֿאַרכנסן וויל זײַן שׂרהלע,
נאָר קיין מזומן האָט ער ניט,
פֿאַרזעצט ער די קאַפּאָטקעלעך,
נעמענדיק די זלאָטקעלעך
און ער פֿאָרט מיט איר צו אַ גוטן ייִד.

זיצט זיך דאָרט אַ צדיקל
ר׳ שלמהלע אין ספּאָדיקל,
פּדיונית נעמט ער שוין אַ לאַנגע צײַט,
ציטערט אויף דער רביניו,
ווען ער נעמט דעם שנײַדערס פּדיון צו
פֿאַרחלומט און ער מורמלט שטילערהייט. . .

– ס׳איז דאָך שׂרהלע, שׂרהלע, שׂרהלע,
וואָס איז עס פֿאַר אַ כּוח, פֿאַר אַ מאַכט?
– שלמהלע, שלמהלע, שלמהלע,
איך חלום וועגן דיר טאָג און נאַכט.

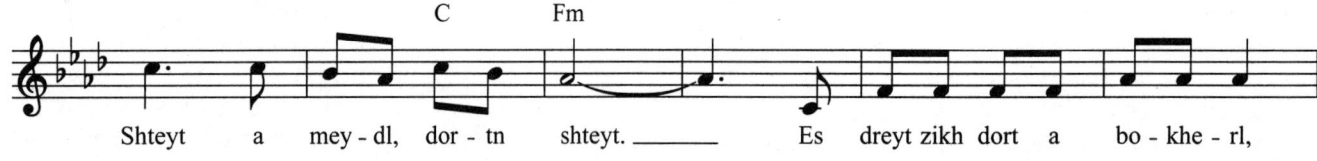

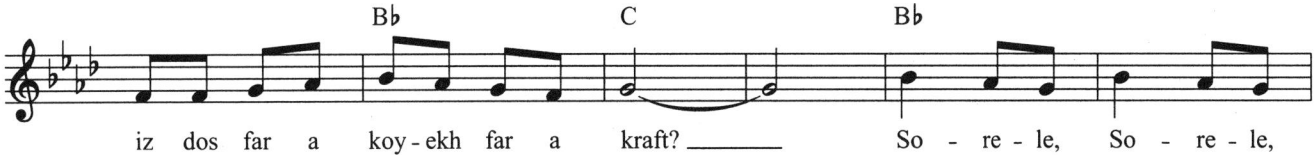

In the narrow little street, near a water barrel, stands a girl. Nearby a young man is hanging around, a young fellow with a gartled coat who twirls his sidecurls. In his hand he holds a small volume of the Talmud, but he keeps thinking about Sorele: Has she noticed him? He glances at the barrel and trembles in the little street. Did anyone see him there?

Sorele, what kind of power do you have over me? Sorele, I dream about you day and night.

Her father is a tailor. He sits at a table in a narrow room and sews. Not far from the tailor's little house is the rabbi's little synagogue, and there the girl waits. In the narrow street, the girl looks at her reflection in the water barrel and thinks about the rabbi's young son, the fellow with the sidecurls who smiled and laughed to her.

Shloymele, what kind of power do you have over me? Shloymele, I dream about you day and night.

The tailor, Urele, wants to get his daughter betrothed, but he has no money, so he pawns his coats, takes the few zlotys and goes with her to the rabbi. Sitting there is a young Rebbe - Reb Shloymele, wearing a fur hat. He has been taking fees for advice for a long time. The rabbi gets excited when he takes the tailor's money and murmurs softly and dreamily:

It's Sorele, after all—Sorele. What kind of power do you have over me? - Shloymele, I dream about you day and night.

IN DER FINTSTER

אין דער פֿינצטער

In the Darkness

Words by Zishe Landau (1889–1937); composer unknown. Published in M. Gelbart, *Lomir zingen*, 1938–39.

In der fintster—zaynen dayne oygn shener,	אין דער פֿינצטער—זײַנען דײַנע אויגן שענער,
In der fintster—zaynen dayne hentlekh klener,	אין דער פֿינצטער—זײַנען דײַנע הענטלעך קלענער,
In der fintster—vayt fun dir mit shtiler ru,	אין דער פֿינצטער—ווײַט פֿון דיר מיט שטילער רו,
In der fintster—veykher, tsarter, boygzamer bistu.	אין דער פֿינצטער—װײכער, צאַרטער, בויגזאַמער ביסטו.
In der fintster—iz dayn ponim bleykher, bleykher,	אין דער פֿינצטער—איז דײַן פּנים בלייכער, בלייכער,
In der fintster—zaynen dayne finger veykher,	אין דער פֿינצטער—זײַנען דײַנע פֿינגער װײכער,
In der fintster—ven du makhst di lodn tsu,	אין דער פֿינצטער—װען דו מאַכסט די לאָדן צו,
In der fintster—veykher, tsarter, boygzamer bistu.	אין דער פֿינצטער—װײכער, צאַרטער, בויגזאַמער ביסטו.
In der fintster—iz dayn ponem milder, milder,	אין דער פֿינצטער—איז דײַן פּנים מילדער, מילדער,
In der fintster—klapt dayn harts alts vilder,	אין דער פֿינצטער—קלאַפּט דײַן האַרץ אַלץ װילדער,
In der fintster—rufstu mikh, ikh veys nit vu,	אין דער פֿינצטער—רופֿסטו מיך, איך װײס ניט װוּ,
In der fintster—veykher, tsarter, boygzamer bistu.	אין דער פֿינצטער—װײכער, צאַרטער, בויגזאַמער ביסטו.

In the darkness, your eyes are prettier. In the darkness, your hands are more delicate. In the darkness, when I'm resting quietly far from you, you are softer, gentler, more pliant. In the darkness, your face is paler. In the darkness, your fingers are softer. In the darkness, when you close the shutters, you are softer, gentler, more pliant. In the darkness, your face is gentler. In the darkness, your heart beats more and more wildly. In the darkness, if you call me, I don't know where—you are softer, gentler, more pliant.

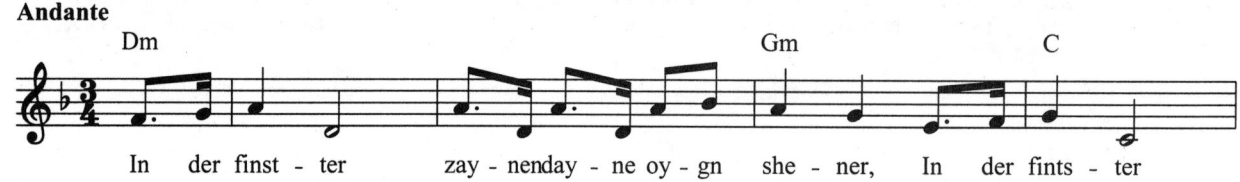

IN MAYN GORTN

אין מײַן גאָרטן

In My Garden

Part of a poem by Chaim Nachmen Bialik (1873–1934). This is one of his charming folk themes written originally in Hebrew "Yesh li gan," and translated into Yiddish by I. Ma Yofis. Published in M. Gelbart, *Lomir zingen*, 1938-39. Albert Bitter also wrote music to the poem.

In mayn gortn hot a brunem
Mit an emer zikh gefunen,
Ale shabes kumt deriber,
Trinken vaser dort mayn liber.

Vi mayn harts, der emer vakht,
Trift zayn gold in brunem zakht;
Trift a perl, trift a tsveyter —
Ot-o geyt er, ot-o geyt er!

Sha, mir dukht es klingen trit. . .
Iz dos er?—un efsher nit?
Gikher, gikher, kum, mayn sheyner!
Kh'bin aleyn un vayter keyner. . .

Zetsn mir zikh do baym vant,
Kop tsu aksl, hant in hant. . .
- Kh'vel dikh fregn a por zakhn,
Zolst, ikh bet dikh, nor nit lakhn.

Zog, fun vanen kumt der shmarts,
Vi a vorem nogt dos harts? -
S'hot gehert mayn mame reydn,
Az du vilst mit mir zikh sheydn.

Zogt mayn liber: Gey shoyn, gey,
Sonim zogn dos azoy,
Nokh a yor, az got vet veln,
Veln mir a khupe shteln. . .

אין מײַן גאָרטן האָט אַ ברונעם
מיט אַן עמער זיך געפֿונען,
אַלע שבת קומט דעריבער
טרינקען װאַסער דאָרט מײַן ליבער.

װי מײַן האַרץ, דער עמער װאַכט,
טריפֿט זײַן גאָלד אין ברונעם זאַכט;
טריפֿט אַ פּערל, טריפֿט אַ צװײטער —
אָט-אַ גײט ער, אָט-אַ גײט ער!

שאַ, מיר דוכט עס קלינגען טריט. . .
איז דאָס ער? -- און אפֿשר ניט?
גיכער, גיכער! קום, מײַן שײנער!
כ'בין אַלײן און װײַטער קײנער. . .

זעצן מיר זיך דאָ בײַם װאַנט,
קאָפּ צו אַקסל, האַנט אין האַנט. . .
– כ'װעל דיך פֿרעגן אַ פּאָר זאַכן,
זאָלסט, איך בעט דיך, נאָר ניט לאַכן.

זאָג, פֿון װאַנען קומט דער שמאַרץ,
װי אַ װאָרעם נאָגט דאָס האַרץ? –
ס'האָט געהערט מײַן מאַמע רײדן,
אַז דו װאָלסט מיט מיר זיך שײדן.

זאָגט מײַן ליבער: - גײ שױן, גײ,
שׂונאים זאָגן דאָס אַזױ, –
נאָך אַ יאָר, אַז גאָט װעט װעלן,
װעלן מיר אַ חופּה שטעלן. . .

In my garden there's a well with a bucket. Every Sabbath my beloved comes here to drink water. Like my heart, the bucket keeps watch; its gold drips peacefully into the well— one pearl drips, then another. Here he comes, here he comes! Ssh! I think I hear the sound of footsteps. Is that him? Maybe not. Faster, faster! Come, my handsome boy, I'm alone and there's no one else around. We sit here near the well, hand in hand, my head on his shoulders.— I want to ask you something— just don't laugh at me, I beg you. Tell me, where does the pain come from that gnaws at my heart like a worm? My mother heard someone say you want to leave me.— Don't be silly, my beloved answers. Only our enemies say such things. Another year, God willing, and we'll get married.

There Is Still Such a Flower

ES IZ NOKH FARAN AZA BLUM

עס איז נאָך פֿאַראַן אַזאַ בלום

Submitted by Sara Rosenfeld, Montreal, who writes that the song was popular among the Jewish youth of Poland before World War II.

Ven di goldn zun fargeyt,
Farganve ikh zikh shtilerheyt,
Dort in tol vu s'rut mayn blum,
Ikh ze zi shtendik umetum.
Faln letste shtraln vi shafirn,
Gingoldene shtraln rund un arum.
Zingt der vald far mir a shir-hashirim,
Beygt dos kepele far mir mayn blum.

Aha, aha— zingt a vintele in tol,
Aha, aha— zingt far mir tsum letstn mol.

Refrain:
Es iz nokh faran aza blum,
Vos keyner veyst nit ir sheynkeyt,
Ikh lib zi shtendik in geheym,
Zi mikh shtum.

Ven di goldn zun vakht oyf,
Zogt tsu mir der tol:— Antloyf,
Dort vu bist a mol geven,
Es darf dikh keyner do nit zen,
Loyft dos taykhele dem vald ontrinken,
Nase beymer kroynen rund un arum.
Zingt der vint tsu mir a shir-hashirim,
Beygt dos kepele far mir mayn blum.

Aha, aha— zingt a vintele in tol,
Aha, aha— zingt far mir tsum letstn mol.

When the golden sun sets, I steal silently down to the valley where my flower rests. I see her always, all around. Last rays fall like sapphires, with pure gold everywhere. The forest sings for me the Song of Songs, and my flower bows her head to me. Aha, aha, sings a wind in the valley. Aha, aha, it sings to me for the last time. There is still such a flower, whose beauty no one knows. I love her always in secret— she loves me in silence.

When the golden sung awakes, the valley says to me: run away, to where you once were. No one has to see you there. The creek flows to water the forest— wet trees crown everywhere.

O, DI VELT VET VERN SHENER
SONGS OF WORK AND HOPE

אָ, די וועלט וועט ווערן שענער

EYDER IKH LEYG ZIKH SHLOFN　　　　　　　　　　　　　　　　אײדער איך לייג זיך שלאָפֿן

No Sooner Do I Lie Down to Sleep

Lament of the seamstress published in 1912 by Y. L. Cahan. This is one of the workers' folksongs that Cahan designated as part of the older folksong repertoire, in which the singer is an individual, rather than the collective "we" of later workers' songs (see Cahan, *Shtudyes*).

Eyder ikh leyg zikh shlofn,　　　　　　　　　　　　　　　אײדער איך לייג זיך שלאָפֿן,
Darf ikh shoyn oyfshteyn,　　　　　　　　　　　　　　　　דאַרף איך שוין אויפֿשטיין,
Mit mayne kranke beyner　　　　　　　　　　　　　　　　מיט מײַנע קראַנקע ביינער
Tsu der arbet geyn.　　　　　　　　　　　　　　　　　　　צו דער אַרבעט גיין.

Refrain:　　　　　　　　　　　　　　　　　　　　　　　**רעפֿרײן:**
Tsu got vel ikh veynen　　　　　　　　　　　　　　　　　 צו גאָט וועל איך וויינען
Mit a groys geveyn:　　　　　　　　　　　　　　　　　　מיט אַ גרויס געוויין:
Tsu vos ikh bin geboyrn　　　　　　　　　　　　　　　　צו וואָס איך בין געבוירן
A neytorin tsu zyn　　　　　　　　　　　　　　　　　　 אַ נייטאָרין צו זײַן!

Kh'kum shpet tsu der arbet,　　　　　　　　　　　　　　כ׳קום שפּעט צו דער אַרבעט,
S'iz vayt der veg,　　　　　　　　　　　　　　　　　　　ס׳איז ווײַט דער וועג,
Shlogt men mir op　　　　　　　　　　　　　　　　　　 שלאָגט מען מיר אָפּ
Far halbe teg.　　　　　　　　　　　　　　　　　　　　 פֿאַר האַלבע טעג.

Nodlen vern tsebrokhn　　　　　　　　　　　　　　　　　נאָדלען ווערן צעבראָכן
Fuftsn a minut,　　　　　　　　　　　　　　　　　　　　 פֿופֿצן אַ מינוט,
Di finger vern tseshtokhn,　　　　　　　　　　　　　　 די פֿינגער ווערן צעשטאָכן,
S'rint fun zey dos blut.　　　　　　　　　　　　　　　 ס׳רינט פֿון זיי דאָס בלוט.

Ikh layd shtendik hunger,　　　　　　　　　　　　　　　איך לײַד שטענדיק הונגער,
Kh'hob nisht vos tsu esn,　　　　　　　　　　　　　　　 כ׳האָב נישט וואָס צו עסן,
Vil ikh gelt betn,　　　　　　　　　　　　　　　　　　　וויל איך געלט בעטן,
Heyst men mir fargesn.　　　　　　　　　　　　　　　　 הייסט מען מיר פֿאַרגעסן.

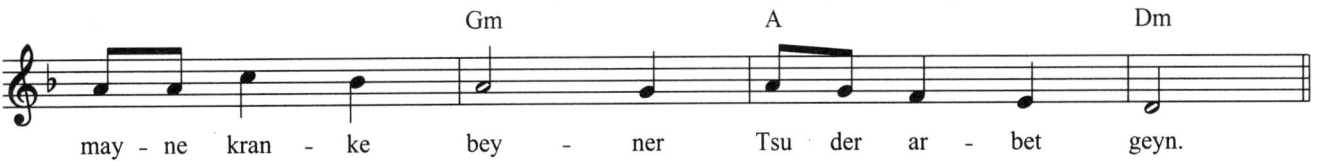

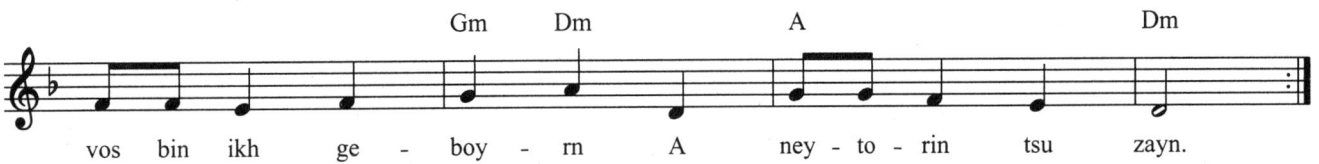

No sooner do I lie down to sleep, I already must get up, and with my aching bones, must go off to work.

To God I will cry with a great outcry: Why was I born to be a seamstress?

I come late to work—the way is long, and they dock me for half a day.

Needles get broken, fifteen every minute. Fingers get stuck and blood runs from them.

I'm always hungry, I have nothing to eat. If I ask for my pay, they tell me to forget it.

S'FALT A SHNEY

סי'פֿאַלט אַ שניי

Snow Is Falling

This folksong has several melodies, two of which are presented here. One was printed in the arrangement of E. Sheinin for chorus in *Gezang un kamf*, no. 3 (1935); it was also published by Michel Gelbart (1951). The second melody was collected by the compilers from composer Ben Yomen. The stanza, beginning with "Hodi dir tsu veynen" derives from a poem "Der arbeter" (The Worker) by David Edelshtat. 34 folk variants of Edelshtat's song were collected and analyzed by folklorist S. Z. Pipe (see Dov Noy and Meir Noy, *Yidishe lider fun galitsye*). Edelshtat's original poem was published in the New York *Varheyt* on June 7, 1889. There he called it an adaptation from the Russian poet Nekrasov. Pipe however found that the poet adapted the first three stanzas from a poem "Duma tkatcha" by Sergei Siniegub. Edelshtat's poem was also folklorized in the song "Shnel loyfn di reder" in this book. R. Pups notes an adaptation that was sung during the Holocaust in Bielsk and Bendin: "Her shoyn oyf tsu veynen/ Un trern tsu fargisn, / Di tsayt fun shtarbn kumt shoyn on, / Oy vey! oy vey! oy vey!"

S'falt a shney, s'falt a shney,
Tog un nakht, tog un nakht,
Nor ikh ney, nor ikh ney,
Un ikh trakht, un ikh trakht.

In droysn geyt a regn,
In droysn geyt a regn,
Un es falt a shney, a shney,
Un es falt a shney, a shney,
Mayne yunge yorn
Hob ikh ongevorn
Zitsndik shtendik baym geney.

Zumer geyt a regn

Zumer geyt a regn
Zumer geyt a regn,
Zumer geyt a regn
Un vinter falt a shney,
Un vinter falt a shney;
Mayne yunge yorn
Hob ikh ongevorn
Baym fintstern geney.

Hodi dir tsu veynen,
Hodi dir tsu klogn,
Du vest makhn oyf der arbet a flek;
Bald vet arayn
Der mayster, der merder,
Traybt er dikh fun der arbet avek.

Snow is falling day and night. But I sew and I brood.

Outside it's raining and snow is falling, My youthful years I've frittered away, sitting always at my sewing.

Stop your crying, stop your weeping—you will leave a stain on your work. Soon the cruel foreman will come and drive you away altogether.

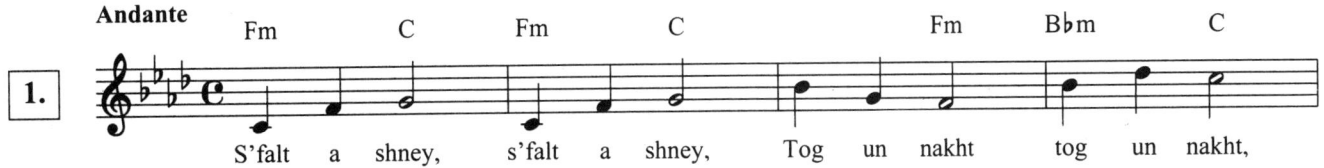

ALEF—INDIKES

אַלף-אינדיקעס

A is for Turkeys

Folksong which uses the Hebrew alphabet to humorously contrast the differences between rich and poor. Published by Menakhem Kipnis in 1925. The melody is based on the traditional Ashkenazic tune for the Akdomes poem. (see Max Wohlberg, "The Music of the Synagogue as a Source of the Yiddish Folk Song"). Kipnis has another tune with the Akdomes motive: "Alef—an odler tut untern himl flien" (A is for an eagle that flies beneath the sky).

Alef—indikes est der nogid, Beyz—beyndelekh grizhet der oreman.	אַלף-אינדיקעס עסט דער נגיד, בית-בײנדעלעך גריזשעט דער אָרעמאַן.
Giml—gendzelekh est der nogid, Daled—dem dales hot der oreman.	גימל-גענדזעלעך עסט דער נגיד, דלת-דעם דלות האָט דער אָרעמאַן.
Hey—hindelekh gepreglte est der nogid, Vov—veytikn hot der oreman.	הא-הינדעלעך געפרעגלטע עסט דער נגיד, ואו-ווייטיקן האָט דער אָרעמאַן.
Zayen—zeml mit puter est der nogid, Khes—khalasn hot der oreman.	זין-זעמל מיט פּוטער עסט דער נגיד, חית-חלאתן האָט דער אָרעמאַן.
Tes—taybelekh gebrotene est der nogid, Yud—yesurim hot der oreman.	טית-טײַבעלעך געבראָטענע עסט דער נגיד, יוד-יסורים האָט דער אָרעמאַן.
Kof—kaloshn trogt der nogid, Lamed—laptshes trogt der oreman.	כּף-קאַלאָשן טראָגט דער נגיד, למד-לאַפּטשעס טראָגט דער אָרעמאַן.
Mem—mashke trinkt der nogid, Nun—nikhter iz der oreman.	מם-משקה טרינקט דער נגיד, נון-ניכטער איז דער אָרעמאַן.
Samekh—sametene kleyder trogt der nogid, Ayen—opgerisn geyt der oreman.	סמך-סאַמעטענע קליידער טראָגט דער נגיד, עין-(ע)אָפּגעריסן גייט דער אָרעמאַן.
Pey—pupkes gebrotene est der nogid, Tsadik—tsores hot der oreman.	פּא-פּופּקעס געבראָטענע עסט דער נגיד, צדיק-צרות האָט דער אָרעמאַן.
Kuf—kotletn gepreglte est der nogid, Reysh—retekh grizhet der oreman.	קוף-קאָטלעטן געפרעגלטע עסט דער נגיד, ריש-רעטעך גריזשעט דער אָרעמאַן.
Shin—Shereshevskis* papirosn reykhert der nogid, Tof—tutin pipket der oreman.	שין-שערעשעווסקיס* פּאַפּיראָסן רייכערט דער נגיד, תיו-תותין (טוטין) פּיפּקעט דער אָרעמאַן.

---

* A factory in Grodno, Poland.

* אַ פֿאַבריק אין גראָדנע, פּוילן

A - lef in - di - kes est der no - gid, Beyz beyn-de-lekh gri-zhet der o - re - man.

Alef, A is for turkeys the rich man eats: Beyz, B is for bones the poor man gnaws. Giml, G is for geese the rich man eats; Daled, D is for poverty the poor man has. Hey, H is for fried chicken the rich man eats; Vov, V are the aches the poor man has. Zayen, Z is for the rolls and butter the rich man eats; Khes is for sickness the poor man has. Tes, T is for the roast pigeons the rich man eats; Yud, Y is for the suffering the poor man has. Kof, K is for the galoshes the rich man wear.; Lamed, L is for the straw shoes the poor man wears. Mem, M is for the whiskey the rich man drinks; Nun, N is for sober that the poor man is. Samekh, S is for the velvet clothes the rich man wears; Ayin is for ragged the poor man is. Pey, P is for the gizzards the rich man eats; Tsadik is for the troubles the poor man has. Kuk is for fried chops the rich man eats.; Reysh, R is for the radishes the poor man gnaws. Shin is for Shereshevsky's cigarettes the rich man smokes; Tof is for tutin, the weeds the poor man puffs.

SHLOF, MAYN KIND, SHLOF KESEYDER

שלאָף מײַן קינד, שלאָף כּסדר

Sleep, My Child, Keep Sleeping

A folk lullaby that tells the child of the inequitable conditions that he will encounter in the world. The theme of the poor who build the palaces for the rich and are themselves forced to live in squalor and unhealthy surroundings recurs in the early protest songs of workers. The song was published by Y. L. Cahan in 1912.

Shlof, mayn kind, shlof keseyder,
Zingen vel ikh dir a lid;
Az du, mayn kind, vest elter vern,
Vestu visn an untershid.

Az du, mayn kind, vest elter vern,
Vestu vern mit laytn glaykh;
Demlt vestu gevoyre vern,
Vos heyst orem un vos heyst raykh.

Di tayerste palatsn, di tayerste hayzer,
Dos alts makht der oreman;
Nor, veystu, ver es tut in zey voynen? –
Gornisht der, nor der raykher man.

Der oreman, er ligt in keler,
Der vilgotsh rint im fun di vent;
Derfun bakumt er a rematn-feler
In di fis un in di hent.

שלאָף מײַן קינד, שלאָף כּסדר,
זינגען וועל איך דיר אַ ליד;
אַז דו, מײַן קינד, וועסט עלטער ווערן,
וועסטו וויסן אַן אונטערשיד.

אַז דו, מײַן קינד, וועסט עלטער ווערן,
וועסטו ווערן מיט לײַטן גלײַך;
דעמלט וועסטו געוווירע* ווערן
וואָס הייסט אָרעם און וואָס הייסט רײַך.

די טײַערסטע פּאַלאַצן, די טײַערסטע הײַזער, –
דאָס אַלץ מאַכט דער אָרעמאַן;
נאָר, ווייסטו, ווער עס טוט אין זיי ווינען? –
גאָרנישט דער, נאָר דער רײַכער מאַן.

דער אָרעמאַן, ער ליגט אין קעלער,
דער ווילגאָטש רינט אים פֿון די וואַנט;
דערפֿון באַקומט ער אַ רעמאַטן-פֿעלער
אין די פֿיס און אין די הענט.

---
*געוווּיער ווערן

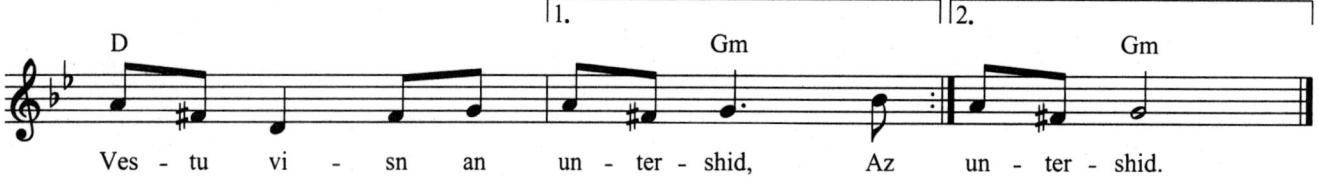

Sleep, my child, keep sleeping, I'll sing you a song. When you get older, my child, you'll know the difference.

When you, my child, get older, you'll be like other people. Then you'll understand what it means to be poor or rich.

The most expensive palaces, the most expensive houses are all built by poor men, but do you know who lives in them? Not they, but rich men.

Poor men live in cellars, moisture runs from their walls. From that they get rheumatism in their feet and hands.

KOYFT A TSAYTUNG!

קויפֿט אַ צייטונג!

Buy a Paper!

Words and music by Simche Schwartz (1900–1974), published under the title "Zeitungverkoifer" in the compilation of Julian Schwartz, 1946. The song was presented in the musical *The Golden Land* by Zalmen Mlotek and Moishe Rosenfeld, 1982–1987. It is notated as sung by compiler in Poland.

Di mame hot mikh fun der heym aroysgetribn,	די מאַמע האָט מיך פֿון דער היים אַרויסגעטריבן,
Un mikh bagleyt mit kloles un mit trern,	און מיך באַגלייט מיט קללות און מיט טרערן,
A shtub mit kinder hot oyf mir gevart	אַ שטוב מיט קינדער האָט אויף מיר געוואַרט
Az ikh, der fardiner zol dernern.	אַז איך, דער פֿאַרדינער זאָל דערנערן.
A kind mit kinder glaykh bin ikh gevezn	אַ קינד מיט קינדער גלײַך בין איך געוועזן
Un nisht hob ikh gehat fun vos tsu zorgn,	און נישט האָב איך געהאַט פֿון וואָס צו זאָרגן,
Nor yorn zenen shoyn farbay	נאָר יאָרן זענען שוין פֿאַרבײַ
Un itst tog nokh tog	און איצט טאָג נאָך טאָג
Vi a hunt iber di gasn muz ikh yogn.	ווי אַ הונט איבער די גאַסן מוז איך יאָגן.

Refrain: / רעפֿריין:

Koyft a tsaytung, ley'nt a tsaytung!	קויפֿט אַ צייטונג, לייענט אַ צייטונג!
Nayesn ful ale ekn velt.	נייעסן פֿון אַלע עקן וועלט.
A royb, a mord, a iberfal,	אַ רויב, אַ מאָרד, אַ איבערפֿאַל,
A katastrofe, a skandal,	אַ קאַטאַסטראָפֿע, אַ סקאַנדאַל,
Blut - blut - taykhn royte	בלוט - בלוט - טײַכן רויטע
Naye tsvantsik toyznt toyte!	נײַע צוואַנציק טויזנט טויטע!
Koyft a tsaytung, ley'nt a tsaytung,	קויפֿט אַ צייטונג, לייענט אַ צייטונג,
Ir hot do ales vos aykh gefelt!	איר האָט דאָ אַלעס וואָס אײַך געפֿעלט!

A hintish lebn hot farsamt mayn kindheyt,	אַ הינטיש לעבן האָט פֿאַרסמט מײַן קינדהייט,
Di noyt hot mikh tsefresn vi a shlang.	די נויט האָט מיך צעפֿרעסן ווי אַ שלאַנג.
A dar shtik broyt hot mir fartoybt dem hunger,	אַ דאַר שטיק ברויט האָט מיר פֿאַרטויבט דעם הונגער,
Mayn nakhtleger a harte, kalte bank.	מײַן נאַכטלעגער אַ האַרטע, קאַלטע באַנק.
Un nokh dem vi di mame iz geshtorbn	און נאָך דעם ווי די מאַמע איז געשטאָרבן
Un oykh di eltste shvester iz avek,	און אויך די עלטסטע שוועסטער איז אַוועק,
Iz vi ikh shtey azoy un ikh derman zikh	איז ווי איך שטיי אַזוי און איך דערמאַן זיך
Tut azoy vey,	טוט אַזוי וויי,
Shray ikh iber alemens geshrey.	שרײַ איך איבער אַלעמענס געשריי.

Es roysht di gas un khvalyes mentshn brumen,	עס רוישט די גאַס און כוואַליעס מענטשן ברומען,
Nor ikh shray iber alemens virvar;	נאָר איך שרײַ איבער אַלעמענס ווירוואַר;
Geyt eyner durkh un tsit mikh farn hitl	גייט איינער דורך און ציט מיך פֿאַרן היטל
A her shpayt oys oyf mir zayn shpits tsigar.	אַ הער שפּײַט אויס אויף מיר זײַן שפּיץ ציגאַר.
Nor kumen vet a tog, ay, vet er kumen,	נאָר קומען וועט אַ טאָג, אײַ, וועט ער קומען,
A likhtikeyt aza in mayn gemit.	אַ ליכטיקייט אַזאַ אין מײַן געמיט.
Iz vi a vint iber di gasn vel ikh tsvalyen,	איז ווי אַ ווינט איבער די גאַסן וועל איך צוואַליען,
Un oystantsn vel ikh a naye lid:	און אויסטאַנצן וועל איך אַ נײַע ליד:

Koyft a tsaytung, ley'nt a tsaytung,
Nayesn fun ale ekn velt!
Oys royb, oys mord, oys iberfal,
Oys katastrofe, oys skandal,
Vald un feld, derfer, shtet
Brenen in a yam fun freyd.
Koyft a tsaytung, ley'nt a tsaytung,
Ir hot do ales, alts vos mir gefelt!

קויפֿט אַ צײַטונג, לייַנט אַ צײַטונג,
נײַעסן פֿון אַלע עקן וועלט!
אויס רויב, אויס מאָרד, אויס איבערפֿאַל,
אויס קאַטאַסטראָפֿע, אויס סקאַנדאַל,
וואַלד און פֿעלד, דערפֿער, שטעט
ברענען אין אַ ים פֿון פֿרייד.
קויפֿט אַ צײַטונג, לייַנט אַ צײַטונג,
איר האָט דאָ אַלעס, אַלץ וואָס מיר געפֿעלט!

My mother drove me out of the house, accompanied by curses and tears. A houseful of children were waiting for me, the breadwinner, to give them food. I was a child like any other child, and I had nothing to worry about. But years have gone by, and now, day after day, I must run along the streets like a dog.

Buy a paper, read a paper—news of all the world: a robbery, a murder, an assault, a catastrophe, a scandal. Blood, blood—red rivers, twenty thousand more dead! Buy a paper, read a paper—Here's everything you like.

A dog's life poisoned my childhood—want ate me up like a snake. A thin crust of bread took the edge off my hunger. My nightly bed was a hard, cold bench. And after my mother died, and my eldest sister too, when I stand here and remember, it hurts so much that I cry out over everyone's shouts.

The street is noisy and waves of people murmur, but I cry out over everyone's tumult. Someone goes by and pulls at my hat. A gentleman spits out the tip of his cigar at me. But there'll come a day—I say it will come—of such joy in my heart! I'll swoop over the streets like the wind and dance to a new tune:

Buy a paper, read a paper, news from all corners of the world: No more robberies, no more murders, no more assaults; no more catastrophes, no more scandals; woods and meadows, villages and cities burn in a sea of joy. Buy a paper, read a paper—Here you have everything I like.

DER KREMER

דער קרעמער

The Shopkeeper

Part of a 25-stanza poem by Abraham Liessin (1872–1938); music attributed to Pinchos Jassinowsky. The original poem was written in Minsk in 1896. Words and music were printed in 1951 by S. Bugatch and Sidor Belarsky. The song was a favorite number in the latter's repertoire.

Zitst zikh a kremer in kreml,
Der hundertster kremer in gas,
Er zitst un er trakht fun a koyne,
In droysn iz fintster un nas.

Es vayzn zikh zeltn di koynim,
Er zitst un er shoydert far kelt,
Un genetst un kholemt khaloymes,
Un trakht zikh mekoyekh der velt.

O, volt ikh gehat nor dem koyekh!
Di erd voltn sonim gekayt,
Un take a melukhe geshafn,
Un take fun undzere layt!

A yidishe melukhe, raboysay,
Tsi kent ir dos gruntik farshteyn?
Dos heyst dokh a melukhe fun geoynim,
A melukhe fun mlokhim aleyn.

Nor plutzling bavayzt zikh a koyne,
Azoy vi an arbes di groys,
Un bet far a kopike hering
Un shlogt im fun dimyen aroys.

Derzeen dos fun vaytn dem pidyen
Di hunderter kremer fun gas,
Zey fresn im oyf mit di oygn,
Mit oygn fun kine un has.

Moderato

The shopkeeper sits in his store, the hundredth one on the block. He sits and waits for a customer. Outside it's dark and wet. Customers seldom show up. He sits and shudders from the cold. He yawns and dreams dreams, and thinks about the world. Oh if only I had the power! My enemies would eat dirt, and I would establish a kingdom just for our people! A Jewish kingdom, people—do you realize what that means? After all, that means a kingdom of geniuses, of veritable kings. But suddenly a customer appears, as big as a bean, who asks for a penny's worth of herring and distracts him from his thoughts. Seeing the paying customer from afar, the hundreds of shopkeepers on the block devour him with their eyes, eyes full of envy and hate.

YIDN SHMIDN

Jews Are Forging

Words by Moishe Broderson (1890–1956), music by David Beigelman (1887–1944). In the children's song anthology *Unter di grininke beymelekh*, compiled by S. Bastomski (1931) some of the words differ: "Noyt un tsores blien / Toyt un hunger vaksn,—/ Darf men ibershmidn / Shtol oyf naye aksn" (Poverty and troubles bloom, death and hunger grow, so we must reforge the steel on new axles). Leizer Wolf paraphrased the song in "Tif in vald baym fayer" for the "Bin" (Bee) Scout Organization of Vilna (*Binishe lider,* 1932). His refrain reads: "Hey, hey, voyl di binen, / Voyl iz zey un gut, / Velder hobn zey in zinen, / Blumenzaft in blut" (Hey, happy are the Bees, happy and well; they have the woods on their minds; petal juice in their blood).

Yidn shmidn, zingen,
Zingen iz der iker;
Klingen ayzns, klingen,
Shpritsn funken shtiker.

Hey, hey, voyl dem shmider,
Voyl iz im un gut,
Zayne shtol—un ayzn-glider
Tsindn on dem mut.

Mentshn, nebekh, blinde,
In der fintster tapn,
Darf men zey atsinder
Podkeves tsuklapn.

Tsar un tsorn glien,
Viln dafke fray zayn,
Darf men ibershmidn
Shverd oyf aker-ayzn.

ייִדן שמידן, זינגען,
זינגען איז דער עיקר;
קלינגען אײַזנס, קלינגען,
שפּריצן פֿונקען שטיקער.

הײ, הײ, װױל דעם שמידער,
װױל איז אים און גוט,
זײַנע שטאָל- און אײַזן-גלידער
צינדן אָן דעם מוט.

מענטשען, נעבעך, בלינדע
אין דער פֿינצטער טאַפּן,
דאַרף מען זײ אַצינדער
פּאָדקעװעס צוקלאַפֿן.

צער און צאָרן גליִען,
װילן דוקא פֿרײַ זײַן,
דאַרף מען איבערשמידן
שװערד אױף אַקער-אײַזן.

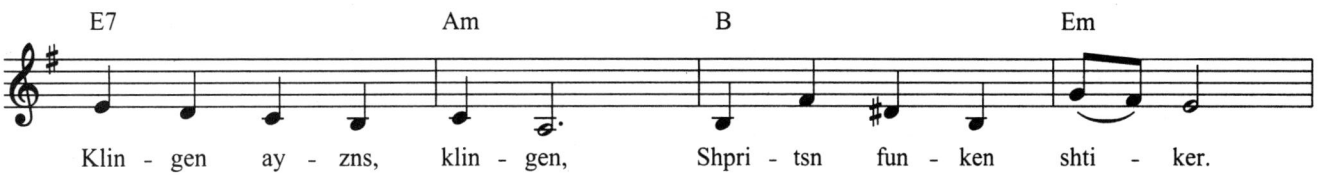

Jews are forging, singing—singing is the most important thing. Iron rings, sparks fly. Hey, hey—things are going well for the blacksmith. His steel and iron limbs kindle our courage. Blind men grope in the dark, so we must shoe them now. Grief and rage glow, seeking to be free, so we must turn swords into plowshares.

DI SVET-SHAP

די סוועט־שאָפּ

The Sweatshop

Part of a song based on the poem "Di mashin" by the "poet of the sweatshop" Morris Rosenfeld (1862–1923). The song has two melodies, both of which are presented here. One was published in the collection of I. Glatstein, *Di fraye muze*, 1918. The second melody was sung to compilers by the late singer David Carrey (1942–1985). R. Pups writes that the poem was adapted in the Lodz Ghetto: "Es roysht azoy vild in resort di mashin" (The machine roars so wildly in the ghetto factory).

Es royshn in shap azoy vild di mashinen,
Az oft mol farges ikh in roysh az ikh bin; -
Ikh ver in dem shreklekhn tuml farlorn,
Mayn ikh vert dort botl, ikh ver a mashin.

Ikh arbet un arbet, un arbet on kheshbn,
Es shaft zikh, un shaft zikh, un shaft zikh on tsol;
Far vos un far vemen? Ikh veys nit, ikh freg nit, -
Vi kumt a mashine tsu denken a mol?

Nito keyn gefil, keyn gedank, keyn farshtand gor; -
Di bitere, blutike arbet dershlogt
Dos eydlste, shenste un beste, dos raykhste,
Dos tifste, dos hekhste vos lebn farmogt;

Es shvindn sekundn, minutn un shtundn
Gor zegl-shnel flien di nekht mit di teg;
Ikh trayb di mashin glaykh ikh vil zey deryogn, -
Ikh yog on a seykhl, ikh yog on a breg.

עס רוישן אין שאַפּ אַזוי ווילד די מאַשינען,
אַז אָפֿט מאָל פֿאַרגעס איך אין רויש אַז איך בין; -
איך ווער אין דעם שרעקלעכן טומל פֿאַרלאָרן,
מיין איך ווערט דאָרט בטל, איך ווער אַ מאַשין.

איך אַרבעט און אַרבעט, און אַרבעט אָן חשבון,
עס שאַפֿט זיך, און שאַפֿט זיך, און שאַפֿט זיך אָן צאָל;
פֿאַר וואָס און פֿאַר וועמען? איך ווייס ניט, איך פֿרעג ניט -
ווי קומט אַ מאַשינע צו דענקען אַ מאָל?

ניטאָ קיין געפֿיל, קיין געדאַנק, קיין פֿאַרשטאַנד גאָר; -
די ביטערע, בלוטיקע אַרבעט דערשלאָגט
דאָס איידלסטע, שענסטע און בעסטע, דאָס רייכסטע,
דאָס טיפֿסטע, דאָס העכסטע וואָס לעבן פֿאַרמאָגט;

עס שווינדן סעקונדן, מינוטן און שטונדן
גאָר זעגל־שנעל פֿליִען די נעכט מיט די טעג;
איך טרייב די מאַשין גלייך איך וויל זיי דעריאָגן, -
איך יאָג אָן אַ שכל, איך יאָג אָן אַ ברעג.

The machines make such wild noise in the shop that I often forget what I am. I get lost in the terrible clamor and think that I'm nothing, just a machine. I work and I work beyond measure. Countless things are manufactured. For what? For whom? I don't know and I don't ask. Where does a machine get off thinking?

No emotion, no thought, no understanding even. The bitter, bloody work beats down the noblest, the most beautiful, the richest, the most profound, and the most exalted things that life offers. Seconds, minutes, and hours disappear. The nights and days fly by speedily. I drive the machine as if I were trying to catch up with it. I chase endlessly, brainlessly.

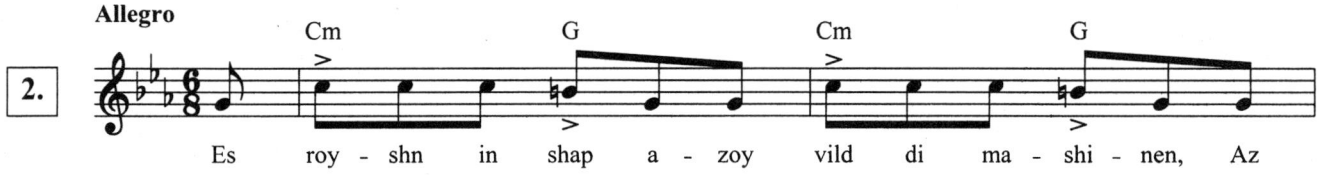

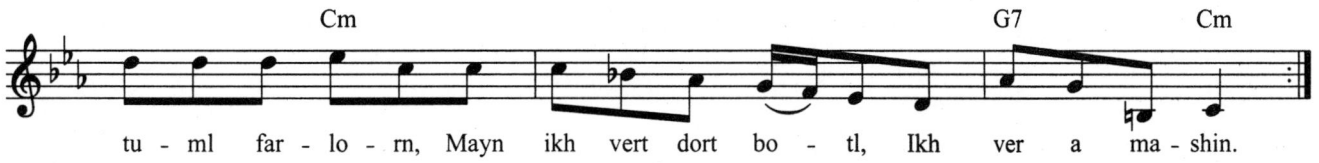

SHNEL LOYFN DI REDER

שנעל לויפֿן די רעדער

The Wheels Turn Fast

Words are by David Edelshtat (1866–1892). This is another offshoot of his poem *Der arbeter* (see "S'falt a shney"). Melodies were written by Jacob Schaefer (1888–1936) and Lazar Weiner (1897–1982). The melody by Weiner, which was written for the Workmen's Circle record *Dos goldene land* (compiled by Joseph Mlotek), was transcribed by the compilers. It was published in *Songs of the American Jewish Experience*, compiled by Neil Levin, Chicago, 1976.

Shnel loyfn di reder,	שנעל לויפֿן די רעדער,
Vild klapn mashinen,	ווילד קלאַפּן מאַשינען,
In shap iz shmutsik un heys,	אין שאָפּ איז שמוציק און הייס,
Der kop vert fartumlt	דער קאָפּ ווערט פֿאַרטומלט,
In oygn vert fintster,	אין אויגן ווערט פֿינצטער,
Fintster fun trern un shveys.	פֿינצטער פֿון טרערן און שווייס.
Ikh fil shoyn bay zikh	איך פֿיל שוין בײַ זיך
Keyn gantsn eyver,	קיין גאַנצן אבֿר,
Tsebrokhn, tsedrikt iz mayn brust,	צעבראָכן, צעדריקט איז מײַן ברוסט,
Ikh ken shoyn far veytik	איך קען שוין פֿאַר ווייטיק
Mayn rukn nit boygn,	מײַן רוקן ניט בויגן,
Bay nakht lozt nit shlofn der hust.	בײַ נאַכט לאָזט ניט שלאָפֿן דער הוסט.
S'loyft um der mayster,	ס'לויפֿט אום דער מײַסטער,
A khaye a vilde,	אַ חיה אַ ווילדע,
Er traybt tsu der shkhite di shof.	ער טרײַבט צו דער שחיטה די שאָף.
O, vi lang vet ir vartn,	אָ, ווי לאַנג וועט איר וואַרטן,
Vi lang vet ir duldn,	ווי לאַנג וועט איר דולדן,
Arbeter-brider, vakht oyf!	אַרבעטער-ברידער, וואַכט אויף!

The wheels turn fast, the machines pound wildly. In the shop it's dirty and hot. My head gets confused, and everything goes dark, dark from tears and sweat.

I don't feel a whole limb anymore. Broken, compressed is my chest. I can't bend my back anymore from pain. At night my cough keeps me from sleeping.

The boss runs around like a wild animal, driving the sheep to slaughter. O how long will you be patient? Brother workers, wake up!

Marcato

1.

Shnel loy - fn di re - der. Vild kla - pn ma - shi - nen, In

shap iz shmu - tsik un heys. Der kop vert far - tu - mlt, In

oy - gn vert fints - ter, Fint - ster fun tre - rn un shveys. Der kop vert far - tu - mlt. In

oy - gn vert fints - ter, Fints - ter fun tre - rn un shveys.

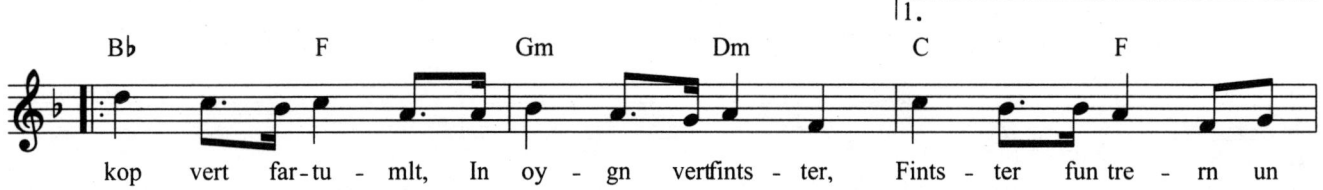

DI LENA   די לענא

The Lena

Part of a poem about an exiled political prisoner in Siberia. Words by Abraham Liessin (1872–1938), music is based on a folk melody. The poem originally entitled "Oyfn vaytn tsofn" (In the Far North) was printed in Minsk in 1896.

In land, vu es kayklt zikh di lena,	אין לאַנד, וווּ עס קײַקלט זיך די לענאַ
In mekhtikn vaser, dem kaltn,	איר מעכטיקן וואַסער, דעם קאַלטן,
Dort shteyt zikh a kleyninke yurte,	דאָרט שטייט זיך אַ קלייניקע יורטע,
In eybike shneyen bahaltn.	אין אייביקע שנייען באַהאַלטן.
Zi shteyt dort a shpil farn shturem,	זי שטייט דאָרט אַ שפּיל פֿאַרן שטורעם,
Farvalgert in mitn dem feld -	פֿאַרוואַלגערט אין מיטן דעם פֿעלד -
Dort shmakht in zayn ayzikn elnt	דאָרט שמאַכט אין זײַן אײַזיקן עלנט
Der kranker, der shtarbnder held.	דער קראַנקער, דער שטאַרבנדער העלד.
Es tsit zikh tseyushet der vinter,	עס ציט זיך צעיושעט דער ווינטער,
Di blinde, di brumende makht;	די בלינדע, די ברומענדע מאַכט;
Es tsit zikh farpantsert der khoyshekh	עס ציט זיך פֿאַרפּאַנצערט דער חושך,
Di toybe, di eybike nakht.	די טויבע, די אייביקע נאַכט.

In the land where the Lena flows, a mighty river and cold, there stands a little tent hidden amid the eternal snows. It stands there for the storms to toy with, far-flung in the midst of the field. There in deep loneliness languishes the sick, dying hero.

The winter drags on like a storm—the blind, roaring power; the darkness, armored, drags on—the unhearing eternal night.

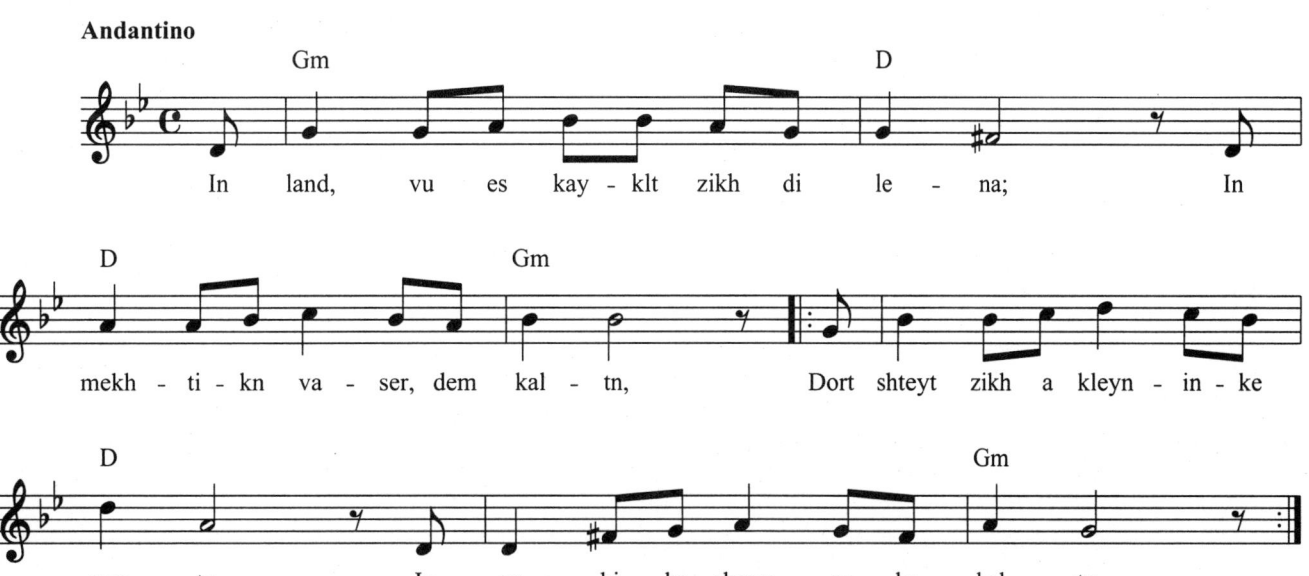

BARIKADN / באַריקאַדן

Barricades

Words by Vilna poet-partisan Shmerke Kaczerginsky (1908-1954), written in 1926. The song was popular in Europe and the U.S. in the 1930s. It was published as an anonymous song by A. Bitter in 1940. In the Memorial Book for S. Kaczerginsky (*Shmerke Katsherginski-ondenk-bukh*), 1955, writer Moishe Knapheis describes in his article "Di freydik lid" (The Joyful Song), how the song "rolled through the Jewish towns of Poland like a golden coin. . . .from all the poor homes and workers' locals, cellars and garrets, from everywhere, the joyful singing spread, trilled out by young, thin little voices."

Tates, mames, kinderlekh Boyen barikadn, Oyf di gasn geyen arum Arbeter-otryadn.	טאַטעס, מאַמעס, קינדערלעך בויען באַריקאַדן, אויף די גאַסן גייען אַרום אַרבעטער-אָטריאַדן.
S'iz der tate fri fun shtub Avek oyf der fabrik, Vet er shoyn in shtibele Nit kumen haynt tsurik.	ס׳איז דער טאַטע פֿרי פֿון שטוב אַוועק אויף דער פֿאַבריק, וועט ער שוין אין שטיבעלע ניט קומען הײַנט צוריק.
S'veysn gut di kinderlekh, Der tate vet nit kumen, S'iz der tate haynt in gas Mit zayn biks farnumen.	ס׳ווייסן גוט די קינדערלעך, דער טאַטע וועט ניט קומען, ס׳איז דער טאַטע הײַנט אין גאַס מיט זײַן ביקס פֿאַרנומען.
S'iz di mame oykh avek In gas farkoyfn epl, Shteyen in kikh faryosemte Di teler mitn tepl.	ס׳איז די מאַמע אויך אַוועק אין גאַס פֿאַרקויפֿן עפּל, שטייען אין קיך פֿאַריתומטע די טעלער מיטן טעפּל.
- S'vet nit zayn keyn vetshere - Zogt Khanele di yatn, - Vayl di mame iz avek Tsuhelfn dem tatn. . .	- ס׳וועט ניט זײַן קיין וועטשערע - זאָגט חנהלע די יאַטן, - ווײַל די מאַמע איז אַוועק צוהעלפֿן דעם טאַטן. . .
Plutsling—trakh! a pule iz Arayn in kleynem shtibl, Farbaygefloygn Khanelen, Gemakht in vant a gribl.	פּלוצלינג - טראַך! אַ פּולע איז אַרײַן אין קליינעם שטיבל, פֿאַרבײַגעפֿלויגן חנהלען, געמאַכט אין וואַנט אַ גריבל.
- Oyb azoy—zogt Khanele - - Kinder, kumt mit mir! Motye, nem di groyse korb, Meyerke—di tir.	- אויב אַזוי - זאָגט חנהלע - - קינדער, קומט מיט מיר! מאָטיע, נעם די גרויסע קאָרב, מאירקע - די טיר.

Di shuflodn fun kamod, Mit an altn fas, A barikade shteln mir Oyf in mitn gas.	די שופֿלאָדן פֿון קאָמאָד, מיט אַן אַלטן פֿאַס, אַ באַריקאַדע שטעלן מיר אויף אין מיטן גאַס.
Di barikade oyfgeshtelt, In shtibl nito keyner, Loyfn politsey farbay, Di kinder varfn shteyner.	די באַריקאַדע אויפֿגעשטעלט, אין שטיבל ניטאָ קיינער, לויפֿן פּאָליציי פֿאַרבײַ, די קינדער װאַרפֿן שטיינער.
Vos mir, ven mir vetshere, Es dunern harmatn, Di kinderlekh fun shtibele Helfn mamen-tatn...	װאָס מיר, װען מיר װעטשערע, עס דונערן האַרמאַטן, די קינדערלעך פֿון שטיבעלע העלפֿן מאַמען-טאַטן...
Tates, mames, kinderlekh Boyen barikadn, Oyf di gasn geyen arum Arbeter-otryadn.	טאַטעס, מאַמעס, קינדערלעך בויען באַריקאַדן, אויף די גאַסן גייען אַרום אַרבעטער-אָטריאַדן.

Fathers, mothers, and little children are building barricades. Patrolling the streets are worker brigades. Father left the house early to go to the factory. Back to the house he will not come today. Father's in the street today, busy with his gun.

Mother's gone away as well to sell her apples in the street. Standing in the kitchen like orphans are all the pots and dishes. "There won't be any supper" says Khanele to the boys, "for mother's gone to help out father."

Suddenly—bang! A bullet enters the little house, flies past Khanele, and buries itself in the wall. "In that case," says Khanele, "children, come with me! Motye, take the big basket—Meyer, get the door!"

"We'll take the dresser drawers and an old barrel, and put up a barricade in the middle of the street."

The barricade is up, nobody's at home; police run past, the children throw stones.

Who cares about supper (when) cannons thunder; the children from the little house are helping mother and father.

DI TSUKUNFT

די צוקונפֿט

The Future

Words by Morris Winchefsky (1856–1932), pen name of Lipe Bentsion Novochovitch. The song is sung in a recent play *A sheyne meydl* (A Pretty Girl), dealing with the Holocaust, which was presented at numerous colleges. At the end of a TV retrospective on the work of artist Yosl Bergner, he plays this melody on his harmonica.

O, di velt vet vern yinger,	אָ, די וועלט וועט ווערן ייִנגער,
Un dos lebn laykhter, gringer,	און דאָס לעבן לײַכטער, גרינגער,
Yeder kloger vet a zinger	יעדער קלאָגער וועט אַ זינגער
Vern, brider, bald!	ווערן, ברידער, באַלד!
Loz dos folk nor vern kliger,	לאָז דאָס פֿאָלק נאָר ווערן קליגער,
Un faryogn dem batriger,	און פֿאַריאָגן דעם באַטריגער,
Im, dem fuks, un oykh dem tiger	אים, דעם פֿוקס, און אויך דעם טיגער
Fun zayn sheynem vald.	פֿון זײַן שיינעם וואַלד.
O, di velt vet vern shener,	אָ, די וועלט וועט ווערן שענער,
Libe greser, sine klener,	ליבע גרעסער, שׂינאה קלענער,
Tsvishn froyen, tsvishn mener,	צווישן פֿרויען, צווישן מענער,
Tsvishn land un land;	צווישן לאַנד און לאַנד;
O, di velt vet vern frayer,	אָ, די וועלט וועט ווערן פֿרײַער,
Frayer, shener, yinger, nayer,	פֿרײַער, שענער, ייִנגער, נײַער,
Un in ir di varheyt tayer,	און אין איר די וואַרהײַט טײַער,
Tayer vi a fraynd.	טײַער ווי אַ פֿרײַנד.
O, di velt vet vern dreyster	אָ, די וועלט וועט ווערן דרייסטער
Un es vet nit zayn a mayster,	און עס וועט ניט זײַן אַ מײַסטער,
Nit di kroyn un nit der tayster, -	ניט די קרוין און ניט דער טײַסטער, -
Nit dem zelners shverd.	ניט דעם זעלנערס שווערד.
Alzo mutik in di reyen,	אַלזאָ מוטיק אין די רייען,
In di reyen, tsu bafrayen,	אין די רייען, צו באַפֿרײַען,
Tsu bafrayen un banayen	צו באַפֿרײַען און באַנײַען
Undzer alte velt!	אונדזער אַלטע וועלט!

O the world will grow younger, and life will be easier. Every complainer will become a singer soon, brothers! Only let the people become wiser and chase away the traitor; the fox and the tiger too from their beautiful forest.

O the world will become more beautiful. Love will grow greater, hatred less between wives and husbands, between countries. O, the world will become freer, more just, younger, newer. And in it the truth will be valued, valued as a friend.

O the world will get bolder and there will be no master. Not the crown nor the purse, nor the soldier's sword. So let's have courage in the ranks to free our old world!

ZINGENDIK זינגענדיק

Singing

Words by Zisha Weinper (1893–1957); music by Paul Lamkoff. Published in the composer's collection *Ten Hebrew Song Classics*, Los Angeles, 1929. The song was also published in *Zingendik, lider far yugnt,* compiled by Raley (Vilna, 1936), and in the *Kinder-Fraynd* (Muzikalishe biblyotek, no. 6, [Warsaw, November 1937], as part of a play *Tsu der zun* (with texts by A. Katz and Z. Weinper, music and arrangements by I. Troupianski). It was sung in the film of the Medem Sanitarium *Mir kumen on* (We Are Coming) (see songs "Mir kumen on" and "Nor a mame").

Zingendik,
Treyst zikh di velt di farvundete,
Un durkh gezang
Efenen zikh di hent gebundene.

Refrain:
Zingen mir, zingen mir, zingen mir,
Un ale veltn farklingen mir.

Zingendik,
Vakht oyf di velt di farmaterte,
Un durkh gezang,
Mit fener royte un tseflaterte.

Zingendik,
Vakht oyf di velt di farblutikte,
Un durkh gezang
Freyen zikh hertser gemutikte.

זינגענדיק,
טרייסט זיך די וועלט די פֿאַרוווּנדעטע,
און דורך געזאַנג
עפֿענען זיך די הענט געבונדענע.

רעפֿרײן:
זינגען מיר, זינגען מיר, זינגען מיר,
און אַלע וועלטן פֿאַרקלינגען מיר.

זינגענדיק,
וואַכט אויף די וועלט די פֿאַרמאַטערטע,
און דורך געזאַנג,
מיט פֿענער רויטע און צעפֿלאַטערטע.

זינגענדיק,
וואַכט אויף די וועלט די פֿאַרבלוטיקטע,
און דורך געזאַנג
פֿרייען זיך הערצער געמוטיקטע.

Singing, the wounded world consoles itself. And through song our clenched fists open up.

We sing, we sing, and our song resounds throughout the world!

Singing, the tired old world awakes through song with red and flapping banners.

Singing, the bloody world awakes. And through song encouraged hearts rejoice.

MAYNE KHAVEYRIM

מײַנע חבֿרים

My Comrades

Words by Joseph Mlotek (born 1918) in 1936, music by Jacob Glatstein, director of the chorus of the Tsukunft Youth Organization of the Bund in Warsaw. Submitted by Sara Rosenfeld and Chana Gonshar, Montreal, members of the Tsukunft chorus.

Mayne khaveyrim—bloyz arbeter-yatn,	מײַנע חבֿרים - בלויז אַרבעטער־יאַטן,
Mit hent fun mazoles un hart,	מיט הענט פֿון מאַזאָלעס און האַרט,
Fintstern op zey're teg in varshtatn,	פֿינצטערן אָפּ זייערע טעג אין וואַרשטאַטן,
Vu tog vert farbitn oyf nakht.	וווּ טאָג ווערט פֿאַרביטן אויף נאַכט.
Mayne khaveyrim, koym yinglekh fun akhtsn,	מײַנע חבֿרים, קוים ייִנגלעך פֿון אַכצן,
Gevebt zikh khaloymes fun glik.	געוועבט זיך חלומות פֿון גליק,
Itst vern di troymen fun mayne khaveyrim	איצט ווערן די טרוימען פֿון מײַנע חבֿרים
Tsemoln oyf shtoyb fun fabrik.	צעמאָלן אויף שטויב פֿון פֿאַבריק.
Derfar geyen khevre avek fun fabrikn,	דערפֿאַר גייען חברה אַוועק פֿון פֿאַבריקן,
Glaykh inem klub, in fareyn;	גלײַך אינעם קלוב, אין פֿאַראײַן;
Un trefn zikh dortn mit mentshn fun arbet,	און טרעפֿן זיך דאָרטן מיט מענטשן פֿון אַרבעט,
Mit brider fun noyt un fun payn.	מיט ברידער פֿון נויט און פֿון פּײַן.
Un bindn tsunoyf zeyer goyrl dem shvern,	און בינדן צונויף זייער גורל דעם שווערן,
Mit brider fun nont un fun vayt;	מיט ברידער פֿון נאָנט און פֿון ווײַט;
Un zeyen a has kegn di vos farshmakhtn	און זייען אַ האַס קעגן די וואָס פֿאַרשמאַכטן
A yugnt aza far der tsayt.	אַ יוגנט אַזאַ פֿאַר דער צײַט.
Derfar hobn khevre a shvue geshvoyrn,	דערפֿאַר האָבן חברה אַ שבֿועה געשוווירן,
A shvue oyf lebn un toyt.	אַ שבֿועה אויף לעבן און טויט,
Derfar hobn khevre zey're blikn gevondn	דערפֿאַר האָבן חברה זייערע בליקן געוואָנדן
Tsum morgn, vos shaynt oyf hel-royt.	צום מאָרגן, וואָס שײַנט אויף העל רויט.

My comrades, just working lads with callused hands, live out their days in darkness in shops where day is turned into night. My comrades, barely eighteen years old, dream dreams of happiness. Now my comrades' dreams are ground up into the dust of the factories. That's why friends leave factories, go right into clubs and unions, and meet working men, brothers of need and pain. They join their harsh fate with brothers from near and far, and sow hatred for those who strike down their youth so prematurely. That's why friends have sworn an oath, an oath of life and death. That's why friends have turned their eyes toward tomorrow, which shines bright red.

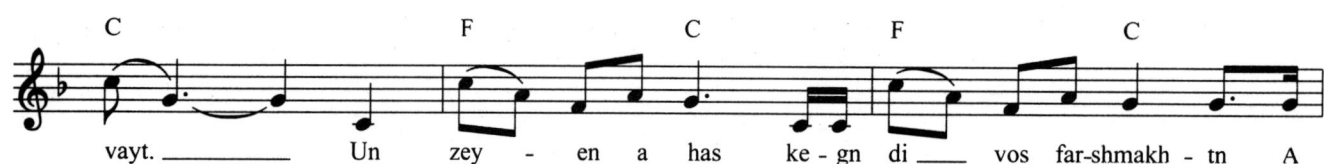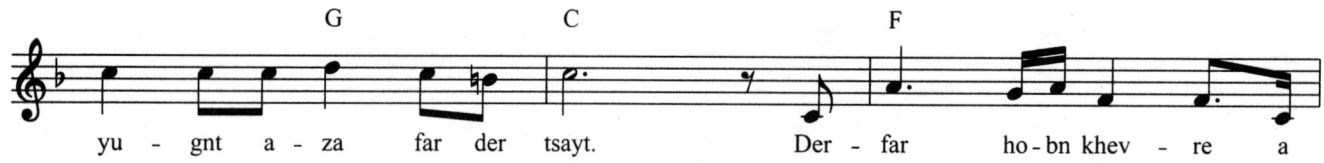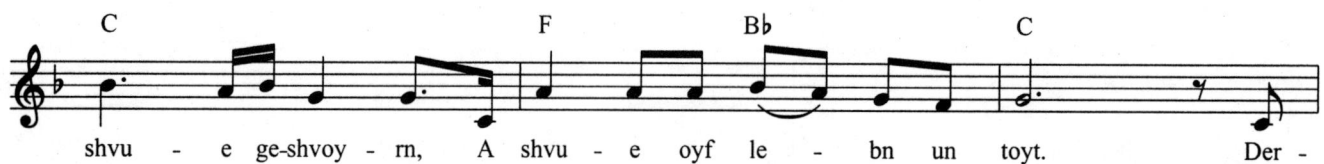

DOS NAYE LID   דאָס נייע ליד

The New Song

Words by Abraham Reisen (1875–1953), composer unknown. Published with this melody in *Di fraye muze,* 1918 and *Binishe lider.* 1932. The song was popular in the Yiddish schools in this country and was sung annually at the traditional Third Seyder of the Workmen's Circle. It was also sung during the Holocaust. Poet Abraham Sutzkever writes that he heard the children of I. Gershteyn's chorus singing this song in the Vilna Ghetto: "[Gershteyn] brought the children closer, arranged them according to their voices, and over the garret, over the ghetto, over the whole world rang out 'Un zol vi vayt'. . ." Another melody by J. S. Roskin, printed in Hasomir's *Sangbog* was arranged for chorus by Zavel Zilberts.

Un zol vi vayt nokh zayn di tsayt
Fun libe un fun sholem,
Dokh kumen vet, tsi fri, tsi shpet,
Di tsayt—es iz keyn kholem!

Ikh her dos lid fun libe, frid,
Di mekhtike gezangen;
Un yeder ton fun lid zogt on:
Di zun iz oyfgegangen!

Es ekt di nakht, di velt dervakht
Ful hofnung, lust un shtrebn.
Du herst—in luft a shtime ruft:
Tsu glik un freyd un lebn!. . .

און זאָל ווי ווײַט נאָך זײַן די צײַט
פֿון ליבע און פֿון שלום,
דאָך קומען וועט, צי פֿרי, צי שפּעט,
די צײַט - עס איז קיין חלום.

איך הער דאָס ליד פֿון ליבע, פֿריד,
די מעכטיקע געזאַנגען;
און יעדער טאָן פֿון ליד זאָגט אָן:
די זון איז אויפֿגעגאַנגען.

עס עקט די נאַכט, די וועלט דערוואַכט
פֿול האָפֿנונג, לוסט און שטרעבן.
דו הערסט - אין לופֿט אַ שטימע רופֿט
צו גליק און פֿרייד און לעבן!

No matter how far away the time of love and peace, still it will come, whether soon or late, that time, it's no dream!

I hear the song of love and peace, the mighty singing. And every note of the song asserts: the sun has risen!

The night is ending, the world is awakening with hope and joy and striving.

You hear—in the air a voice calls to happiness, to joy, to life.

HUMOR UN OYF SIMKHES
HUMOROUS SONGS AND
SONGS FOR CELEBRATIONS AND PARTIES
הומאָר און אויף שׂימחות

Lekhayim! לחיים

Words by Sam Liptzin (1893–1980), music by Joseph Shrogin (1902–1974). Originally published in *Zingen mir*, 1949 to the tune of "Lomir bagrisn." In the *Anthology of Yiddish Folksongs*, IV (1987), there are additional words that new immigrants from Soviet Russia sang in Israel: "Lekhayim for Jerusalem" . . . "for our army". . . "for our sunny land."

Lekhayim—a shnepsl lomir makhn,
Lekhayim—far ale gute zakhn.

To heybt di glezlekh un raglayim,
Lomir ale trinken lekhayim.
Lekhayim, lekhayim!

Lekhayim—fun tsores mer nit visn,
Lekhayim—nor fun freyd genisn.

Lekhayim—far sholem lomir shtrebn,
Lekhayim—far glik un freyd un lebn!

Lekhayim—far dem land dem nayem,
Lekhayim—far dem land dem frayen.

לחיים - אַ שנעפּסל לאָמיר מאַכן,
לחיים - פֿאַר אַלע גוטע זאַכן.

טאָ הייבט די גלעזלעך און רגלים,
לאָמיר אַלע טרינקען לחיים.
לחיים, לחיים!

לחיים - פֿון צרות מער ניט וויסן,
לחיים - נאָר פֿון פֿרייד געניסן.

לחיים - פֿאַר שלום לאָמיר שטרעבן,
לחיים - פֿאַר גליק און פֿרייד און לעבן!

לחיים - פֿאַר דעם לאַנד דעם נײַעם,
לחיים - פֿאַר דעם לאַנד דעם פֿרײַען.

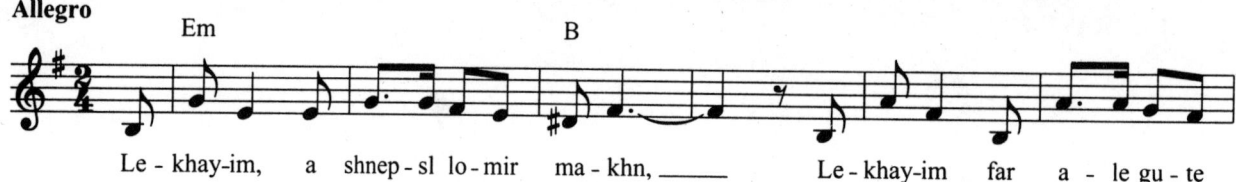

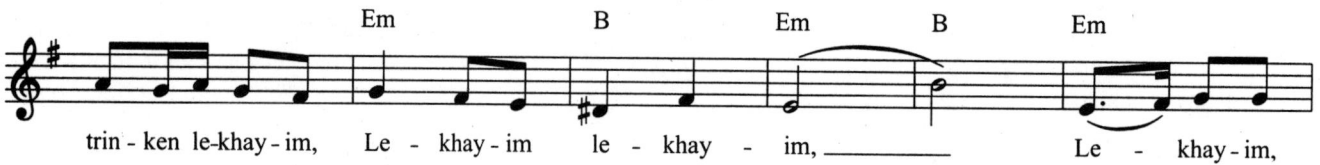
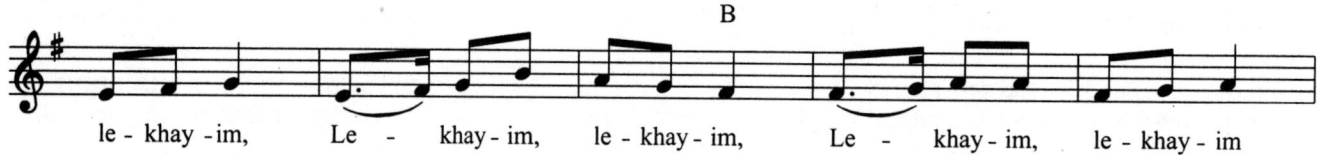

Lekhayim! To life! Let's drink a toast for all the good things here!

So raise your glasses and dance, and let's all drink lekhayim!

Let us know no more sorrow, let's only enjoy happiness! Let's strive for peace, for joy, good fortune and life! Lekhayim for the new land, the free land!

Khatskele

כאַצקעלע

Folksong. Text published by S. Ginzburg and P. Marek in 1901; text and music published in 1905 in *Ost und West* and by the Society for Jewish Folk Music in St. Petersburg in 1909, in the arrangement of Ephraim Shkliar. Y. L. Cahan has additional variants in 1912, with other names like "Sorele, the rabbi's wife" and "Reb Abe." He and, Moishe Beregovski and Joachim Stutchewsky cite this song in connection with the names of the dances mentioned: "kozatske," "dume" and "semele." Isa Kremer brings other stanzas about giving charity in her *Album* like "Brider, oy yidelekh, shenkt a nedove, / Far di yesoymelekh, der mume Slove" (Brothers, oh fellow Jews, give charity, for the orphans, for Aunt Slove) and A. Litvin published a parody in his column in the *Haynt* about the nauseous Legionnaires on the ship going to Palestine.

Khatskele, Khatskele, shpil mir a kazatskele!
Khotsh an oreminke, dokh a khvatskele!
Orem iz nit gut, orem iz nit gut,
Lomir zikh nit shemen mit undzer eygn blut!

כאַצקעלע, כאַצקעלע, שפּיל מיר אַ קאַזאַצקעלע!
כאָטש אָן אָרעמינקע, דאָך אַ כוואַטסקעלע!
אָרעם איז ניט גוט, אָרעם איז ניט גוט,
לאָמיר זיך ניט שעמען מיט אונדזער אייגן בלוט!

Khatskele, Khatskele, shpil zhe mir a dume!
Un khotsh an oreme, abi a frume!
Orem iz nit gut, orem iz nit gut,
Lomir zikh nit shemen mit eygenem blut!

כאַצקעלע, כאַצקעלע, שפּיל זשע מיר אַ דומע!
און כאָטש אַן אָרעמע, אַבי אַ פֿרומע!
אָרעם איז ניט גוט, אָרעם איז ניט גוט,
לאָמיר זיך ניט שעמען מיט אייגענעם בלוט!

Khatskele, Khatskele, shpil zhe mir a semele
Far a drayerl oyf Khaskes kremele!
Orem iz nit gut, orem iz nit gut,
Lomir zikh nit shemen mit eygenem blut!

כאַצקעלע, כאַצקעלע, שפּיל זשע מיר אַ סעמעלע
פֿאַר אַ דרײַערל אויף כאַסקעס קרעמעלע!
אָרעם איז ניט גוט, אָרעם איז ניט גוט,
לאָמיר זיך ניט שעמען מיט אייגענעם בלוט!

Khotsh an oreminke, fort a mume,
Nit keyn gebetene, aleyn gekumen!
Orem iz nit gut, orem iz nit gut,
Lomir zikh nit shemen mit eygenem blut!

כאָטש אַן אָרעמינקע, פֿאָרט אַ מומע,
ניט קיין געבעטענע, אַליין געקומען!
אָרעם איז ניט גוט, אָרעם איז ניט גוט,
לאָמיר זיך ניט שעמען מיט אייגענעם בלוט!

Khatskele, Khatskele, play me a kozatska. Though I'm poor, I'm still nimble.
Being poor isn't good, but don't be ashamed of your own flesh and blood.
Khatskele, Khatskele, play me a duma, Though I'm poor, I'm still pious.
Khatskele, Khatskele, play me a semele. Here are three cents for Khatske's store.
Though I'm poor, I'm still an aunt. Though uninvited, I still came on my own.

לאָמיר אָנהייבן צו דערקלערן

LOMIR ONHEYBN TSU DERKLERN

Let's Begin to Explain

Folksong collected by the compilers from Charles Leikin, Bronx, N.Y. Textual variant was published by S. Ginzburg and P. Marek, 1901. This riddle song was sung at weddings usually by a badkhn (wedding entertainer) or marshelik (jester.) In some versions the "khasene-hoyz" (the wedding house) instead of the "khosns tish" (the groom's table) leads off the string of riddles. The day of feasting and dancing and leaping is the usual metaphor of a wedding. Other versions appear in *Filologishe shriftn*, V; Dov and Meir Noy, *Yidishe folkslider fun galitsye* and elsewhere). Additional versions were submitted by Gelle Fishman (Bronx, N. Y.) and Dvoyre Neustempel (Rego Park).

Lomir onheybn tsu derklern Vos fun eyns ken alts vern: Eyns iz dem khosns tish Vu men est un vu men trinkt, Vu men tantst un vu men shpringt. Tra-la-la-la. . .	לאָמיר אָנהייבן צו דערקלערן וואָס פֿון איינס קען אַלץ ווערן. איינס איז דעם חתנס טיש ווי מען עסט און ווי מען טרינקט, ווי מען טאַנצט און ווי מען שפּרינגט. טראַ־לאַ־לאַ־לאַ . . .
Lomir onheybn tsu derklern Vos fun tsvey ken alts vern: Tsvey zenen khosn-kale, Vos zey geyen iber ale, Eyns iz dem khosns tish. . .	לאָמיר אָנהייבן צו דערקלערן וואָס פֿון צוויי קען אַלץ ווערן: צוויי זענען חתן־כּלה, וואָס זיי גייען איבער אַלע, איינס איז דעם חתנס טיש . . .
Lomir onheybn tsu derklern Vos fun dray ken alts vern: Dray zenen di mekhutonim, Vos zey zogn tsu mezumonim. Tsvey zenen khosn-kale, Vos zey geyen iber ale, Eyns iz dem khosns tish. . .	לאָמיר אָנהייבן צו דערקלערן וואָס פֿון דרײַ קען אַלץ ווערן: דרײַ זענען די מחותּנים, וואָס זיי זאָגן צו מזומנים. צוויי זענען חתן־כּלה, וואָס זיי גייען איבער אַלע, איינס איז דעם חתנס טיש . . .
Lomir onheybn tsu derklern Vos fun fir ken alts vern: Fir zenen di khupe-shtangen Vu khosn-kale vern gefangen. Dray zenen di mekhutonim, Vos zogn tsu mezumonim. Tsvey zenen di khosn-kale, Vos zey geyen iber ale, Eyns iz dem khosns tish. . .	לאָמיר אָנהייבן צו דערקלערן וואָס פֿון פֿיר קען אַלץ ווערן: פֿיר זענען די חופּה־שטאַנגען ווי חתן־כּלה ווערן געפֿאַנגען, דרײַ זענען די מחותּנים, וואָס זאָגן צו מזומנים, צוויי זענען די חתן־כּלה, וואָס זיי גייען איבער אַלע, איינס איז דעם חתנס טיש . . .

Lomir onheybn tsu derklern
Vos fun finf ken alts vern:
Finf zenen di klezmorim
Vos zey shpiln far raykh un orem,
Fir zenen di khupe-shtangen,
Vu khosn-kale vern gefangen,
Dray zenen di mekhutonim
Vos zogn tsu mezumonim.
Tsvey zenen khosn-kale
Vos zhe geyen iber ale,
Eyns iz dem khosns tish. . .

Lomir onheybn tsu derklern
Vos fun zeks ken alts vern:
Zeks zenen di zeks teg
Vos keyner tor nisht un khosn-kale meg,
Finf zenen di klezmorim
Vos zey shpiln far raykh un orem.
Fir zenen di khupe-shtangen,
Vu khosn-kale vern gefangen,
Dray zenen di mekhutonim
Vos zogn tsu mezumonim.
Tsvey zenen khosn-kale,
Vos zhe geyen iber ale,
Eyns iz dem khosns tish. . .

Lomir onheybn tsu derklern
Vos fun zibn ken alts vern:
Zibn zenen di sheyve brokhes,
Me zogt tsu nadn, me git s'kadokhes.
Zeks zenen di zeks teg
Vos keyner tor nisht un khosn-kale meg,
Finf zenen di klezmorim,
Vos zey shpiln far raykh un orem,
Fir zenen di khupe-shtangen,
Vu khosn-kale vern gefangen.
Dray zenen di mekhutonim,
Vos zey zogn tsu mezumonim,
Tsvey zenen khosn-kale,
Vos zey geyen iber ale,
Eyns iz dem khosns tish
Vu men est un vu men trinkt,
Vu men tantst un vu men shpringt.
Tra-la-la-la. . .

לאָמיר אָנהייבן צו דערקלערן
וואָס פֿון פֿינף קען אַלץ ווערן:
פֿינף זענען די קלעזמאַרים
וואָס זיי שפּילן פֿאַר רײַך און אָרעם,
פֿיר זענען די חופּה-שטאַנגען
ווו חתן-כּלה ווערן געפֿאַנגען,
דרײַ זענען די מחותּנים,
וואָס זאָגן צו מזומנים,
צוויי זענען חתן-כּלה,
וואָס זיי גייען איבער אַלע,
איינס איז דעם חתנס טיש . . .

לאָמיר אָנהייבן צו דערקלערן
וואָס פֿון זעקס קען אַלץ ווערן:
זעקס זענען די זעקס טעג
וואָס קיינער טאָר נישט און חתן-כּלה מעג,
פֿינף זענען די קלעזמאַרים
וואָס זיי שפּילן פֿאַר רײַך און אָרעם,
פֿיר זענען די חופּה-שטאַנגען
ווו חתן-כּלה ווערן געפֿאַנגען,
דרײַ זענען די מחותּנים,
וואָס זאָגן צו מזומנים,
צוויי זענען חתן-כּלה,
וואָס זיי גייען איבער אַלע,
איינס איז דעם חתנס טיש . . .

לאָמיר אָנהייבן צו דערקלערן
וואָס פֿון זיבן קען אַלץ ווערן:
זיבן זענען די שבֿע ברכות,
מע זאָגט צו נדן, מע גיט ס'קדחת.
זעקס זענען די זעקס טעג
וואָס קיינער טאָר נישט און חתן-כּלה מעג,
פֿינף זענען די קלעזמאַרים,
וואָס זיי שפּילן פֿאַר רײַך און אָרעם,
פֿיר זענען די חופּה-שטאַנגען
ווו חתן-כּלה ווערן געפֿאַנגען,
דרײַ זענען די מחותּנים,
וואָס זיי זאָגן צו מזומנים,
צוויי זענען חתן-כּלה,
וואָס זיי גייען איבער אַלע,
איינס איז דעם חתנס טיש,
ווו מען עסט און ווו מען טרינקט,
ווו מען טאַנצט און ווו מען שפּרינגט.
טראַ-לאַ-לאַ-לאַ . . .

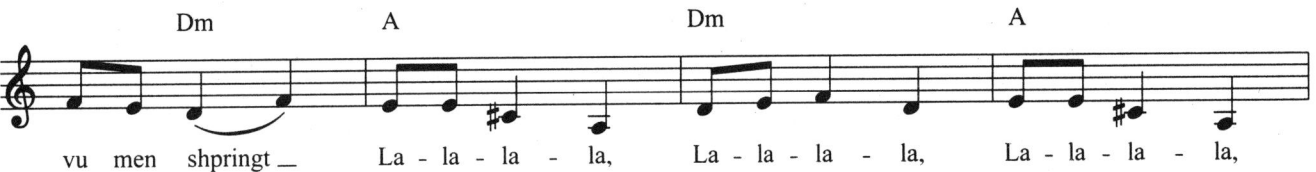

Let's begin to explain all the things that come from "one:"

"One" is the bridegroom's table where they eat and drink, where they dance and leap.

"Two" are the bride and groom who are better than every one else.

"Three" are the in-laws who promise to pay for the wedding in cash.

"Four" are the canopy poles where bride and groom are captured,

"Five" are the five musicians who play for both rich and poor.

"Six" are the six days during which others may not, but bride and groom may.

"Seven" are the seven blessings. They pledge a dowry, but give you nothing.

FUNEM SHEYNEM VORTSL AROYS פֿונעם שײנעם װאָרצל אַרױס

From the Beautiful Root

A song of cumulative rhymes that begins with the creation of the earth and the sky. Published by M. Beregovski and Itzik Fefer in 1938. The compilers heard the children in a Yiddish school in Buenos Aires and in Camp Hemshekh, New York, in the 1960s ending the song with "from the pillow came a dream." There is a variation in N. Prilutsky, I: "Got hot bashafn himl un erd,/ Fun der erd—korien aroys" (God created heaven and earth; a root came from the earth." It ends with "Funem bokher—di toyre aroys" (From the boy came the Torah).

Funem sheynem vortsl aroys
Iz a sheyner boym aroys.
   Boym funem vortsl,
   Vortsl fun der erd,
   Zint s'iz bashafn himl un erd.

Funem sheynem boym aroys
Iz a sheyner tsvayg aroys.
   Tsvayg funem boym,
   Boym funem vortsl,
   Vortsl fun der erd,
   Zint s'iz bashafn himl un erd.

Funem sheynem tsvayg aroys
Iz a sheyner nest aroys.
   Nest funem tsvayg. . .

Funem sheynem nest aroys
Iz a sheyner foygl aroys.
   Foygl funem nest. . .

Funem sheynem foygl aroys
Iz a sheyner feder aroys.
   Feder funem foygl. . .

Funem sheynem feder aroys
Iz a guter kishn aroys.
   Kishn funem feder. . .

Fun dem gutn kishn aroys
Iz a sheyne meydl aroys,
   Meydl fun dem kishn,
   Kishn funem feder,
   Feder funem foygl,
   Foygl funem nest,
   Nest funem tsvayg,
   Tsvayg funem boym,
   Boym funem vortsl,
   Vortsl fun der erd,
   Zint s'iz bashafn himl un erd.

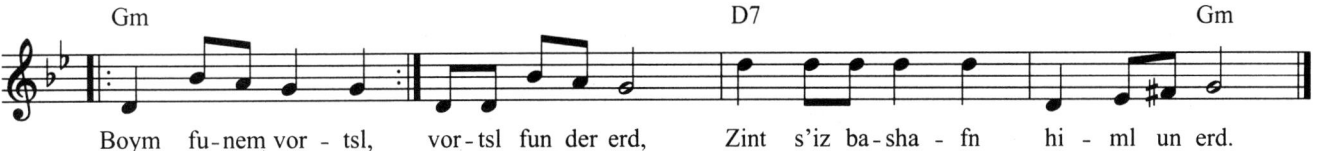

From the beautiful root came a beautiful tree. Tree from the root, root from the earth—since heaven and earth were created.

From the beautiful tree came a beautiful branch. Branch from the tree. . .

From the beautiful branch came a beautiful nest. Nest from the branch. . .

From the beautiful nest came a beautiful bird. Bird from the nest. . .

From the beautiful bird came a beautiful feather. Feather from the bird. . .

From the beautiful feather came a beautiful pillow. Pillow from the feather. . .

From the beautiful pillow came a beautiful girl. Girl from the pillow.

Pillow from the feather. Feather from the bird. Bird from the nest. Nest from the branch. Branch from the tree. Tree from the root. Root from the earth. Since heaven and earth were created.

TONU RABONEN

תנו רבנן

O Great Teachers

Humorous interpretation of the sayings of the sages was collected by compiler in Poland from Jacob Pat, Yiddish writer and cultural leader, who sang it at a summer colony of the SKIF (Jewish Socialist Children's Association) prior to World War II. A different melody was published by Schack and Cohen in 1924. The refrain of the vocables "ay-ay-ay" is sung by the audience each time with increasing fervor until the humorous climax (or anti-climax) is reached. The words "Tonu rabonen" which introduce many passages of the Talmud enhance the humor, combining the serious with the mundane.

Tonu rabonen
Hobn undzere khakhomim gelernt:
Vos volt zayn, vos volt zayn,
Vos volt zayn,
Ven fun ale poyerim
In der gantsener velt,
Volt vern, volt vern, volt vern
Eyn groyser poyer?
- Ay, volt dos a poyer geven!
Ay-ay-ay...!

Tonu rabonen
Hobn undzere khakhokhim vayter gelernt:
Vos volt zayn, vos volt zayn,
Vos volt zayn,
Ven fun ale beymer
Fun der gantsener velt
Volt vern, volt vern, volt vern
Eyn groyser boym?
- Ay, volt dos a boym geven!
Ay-ay-ay...!

Tonu rabonen
Hobn ober undzere khakhomim nokh vayter gelernt:
Vos volt zayn, vos volt zayn,
vos volt zayn,
Ven fun ale hek
Fun der gantser velt,
Volt vern, volt vern, volt vern
Eyn groyse hak?
- Ay, volt dos a hak geven!
Ay-ay-ay...!

Tonu rabonen	תּנו רבנן
Hobn ober undzere khakhomim nokh vayter gelernt:	האָבן אָבער אונדזערע חכמים נאָך ווײַטער געלערנט:
Vos volt zayn, vos volt zayn, vos volt zayn,	וואָס וואָלט זײַן, וואָס וואָלט זײַן, וואָס וואָלט זײַן,
Ven fun ale taykhn	ווען פֿון אַלע טײַכן
Fun der gantser velt	פֿון דער גאַנצער וועלט,
Volt vern, volt vern, volt vern	וואָלט ווערן, וואָלט ווערן, וואָלט ווערן
Eyn groyser vaser?	אײן גרויסער טײַך?
- Ay, volt dos a taykh geven!	–אײַ, וואָלט דאָס אַ טײַך געווען!
Ay-ay-ay...!	אײַ-אײַ-אײַ!...
Tonu rabonen	תּנו רבנן
Hobn ober undzere khakhomim alts vayter gelernt:	האָבן אָבער אונדזערע חכמים אַלץ ווײַטער געלערנט:
Vos volt zayn, vos volt zayn, vos volt zayn,	וואָס וואָלט זײַן, וואָס וואָלט זײַן, וואָס וואָלט זײַן,
Ven der doziker poyer	ווען דער דאָזיקער פּויער
Volt a nem geton di dozike hak,	וואָלט אַ נעם געטאָן די דאָזיקע האַק,
Un mit der doziker hak	און מיט דער דאָזיקער האַק
Volt er a hak geton in dozikn boym	וואָלט ער אַ האַק געטאָן אין דאָזיקן בוים
Un der doziker boym	און דער דאָזיקער בוים
Volt a fal geton in dozikn vaser,	וואָלט אַ פֿאַל געטאָן אין דאָזיקן וואַסער,
- Ay, volt es demolt a plyukhke geton!	–אײַ, וואָלט עס דעמאָלט אַ פּליוכקע געטאָן!
Ay-ay-ay!	אײַ-אײַ-אײַ!

O great teachers, this is what our wise men taught: What would happen if all the peasants in the whole wide world were turned into one gigantic peasant? Oh, what a peasant that would be!

O great teachers, this is what our wise men further taught: What would happen if all the trees in the whole wide world were turned into one gigantic tree? Oh, what a tree that would be!

O great teachers, this is what our wise men still further taught: What would happen if all the axes in the whole wide world were turned into one gigantic axe? - Oh, what an axe that would be!

O great teachers, this is what our wise men even further taught: What would happen if all the rivers in the whole wide world were turned into one gigantic river? - Oh, what a river that would be!

O great teachers, this is what our wise men taught at the very end:

What would happen if that very peasant should get hold of that very axe, and with that axe should chop down that very tree, and that tree would fall into that very river? - Oh, would that make a splash! Ay-ay-ay!

HOB IKH MIR A MANTL

האָב איך מיר אַ מאַנטל

I Have a Coat

    Folksong published in *Tsaytshrift*. . . II-III (1927–1928) There are various endings of the song. The coat ultimately evolves into: "a knepl" (a button): in A. Bitter; "a lidl" (a song): in M. Gelbart and Sidor Belarsky; "a lidele" (a little song): in *Klezkamp Songbook* and Hai and Topsy Frankel; "a gornisht" (a nothing): in *Klezkamp Songbook,* 1989; "a gornisht fun gornisht" (a nothing from nothing): in Abrasha Vayner; "a kestele" (a box to bury the vest): in Moishe Beregovski, 1962; "a nayem mantl fun a late" (a new coat from a patch): in Sam Liptzin, 1949; and finally "funem pekele oysgelakht" (I scoffed at the bundle [of old cloth]): in *Tsaytshrift*. . . II-III

Hob ikh mir a mantl fun fartsaytikn tukh,	האָב איך מיר אַ מאַנטל פֿון פֿאַרצײַטיקן טוך,
Tra-la-la-la, la-la-la-la, la,la,la	טראַ־לאַ־לאַ־לאַ, לאַ־לאַ־לאַ־לאַ, לאַ, לאַ, לאַ.
Iz in im nishto keyn gantsener dukh,	איז אין אים נישטאָ קיין גאַנצענער דוך,
Tra-la-la-la,. . .	טראַ־לאַ־לאַ־לאַ. . .
Darum hob ikh zikh batrakht	דאַרום האָב איך זיך באַטראַכט
Un fun dem mantl a rekl gemakht.	און פֿון דעם מאַנטל אַ רעקל געמאַכט.
Tra-la-la-la, la-la-la,	טראַ־לאַ־לאַ־לאַ, לאַ־לאַ־לאַ. . .
Un fun dem mantl a rekl gemakht.	און פֿון דעם מאַנטל אַ רעקל געמאַכט.
Hob ikh mir a rekl fun fartsaytikn tukh. . .	האָב איך מיר אַ רעקל פֿון פֿאַרצײַטיקן טוך. . .
Iz in im nishto keyn gantsener dukh. . .	איז אין אים נישטאָ קיין גאַנצענער דוך. . .
Darum hob ikh zikh batrakht	דאַרום האָב איך זיך באַטראַכט,
Un fun dem rekl a vestl gemakht. . .	און פֿון דעם רעקל אַ וועסטל געמאַכט. . .
Hob ikh mir a vestl fun fartsaytikn tukh. . .	האָב איך מיר אַ וועסטל פֿון פֿאַרצײַטיקן טוך. . .
Iz in im nishto keyn gantsener dukh. . .	איז אין אים נישטאָ קיין גאַנצענער דוך. . .
Darum hob ikh zikh batrakht,	דאַרום האָב איך זיך באַטראַכט,
Un fun dem vestl a hitl gemakht. . .	און פֿון דעם וועסטל אַ היטל געמאַכט. . .
Hob ikh mir a hitl fun fartsaytikn tukh. . .	האָב איך מיר אַ היטל פֿון פֿאַרצײַטיקן טוך. . .
Iz in im nishto keyn gantsener dukh. . .	איז אין אים נישטאָ קיין גאַנצענער דוך. . .
Darum hob ikh zikh batrakht,	דאַרום האָב איך זיך באַטראַכט,
Un fun dem hitl a keshene gemakht. . .	און פֿון דעם היטל אַ קעשענע געמאַכט. . .
Hob ikh mir a keshene fun fartsaytikn tukh. . .	האָב איך מיר אַ קעשענע פֿון פֿאַרצײַטיקן טוך. . .
Iz in ir nishto keyn gantsener dukh. . .	איז אין איר נישטאָ קיין גאַנצענער דוך. . .
Darum hob ikh zikh batrakht,	דאַרום האָב איך זיך באַטראַכט,
Un fun der keshene a henger gemakht. . .	און פֿון דער קעשענע אַ הענגער געמאַכט. . .
Hob ikh mir a henger fun fartsaytikn tukh. . .	האָב איך מיר אַ הענגער פֿון פֿאַרצײַטיקן טוך. . .
Iz in im nishto keyn gantsener dukh. . .	איז אין אים נישטאָ קיין גאַנצענער דוך. . .
Darum hob ikh zikh batrakht,	דאַרום האָב איך זיך באַטראַכט,
Un fun dem henger a shnipsl gemakht. . .	און פֿון דעם הענגער אַ שניפסל געמאַכט. . .
Hob ikh mir a shnipsl fun fartsaytikn tukh. . .	האָב איך מיר אַ שניפסל פֿון פֿאַרצײַטיקן טוך. . .
Iz in im nishto keyn gantsener dukh. . .	איז אין אים נישטאָ קיין גאַנצענער דוך. . .
Darum hob ikh zikh batrakht,	דאַרום האָב איך זיך באַטראַכט,
Un fun dem shnipsl a gornisht gemakht. . .	און פֿון דעם שניפסל אַ גאָרנישט געמאַכט. . .

Hob ikh mir a gornisht fun fartsaytikn tukh. . .	. . . האָב איך מיר אַ גאָרנישט פֿון פֿאַרצײַטיקן טוך
Iz in im nishto keyn gantsener dukh. . .	. . . איז אין אים נישטאָ קיין גאַנצענער דוך
Darum hob ikh zikh batrakht,	,דאַרום האָב איך זיך באַטראַכט
Un fun dem gornisht a lidl gemakht. . .	. . . און פֿון דעם גאָרנישט אַ לידל געמאַכט

I have a coat made of ancient cloth, without a whole piece of material. So I reflected on what to do—and made the coat into a jacket.

I have a jacket made of ancient cloth without a whole piece in it. So I reflected on what to do—and made the jacket into a vest.

I made the vest into a hat. . . I made the hat into a pocket. . . I made the pocket into a hanger loop. . . I made the hanger loop into a bowtie. . . I made the bowtie into a nothing. . . I made the nothing into a song. . .

Hirsh Dovid

Words by Moishe Broderson (1890–1956); music by David Beigelman (1887–1944). The sung was published as an anonymous song with a slightly different text by Albert Bitter in 1940. The late Avram Kahn submitted a text by Hal Colter that was sung by the Jewish People's Philharmonic Chorus, which begins:

"A gut-morgn dir, Hersh-Dovid, / A gut-morgn, Frume, / Kh'hob gehert du host dos veyts / Un hey aropgenumen. (Good morning, Hersh Dovid, good morning, Frume, I heard you gathered the wheat and hay.)

In his compilation *The Yiddish Song Book*, Jerry Silverman includes a humorous parody of the song entitled "To gey zikh lernen tantsn." The first stanza is: - A gut-morgn, dir, Reb Berl, / - A gut-morgn, Sammy, / - Ikh hob gehert az geyst mit mazl / Blaybn in Miami. / Trogst oyf zikh koym zibn tsendlik / Yorelekh in gantsn; / Heybstu on a tsveyte yugnt, / To gey zikh lernen tantsn" (- Good morning Berl, - Good morning, Sammy, - I heard that you're going to stay in Miami. You're barely 70, you're starting your second youth. So go learn to dance).

- A gut-morgn dir, Hirsh-Dovid!
- A gut-morgn, Borekh!
Kh'hob gehert, du host mit mazl
Oysfarkoyft dem tsvorekh.

- Nisht dem tsvorekh,
Nor dos milkhiks,
Oysfarkoyft in gantsn,
Abi dos gelt iz do in baytl,
Vilt zikh take tantsn

    Au-di didi-di, ay-ra, ay-ra, ay-ra. . .

- O, Hirsh-Dovid, vos makht dayn vaybl,
Kh'meyn dayn Sore-Khaye?
- Ot di kobile zi shert zikh
Loyt di modes naye.
Oysgeton fun zikh dos shaytl,
Yidishkeyt in gantsn -
Iber koymens, iber dekher
Geyen sheydim tantsn.

- Kh'hob a moyd, a kosher kelbl,
Du a zun, Efroyim,
M'vet zey makhn a gevelbl,
Lomir shraybn tnoyim.
- Kha-kha-kha, tsvey meyes zilber
Gib ikh zey in gantsn,
Iber felder, iber velder
Veln yidn tantsn.

— אַ גוט-מאָרגן דיר, הירש-דוד!
— אַ גוט-מאָרגן, ברוך!
כ'האָב געהערט, דו האָסט מיט מזל
אויספֿאַרקויפֿט דעם צוואַרעך.

— נישט דעם צוואַרעך,
נאָר דאָס מילכיקס,
אויספֿאַרקויפֿט אין גאַנצן,
אַבי דאָס געלט איז דאָ אין בײַטל,
ווילט זיך טאַקע טאַנצן!

איי-די דידל-די, איי-ראַ, איי-ראַ, איי-ראַ. . .

— אַ, הירש-דוד, וואָס מאַכט דײַן ווײַבל,
כ'מיין דײַן שרה-חיה?
— אָט די קאָבילע זי שערט זיך
לויט די מאָדעס נײַע.
אויסגעטאָן פֿון זיך דאָס שנײטל
ייִדישקייט אין גאַנצן -
איבער קוימענס, איבער דעכער
גייען שדים טאַנצן.

— כ'האָב אַ מויד, אַ כשר קעלבל,
דו אַ זון, אפֿרים,
מ'וועט זיי מאַכן אַ געוועלבל,
לאָמיר שרײַבן תּנאים.
— כאַ-כאַ-כאַ, צוויי מאות זילבער
גיב איך זיי אין גאַנצן,
איבער פֿעלדער, איבער וועלדער
וועלן ייִדן טאַנצן.

Con brio

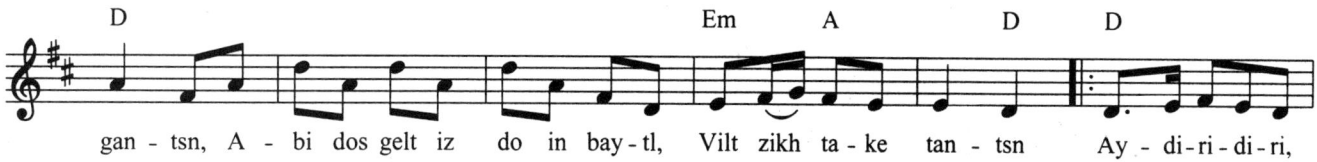

Good morning, Hirsh Dovid! Good morning, Borekh! I heard you sold out your pot cheese. Not only the pot cheese, but all the dairy food. . . I sold out everything. So let's put our arms on each other's shoulders, let's dance!

O, Hirsh Dovid, how's your wife? I mean your Sore Khaye? The old bag has bobbed her hair in the latest style. She's taken off her wig and dropped all her Jewish ways. Above the chimneys, on the roofs, demons will go dancing.

I have a daughter, a nice young thing. You have a son, Ephraim. Let's buy a little store for them and betroth them. Ha-ha-ha, I'll give them all of 200 in silver. Through the fields and the woods people will go dancing!

KOL MEKADESH SHEVII

כּל מקדש שביעי

All Who Keep the Sabbath Holy

Humorous parody of a Sabbath table song, an adaptation of a song by N. Jasnogorodski, published circa 1910. There the wife's name is Gnendl. This version was collected from Aaron Feiner, Toronto. The song quotes the original Hebrew lines of the song. As the singer cites these lines, he addresses his thoughts to his wife Tsipkenyu, telling her how respected and admired he is, how God has favored her by giving her such a special husband.

Kol mekadesh shevii koroui loy
Kol shoymer shabos kados meykhaleloy,
Tsipkenyu, mayn tayer vaybele,
Far vos vilstu mikh nit farshteyn,
Az du host a man mit toyre un mit kheyn,
Mit aza min metsiye hot dir got bashert,
Un efsher bistu im take gornisht vert,
Vayl nisht yeder Moyshe iz azoy,
Ish al makhneyhu veish al digloy.

Ay-bay, ay-bay, ay-bay-ba. . .

Tsipkenyu, mayn vayb,
Darfst zen vi men hot far mir moyre,
In shil ven me leyent in der heyliker toyre,
Oyfn balemer shtey ikh eyner aleyn,
Un veys vemen oystsurufn un vemen—neyn,
Vayl eyn Moyshe hot aza zkhiye,
Un a tsveyter take—loy,
Ze hayoym oso hashem, nogilo venismekho voy.

Tsipkenyu, mayn vaybele,
Gib zikh nor a kuk arum in a zayt,
Oyf di hayntike tsores mit di hayntike yungelayt,
Poyln, lite, mizrekh, krim,
Un ale shtetelekh arim un arim,*
Badarfstu mikh onkukn, un kveln on a tsol,
Borukh hashem asher nosan menukho leamoy yisroel.

Tsipkenyu, mayn vaybele,
Zolst zen vi men git mir op koved,
In shil oyfn mizrekh shtey ikh lebn Reb Dovid,
Un az ikh gib zikh a hil arum
Mitn tales mit der gildener atore,
Azoy krign ale yunge vaybelekh
Far mir di kapore,
Un fun untern tales vayz ikh zey ale a fayg a groyse,
Kol adas yisroel yaasu oysoy.

Tsipkenyu, mayn vaybele,	ציפקעניו, מײַן װײַבעלע,
Zolst zen vi me hot far mir derekh-erets,	זאָלסט זען װי מע האָט פֿאַר מיר דרך־ארץ,
In shil baym kool oder lehavdil in merkhets;	אין שיל בײַם קהל אָדער להבֿדיל אין מרחץ;
Dos beziml krig ikh, ay, dos beste,	דאָס בעזימל קריג איך, אײַ, דאָס בעסטע,
Un dos shefele, ay-ay-ay, dos greste,	און דאָס שעפֿעלע, אײַ־אײַ־אײַ, דאָס גרעסטע,
Ikh krikh mir aroyf oyfn eybershtn bank,	איך קריך מיר אַרױף אױפֿן אײבערשטן באַנק,
Ikh heyb zikh on tsu flyasken,	איך הײב זיך אָן צו פֿליאַסקען,
Iz venakhal adonekho sashkeym.	איז ונחל עדניך תשקם.

Fun ale mayne mayles, Tsipkenyu, mayn vaybele,	פֿון אַלע מײַנע מעלות, ציפקעניו, מײַן װײַבעלע,
Hob ikh dir nisht dermont,	האָב איך דיר נישט דערמאָנט,
Az bay der khevre-kadishe	אַז בײַ דער חבֿרה־קדישא
Bin ikh di ershte hant,	בין איך די ערשטע האַנט,
Oy, shtarbn, shtarbt nebekh der oremer	אױ, שטאַרבן, שטאַרבט נעבעך דער אָרעמער
Tsu glaykh mitn raykhn,	צו גלײַך מיטן רײַכן,
Un az eyner hot nit keyn takhrikhim,	און אַז אײנער האָט ניט קײן תּכריכים,
Muz men im makhn.	מוז מען אים מאַכן,
Ober dikh, Tsipkenyu, mayn tayer vaybele,	אָבער דיך, ציפקעניו, מײַן טײַער װײַבעלע,
Vel ikh bagrobn on a groshn mezumonim,	װעל איך באַגראָבן אָן אַ גראָשן מזומנים,
Hashem elokey yisroel teshuas oylomim.	ד' אלוקי ישראל תשועת עולמים.

---

* arum

"All who sanctify the Sabbath properly. . . All who keep the Sabbath unprofaned"

Tsipkele, my dear little wife, why don't you want to understand that you have a husband with learning and charm? God has given you such a bargain, for not every Moyshe is that way.

"Each man in his tribe and each under his own banner."

Tsipkenyu, my wife, you should see how people fear me. In the synagogue, when they read from the holy Torah, I stand all alone on the platform and I know whom to call and whom not. Only one Moyshe has such an honor, and others don't.

"This is the day God designated, so let's be happy and rejoice in it."

Tsipkenyu, my wife, just look around you at today's troubles and today's young people. Poland, Lithuania, the Orient, Crimea, and all the little villages around them. You should look at me and swell with pride. "Blessed be God who granted rest to the people of Israel."

Tsipkenyu, my wife, you should see how they honor me. In the synagogue I stand at the eastern wall, next to Reb Dovid. And when I wrap myself in the talis with the golden embroidery, all the young women are ready to do anything for me. But from beneath the talis, I give them all the finger.

"And the people of Israel should do thus."

Tsipkenyu, my wife, you should see how they respect me. In the synagogue with the chant, or in the bathhouse (forgive my mentioning them in one breath). I get the broom, the best one, and the basin, the biggest one. I climb up to the topmost bench and start to whisk myself.

"And let them drink from your river of pleasure."

All my virtues, Tsipkenyu, my wife, I haven't mentioned—that I am the leader of the burial society. The poor man, unfortunately, dies just as the rich man does. And if someone doesn't have a shroud, we must make one for him. But you, Tsipkenyu, I'll bury without paying a cent.

"The Lord of Israel is our eternal help."

Recitativo

In a Little Town Pitshepoy

אין אַ שטעטעלע פּיטשע-פּוי

Humorous dialect song collected from Moshe Kligsberg by compilers, in 1947. According to informant the song was by Moishe Broderson (1890–1956). The text appears in Ruth Rubin's *Voices of a People* as an anonymous children's song. Also Leyzer Ran analyzes it as a children's song in *Di goldene keyt,* 110–111, 1983. In the second and third stanzas, the words are formed from dialectal elisions: "Tsoteki" means "Ets hot di ki?" (Do you have the cows?), "Moteki" means "Me hot di ki" (I have the cows) and others.

The name of the town "Pitshepoy" has several meanings. It is used as a synonym for an anonymous town, for a remote or nonsensical place like Hotseplots. During the Holocaust the children of the internment camp in the Parisian suburb of Drancy came up with the name "Pitchipoi" as an unknown, mysterious place to which they would be taken and which turned out to be Auschwitz.

In a shtetele pitshe-poy
Shteyen hayzelekh gedekt mit shtroy.
Trift a regndl, falt a shney,
Voynen dort shkheynimlekh tsvey.

Refrain:
Tsoteki, moteki,
Tsotse, motse
Abi tsotse*
Ruft men zey.

Tsotse di metsotse**,
Di metsotse di ki,
Kumt, reb Mekhele, nenter tsi.***
Lam-tsi-di-ri-ri, lam-tsi-di-ray,
Lomir beyde a tentsele gayn [geyn].

אין אַ שטעטעלע פּיטשע-פּוי
שטייען הײַזעלעך געדעקט מיט שטרוי
טריפֿט אַ רעגנדל, פֿאַלט אַ שניי,
ווינען דאָרט שכנימלעך צוויי.

רעפֿרײן:
צאָטעקי, מאָטעקי,
צאָצע, מאָצע,
אַבי צאָצע
רופֿט מען זיי.*

צאָצע די מעצאָצע,
די מעצאָצע די קי,**
קומט, ר׳ מעכעלע, נענטער צי,
לאַם-צי-די-רי-רי, לאַם-צי-די-רײַ,
לאָמיר ביידע אַ טענצעלע גײַן (גיין).

---

* Ets (ir) hot di ku? Me hot di ku. Ets (ir) hot zi? Me hot zi.
Abi ets (ir) hot zi.
** Ets (ir) hot di metsie di ku?
*** tsu

*צאָטעקי, מאָטעקי: עץ האָט די קי? מע האָט די קי.
צאָצע, מאָצע: עץ האָט זי? מע האָט זי.
אַבי צאָצע: אַבי עץ האָט זי.
**צאָצע די מעצאָצע: עץ האָט זי די מציאה.

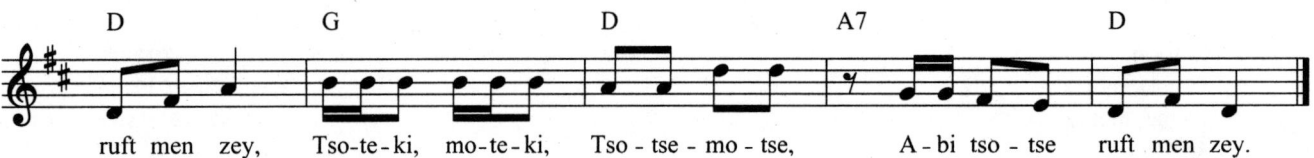

In a little town Pitshepoy there are little houses thatched with straw.

Comes a shower, snow falls. Two neighbors live there.

Do you have the cow? one says. I have the cow, the other replies.

Do you have her? I have her. As long as you have her, come closer, Reb Mikhl, and let's dance.

ITSIK SHPITSIK / איציק שפיציק

Itsik Shpitsik

Words by Itsik Manger (1901–1969), music by N. Hirsh transcribed by the compilers from the record *Poems and Songs by Itzik Manger*, (CBS 52568). The original words come from the second part of Manger's poem "Gram shtram far Note." Manger imitates the opening lines of a popular children's folksong: "Itsik shpitsik nodl-teshl / Gey in kleyt, khap a fleshl."

Different versions of the folksong were discussed by Alfred Landau in an interesting article "Bamerkungen tsum yidishn folklor," *Filologishe shriftn fun YIVO*, I, 1926. In Manger's printed text there is a misprint which he corrects in the supplement of the book. The first line should read: "Itsik, shpitsik, got-mit-dir," as in the familiar expression "Got iz mit dir" instead of "geyt mit dir."

Itsik shpitsik, got-mit-dir, Loyf un koyf a fleshl bir, Loyf un koyf a fleshl vayn, Veln mir ale freylekh zayn.	איציק שפיציק, גאָט־מיט־דיר, לויף און קויף אַ פֿלעשל ביר, לויף און קויף אַ פֿלעשל ווײַן, וועלן מיר אַלע פֿריילעך זײַן.
Loyf ikh, koyf ikh, kum tsurik, Ze ikh epes an antik: Der frumer Reb Elkone Shpringt kegn der levone.	לויף איך, קויף איך, קום צוריק, זע איך עפּעס אַן אַנטיק: דער פֿרומער ר׳ אלקנה, שפּרינגט קעגן דער לבֿנה.
Er redt tsu ir azoyne reyd, Az zi tayet on far freyd: - Ay, ay, ay, bal-tavetse, Ay, ay, ay, krasavitse.	ער רעדט צו איר אַזוינע רייד, אַז זי טײַעט אָן פֿאַר פֿרייד: – אײַ, אײַ, אײַ, בעל־תּאווהצע, אײַ, אײַ, אײַ, קראַסאַוויצע.
Un ale yidn mit a mol Khazern iber oyf a kol: - Ay, ay, ay, bal-tavetse, Ay, ay, ay, krasavitse.	און אַלע ייִדן מיט אַ מאָל חזרן איבער אויף אַ קול: – אײַ, אײַ, אײַ, בעל־תּאווהצע, אײַ, אײַ, אײַ, קראַסאַוויצע.
Veys ikh nisht, vu oys vu ayn, Trink ikh oys dos fleshl vayn. Vert mir likhtik oyfn harts, Royt iz grin un blo iz shvarts.	ווייס איך נישט, וווּ אויס ווו אײַן, טרינק איך אויס דאָס פֿלעשל ווײַן. ווערט מיר ליכטיק אויפֿן האַרץ, רויט איז גרין און בלאָ איז שוואַרץ.
Trink ikh oys dos fleshl bir, Fil ikh, mir zol zayn far ir. Shpring ikh oykh arayn in kon, Reb Elkone oybn on.	טרינק איך אויס דאָס פֿלעשל ביר, פֿיל איך, מיר זאָל זײַן פֿאַר איר. שפּרינג איך אויך אַרײַן אין קאָן, ר׳ אלקנה אויבן אָן.
Un der tate nebn mir, Khazert iber on a shir: - Ay, ay, ay, bal-tavetse, Ay, ay, ay, krasavitse.	און דער טאַטע נעבן מיר, חזרט איבער אָן אַ שיעור: – אײַ, אײַ, אײַ, בעל־תּאווהצע, אײַ, אײַ, אײַ, קראַסאַוויצע.

Un ale yidn mit a mol
Khazern iber oyf a kol:
Ay, ay, ay, bal-tavetse,
Ay, ay, ay, krasavitse.

און אלע יידן מיט אַ מאָל
חזרן איבער אויף אַ קול:
– אַיַ, אַיַ, אַיַ, בעל-תּאװוהצע,
אַיַ, אַיַ, אַיַ, קראַסאָװיצע.

Itsik Shpitsik, have a heart!—run and buy a flask of beer. Run and buy a flask of wine and we'll have a good time.

I run, I buy, and run right back, and see something really wondrous: Pious Reb Elkone jumping toward the moon.

He says such things to her that she covers her face from embarassment. Oh, you, passionate thing, oh, you beauty! which all the men repeat.

So completely confused am I that I drink the flask of wine. I get so light-hearted that colors begin to change.

When I drink the flask of beer, I feel so compassionate for her and jump into the circle. And my father, next to me, keeps repeating, together with all the men: Oh, you passionate thing, oh, you beauty!

A GUT-MORGN, FEYGE-SOSHE

אַ גוט-מאָרגן, פֿייגע-סאָשע

Good Morning, Feyge Soshe

Folksong published by Moishe Beregovski in 1962 and reprinted by Mark Slobin in *Old Jewish Folk Music*. Slobin notes that the humor in this song is enhanced by the interpolation of Russian rhyming words "giving a 'highfalutin' air." Mascha Benya Matz submitted a slightly different version with an introduction and epilogue.

- A gut-morgn, Feyge-Soshe,
Vos zitst ir azoy asobene?
- A gut-yor aykh, Fayve-Yose
Vayl s'iz mir udobne.

Efsher vilt ir, Fayve-Yose,
Farzukhn fun mayn prodovolstvye?
- A shabesdikn lokshn-kugl—
S'ara udovolstvye!

Shabes nokhn kugl
Bin ikh di emese krasavitse,
Oysgeputst un ongeton zikh,
Kak ya vam naravitsa?

- Efsher vilt ir, Feyge-Soshe,
Mit semetshkes aykh ugozhayeven?
- Vayl bay aykh, Fayve-Yose,
Vel ikh prinimayeven.

- Efsher vilt ir, Feyge-Soshe,
Geyn mit mir gulayeven?
- Vayl mit aykh, Fayve-Yose,
Vel ikh ispolnayeven.

Good morning, Feyge Soshe. Why are you sitting there like that? - Good morning, Fayve Yose. It's because I'm comfortable this way.

Perhaps, Fayve Yose, you'd like to try some of my wares? A Sabbath noodle pudding? - That would be a pleasure! On the Sabbath, after making the pudding, I'm a real beauty—all dolled up. How do you like me?

Perhaps, Feyge Soshe, you'd like some sunflower seeds? - I'd like to try some, Fayve Yose. - Perhaps, Feyge Soshe, you'd like to go for a stroll with me? Fayve Yose, I'd like to do just that.

YOSL UN SORE-DVOSHE

Yosl and Sore Dvoshe

Popular duet of the revue theatres in Poland. Words by Kasriel Broydo of Vilna (1907—killed by the Nazis); composer unknown. The song was submitted by actress-singer Mina Bern, who informed the compilers that she originally sang it with Joseph Widetzky in Vilna before World War II, later as a solo number in Israel in the late 1940s and finally with her husband Ben Bonus in New York. Sender Wajsman, Miami Beach, submitted a slightly different version.

- Akh, mayn libe Sore-Dvoshe,
Vos zhe zitstu do in gas
Un kukst oyf der levone?
Akh, antshuldik, kh'hob fargesn,
Binst nokh alts oyf mir in kas,
Mayn likhtike madone.

Zog mir vos di sibe iz
Fun nokh anander broygez zayn,
Lomir shoyn sholem makhn.
Lyubov moya, vedya lyublyu tyebya,
Mayn Sore-Dvoshele, povyer-zhe mnye.

- Yosl, vos zingstu mir a serenade
Un lozt nit zitsn a sheyne meydele in gas!
Du koyf mir beser a groyse plite shtshikolade,
Veln mir geyn shpatsirn
Un ikh vel mer nit zayn in kas.

- Akh, a plite shtshikolade, narishkeyt, nu, zog, aleyn,
Es kost nit mer vi a zlote,
Lomir beser in yidishn teater geyn, teater geyn,
Dort kost mir nit keyn prute,
Der balebos vos zitst baym tir,
Er iz mayns a feter, er lozt arayn,
Er iz a yid a guter,
Lyubov moya, vedya lyublyu tebya,
Mayn Sore-Dvoshele, povyer-zhe mnye.

- Yosl, mir veln zitsn ershte reye,
Un zikh lyuboyen mit Velvele,
Vos est kompot,
Du vest mir koyfn a bisl semetshkes tsum kayen,
A por tsukerkes tsu smotshkenen
Volt nit geshat.

- Akh, mayn libe Sore-Dvoshe,
Vi derlebt men di minut
Dir tsu der khupe firn,
Du a galande, ikh a smoking,
A vaysn shnipsele dertsu
Veln mir in zal shpontsirn.

Di mekhutonim groys un kleyn
Oysgeputst dokh zeyer sheyn
In esik un in honik
Lyubov moya, vedya lyublyu tebya
Mayn Sore-Dvoshele, povyer zhe mnye.

- Yosl, mir veln a tsendlik kinder hobn
Un geyn shpatsirn mit zey iber der breyter gas
A tsendlik hering, a pud kartoflyes optsushobn,
S'vet zayn a lebn, oy, zis vi tsuker un epl-kvas.

די מחותנים גרויס און קליין
אויסגעפוצט דאָך זייער שיין
אין עסיק און אין האָניק.
ליובאַוו מאַיאַ, וועדיאַ ליובליו טעביאַ
מײַן שׂרה-דוואָשעלע, פּאָווער זשע מניע.

- יאָסל, מיר וועלן אַ צענדליק קינדער האָבן
און גיין שפּאַצירן מיט זיי איבער דער ברייטער גאַס,
אַ צענדליק הערינג, אַ פּוד קאַרטאָפֿליעס אָפּצושאָבן,
ס'וועט זײַן אַ לעבן, אוי זיס ווי צוקער, און עפּל קוואַס.

- Ah, my dear Sore Dvoshe, why are you sitting here on the street and looking at the moon? Ah, forgive me, I forgot—you're still mad at me, my radiant madonna. Tell me what's the reason for always being angry. Let's make peace already. My darling, know that I love you, my little Sore Dvoshe, believe me.

- Yosl, why are you serenading me and not letting a pretty girl sit on the street? You'd do better to buy me a big piece of chocolate, and then we'll take a stroll and I won't be mad anymore.

- Ah, a piece of chocolate. A trifle, don't you agree? It only costs a zloty. Let's rather go to the Yiddish theater, to the theater—there it doesn't cost me a cent. The manager who sits at the door is my uncle—he'll let us in; he's a good fellow. My darling, know that I love you, my little Sore Dvoshe, believe me.

- Yosl, we'll sit in the first row and cuddle with Velvele, who eats stewed fruit. You'll buy me some sunflower seeds to chew, and a couple of cookies to munch wouldn't hurt either.

- Ah, my dear Sore Dvoshe, how will I be able to last till the time of our wedding? You in a wedding gown, I in a tuxedo, with a white tie in addition. We'll stroll into the hall. The in-laws, big and small, all decked out beautifully in finery. My darling, know that I love you. My little Sore Dvoshe, believe me.

- Yosl, we'll have a dozen children and we'll promenade with them on the broad avenues. A dozen herrings, a bushel of potatoes to peel. What a life it'll be—sweet as sugar and apple cider.

VARNITSHKES וואַרניטשקעס

Dumplings

Folksong. Text published by Y. L. Cahan; text and music published by Moishe Beregovski, 1962. In the version that Y. L. Cahan brings, the song ends with: "Avu nemt men a vaybele? / Volt ikh gehat a vaybele, / Volt zi mir gemakht vartsiklekh" (Where does one get a wife? If I had a wife, she would make me dumplings.) The song was also published by M. Goldin in 1972. It was popularized by Mascha Benya Matz in the arrangement of Harry Anik and was also a popular repertory piece of the Soviet-Yiddish singer Misha Alexandrovich, who has a different closing stanza: "Vu nemt men a bokher tsu esn di varnishkes, / Ven ikh bin aleyn on zalts, on fefer un on shmalts" (Where can I get a boy to eat the varnishkes when I myself am without salt, without pepper and without spice? [literally: chicken fat]).

Gevald, vu nemt men?	געוואַלד, וווּ נעמט מען?
Vu nemt men, vu nemt men -	וווּ נעמט מען, וווּ נעמט מען -
A lokshnbret oyf katshen	אַ לאָקשנברעט אויף קאַטשען
Di varnitshkes?	די וואַרניטשקעס?
On heyvn, un on shmalts,	אָן הייוון, אָן אָן שמאַלץ,
Un on fefer, un on zalts -	און אָן פֿעפֿער, און אָן זאַלץ -
Oy, a lokshnbret tsu katshen	אוי, אַ לאָקשנברעט צו קאַטשען
Di varnitshkes!	די וואַרניטשקעס!
Gevald, vu nemt men?	געוואַלד, וווּ נעמט מען?
Vu nemt men, vu nemt men -	וווּ נעמט מען, וווּ נעמט מען -
A meser oyf tsu shnaydn	אַ מעסער אויף צו שנײַדן
Di varnitshkes?	די וואַרניטשקעס?
On heyvn, un on shmalts,	אָן הייוון, אָן אָן שמאַלץ,
Un on fefer, un on zalts -	און אָן פֿעפֿער, און אָן זאַלץ -
Oy, a meser oyf tsu shnaydn	אוי, אַ מעסער אויף צו שנײַדן
Di varnitshkes!	די וואַרניטשקעס!
Gevald, vu nemt men?	געוואַלד, וווּ נעמט מען?
Vu nemt men, vu nemt men -	וווּ נעמט מען, וווּ נעמט מען -
A tepl oyf tsu kokhn	אַ טעפּל אויף צו קאָכן
Di varnitshkes?	די וואַרניטשקעס?
On heyvn, un on shmalts,	אָן הייוון, אָן אָן שמאַלץ,
Un on fefer, un on zalts -	און אָן פֿעפֿער, און אָן זאַלץ -
Oy, a tepl oyf tsu kokhn	אוי, אַ טעפּל אויף צו קאָכן
Di varnitshkes?	די וואַרניטשקעס!
Gevald, vu nemt men?	געוואַלד, וווּ נעמט מען?
Vu nemt men, vu nemt men -	וווּ נעמט מען, וווּ נעמט מען -
A bokher oyf tsu esn	אַ בחור אויף צו עסן
Di varnitshkes?	די וואַרניטשקעס?
On heyvn, un on shmalts,	אָן הייוון, אָן אָן שמאַלץ,
Un on fefer, un on zalts -	און אָן פֿעפֿער, און אָן זאַלץ -
Oy, a bokher oyf tsu esn	אוי, אַ בחור אויף צו עסן
Di varnitshkes!	די וואַרניטשקעס!

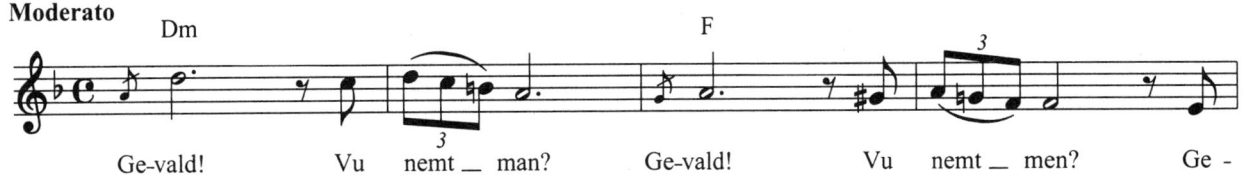

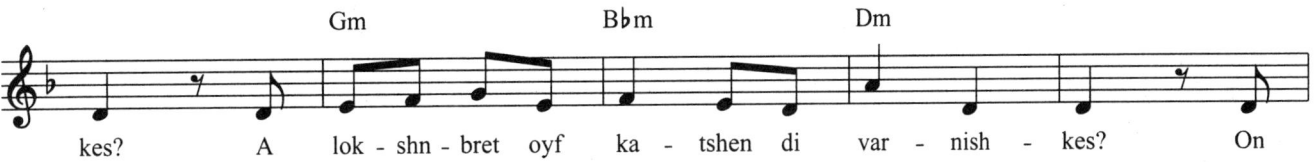

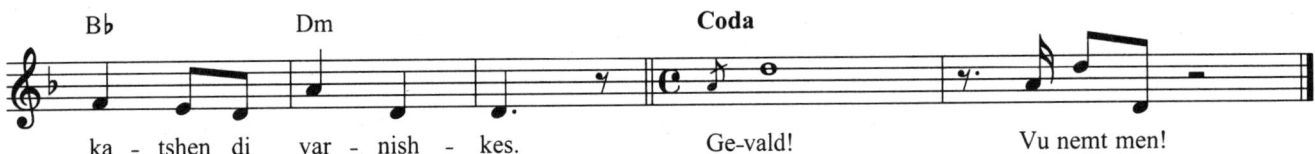

Oh, help, where can I get? A (wooden) noodle board to roll out the dumplings? Without any yeast, without any fat, without any pepper and without any salt. Oh a noodle board to roll out the dumplings!

Oh, help, where can I get? A knife to cut the dumplings?

Oh, help, where can I get? A pot to cook the dumplings?

Oh, help, where can I get? A young man to eat the dumplings?

The Treasure

Words by Z. Telesin (1905–1996), music by Lev Kogan. The song was submitted by actress-singer Mina Bern.

Bay mir iz an oytser faran,
Nit keyn kleyner,
Haynt veyst ir fun vos er bashteyt:
Nit fun keyn gold,
Fun keyn tayere shteyner,
An oytser fun emeser freyd.
Ikh hob a farmegn
Bay hayntikn tog,
Helft mir barekhenen
Vos ikh farmog.

Refrain:
Tsvelef zin un tekhter,
Bilder sheyne,
Tsvelef shnir un eydems,
Eyns un eyne,
Fun di eydems un di shnir,
Mekhutonim tsvantsik-fir,
Un dertsu kol-boyniklekh,
Dray un draysik eyniklekh,
Dray un draysik,
Aza yor oyf mir!

Oyf eygene felder
Iz mayn land mir tayer,
Oyf boy-pletser klingt undzer trot;
Dos lebn vert shener,
Dos lebn vert frayer,
In yetvedn shtetl un shtot.
Un alts vos geflantst
Un geboyt vert in land
Tsu dem leygn tsu
Yedn tog zeyer hant -

Tsvelef zin un tekhter. . .

Es vakst mayn mishpokhe
Alts greser un breyter,
Di oystres tseblien zikh shnel;
Men pravet oykh khasenes,
Eyns nokh der tsveyter,

בײַ מיר איז אַן אוצר פֿאַראַן,
ניט קיין קליינער,
הײַנט ווייסט איר פֿון וואָס ער באַשטייט;
ניט פֿון קיין גאָלד,
פֿון קיין טײַערע שטיינער,
אַן אוצר פֿון אמתער פֿרייד.
איך האָב אַ פֿאַרמעגן
בײַ הײַנטיקן טאָג,
העלפֿט מיר באַרעכענען
וואָס איך פֿאַרמאָג.

רעפֿריין:
צוועלעף זין און טעכטער,
בילדער שיינע,
צוועלעף שניר און איידעמס,
איינס און איינע,
פֿון די איידעמס און די שניר,
מחותּנים צוואַנציק-פֿיר,
און דערצו כּל-בוניקלעך,
דרײַ און דרײַסיק אייניקלעך,
דרײַ און דרײַסיק,
אַזאַ יאָר אויף מיר!

אויף אייגענע פֿעלדער
איז מײַן לאַנד מיר טײַער,
אויף בוי-פּלעצער קלינגט אונדזער טראָט;
דאָס לעבן ווערט שענער,
דאָס לעבן ווערט פֿרײַער,
אין יעטוועדן שטעטל און שטאָט.
און אַלץ וואָס געפֿלאַנצט
און געבויט ווערט אין לאַנד
צו דעם לייגן צו
יעדן טאָג זייער האַנט -

צוועלעף זין און טעכטער. . .

עס וואַקסט מײַן מישפּחה
אַלץ גרעסער און ברייטער,
די אוצרות צעבלײַען זיך שנעל;
מען פּראַוועט אויך חתונות,
איינס נאָך דער צווייטער,

Fun dem ver ikh yinger un kvel.
Dem ershtn tants
Tants ikh aleyn in der mit,
Tsuzamen in redl
Mit mir tantsn mit -

Tsvelef zin un tekhter...

פֿון דעם װער איך יונגער און קװעל.
דעם ערשטן טאַנץ
טאַנץ איך אַליין אין דער מיט,
צוזאַמען אין רעדל
מיט מיר טאַנצן מיט -

צװעלעף זין און טעכטער...

I have a treasure, you see—not a small one. Do you know of what it consists? Not of gold, nor precious stones—A treasure of actual joy. I have a great treasure at the present time. Help me count up all I possess.

Twelve sons and daughters, pretty as pictures. Twelve wives and husbands one for each. From the wives and the husbands I have twenty-four in-laws, and besides that I have little rascals. Three-and thirty grandchildren. Three-and-thirty—Heaven help me!

On fields of my own my land is dear to me. Our steps ring out on building sites, Our life keeps getting freer in each little town and city. Every day, they put their hands to each thing that is planted and built on our land.

It grows, my family, quite bigger and bigger. The first dance I dance by myself. Then, together in the circle, they dance with me.

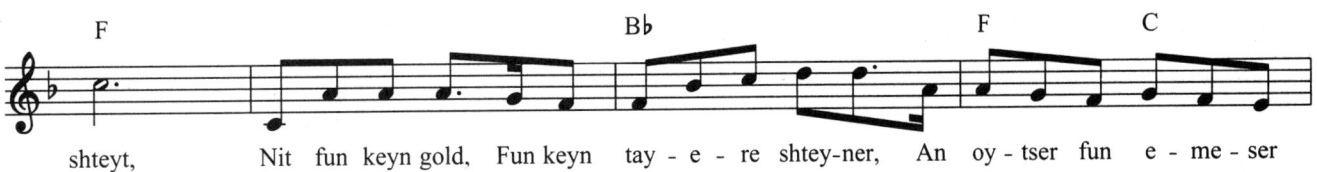
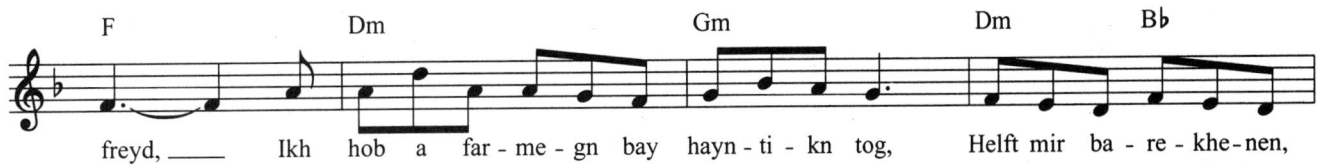

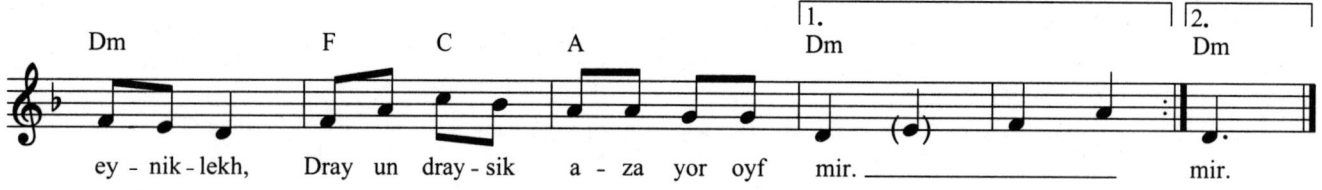

Miracles

NISIM, NISIM / נסים, נסים

Words by Moishe Broderson (1890–1956), music by David Beigelman (1887–1944). Transcribed by the compilers from a record of Menashe Oppenheim.

Ay, nisim, nisim, nisim, nisim,
Nisim min hashomayim,
Ay, nisim, nisim, nisim,
Nisim on a shir.
Zingt men, tantst men, oy-vey!
Makht men a lekhayim.
Tate ziser, al khezhbn hagevir.

Ruft zikh opet a khosidl:

Ikh bin a mol geforn oyf a taykh,
Un a shturem-vint hot zikh dan gemakht,
Treft vos zhe iz geven?
Treft vos zhe iz geshen?
A nes, a nes, a nes.
Un ikh hob nit lang getrakht,
Un bald mit di hent azoy gemakht:
Vaser ahin, vaser aher,
Un ikh bin mesukn
Bald aroys trukn.

Ruft zikh opet a litvakl:

Un ikh hob a mol badarft tsu forn
Un sabes* hot zikh dan gemakht,
Treft vos zhe iz geven?
Treft vos zhe iz gesen**?
A nes, a nes, a nes.
Un ikh hob take lang getrakht
Un mit di hent azoy gemakht:
Sabes ahin, sabes aher,
Treft vos iz gevorn?
Gornit nit! Kh'bin zhikh*** vayter geforn.

---

* shabes (Lithuanian pronunciation)
** geshen
***zikh

אײַ, נסים, נסים, נסים, נסים,
נסים מן השמים,
אײַ, נסים, נסים, נסים,
נסים אָן אַ שיעור,
זינגט מען, טאַנצט מען, אױ־װײ!
מאַכט מען אַ לחיים,
טאַטע זיסער, על חשבון הגביר.

רופֿט זיך אָפֿעט אַ חסידל:

איך בין אַ מאָל געפֿאָרן אױף אַ טײַך,
און אַ שטורעמװינט האָט זיך דאַן געמאַכט,
טרעפֿט װאָס זשע איז געװען?
טרעפֿט װאָס זשע איז געשען?
אַ נס, אַ נס, אַ נס.
און איך האָב ניט לאַנג געטראַכט,
און באַלד מיט די הענט אַזױ געמאַכט,
װאַסער אַהין, װאַסער אַהער,
און איך בין מסוכּן
באַלד אַרױס טרוקן.

רופֿט זיך אָפֿעט אַ ליטװאַקל:

און איך האָב אַ מאָל באַדאַרפֿט צו פֿאָרן
און סאַבעס*) האָט זיך דאַן געמאַכט,
טרעפֿט װאָס זשע איז געװען?
טרעפֿט װאָס זשע איז געסען*)?
אַ נס, אַ נס, אַ נס.
און איך האָב טאַקע לאַנג געטראַכט
און מיט די הענט אַזױ געמאַכט:
סאַבעס*) אַהין, סאַבעס אַהער,
טרעפֿט װאָס איז געװאָרן?
גאָרניט ניט! כ'בין זשיך*) װײַטער געפֿאָרן.

---

* שבת, געשען, זיך

Miracles, miracles from Heaven. Miracles without end. Sing, dance, raise a glass of cheer. Dear Father, the rich man's paying for it.

A little Hassid speaks up: I was once traveling on a river and a tempest arose. Guess what happened! A miracle! I didn't think about it long and I gestured thus with my hands: Water here and water there—I was saved from danger and came out dry.

A Litvak speaks up: Once I had to travel and the Sabbath came upon me.

Guess what happened! A miracle! I did think about it long and I gestured thus with my hands: Sabbath here, Sabbath there. Guess what happened! Nothing! I continued my journey.

NISIM VENIFLOES

ניסים ונפלאות

Miracles and Wonders

Folksong, published in *90 geklibene yidishe folkslider*, Warsaw, 1926. The song was also published in different versions by S. Alman, J. Jacobsen and Erwin Jospe, among others.

A children's song "Undzer krolik" (Our Rabbit) in *Unter di grininke beymelekh* (1935) adapted the theme: "Undzer krolik ken ton nisim, / Kh'bin derbay gezesn, / M'hot derlangt a mer a groysn, / Hot er oyfgegesn!" (Our rabbit can perform miracles, I was there when he did them. They handed him a large carrot, and he ate it up.) The melody was also used in a Hebrew Purim song "Maseichos," words by L. Kipnis, in S. Altman, *The Judaean Songster,* 1934.

Der rebe tut vunder,
Ikh hob aleyn gezen:
Er geyt arayn in vaser,
Un kumt aroys a naser.

Refrain:
Ay, ay, ay, ay, ay, ay, ay,
Nisim venifloes!

Der rebe tut vunder,
Hob ikh aleyn gezen:
Er iz arayn in blote,
Un shmirt oys di kapote.

Der rebe tut vunder,
Hob ikh aleyn gezen:
Er iz arayn in keler
Un iz aroys a geler.

Der rebe tut vunder
In laydn un in freydn,
Es iz arayn a shtumer,
Hot er im nit geheysn reydn.

Der rebe tut vunder,
Hert vos iz geven:
Es iz arayn a blinder,
Hot er im nit geheysn zen.

Der rebe tut vunder,
Kent ir gut farshteyn,
Es iz arayn a krumer,
Hot er im nit geheysn geyn.

דער רבי טוט וווּנדער,
איך האָב אַליין געזען.
ער גייט אַרײַן אין וואַסער,
און קומט אַרױס אַ נאַסער.

רעפֿרײן:
אַיַ, אַיַ, אַיַ, אַיַ, אַיַ, אַיַ,
ניסים ונפלאות!

דער רבי טוט וווּנדער,
האָב איך אַליין געזען:
ער איז אַרײַן אין בלאָטע,
און שמירט אויס די קאַפּאָטע.

דער רבי טוט וווּנדער,
האָב איך אַליין געזען:
ער איז אַרײַן אין קעלער
און איז אַרויס אַ געלער.

דער רבי טוט וווּנדער,
אין ליידן און אין פֿריידן,
עס איז אַרײַן אַ שטומער,
האָט ער אים ניט געהייסן ריידן.

דער רבי טוט וווּנדער,
הערט וואָס איז געווען:
עס איז אַרײַן אַ בלינדער,
האָט ער אים ניט געהייסן זען.

דער רבי טוט וווּנדער,
קענט איר גוט פֿאַרשטיין.
עס איז אַרײַן אַ קרומער,
האָט ער אים ניט געהייסן גיין.

Allegro

The rabbi does wonders, I've seen them myself: He goes into the water and comes out all wet.

Ay, ay, ay—Miracles and wonders!

The rabbi does wonders, I saw them myself: He goes into the mud and comes out with a dirty caftan.

The rabbi does wonders, I saw them myself: He goes into the cellar and comes out all yellow.

The rabbi does wonders in suffering and joy: A mute came into the house, and he didn't tell him to speak.

The rabbi does wonders, listen to what happened: A blind man came into the house, and he didn't tell him to see.

The rabbi does wonders, you can understand it very well: A cripple came into the house, and he didn't tell him to walk.

Tshiribim

טשיריבים

Folksong published in Leye Bloch-Lederer, *Di shenste geklibene yidishe lider...*, 1992. There are different words in Nokhem Shakhnovski's *Lider gezungen funem folk*, Paris, 1958. The song was parodied in the Warsaw Ghetto: "In dzhoynt kumt tsu geyn a yid" (A Jew comes to the Joint [Joint Distribution Committee]).

Lomir zingen, kinderlekh,	לאָמיר זינגען, קינדערלעך,
A zemerl tsuzamen,	אַ זמרל צוזאַמען,
A nigndl a freylekhn	אַ ניגונדל אַ פֿריילעכן
Mit verter vos es gramen.	מיט ווערטער וואָס עס גראַמען.
Di mame kokht a lokshn-zup,	די מאַמע קאָכט אַ לאָקשן זופּ,
Mit kashe in di kneydlekh,	מיט קאַשע אין די קניידלעך,
Vet kumen der yomtev khanike,	וועט קומען דער יום-טובֿ חנוכּה,
Veln mir shpiln zikh in dreydlekh.	וועלן מיר שפּילן זיך אין דריידלעך.
Tshiribim, tshiribam...	טשיריבים, טשיריבאַם...
A mol iz undzer rebenyu	אַ מאָל איז אונדזער רבינו
Gegangen unter vegn,	געגאַנגען אונטער וועגן,
Mit a mol fangt on tsu plyukhenen,	מיט אַ מאָל פֿאַנגט אָן צו פּליוכענען,
Gisn, oy, a regn.	גיסן, אוי, אַ רעגן.
Shrayt der rebe tsu der khmare:	שרײַט דער רבי צו דער כמאַרע:
Her oyf gisn vaser.	הער אויף גיסן וואַסער.
Zaynen ale khsidim trukn aroys,	זײַנען אַלע חסידים טרוקן אַרויס,
Nor der rebe iz aroys a naser.	נאָר דער רבי איז אַרויס אַ נאַסער.
Tshiribim, tshiribam...	טשיריבים...
Me zogt az in dem shtetl khelm	מ'זאָגט אַז אין דעם שטעטל כעלם
Vaksn nor naronim,	וואַקסן נאָר נאַראָנים,
Oyb mir zaynen di klige,	אויב מיר זײַנען די קליגע,
Hobn mir a sheynem ponem.	האָבן מיר אַ שיינעם פּנים.
Ikh her nor lakhn tog un nakht,	איך הער נאָר לאַכן טאָג און נאַכט,
Tsu lokhes di gazlonim,	צו להכעיס די גזלנים,
Zogt ver zaynen di narishe,	זאָגט ווער זײַנען די נאַרישע,
Ver zaynen di khakhomim.	ווער זײַנען די חכמים.
Tshiribim, tshiribam...	טשיריבים...

Let's sing a little song together, children; a happy little tune with words that rhyme. Mother is cooking noodle soup, with kasha in the matzo balls. When the Hanukkah holiday comes, we'll play with dreydls. Tshiri-bim, tshiri-bam.

Once our dear rabbi was traveling on the road, when a sudden downpour began. The rabbi cried out to the clouds: Stop pouring out water! So all the Hassidim came out dry, but the rabbi came out wet.

They say the town of Chelm produces only fools. If we are the smart ones, then we play the part well. We laughed day and night despite the robbers. So tell me, who are the fools and who the wise ones?

HISTORISHE LIDER
HISTORICAL SONGS

היסטאָרישע לידער

LID FUN MENDL BEYLIS

לִיד פֿון מענדל בייליס

The Song of Mendel Beilis

    Mendel Beilis (1874–1934) was the victim of one of the most notorious blood-libel accusations in Russia in 1911. He was the superintendent of a brick kiln in Kiev, where 12-year-old Andrei Yushchinsky had been seen playing before his murder. Beilis was arrested for allegedly using the boy's blood for ritual purposes, even though the leader of a gang of thieves, Vera Cheberiak, was implicated. The trial took place in Kiev, September 25–October 28, 1913, at which anti-Semitic statements were brazenly pronounced by the chief prosecutor A. I. Vipper. The case attracted world-wide attention and protests, and finally, Beilis was acquitted. The song was sent in to the YIVO magazine *Yidisher folklor*. It was adapted from the song "Vi halt ikh dos oys?" (How do I bear it?) by Mark Warshawsky.

Vi halt men dos oys?
Der yid fregt farvundert,
Zayn eydeler moyekh kon dos nisht farshteyn.
Bay der yetstiker tsayt,
In tsvantsikstn yorhundert,
Aza min retsikhe zol kenen geshen.
Teologn, gelernte, zey bagrayfn dos kam*,
Mit sharfe protestn zey tretn aroys
Kegn dem bilbl fun aliles-dam.
Zey shrayen, zey fregn:
Vi halt men dos oys?

Az dort in kiev, di shvartse khavruse,
Gemeyne farbrekher, zey teytn dos kind.
Mendl Beylis umshuldik, im varft men in tfise
Un im klogt men on in der shreklekher zind,
Tsu makhn a bilbl fun aliles-dam,
Der tiran Zamislavski tret khutspish aroys,
Kedey oyfhetsn a vildn pogrom.
Vi halt men dos oys,
Vi halt men dos oys!

Tsu zayn in gerikht di taynes oystsuhern
Fun dem roshe Viper, dem prokuror,
In di oygn zikh shteln heys-blutike trern
Tsu zen dos falshkeyt vos dortn geyt for.
Vi er zukht tsu fartumlen yedes emese vort,
Vos di erlekhe eydes zogn dort oys,
Tsu bavayzn az Beylis iz shuldik in dem mord.
Vi halt men dos oys,
Vi halt men dos oys!

Ver es zet nisht dem merder, dem vildn rotseyakh,
Dem yid vos er dorsht nokh krishtlekhn blit (blut),
Der rukn geboygn, dos ponem vist un bleykh,
Der shtempl fun dem goles, der dershlogener yid,
Er kukt vi fartsveyflt tsu di sonim akegn,

---

* koym

A zifts fun dem hartsn im rayst zikh aroys.
Zayne trukene lipn eyn shayle zey fregn:
Vi halt men dos oys,
Vi halt men dos oys?

Dort in der tfise, in a fintstern kheyder,
In dem shvartsn paroykhes kumt di nakht.
Dort zitst Mendl Beylis farkimert keseyder,
Nokh zayn vayb un kinder er benkt un er shmakht.
Dos lozt im nisht ruen, dos lozt im nisht shlofn,
Er veynt shtil un bet: Got, helf mir aroys!
Genug shoyn, tsu fil, got, tustu mikh shtrofn,
Ikh halt es nisht oys,
Ikh halt es nisht oys!

אַ זיפֿץ פֿון דעם האַרצן אים רײַסט זיך אַרויס,
זײַנע טרוקענע ליפּן איין שאלה זײ פֿרעגן:
ווי האַלט מען דאָס אויס?
ווי האַלט מען דאָס אויס?

דאָרט אין דער תּפֿיסה, אין אַ פֿינצטערן חדר,
אין דעם שוואַרצן פרוכת קומט די נאַכט,
דאָרט זיצט מענדל בײליס פֿאַרקימערט כּסדר,
נאָך זײַן ווײַב און קינדער ער בענקט און ער שמאַכט.
דאָס לאָזט אים נישט רוען, דאָס לאָזט אים נישט שלאָפֿן,
ער וויינט שטיל און בעט: גאָט, העלף מיר אַרויס!
גענוג שוין, צו פֿיל, גאָט, טוסטו מיך שטראָפֿן,
איך האַלט עס נישט אויס!
איך האַלט עס נישט אויס!

How can one bear it? the Jew asks confused. His naive mind cannot fathom—that in these present times in the twentieth century, how such an outrage can be borne? Theologians, learned men cannot comprehend, they come forth with sharp protests against the dreadful blood-libel. They cry out, they ask: How can one bear it?

There in Kiev that black gang of ugly criminals murders a child. Mendel Beilis, innocent, is thrown in prison and they accuse him of the dreadful crime, the terrible blood-libel. The tyrant Zamislavski comes forth arrogantly to incite a wild pogrom. How can one bear it?

To sit in the court and hear the charges of the evil Vipper, the prosecutor, brings hot tears to one's eyes. To see the falseness that takes place there, how he tries to confound every truthful word that the honest witnesses say there in order to prove that Beilis is guilty of the murder. How can one bear it?

Who does not see the "murderer," the "wild, savage butcher," "the Jew who thirsts for Christian blood." His back is bent, his face pale and downcast, the stamp of his exile, the downhearted Jew. He looks with confusion at his enemies. A sigh wrenches itself from his heart. His dry and cracked lips ask a question: How can one bear it?

There in the prison, in a dark cell, nightfall like a black Torah curtain has come. There Mendel Beilis sits, constantly worried. He longs and yearns for his wife and children. It won't let him rest and it won't let him sleep. He weeps softly and prays: God, please help me! Enough, God, too much do You punish me! I cannot bear it!

DOS LID FUN LEO FRENK

ליאָ פֿרענק

Leo Frank

On August 17, 1915, the American Jew Leo Frank (born 1884) was lynched by an anti-Semitic mob near Atlanta, Georgia. He had been charged in 1913 with murdering Mary Phagan, a 14-year old employee of a pencil factory where he was the superintendent. Despite inconclusive evidence, the jury found Frank guilty. The case was retried a few times and was finally brought by Louis Marshall before the United States Supreme Court, without success. Hundreds of thousands of petitions were sent to the governor of Georgia, John Slaton, urging him to commute the sentence of death by hanging to life imprisonment and on June 21, the day before the scheduled execution, Governor John Slaton commuted Frank's sentence to life imprisonment. A few months later the inflamed mob kidnapped Frank from jail and lynched him. The case had wide repercussions. From the Knights of Mary Phagan reemerged the Ku Klux Klan and as a result of the case, the Anti-Defamation League of the B'nai B'rith was created (Frank had been president of the local chapter of B'nai B'rith).

On March 7, 1982 The Tennessean published an article "An Innocent Man Was Lynched" in which it stated that after seventy-five years a witness Alonzo Mann, then 14 years old, had come forth and sworn that he had seen Conley carrying the body of Mary Phagan, but at the time his mother had forced him to remain silent. Now however, he felt with death approaching, he had to speak out.

In American folklore, however, in the Ballad of Mary Phagan, Leo Frank is not exonerated: "I have an idea in my mind, when Frankie comes to die,/ And stands examination in the courthouse in the sky/ He'll be so astonished to what the angels say,/ How he killed little Mary upon that holiday./ Judge Roan passed the sentence; he passed it very well;/ The Christian doers of heaven sent Leo Frank to hell. . ."

The Yiddish song entitled "Frank's Tragedy" expresses hope that Frank will be exonerated. The words and music by Yankev Krakovski were printed on a broadside in Toronto. The song mentions Sherbakova (Vera Cheberiak) who with her gang were implicated in the murder of the 12-year old boy Andrei Yushchinsky (see *Dos lid fun Mendl Beylis*).

The trial of Leo Frank also had an impact in the Yiddish theatre. The second stanza of the popular song *Lebn zol Columbus* goes: "A bilbl hot men oysgetrakht/ Oyf undzern a yidl. . ." (They made up a blood libel about one of our Jews).

Fintster in tfise, keytn klingen,
Der talyen halt dem shtrik un lakht,
Oyf Leo Frenk vart er tsum hengen,
Langvaylik iz im di nakht;
Plutslung laykht oyf Frenks a shtern
Un er shaynt im in tfise arayn;
Er treyst im un visht zayne trern
Mit lebns-lider shlefert er im ayn.

פֿינצטער אין תּפֿיסה, קייטן קלינגען,
דער תּלין האלט דעם שטריק און לאַכט,
אויף ליאַ פֿרענק ווארט ער צום הענגען,
לאַנגווײַליק איז אים די נאַכט;
פּלוצלונג לײַכט אויף פֿרענקס אַ שטערן
און ער שײַנט אים אין תּפֿיסה אַרײַן;
ער טרייסט אים און ווישט זײַנע טרערן
מיט לעבנס-לידער שלעפֿערט ער אים אײַן.

Refrain:
Hob nit keyn moyre, got iz mit dir;
Dem yidns tlie iz tsebrokhn,
Tsebrokhn on a shir.
Shrek nit, yidl, zey veln shtumen,
Ale tsores vestu iberkumen,
Hob nit keyn moyre, got iz mit dir,
Hob nit keyn moyre, got iz mit dir.
Dem yidns tlie iz tsebrokhn,
Tsebrokhn on a shir.
Far Beylises bilbulim un far Frenkn
Vet Shterbakova un Konli krenken.
Hob nit keyn moyre, got iz mit dir.

רעפֿריין:
האָב ניט קיין מורא, גאָט איז מיט דיר;
דעם ייִדנס תּליה איז צעבראָכן,
צעבראָכן אָן אַ שיעור.
שרעק ניט, ייִדל, זיי וועלן שטומען,
אַלע צרות וועסטו איבערקומען,
האָב ניט קיין מורא, גאָט איז מיט דיר,
האָב ניט קיין מורא, גאָט איז מיט דיר.
דעם ייִדנס תּליה איז צעבראָכן,
צעבראָכן אָן אַ שיעור.
פֿאַר בייליסעס' בילבולים און פֿאַר פֿרענקן
וועט שטערבאַקאָואַ און קאָנלי קרענקען.
האָב ניט קיין מורא, גאָט איז מיט דיר.

Tsvey toyznt yor bald farfloygn,	צװײ טױזנט יאָר באַלד פֿאַרפֿלױגן,
In yedn dor a Homen tlies shtelt.	אין יעדן דור אַ המן תּליות שטעלט.
Men makht nor bilbulim blut zoygn,	מען מאַכט נאָר בילבולים בלוט זױגן,
Yetst kumt a Konli, a Homen oyf der velt.	יעצט קומט אַ קאָנלי, אַ המן אױף דער װעלט,
Muz got oykh a Mordkhe shafn,	מוז גאָט אױך אַ מרדכי שאַפֿן,
A Governor Sleyton in tsayt,	אַ גאָװערנאָר סלײטאָן אין צײַט,
Vos gleybt nit in tlies, in vafn,	װאָס גלײבט ניט אין תּליות, אין װאַפֿן,
Un Frenkn fun toyt bafrayt.	און פֿרענקען פֿון טױט באַפֿרײַט.
Nokh nit opgetriknt di trern	נאָך ניט אָפּגעטריקנט די טרערן
Fun Mendl Beylises alilas-dam,	פֿון מענדל בײליסעס׳ עלילת-דם,
Darfn mir, yidn, vayter hern	דאַרפֿן מיר, ייִדן, װײַטער הערן
A Feygans bilbl groys vi der yam.	אַ פֿײגאַנס ביבול גרױס װי דער ים.
Kent ir got, dem yidishn tatn?	קענט איר גאָט, דעם ייִדישן טאַטן?
Fun yedn umglik helft er zey.	פֿון יעדן אומגליק העלפֿט ער זײ.
Nit geshat Beylisn un s'vet im nit shatn,	ניט געשאַט בײליסן און ס׳װעט אים ניט שאַטן,
Un Frenk vet oykh vern gants fray.	און פֿרענק װעט אױך װערן גאַנץ פֿרײַ.
Mit mut un simkhe veln yidn dermonen	מיט מוט און שׂימחה װעלן ייִדן דערמאָנען,
Dzhan Sleyton, der emes "governor,"	דזשאַן סלײטאָן, דער אמת גאָװערנאָר,
Un bentshn dem tatn un der mamen,	און בענטשן דעם טאַטן און דער מאַמען,
Vos hobn 'zoy a zun gebrengt aher,	װאָס האָבן ׳זױ אַ זון געברענגט אַהער,
Fun tlie aropgenumen milyonen,	פֿון תּליה אַראָפּגענומען מיליאָנען,
Reyn gevashn dem yidishn natsyon,	רײן געװאַשן דעם ייִדישן נאַציאָן,
Ver volt 'zoy vos nokh konen	װער װאָלט ׳זױ װאָס נאָך קאָנען
Ven nit du, Governor Sleyton.	װען ניט דו, גאָװערנאָר סלײטאָן.

It's dark in prison—chains clang. The hangman holds the noose and laughs. He's waiting to hang Leo Frank. The night drags for him. Suddenly a star lights up for Frank and shines for him in the prison. It comforts him and wipes away his tears, and sings him to sleep with songs of life.

Have no fear, God is with you. The Jew's gallows is broken, shattered. Don't be afraid, little Jew, they will be silent; you'll overcome all your troubles. Have no fear, God is with you. The Jew's gallows is broken, shattered. For Beilis' libels and for Frank, Shterbakova and Conley will suffer. Have no fear, God is with you.

Two thousand years have flown by quickly, in every generation a Haman puts up a gallows; They keep promulgating libels of drinking blood. Now a Haman a Conley appears in the world, so God must also create a Mordecai, a Governor Slayton, in time, who doesn't believe in gallows, in weapons, and frees Frank from the death sentence.

The tears are not yet dried from Mendel Beilis' blood libel, and we Jews must hear again a Phagan libel as broad as an ocean. Do you know God, the Jewish father? He helps them out of every misfortune. It didn't hurt Beilis and it won't hurt him, and Frank will also be freed.

With courage and joy, Jews will remember John Slayton, the true governor, and bless his father and mother who brought such a saint into the world. He saved millions from the gallows and exonerated the Jewish nation. Who else could have done something like that, If not for you, Governor Slayton?

KHURBN TITANIK

חורבן טיטאַניק

The Destruction of the Titanic

Words and music by Solomon Smulewitz-Small (1868–1943), music by Henry A. Russotto. Published in July, 1912 by the Hebrew Publishing Co. The song was later included in the author's collected poems *Lider* (N.Y., 1913), with the omission of the lines about Ida Strauss, who refused to be separated from her husband when the ship went down. On the sheet music the song closes with the lines: "Zoln ern kleyn un groys / Dem nomen Ida Shtroys!" (Let young and old honor the name Ida Strauss!). In the book, the song ends on a moralizing note. Other melodies to the poem were written by Meir Posner and A. Garfinkel, London. The subject of the Titanic tragedy is also represented in Yiddish folksong (see *Pearls of Yiddish Song*). "The Ballad of the Steamship Titanic"/ "Parakhod Titanik" was recently collected and recorded by Michael Alpert on the cassette of the Brave Old World Klezmer Ensemble.

Akh, troyert, badoyert	אָך, טרויערט, באַדויערט
Dem groysn, frishn brokh!	דעם גרויסן, פֿרישן בראָך!
Zoln trern zikh mern	זאָלן טרערן זיך מערן
Un flisn nokh un nokh.	און פֿליסן נאָך און נאָך.
Zoln veynen raykh un orem.	זאָלן וויינען רייך און אָרעם,
Nit zhaleven keyn trer,	ניט זשאַלעווען קיין טרער,
Oyf di tife, nase kvorim	אויף די טיפֿע, נאַסע קבֿרים
Fun shoyderlekhn mer.	פֿון שוידערלעכן מער.
Dem yam iz yetst gelungen	דעם ים איז יעצט געלונגען
Zayn vilde tayvl-shpil,	זײַן ווילדע טײַוול-שפּיל,
In opgrunt hot er farshlungen	אין אָפּגרונט האָט ער פֿאַרשלונגען
Korbones, lebns fil.	קרבנות, לעבנס פֿיל.
Er hot getsaygt zayn kraft,	ער האָט געצײַגט זײַן קראַפֿט,
Akh! shreklekh! shoyderhaft!	אָך! שרעקלעך! שוידערהאַפֿט!
Refrain:	**רעפֿרײן:**
Mentsh, megst am bestn	מענטש, מעגסט אַם בעסטן
Sharfn dayn moyekh,	שאַרפֿן דײַן מוח,
Kenst zikh nit mestn	קענסט זיך ניט מעסטן
Mit dem yams koyekh.	מיט דעם ימס כּוח.
Megst zikh vi klign,	מעגסט זיך ווי קליגן,
Er iz dir geyver*,	ער איז דיר גײַװער (גובר),
Ot mustu lign	אָט מוזסטו ליגן
In zayn nasn keyver. . .	אין זײַן נאַסן קבֿר.
Di freydn fun yedn	די פֿריידן פֿון יעדן
Vos iz in shif arayn,	וואָס איז אין שיף אַרײַן,
Oyf dizn, dem rizn,	אויף דיזן, דעם ריזן,
A pasazhir tsu zayn.	אַ פּאַסאַזשיר צו זײַן.
Titanik vet zey firn,	טיטאַניק וועט זיי פֿירן,
Keyn shpas, es iz a glik,	קיין שפּאַס, עס איז אַ גליק,
Men vet zikh amuzirn	מען וועט זיך אַמוזירן
Mit teater, mit muzik.	מיט טעאַטער, מיט מוזיק.
A regele komedye,	אַ רעגעלע קאָמעדיע,

A lebedike velt,	אַ לעבעדיקע וועלט,
Dokh oyf aza tragedye	דאָך אויף אַזאַ טראַגעדיע
Hot zikh keyner forgeshtelt.	האָט זיך קיינער פֿאָרגעשטעלט.
Dertrunken iz di freyd,	דערטרונקען איז די פֿרייד,
Geblibn iz di leyd.	געבליבן איז די לייד.
Ot shteyen, mit veyen,	אָט שטייען, מיט וויִען,
Di toyznter in noyt,	די טויזנטער אין נויט,
Un veysn az shtoysn	און ווייסן אַז שטויסן
Vet zey tsu grunt der toyt.	וועט זיי צו גרונט דער טויט.
Ot shrayt men: "Geyt zikh retn	אָט שרײַט מען: ״גייט זיך רעטן
In shiflekh, froyen, shnel!	אין שיפֿלעך, פֿרויען, שנעל!
Nit vagn zol batretn	ניט וואַגן זאָל באַטרעטן
Keyn man gor yene shtel."	קיין מאַן גאָר יענע שטעל.״
Dokh hert a froyen-zele,	דאָך הערט אַ פֿרויען-זעלע,
Vos ken a zog ton dan:	וואָס קען אַ זאָג טאָן דאַן:
"Ikh gey nit fun der shtele,	״איך גיי ניט פֿון דער שטעלע,
Ikh shtarb do mit mayn man..."	איך שטאַרב דאָ מיט מײַן מאַן . . .
Zoln ern kleyn un groys	זאָלן ערן קליין און גרויס
Dem nomen Ida Shtroys!	דעם נאָמען אידאַ שטרויס!

---
* goyver

Oh, bewail, bemoan the terrible recent catastrophe. Let tears multiply and flow more and more. Let rich and poor weep, don't be stingy with tears, over the deep, watery graves. The ocean has now won its wild, diabolical game. It has swallowed up in the abyss many victims and lives. It has shown its power. Oh frightful, horrible!

Man, no matter how well you sharpen your mind, you cannot fight the ocean's strength. As clever as you may be, it is stronger than you. Here you must lie, in its watery grave.

The joy of each one who got on the ship! On this giant ship to be a passenger! The Titanic will carry them—no joke, it's a pleasure. They'll have a good time with theater and music, a moment of comedy, a world of activity. But such a tragedy was not imagined by anyone. Drowned is all the joy—what remains is the suffering.

Here they stand in pain, the thousands in need, knowing that Death will push them into the depths. There they shout: "Save yourself—women to the lifeboats—hurry! Let no man dare to step into them!" But just listen to one woman who says then: "I'm not leaving this place, I'll die here with my husband." Let young and old honor the name of Ida Strauss!

LID FUN KISHENEVER POGROM

לִיד פֿונעם קישענעווער פּאָגראָם

Song of the Kishenev Pogrom

The pogrom in Kishenev in 1903 evoked a number of laments. This song, originally titled "Hot rakhmones oyf di milkhome-korbones" (Have Pity on the War Sufferers) was written by Simon S. Frug (1860–1916), music by Abraham M. Bernstein (1865–1932), published in *Der fraynd,* St. Petersburg (Supplement no. 142, June 28, 1903:5-6). When news about the Kishinev pogrom broke in this country, the three-year-old actress Stella Adler stood on the stage of her father Jacob P. Adler's theater and recited this poem. After she finished, her father came down from the platform and went through the audience with his tophat in hand, repeating the last lines. "People wept and emptied their pockets. Women with no money to give threw their wedding rings in his hat." (Lulla Rosenfeld, *Bright Star of Exile, Jacob Adler and the Yiddish Theater,* N. Y. , 1977). Other melodies to the poem were written by Henry A. Russotto, Nathan Spector, Henry Lefkowitch, A. Garfinkel and Herman S. Shapiro. An anonymous song of the Kishenev pogrom was published in *Mir Trogn A Gezang.*

Shtromen blut un taykhn trern	שטראָמען בלוט און טײַכן טרערן
Zidn, flisn tif un breyt. . .	זידן, פֿליסן טיף און ברייט. . .
Undzer alte, groyser umglik	אונדזער אַלטער, גרויסער אומגליק
Hot zayn hant oyf undz farshpreyt.	האָט זײַן האַנט אויף אונדז פֿאַרשפּרייט.
Hert ir dort vi muters klogn	הערט איר דאָרט ווי מוטערס קלאָגן
Un fun kinder dos geshrey?	און פֿון קינדער דאָס געשריי?
Toyte lign in di gasn,	טויטע ליגן אין די גאַסן,
Kranke faln nebn zey.	קראַנקע פֿאַלן נעבן זיי. . .
Refrain:	**רעפֿריין:**
Brider, shvester, hot rakhmones!	ברידער, שוועסטער, האָט רחמנות!
Groys un shreklekh iz di noyt,	גרויס און שרעקלעך איז די נויט;
Git di toyte oyf takhrikhim,	גיט די טויטע אויף תּכריכים,
Git di lebedike broyt!. . .	גיט די לעבעדיקע ברויט!. . .
Shtromen blut un taykhn trern	שטראָמען בלוט און טײַכן טרערן
Zidn, flisn on a shir. . .	זידן, פֿליסן אָן אַ שיעור. . .
Eymes-moves kukt in fentster	אימת־מוות קוקט אין פֿענצטער
Un der hunger klapt in tir. . .	און דער הונגער קלאַפּט אין טיר. . .
Shlaf iz undzer hant tsu shtraytn,	שלאַף איז אונדזער האַנט צו שטרײַטן,
Shtark un shver iz undzer shmarts. . .	שטאַרק און שווער איז אונדזער שמאַרץ. . .
Kum zhe, du, mit treyst un libe,	קום זשע, דו, מיט טרייסט און ליבע,
Gutes, heyses, yidish harts!	גוטעס, הייסעס, ייִדיש האַרץ!

Streams of blood and rivers of tears, wide and deep they flow and boil. Our ancient great misfortune has unleashed itself upon us.

Do you hear mothers wailing, and the children's frightened cry? Corpses lie in the streets here, and the sick fall down near them wounded?

Brothers, sisters, please have pity; great and awful is our need. Give to the dead for shrouds, give bread to the living ones!

Streams of blood and endless tears boil and flow now more and more. The face of death looks in the window and there's hunger at the door.

Our had is feeble to fight, our pain—great and heavy. Come then, with comfort and love, you, good, warm Jewish heart!

DI KHASENE IZ GEVEN IN DER KAZARME   די חתונה איז געווען אין דער קאַזאַרמע

The Wedding Was in the Barracks

Folksong of a recruit in the Czar's army, collected from Russian singer Emil Gorovets, who states that the song was made popular in the Soviet Union in the 1930s and 1940s by the folk singer Mikhail Apelbaum. Like other East European recruits, the Jewish recruit compared his draft to marriage with the Czar. A different version was submitted to the *Perl* by Moyshe Aaron Buchvald (Brooklyn, N.Y.) from Biala, Siedlec province.

In prisutsvye hot men mikh gebrakht,	אין פריסוסטווע האָט מען מיך געבראַכט,
Di mos hob ikh gekhapt akurat,	די מאָס האָב איך געכאַפט אַקוראַט,
Di doktoyrim, zey tuen mir zogn:	די דאָקטוירים, זיי טוען מיר זאָגן:
- Bist godyen tsu zayn a soldat.	- ביסט גאָדיען צו זײַן אַ סאָלדאַט.
Pozdravet hot mikh di visoko blagorodye,	פאָזדראַוועט האָט מיך די וויסאָקאָ בלאַגאָראָדיע,
Un oysgetrunken a glezele derbay.	און אויסגעטרונקען אַ גלעזעלע דערבײַ.
A trask in pleytse hot er mir gegebn,	אַ טראַסק אין פלייצע האָט ער מיר געגעבן,
Zolst dinen dem keyser getray.	זאָלסט דינען דעם קיסר געטרײַ.
Di khasene iz geven in der kazarme,	די חתונה איז געווען אין דער קאַזאַרמע,
Der kazyoner rabiner iz oykh geven derbay,	דער קאַזיאָנער ראַבינער איז אויך געווען דערבײַ,
Oy, a shvue hot er bay mir genumen,	אוי, אַ שבֿועה האָט ער בײַ מיר גענומען,
Kh'zol dinen dem keyser getray.	כ'זאָל דינען דעם קיסר געטרײַ.
Zay zhe mir gezunt, mayn tayere nekhomenyu,	זײַ זשע מיר געזונט, מײַן טײַערע נחמהניו,
Oy, shver iz zikh mir sheydn mit dir.	אוי, שווער איז זיך מיר שיידן מיט דיר.
Oy, benken nokh dir vel ikh, neshomenyu,	אוי, בענקען נאָך דיר וועל איך, נשמהניו,
Mayn harts vet nor tsien tsu dir.	מײַן האַרץ וועט נאָר ציִען צו דיר.

They brought me to the Recruiting Board. I measured up precisely. The doctor told me: You're fit to be a soldier. Congratulations—the high-ranking official said to me while drinking a glass of whiskey. He slapped me on the shoulder: Serve the Czar faithfully.

The wedding was in the barracks. The official rabbi was there too. Oh, he administered an oath to me, to serve the Czar faithfully. - Farewell, my darling. It's hard for me to leave you. I'll miss you, my darling. My heart will long only for you.

Zishe Breitbard

זישע ברייטבארד

Song transmitted by Tova Blum Dobkin which she collected from Isaac Milstein, Brooklyn, N. Y., published October 20, 1974 in the *Perl*. Zishe Breitbard (1883–1925) was the youngest son of a Jewish blacksmith in Lodz, Poland, whose prodigious strength brought him fame throughout the world. He presented his feats of strength in theatres of Warsaw, in all capitals of Europe, and also in New York, at the Orpheum and Palace Theaters. The world press hailed him as the "Iron King," the "Polish Apollo," the "Superman of Strength" and the "Modern Samson." At one performance he banged a nail with his hand (the song states that the nail went into his right foot) and he contracted blood-poisoning from which he died. The New York Times of October 16, 1925 devoted an editorial to his death, comparing him to the great and legendary strong men of history.

Part of the melody of this song is adapted from the song "Reyzele dem shoykhets" (*Reyzele, the Ritual Slaughterer's Daughter*), words by Z. Segalovitch, which in turn was based on the Italian song *Sorrento*.

Other songs about Zishe Breitbart were submitted by A. Edelman (Los Angeles), Irene Goldberg (Forest Hills, N. Y.) and Hershl Altman (Bronx, N. Y.).

In a kleynem engn shtibl,	אין אַ קלײנעם ענגן שטיבל,
Nisht bay raykhe tate-mame,	נישט בײַ רײַכע טאַטע-מאַמע,
Hot dertsoygn zikh a bokher -	האָט דערצויגן זיך אַ בחור,
Ir hot dos gehert mistame.	איר האָט דאָס געהערט מסתּמא.
Zishe hot men im gerufn,	זישע האָט מען אים גערופֿן,
Un bakant iz er gevorn	און באַקאַנט איז ער געוואָרן
Als kreftiker un shtarker	אַלס קרעפֿטיקער און שטאַרקער,
Shoyn in zayne kinder-yorn.	שוין אין זײַנע קינדער-יאָרן.
Nokh beysn geyn in kheyder	נאָך בעתן גיין אין חדר,
Hot er ale shoyn geheysn	האָט ער אַלע שוין געהייסן
Brengen zikh nor shtiklekh keytn	ברענגען זיך נאָר שטיקלעך קייטן
Un gepruvt hot er zey raysn.	און געפּרוּווט האָט ער זיי רײַסן.
Zayne shreklekhe gvures	זײַנע שרעקלעכע גבֿורות
Hobn dan bavundert ale,	האָבן דאַן באַוווּנדערט אַלע,
Nisht eyn mame hot ir tokhter	נישט איין מאַמע האָט איר טאָכטער
Im gevolt gebn a kale.	אים געוואָלט געבן אַ כּלה.
Zishe hot nor alts getsoygn	זישע האָט נאָר אַלץ געצויגן
Tsu a svive fun atletn,	צו אַ סבֿיבֿה פֿון אַטלעטן,
Un es hot gornit geholfn,	און עס האָט גאָרניט געהאָלפֿן,
Khotsh zayn mame hot gebetn,	כאָטש זײַן מאַמע האָט געבעטן,
Az er zol keyn kemfer vern,	אַז ער זאָל קיין קעמפּפֿער ווערן,
In keyn tsirkn keyn mol shpiln,	אין קיין צירקן קיין מאָל שפּילן,
Nisht gekont hot ober Zishe	נישט געקאָנט האָט אָבער זישע
Zayn atletn-kheyshek shtiln.	זײַן אַטלעטן-חשק שטילן.
Dan farlozt di tate-mame	דאַן פֿאַרלאָזט די טאַטע-מאַמע
Un zayn kind-shtub fun kinder-yorn,	און זײַן קינד-שטוב פֿון קינדער-יאָרן,
Tsu antviklen zayne gvures	צו אַנטוויקלען זײַנע גבֿורות
Pruvt er in der velt tsu forn.	פּרוּווט ער אין דער וועלט צו פֿאָרן.

Er shpilt a mazl iber alem,
Yeder iz im untertenik,
Un men kroynt im dort in oysland
Mitn nomen "Ayzn-kenig."

Iz zayn nomen bakant gevorn
Iberal in ale krayzn,
Nor plutslung iz geshen an umglik
Mitn kenig fun dem ayzn.

Es iz geven a nakht a sheyne,
Gelaykht di shtern oyfn himl,
Dortn oyf der gas in rodem
Iz a rash un a getiml (getuml).

Es loyfn yung, es loyfn alte,
Yeder eyner loyft bazunder,
Vayl gedarfn hot dort Zishe
Bavayzn zayne groyse vunder.

Vegn im hot shoyn gevust yederer,
Es hot gevust shoyn yeder eyner,
Az dos iz der lodzher Zishe
Vos brekht ayzn mit di tseyner.

Hel iz der tsirk baloykhtn,
Hilkhik shpiln di trumpeytn,
Zishe shteyt in mitn stsene
Un er rayst di grobe keytn.

Dan nemt er a blekh un tshvekes
Un pruvt zey klapn punkt vi nekhtn,
Nor anshtot in di blekhn,
Treft er zikh in fus in rekhtn.

Zishe iz dan krank gevorn,
Nit gekont shoyn mer keynem veyln,
Tsurik keyn oysland opgeforn
Zikh dem fus oysheyln.

Es hot shoyn keyner nit bavizn,
Oy, im tsu erhaltn bay zayn lebn,
Khotsh er hot far di doktoyrim
Zayns a fus avekgegebn.

Tragish iz der held Zishe
Fun di velt avekgekumen,
Es hot a shpitsik shtikl ayzn
Im zayn lebn tsugenumen.

Oyfn berliner beys-hakvores
Iz a bergl dort faranen,
Ver s'tut dortn farbaygeyn,
Muz zikh dem troyer dermonen.

In a little cramped cottage, with parents not wealthy, a boy grew up—you've probably heard about him. Zishe was his name, and he became well known as a strong fellow, even as a child. Even when he was still going to kheyder, he told everyone to bring him pieces of chain and he tried to rip them apart. His awesome strength was admired by all; more than one mother wanted to give him her daughter as a bride.

Zishe was constantly drawn to the world of athletes, and nothing could deter him despite his mother's pleas that he not become a fighter and never become a circus performer. Zishe could not resist his appetite for athletics. Later he left his parents' and his childhood home. To develop his strength he set forth into the world.

He was luckier than anyone, everyone yielded to him. There in the outside world they crowned him "the King of Iron." His name became well known everywhere and in all circles. But suddenly a misfortune befell the King of Iron.

It was a beautiful night, the stars were shining in the sky. Out on the street in Radom, there was a sudden tumult. Young and old came running, each one separately, for Zishe was to show there his great wonders.

Everyone knew about him already, all about him; that this was Zishe from Lodz, who could break iron chains with his teeth.

The circus was brightly lit, the trumpets were blaring. Zishe stood in the middle of the arena and ripped the heavy chains. Then he took some sheet metal and nails and tried to hammer them in, as always, with bare hands. But instead of hitting the nails into the metal, he hit them into his right leg.

Zishe then grew ill and could no longer crush anything. He traveled to foreign lands to heal his right leg. No one was able to keep him alive, even though the doctors removed his leg. Tragically was Zishe the hero taken from the world. A little piece of iron took his life away. The sight of this mound in the Berlin cemetery is a tragic reminder to those who pass by.

AMOL IZ GEVEN...
SONGS OF THE STREET

אַ מאָל איז געווען...

VILNE וױלנע

Vilna

This version of the song which was sung in the Vilna Ghetto, was published by S. Kaczerginski in 1947. He notes that almost every program in the ghetto opened with it. Original words by A. L. Wolfson (1867–1946), and music by Alexander Olshanetsky (1892–1946) were printed in the compilation *Vilne,* 1935. The song was revived by Adrienne Cooper in Irena Klepfisz's play *Bread and Candy,* presented at the Jewish Museum in 1991, and at KlezKamp in 1992. Joseph Rumshinsky also wrote music to the poem.

Vilne—shtot fun gayst un tmimes,
Vilne—yidishlekh fartrakht,
Vu es murmlen shtile tfiles,
Shtile soydes fun der nakht.
Oft mol ze ikh dir in kholem,
Heys-gelibte vilne mayn,
Un di alte vilner geto
In a npeldikn shayn.

Refrain:
Vilne, vilne, undzer heymshtot,
Undzer benkshaft un bager. . .
Akh, vi oft es ruft dayn nomen
Fun mayn oyf aroys a trer.
Vilner geslekh, vilner taykhn,
Vilner velder, barg un tol.
Epes noyet, epes benkt zikh
Nokh di tsaytn fun amol.

Kh'ze dem veldele zakreter
In zayn shotn ayngehilt,
Vu geheym es hobn lerer
Undzer visndursht geshtilt.
Vilne hot dem ershtn fodem
Fun der frayheyts-fon gevebt
Un di libe kinder ire -
Mit a tsartn gayst balebt.

Vilna—city of spirit and innocence. Vilna—conceived in Jewish ways, where quiet prayers murmured soft secrets of the night. I often see you in my dreams, dearly beloved Vilna of mine, and the old Vilna ghetto in a foggy glow.

Vilna, Vilna, our hometown, our longing and desire. Ah, how often your name calls forth a tear from my eye. Vilna streets, Vilna rivers, Vilna forests, mountains and valleys. Something gnaws at me, makes me yearn for the days of long ago.

I see the Zakret forest, enveloped in its shadows, where teachers secretly slaked our thirst for knowledge. Vilna sewed the first thread of our flag of freedom, and inspired its children with a gentle spirit.

Sore and Rifke

שרה און רבֿקה

SORE UN RIFKE

Words by folk poet Mark Warshavsky (1840–1907), author and composer of popular Yiddish songs: *Oyfn pripetshik, Di mizinke oysgegebn, Tayere Malke* and others. *Sore and Rivke* was sung, in addition to its original melody, to the melody of *Der rebe hot geheysn freylekh zayn* (The Rabbi Bade Us Be Merry) (see *Pearls of Yiddish Song*). This melody is the one that compilers heard from Sara Rosenfeld, Montreal. It also appears in Ruth Zahava, *Jewish Dances* (Los Angeles, 1950), entitled "Yoshke, Yoshke (Rachmistrifke)," with the first stanza of the song.

Az ikh bin gekumen keyn rakhmestrivke,
Tsvey sheyne shvesters hob ikh dort gezen;
Eyne heyst Sore, di andere Rifke,
Tsvey sheyne kales zaynen dos geven.
Yede fun zey hot gehat an ander mayle,
Do hot zikh fardreyt mir der kop oyfn ort:
Velkhe fun zey zol ikh nemen far a kale,
Velkher fun beyde zol ikh gebn dos vort?

    Refrain:
    Sore, Sore, Sore, Rifke,
    Sore, Sore, Rifke—
    Sore, Sore, Sore, Rifke,
    Fun shtetele rakhmestrivke.

In Soreles oygn ken men glaykh nisht kukn,
Vi di zun in tamez azoy shaynen zey.
Zey shmeykhlen, zey lakhn, zey reydn, zey kvikn
Dos harts, az zi tut a kuk nor mit zey.
Ober Rifkes oygn brenen vi fayer,
Shvarts vi di koyln, vos tif in der erd:
Az zi heybt zey oyf, vert dos lebn tayer,
Az zi lozt zey arop—hot dos lebn keyn vert...

Azelkhe vi Sore gefint ir nit in di bikhlekh,
Goldene hent hot zi—ir zolt nor zen...
Zi hot oysgeheft far zikh a por goldene shikhlekh,
"In zey"—zogt zi—"vel ikh tsu der khupe geyn."
Rifke hot in eyn fraytik oyfgeneyt a kleydl,
Un shabes hot zi es ongeton tsulib mir in der fri...
Gliklekh vet zayn der, ver s'vet nemen ot dos meydl,
Ver farmogt ir sheynkeyt? kukt aykh nor tsi*!

---

* tsu

Ikh hob a mol a sod in oyer ayngeroymt Soren -
Hot zi zikh tseveynt vi a pitsele kind.
"Akegn vos"—fregt zi mikh—"bistu gekumen tsu forn,
Tsu vos hot dikh gebrakht ahertsu der vint?"
Az es hot zikh in mir tseshpilt di vilde klipe,
Hob ikh Rifken ayngeroymt dem eygenem sod,
"Nar! du vilst a kush?—shtel frier a khipe!*
Ikh bin dir nit Hopke, du bist nit Fedot!"

Kh'hob geklert un getrakht, un gegebn mir eytses,
Biz ikh hob avekgeleygt di bushe oyf a zayt;
Ot a ponem me muz nemen di fis oyf di pleytses,
Azoy hob ikh gelernt in der gemore a pshat.
Fun denstmol on hob ikh mer nit geklibn,
Nor Soren un Rifken gedenk ikh gants git (gut)…
Oy, ikh bin an alter bokher geblibn…
Oyb ikh hob kharote, freg mikh shoyn nit!

** khupe

איך האָב אַ מאָל אַ סוד אין אויער אײַנגערוימט שׂרהן -
האָט זי זיך צעוויינט ווי אַ פּיצעלע קינד.
„אַקעגן וואָס - פֿרעגט זי מיך - „ביסטו געקומען צו פֿאָרן,
צו וואָס האָט דיך געבראַכט אַהערצו דער ווינט?"
אַז עס האָט זיך אין מיר צעשפּילט די ווילדע קליפה,
האָב איך רבֿקהן אײַנגערוימט דעם אייגענעם סוד,
„נאַר! דו ווילסט אַ קוש? - שטעל פֿריִער אַ חופה!
איך בין דיר ניט האָפּקע, דו ביסט ניט פֿעדאָט!"

כ׳האָב געקלערט און געטראַכט, און געגעבן מיר עצות,
ביז איך האָב אַוועקגעלייגט די בושה אויף אַ זייט;
אָט אַ פּנים מע מוז נעמען די פֿיס אויף די פּלייצעס,
אַזוי האָב איך געלערנט אין דער גמרא אַ פּשט.
פֿון דענטסמאָל אָן האָב איך מער ניט געקליבן,
נאָר שׂרהן און רבֿקהן געדענק איך גאַנץ גיט (גוט)…
אוי, איך בין אַן אַלטער בחור געבליבן…
אויב איך האָב חרטה, פֿרעג מיך שוין ניט!

When I came to the town of Rakhmestrivke, two lovely sisters there I did see: One was called Sore, the other one Rifke. Two pretty brides were they. Each of them had a different virtue. My head began to whirl on the spot. Which of them should I take for a bride? To whom should I pledge my troth?

Sore, Sore, Sore, Rifke—From the little town Rakhmestrivke.

You cannot look directly into Sore's eyes, like the summer sun they shine. They smile, they laugh, they speak. They gladden your heart when she looks at you. But Rifke's eyes burn like fire. They're black as the coal from deep in the earth. When she raises them, your life is more dear to you. When she lowers them, then life has no worth.

Girls like Sore you don't find in books, she has golden hands—you ought to see. She embroidered herself a pair of golden slippers. In them, she says, she will be married. Rifke made herself a dress one Friday, and on the Sabbath morning she wore it for me. Happy the man who marries this maiden! Who has her beauty? Just look at her!

I told Sore a secret one day. Like a little child, she started to cry. - Why, she asked, - did you come here? Why did the wind have to bring you here? When my passion grew stronger, I told the same secret to Rifke. Fool, you want a kiss? First have the wedding! I'm not your doxie, you're not my swell!

So I thought and thought and took counsel, till I put aside my shame. I guess I have to scram out of here, this I learned from the old books. Since then I haven't been so picky, but Sore and Rifke I remember well. Oh yes, I've remained an old bachelor. Do I regret it? Better not ask.

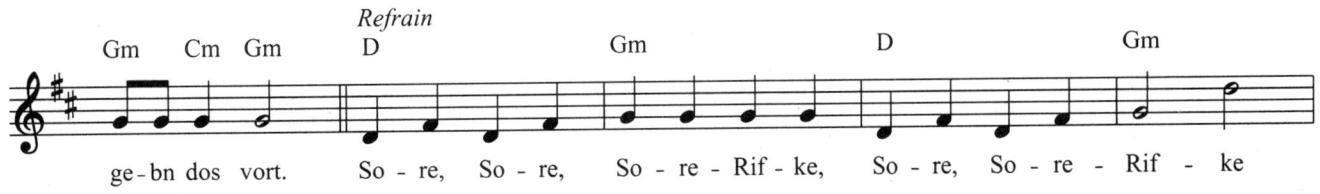

KROKHMALNE GAS

קראָכמאַלנע גאַס

Krokhmalne Street

Song has been attributed to Ben Zion Wittler (1907–1961). The compilers heard the song from Aaron Irlicht of Montreal. Krochmalne Street was the ambience of the underworld in Warsaw, which Yiddish writer Isaac Bashevis Singer often described in his stories.

Krokhmalne gas, ikh ken zi gut,	קראָכמאַלנע גאַס, איך קען זי גוט,
Ikh bin in ir geboyrn,	איך בין אין איר געבוירן,
On der gas volt ikh gevis	אָן דער גאַס וואָלט איך געוויס
Shoyn lang geven farloyrn.	שוין לאַנג געווען פֿאַרלוירן.
Der faykhter bruk, mit shmuts badekt,	דער פֿײַכטער ברוק, מיט שמוץ באַדעקט,
Dos hoyz vos halt in foyln,	דאָס הויז וואָס האַלט אין פֿוילן,
Der yid vos raybt di hent fun kelt	דער ייִד וואָס רײַבט די הענט פֿון קעלט
Un trakht: Vu nemt men koyln?	און טראַכט: וווּ נעמט מען קוילן?
Di froy vos shteyt mit beygl tsvey	די פֿרוי וואָס שטייט מיט בייגל צוויי
Un zukht far zay a baln,	און זוכט פֿאַר זיי אַ בעלן,
Der yung vos geyt fun hunger oys	דער יונג וואָס גייט פֿון הונגער אויס
Un shtarkt zikh nisht tsu faln.	און שטאַרקט זיך נישט צו פֿאַלן.
Afile oykh dos meydl dort,	אַפֿילו אויך דאָס מיידל דאָרט,
Vos vil ir layb farkoyfn,	וואָס וויל איר לײַב פֿאַרקויפֿן,
Un oykh der yat, vos khapt a shans	און אויך דער יאַט, וואָס כאַפּט אַ שאַנס
Un tut dermit antloyfn.	און טוט דערמיט אַנטלויפֿן.
Refrain:	רעפֿרײן:
Krokhmalne gas, du bist mir lib,	קראָכמאַלנע גאַס, דו ביסט מיר ליב,
In hartsn ayngebakn,	אין האַרצן אײַנגעבאַקן,
Ikh volt far dir mayn haldz geshtrekt,	איך וואָלט פֿאַר דיר מײַן האַלדז געשטרעקט,
Dem kop gelozt ophakn.	דעם קאָפּ געלאָזט אָפּהאַקן.
Dos pletsl, dos iz mayn heym,	דאָס פּלעצל, דאָס איז מײַן היים,
Di gas, zi iz mayn mame,	די גאַס, זי איז מײַן מאַמע,
Mayn bruder iz der shtoyb fun gas,	מײַן ברודער איז דער שטויב פֿון גאַס,
Di shvester—shteyner same.	די שוועסטער - שטיינער סאַמע.
Kh'hob keyn mol keyn heym gehat,	כ'האָב קיין מאָל קיין היים געהאַט,
Di gas hot mikh geboyrn,	די גאַס האָט מיך געבוירן,
Ikh bin der gas a kind geven,	איך בין דער גאַס אַ קינד געווען,
Di gas hot mikh dertsyogn.	די גאַס האָט מיך דערצויגן.
Keyn mame nisht, keyn tate nisht,	קיין מאַמע נישט, קיין טאַטע נישט,
Vi nisht fun mentsh geboyrn,	ווי נישט פֿון מענטש געבוירן,
Gevalgert zikh in gas aleyn,	געוואַלגערט זיך אין גאַס אַליין,
Gehungert un gefroyrn,	געהונגערט און געפֿרוירן,
Un oyb a mol s'heybt on mayn harts	און אויב אַ מאָל ס'הייבט אָן מײַן האַרץ
Tsitern un klogn,	ציטערן און קלאָגן,
Ikh volt gevolt a mames moyl	איך וואָלט געוואָלט אַ מאַמעס מויל
Zol mir a treyst-vort zogn.	זאָל מיר אַ טרייסט-וואָרט זאָגן.
Loyf ikh aroys tsum "pletsl" dort,	לויף איך אַרויס צום פּלעצל דאָרט,
Tref zikh mit mayne yatn,	טרעף זיך מיט מײַנע יאַטן,

Fartret dos mir di shvester mayne,
Di mamen mit dem tatn.

Az ikh gey a mol in gas aroys
Un vil zikh durkhshpatsirn,
Zikher bin ikh az mayne fis
Veln mikh tsu krokhmalne firn.
Fun kindheyt on bin ikh azoy,
Es vet mikh gornisht maydn,
Es tsit mikh nor tsu oremkeyt,
Tsu mentshn velkhe laydn.
Tsu mentshn velkhe horeven,
Kemfn shreklekh mit der noyt,
Vos far zey—der ideal
Iz a trukn shtikl broyt.
Mentshn azelkhe veysn nisht
Fun luksus un fun prakht,
Tates, mames, yunge kinder
Horeven tog un nakht.

פֿאַרטרעט דאָס מיר די שוועסטער מײַנע,
די מאַמען מיט דעם טאַטן.

אַז איך גיי אַ מאָל אין גאַס אַרויס
און וויל זיך דורכשפּאַצירן,
זיכער בין איך אַז מײַנע פֿיס
וועלן מיך צו קראָכמאַלנע פֿירן.
פֿון קינדהייט אָן בין איך אַזוי,
עס וועט מיך גאָרנישט מײַדן,
עס ציט מיך נאָר צו אָרעמקייט,
צו מענטשן וועלכע לײַדן,
צו מענטשן וועלכע האָרעווען,
קעמפֿן שרעקלעך מיט דער נויט,
וואָס פֿאַר זיי - דער אידעאַל
איז אַ טרוקן שטיקל ברויט.
מענטשן אַזעלכע ווייסן נישט
פֿון לוקסוס און פֿון פּראַכט,
טאַטעס, מאַמעס, יונגע קינדער
האָרעווען טאָג און נאַכט.

Krokhmalne Street, I know it well, I was born there myself. Without that street, I would surely be long ago lost and gone. The damp old pavement all covered with dirt, the house that is falling apart, the man who rubs his hands with cold and thinks: where to get some coal? The woman who stands there selling bagels and looks for an eager buyer, the youth who is dying from hunger, who braces himself so he won't fall. Even the young girl there who wants to sell her body, and also the guy who takes a chance and afterwards runs away.

Krokhmalne Street, you're dear to me, embedded in my heart. I'd stretch out my neck for you and let them chop off my head. The town square, that's my home, the street, that is my mother. My brother is the dust from the street, my sister, the very stones.

I never had a home, the street gave birth to me. I am the street. I was a child and the street brought me up. I had no mother, no father either, like one not born of woman. I was hungry and frozen, I roamed the streets alone. and if sometimes my heart begins to tremble and complain, I would have wanted a mother's mouth to tell me a comforting word; so I run out to the old square and meet all the guys there. The square is my sister, my mother and father.

When I go out in the street sometimes and want to walk around, I'm sure, quite sure, that my old feet will take me to Krokhmalne Street. From childhood on, I've been like this—nothing will ever change me. I'm only drawn to poverty, to people who are suffering, to people who work hard and struggle terribly with need, whose only fantasy is a dry piece of bread. Such people know not of luxury and splendor. Fathers, mothers, young children work hard day and night.

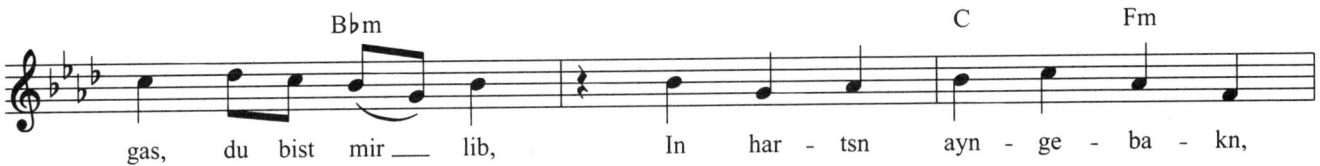

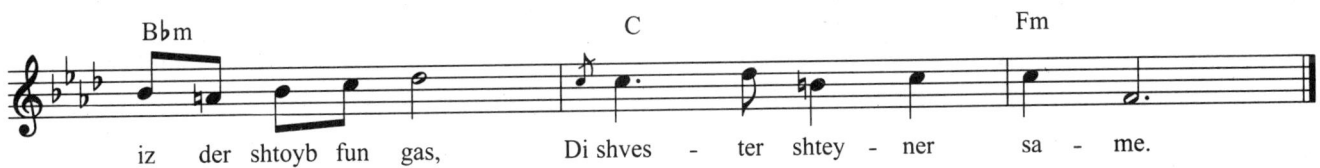

DER YOLD IZ MIKH MEKANE

דער יאָלד איז מיך מקנא

The Fool Is Jealous of Me

Folklorized song of the underworld, published by S. Lehman in Warsaw (1928), who writes that the song arose during the German occupation in Poland during World War I. It also appeared in the YIVO *Filologishe shriftn*, V, 1938. According to the sheet music published in this country, the words are by Gus Goldstein, music by Max Leibowitz, published by S. Schenker Co., N.Y. in 1920. The song was submitted to the *Perl* by the following readers: Sam Adler, Studio City, Ca.; Godl Jacobson, Hallandale, Fla., Abraham Arbetman, LA., Hershl Altman, Bronx, NY., Jacob Schaefer, L.A., Kh. Tselemenski, Montreal, Victor Weitzman, North Miami Beach and Chaim Sheskin, Brooklyn, N.Y. It was sung by Lillian Klempner in the film *Image Before My Eyes* produced by Josh Waletzky.

Der yold iz mikh mekane,	דער יאָלד איז מיך מקנא,
Der yold iz mikh mekane,	דער יאָלד איז מיך מקנא,
Der yold iz mikh mekane	דער יאָלד איז מיך מקנא
Mit mayn laykht shtikele broyt.	מיט מײַן לײַכט שטיקעלע ברויט;
Er vil fun gornisht visn	ער וויל פֿון גאָרנישט וויסן
Az di keshene iz tserisn,	אַז די קעשענע איז צעריסן,
Es kumt mir on shver vi der toyt.	עס קומט מיר אָן שווער ווי דער טויט.
Mayn mame un mayn tate	מײַן מאַמע און מײַן טאַטע
Zey zaynen gevezn blate,	זיי זײַנען געוועזן בלאַטע,
A rebele ikh zol vern	אַ רביל‍ע איך זאָל ווערן
Dos iz zey'r farlang.	דאָס איז זייער פֿאַרלאַנג.
Biz draytsn yor k'seyder	ביז דרײַצן יאָר כּסדר
Hob ikh gelernt in kheyder	האָב איך געלערנט אין חדר
Biz draytsn yor hob ikh gekvetsht di bank.	ביז דרײַצן יאָר האָב איך געקוועטשט די באַנק.
In dem bin ikh gezesn,	אין דעם בין איך געזעסן,
Getrunken un gegesn,	געטרונקען און געגעסן,
Mayn mamenyu fleg mir untershtekn	מײַן מאַמעניו פֿלעג מיר אונטערשטעקן
A kleyn bisele broyt.	אַ קליין ביסעלע ברויט.
Geshtorbn iz der tate,	געשטאָרבן איז דער טאַטע,
Un bald nokh dem di mame,	און באַלד נאָך דעם די מאַמע,
Geblibn bin ikh elnt oyf di velt.	געבליבן בין איך עלנט אויף די וועלט.
A yerushe hob ikh bakumen	אַ ירושה האָב איך באַקומען
Mit andere mezumen,	מיט אַנדערע מזומן,
Kortn-shpiln un koleges	קאָרטן־שפּילן און קאָלעגעס
Arayngelozt zikh shtark.	אַרײַנגעלאָזט זיך שטאַרק.
S'gelt hob ikh farlorn	ס'געלט האָב איך פֿאַרלאָרן
In kortn ongevorn,	אין קאָרטן אָנגעוואָרן,
Geblibn bin ikh reyn on a mark.	געבליבן בין איך ריין אָן אַ מאַרק.
Kum ikh arayn in mark	קום איך אַרײַן אין מאַרק
Un pak a gutn targ,	און פּאַק אַ גוטן טאַרג,
A masematn fun dolarn	אַ משׂא־מתּן פֿון דאָלאַרן
Hot zikh mir gemakht.	האָט זיך מיר געמאַכט.
Kukt oyf mir a yente	קוקט אויף מיר אַ יענטע
Un shikt on oyf mir a mente,	און שיקט אָן אויף מיר אַ מענטע,

M'nemt mikh glaykh	מ'נעמט מיך גלײַך
Un m'tsintevet mir arayn.	און מע צינטעװעט מיר אַרײַן.
In turme bin ikh gezesn	אין טורמע בין איך געזעסן
Un aroysgekukt durkh di kratn,	און אַרױסגעקוקט דורך די קראַטן,
Zumer ze ikh regns gisn,	זומער זע איך רעגנס גיסן,
Vinter ze ikh shney.	װינטער זע איך שנײַ.
Ale mayne yorn	אַלע מײַנע יאָרן
Zenen in tfise opgeforn	זײַנען אין תּפֿיסה אָפּגעפֿאָרן
Un haynt tut mir in yedn eyver vey.	און הײַנט טוט מיר אין יעדן אבֿר װײ.

The fool is envious of me for my little piece of bread. He doesn't want to know that my pockets are torn and I'm having a terribly hard time.

My mother and father were thieves. That I should become a rabbi—that was their demand. Till I was thirteen, I studied in kheyder. Till I was thirteen I weighed down the benches.

I sat on them, ate and drank—my dear mother used to give me a little bread. My father died, and my mother soon after—I remained alone in the world. I received an inheritance of foreign currency. I got deeply involved in playing cards with friends. I lost the money, I lost it at cards, and I was left clean out of money.

So I went ino the market and made some good deals. I stole some dollars—a woman saw me and sent the police after me. They grabbed me and put me in jail. I sat in prison and looked out through the bars. In summer I saw the rain fall, and in winter I saw the snow. All my years were spent in prison, and today every bone in my body aches.

IKH GANVE IN DER NAKHT

איך גנבֿע אין דער נאַכט

I Steal at Night

Words by Moishe Broderson (1890–1956), music by David Beigelman (1887–1944). Written for the Ararat Theatre of pre-war Warsaw. The song, which incorporates the argot of the underworld, was a popular repertory piece of the singer-actors Leon Liebgold and Lilly Liliana. Liebgold submitted the song to Mina Bern who transcribed it for compilers. During the Holocaust the melody was used for two songs in the Lodz Ghetto, collected by Gila Flam: "Kemfn" (Fight) and "Amerike hot erklert" (America Declared). The second states that "America has declared. . . that England must let the Jews have their own country."

Er: Ikh ganve in der nakht,
    Di nakht iz khoyshekh-shvarts,
    Un du host mikh fartshapet,
    Gelatkhnt mir mayn harts.

Zi: Az ikh latkhn iz dokh gut,
    A simen, az ikh toyg,
    Ikh bin dokh a berye,
    Dos vaysl fun dayn oyg.

Refrain:
Undz nisht shatn
Keyn masematn,
Mit shtot-parad zenme blat, zenme blat.
Shpil pavole
Nor di role
Zog mir, yat, harey-at, harey-at.

Zi: Ikh ganve tsu dayn harts,
    Es iz keyn kapital,
    Un du host mikh derdushet,
    Mir tsugedrikt di gal.

Er: Az ikh dushe iz dokh gut,
    Mayn libshaft iz dokh groys,
    Ikh drik fun dir dos beyzkeyt,
    Dos biternish aroys.

Er: Ikh latkhn a brilyant,
    In perelekh a baytsh,
    Tsum sof ze ikh dikh geyn gor
    Mit Yoselen dem daytsh.

Zi: A nafke mine zest
    A daytsh tsi a frantsoyz,
    Bay mir ken er bakumen
    A parekh mit a royz.

S'hot Yosele gezogt,	ס'האָט יאָסעלע געזאָגט,
Az ikh bin an antik,	אַז איך בין אַן אַנטיק,
Er zogt er vet mir shenken	ער זאָגט ער וועט מיר שענקען
A groyse kupe glik.	אַ גרויסע קופּע גליק.

Er: Vos vil der vishtukh, vos,
   Oyf s'nay zikh ongezetst,
   Tsi vil er gor a meser
   In zayt arayngezetst.

   Dos knipekhl er glantst,
   Es shpilt dokh vi a smik,
   Ikh broykh dokh nisht keyn brunes,
   Vayl teykev makh ikh khik.

Zi: Nu shoyn, nu shoyn, nu shoyn,
   Oyf s'nay du drikst di gal,
   Vilst, Vaptshele, shoyn vider
   Arayn in kriminal?

   Nu shoyn, ikh vel nisht geyn,
   Mit Yoselen mer geyn,
   To veln mir keyn Boyne
   Forn bloyz in tsvey'n (tsveyen)

Er: Azoy iz take gut,
   Ikh meyn dokh ot-o dos,
   Vest zayn di baleboste
   Un ikh der balebos.

- I steal at night, the night is inky black. And you've gotten hold of me and stolen my heart.
- If I've stolen it, that's good—it's a sign that I'm capable. After all, I'm skillful, the apple of your eye. No prison will hurt us. We've corrupted everyone in the city, Just play the role slowly. Buster—tell me you'll marry me!
- I steal your heart, it's not a treasure. You've choked me, squeezed my bile.
- If I'm still breathing, that's good! My love is indeed quite great. I squeeze the anger out of you, and the bitterness. I steal a diamond and a string of pearls, and in the end I see you walking with Yosele, the German (dandy).
- You see, it makes no difference—a German or a Frenchman. From me he can get inflamed skin rash. Yosele said that I'm something precious. He says he'll give me a heap of good fortune.
- What does that wiseguy want? Again he's attacked me. Does he indeed want a knife plunged into his side? The switchblade glitters and plays like a bow. I need no weapons for I'll slit his throat.
- Well, well! You're giving me a hard time again. Big shot—do you want to go to prison again? Well, I won't go with Yosele any more. We'll only go together to Buenos Aires.
- That's just fine. That's what I mean. You'll be the mistress of the house, and I'll be the man.

Allegro

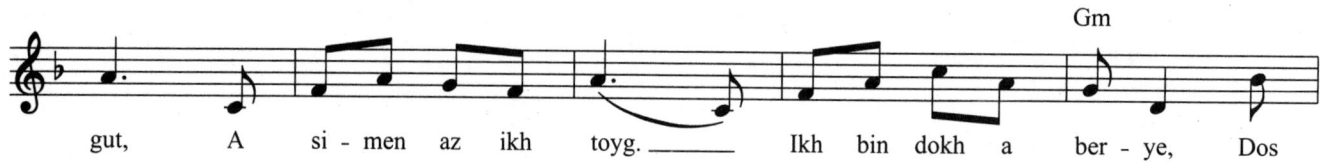

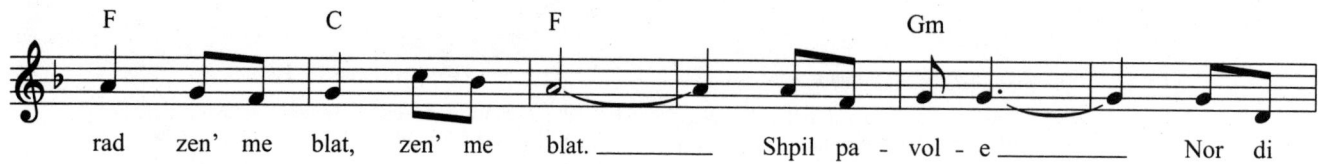

DOS KLEYNE TSIGAYNERL

דאָס קליינע ציגײַנערל

The Little Gypsy

Words by Itsik Manger (1901–1969), music by Herts Rubin (1911–1958). Submitted by singer Mascha Benya Matz, who received the song from Genia Manger, the poet's widow. The version recorded by the late singer David Carrey differs slightly.

Kh'bin a tsigaynerl a kleyner,	כ'בין אַ ציגײַנערל אַ קליינער,
Ober, vi ir zet, a sheyner,	אָבער, ווי איר זעט, אַ שיינער,
Borves, hungerik un freylekh,	באָרוועס, הונגעריק און פֿריילעך,
Leb ikh mir vi a ben-meylekh.	לעב איך מיר ווי אַ בן-מלך.
Kh'veys nit vu ikh bin geboyrn,	כ'ווייס ניט וווּ איך בין געבוירן,
Mayn mame t'mikh in step farloyrn,	מײַן מאַמע ט'מיך אין סטעפּ פֿאַרלוירן,
Mayn tatn hot men oyfgehangen,	מײַן טאַטן האָט מען אויפֿגעהאַנגען,
Ven er iz ganvenen gegangen.	ווען ער איז גנבֿענען געגאַנגען.

Refrain:
רעפֿרײן:

Ekh, du fidl, fidele du mayn,	עך, דו פֿידל, פֿידעלע דו מײַן,
Shpil mayn troyer tsu zey in harts arayn.	שפּיל מײַן טרויער צו זיי אין האַרץ אַרײַן.
Ekh, du khaver mayn,	עך, דו חבֿר מײַן,
Ver veyst vi du aleyn,	ווער ווייסט ווי דו אַליין,
Az eybik, eybik, royt iz	אַז אייביק, אייביק, רויט איז
Blut un vayn.	בלוט און ווײַן.

Fun tatn geyarshnt hob ikh di fidl,	פֿון טאַטן געיאַרשנט האָב איך די פֿידל
Shpil ikh oyf ir "didl, didl,"	שפּיל איך אויף איר „דידל, דידל,"
In mayn fidl kent ir hern	אין מײַן פֿידל קענט איר הערן
Mayn mames tsar, mayn shvesters trern,	מײַן מאַמעס צער, מײַן שוועסטערס טרערן,
In mayn fidl ligt gefangen	אין מײַן פֿידל ליגט געפֿאַנגען
Vi m'hot mayn tatn oyfgehangen.	ווי מ'האָט מײַן טאַטן אויפֿגעהאַנגען.
Ven tsum toyt m'hot im getribn,	ווען צום טויט מ'האָט אים געטריבן,
Iz di fidl mir geblibn.	איז די פֿידל מיר געבליבן.

Dos lid fun roydefn un yogn,	דאָס ליד פֿון רודפֿן און יאָגן,
Dos lid fun nekhtikn, nisht togn,	דאָס ליד פֿון נעכטיקן, נישט טאָגן,
Kh'bin a tsigaynerl a kleyner,	כ'בין אַ ציגײַנערל אַ קליינער,
Kh'zing vi s'zingt nisht keyner, keyner,	כ'זינג ווי ס'זינגט נישט קיינער, קיינער.
Vos far a lid s'vet aykh gefeln,	וואָס פֿאַר אַ ליד ס'וועט אײַך געפֿעלן,
Kent ir zikh bay mir bashteln,	קענט איר זיך בײַ מיר באַשטעלן,
Batsoln darft ir bloyz a drayer,	באַצאָלן דאַרפֿט איר בלויז אַ דרײַער,
S'kost mayn veytik aykh nisht tayer.	ס'קאָסט מײַן ווייטיק אײַך נישט טײַער.

Ekh, du fidl, fidele du mayn,	עך, דו פֿידל, פֿידעלע דו מײַן,
Shpil mayn tsar tsu zey in harts arayn.	שפּיל מײַן צער צו זיי אין האַרץ אַרײַן,
Ekh, du khaver mayn,	עך, דו חבֿר מײַן,
Ver veyst vi du aleyn,	ווער ווייסט ווי דו אַליין,
Az eybik, eybik royt iz	אַז אייביק, אייביק רויט איז
Blut un vayn!	בלוט און ווײַן!

I am a little gypsy, but, as you see, I'm handsome. Barefoot, hungry and happy, I live like a prince. I don't know where I was born—My mother lost me in the steppes. My father was hanged when he went out to steal.

Oh, you fiddle, you fiddle of mine—play my sorrow into their hearts. Oh, you friend of mine—who knows as well as you, that forever red are blood and wine.

From my father I inherited my fiddle and I play on it: "Diddle, diddle." In my fiddling you can hear my mother's sorrow and my sister's tears. In my fiddle is captured the story of my father's hanging. When they drove him to his death, the fiddle remained for me.

The song of persecution and the chase, the song of staying overnight but not during the day—I am a little gypsy and I sing like no one else.

Whatever song you want, you may request from me. You only have to pay a three-penny—my pain doesn't cost you very much.

SHPIL, GITAR!

שפּיל, גיטאַר!

Play, Guitar

This is a translation of the Russian song "Chto mnie gore" by Samuil Iakovlevich Pokrass (1894–1939). Submitted by Arnold Sisk, Hallandale, Fla. It was sung by Lori Wilner in the play *Those Were the Days*. Singers Joanne Borts and Phyllis Berk also popularized the song.

Shpil, gitar, biz mayn tsar vet oyfhern,
Zoln platsn di strunes on a tsol.
Kh'vil mit vayn un shampayn shiker vern, oy,
Un fargesn vos geven iz a mol.

Refrain:
Tsu vos zhe zorgn
Farn morgn,
Fil dem bekher on mit vayn;
Heyb dem bekher
Hekher, hekher,
In dem vayn fargeyt der payn.

Di tsigayner, zey ruen un shlofn,
Un men hert shoyn keyn lidl nisht meyn;
Nor kol-zman s'iz faran vayn a tropn,
Iz dos lebn un der toyt shoyn alts eyns.

Alt un shvakh, on a dakh, iz farblibn
A tsigayner, a held, gants aleyn;
Ferdlekh ganvenen, meydlekh fil libn,
Er flegt zingen dos lid azoy sheyn.

שפּיל, גיטאַר, ביז מײַן צער וועט אויפֿהערן,
זאָלן פּלאַצן די סטרונעס אָן אַ צאָל.
כ׳וויל מיט ווײַן און שאַמפּײַן שיכּור ווערן, אוי,
און פֿאַרגעסן וואָס געווען איז אַ מאָל.

רעפֿרײַן:
צו וואָס זשע זאָרגן
פֿאַרן מאָרגן,
פֿיל דעם בעכער אָן מיט ווײַן;
הייב דעם בעכער,
העכער, העכער,
אין דעם ווײַן פֿאַרגייט דער פּײַן.

די ציגײַנער, זיי רוען און שלאָפֿן,
און מען הערט שוין קיין לידל שוין מיין;
נאָר כּל־זמן ס׳איז פֿאַראַן ווײַן אַ טראָפּן,
איז דאָס לעבן און דער טויט שוין אַלץ איינס.

אַלט און שוואַך, אָן אַ דאַך, איז פֿאַרבליבן
אַ ציגײַנער, אַ העלד, גאַנץ אַליין,
פֿערדלעך גנבֿענען, מיידלעך פֿיל ליבן,
ער פֿלעגט זינגען דאָס ליד אַזוי שיין.

Play, guitar, till my sorrow goes away. Let many strings break. I want to get drunk on wine and champagne, and forget the way things were.

Why worry about tomorrow—fill the goblet with wine; raise the goblet higher, higher—pain dissolves in the wine.

The gypsies rest and sleep, and one no longer hears any songs. But as long as there's a drop of wine, life and death are both the same.

Old and weak, without a roof, all alone is a great big gypsy who used to steal horses and make love to girls, and he used to sing his song so beautifully.

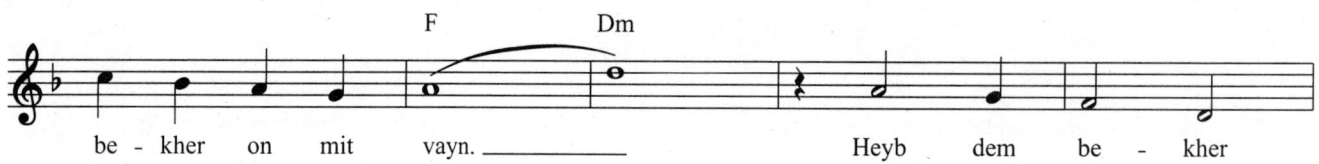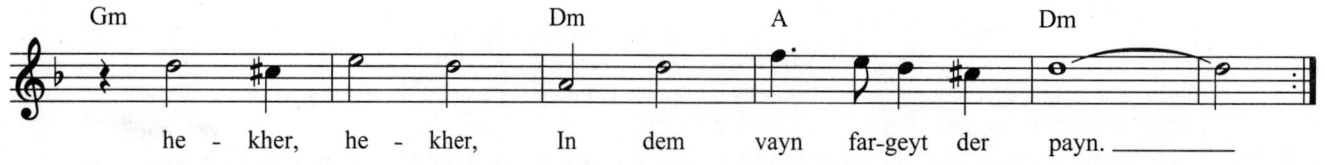

TSION, TSION, MAYN HEYLIK LAND...
HASSIDIC AND NATIONAL SONGS

ציון, ציון, מײַן הייליק לאַנד...

FRAYTIK OYF DER NAKHT

פֿרײַטיק אויף דער נאַכט

Friday After Shul

The song was published in sheet music in this country in 1905, without accreditation to any author or composer, simply that it was sung by Rosa Klug. Theater historian Sholem Perlmutter writes that the song was written by the Galician Jewish composer Khone Wolfsthal (1851–1924). Although Wolfsthal never came to this country, many of his songs were adopted here and credited to others. It was sung in the musical *The Golden Land* by Bruce Adler.

Fraytik oyf der nakht—
Az ikh kum nor fun der shul tsu geyn,
Shteyt shoyn mayn vaybele un lakht—
Oy, iz zi mole-kheyn.

Un di khalelekh tsugedekt,
Mit a servetke vos es lakht,
Nor a yidele veyst vi se shmekt
Der fraytik oyf der nakht.

Nokh dem kidesh a shtikele fish,
Vos mayn vaybele hot aleyn gemakht,
Zi iz vert in piskele a kish—(kush)
Um fraytik oyf der nakht.

Refrain:
Oy, fraytik oyf der nakht
Iz ayeder yid a meylekh.
In yedn vinkele lakht,
Di gantse shtub iz freylekh.

Nokh di lokshn mit yoykh
Dos shtikele fleysh iz oykh zeyer git*,
Dem tam fil ikh oykh—
Vayl ikh bin a yid.

Nokh dem tsimes a glezele vayn—
Dos hot keyn nar nit oysgetrakht,
Un zikh leygn in bet arayn,
Um fraytik oyf der nakht.

Orem oder raykh—
Ayeder zingt tsum esn tsi (tsu),
Damolst iz yeder glaykh—
Biz zuntik in der fri.

Friday after synagogue, when I come home, my young wife waits and smiles.

Oh, she's full of charm! The little khales are covered well, with a napkin that is gleaming. Only a Jew knows the smell of Friday after shul. After kiddush there's a piece of fish, which my wife cooked herself. For that she deserves a special kiss on Friday after shul.

Oh, Friday after shul each and every Jew is a king. Every corner gleams, the house with laughter rings.

After the noodles and the soup, the little piece of meat is very good. I can sense the taste also, because I am a Jew. After the tsimmes, a little glass of wine, no fool thought that up. I lie down on the bed, on Friday after shul. No matter if you're poor or rich—every one sings at his meal. Then all are equal till Sunday morning.

AMOL IZ GEVEN A YID

אַ מאָל איז געווען אַ ייִד

There Once Was a Jew

Words and music by Ben Yomen (1901–1970), published in the composer's collection *Oneg shabbat songs,* 1962. The song, in the repertoire of popular singer Ben Bonus, was revived by his wife actress-singer Mina Bern, in the musical *Those Were the Days.* Bonus added the musical refrain.

Amol iz geven a yid,
Hot er gehat a yidene,
Hot er geheysn, geheysn—
Zi zol im koyfn vayn oyf shabes.

אַ מאָל איז געווען אַ ייִד,
האָט ער געהאַט אַ ייִדענע,
האָט ער געהייסן, געהייסן -
זי זאָל אים קויפֿן ווײַן אויף שבת.

Oy, shabes, shabes, shabes,
Zog, vu nemt men vayn oyf shabes?
S'iz nishto keyn zalts,
S'iz nishto keyn shmalts—
Iz vu nemt men vayn oyf shabes.

אוי, שבת, שבת, שבת,
זאָג, וווּ נעמט מען ווײַן אויף שבת?
ס׳איז נישטאָ קיין זאַלץ,
ס׳איז נישטאָ קיין שמאַלץ -
איז וווּ נעמט מען ווײַן אויף שבת.

Amol iz geven a yid,
Hot er gehat a yidene,
Hot er geheysn, geheysn,
Zi zol im bakn khale oyf shabes.

אַ מאָל איז געווען אַ ייִד,
האָט ער געהאַט אַ ייִדענע,
האָט ער געהייסן, געהייסן,
זי זאָל אים באַקן חלה אויף שבת.

Oy, shabes, shabes, shabes,
Zog, vu nemt men khale oyf shabes?
S'iz nishto keyn zalts,
S'iz nishto keyn shmalts,
Iz vu nemt men khale oyf shabes.

אוי, שבת, שבת, שבת,
זאָג, וווּ נעמט מען חלה אויף שבת?
ס׳איז נישטאָ קיין זאַלץ,
ס׳איז נישטאָ קיין שמאַלץ,
איז וווּ נעמט מען חלה אויף שבת?

Amol iz geven a yid,
Hot er gehat a yidene,
Hot er geheysn, geheysn—
Zi zol im kokhn fleysh oyf shabes.

אַ מאָל איז געווען אַ ייִד,
האָט ער געהאַט אַ ייִדענע,
האָט ער געהייסן, געהייסן -
זי זאָל אים קאָכן פֿלייש אויף שבת.

Oy, shabes, shabes, shabes,
Zog, vu nemt men fleysh oyf shabes?
S'iz nishto keyn zalts,
S'iz nishto keyn shmalts,
Iz vu nemt men fleysh oyf shabes.

אוי, שבת, שבת, שבת,
זאָג, וווּ נעמט מען פלייש אויף שבת?
ס׳איז נישטאָ קיין זאַלץ,
ס׳איז נישטאָ קיין שמאַלץ,
איז וווּ נעמט מען פֿלייש אויף שבת?

Amol iz geven a yid,
Hot er gehat a yidene,
Hot er geheysn, geheysn—
Zi zol im makhn khotsh tsimes oyf shabes.

אַ מאָל איז געווען אַ ייִד,
האָט ער געהאַט אַ ייִדענע,
האָט ער געהייסן, געהייסן -
זי זאָל אים מאַכן כאָטש צימעס אויף שבת.

Oy, shabes, shabes, shabes,
S'iz shoyn bald avek der shabes,
Un s'iz biter vi der toyt,
On a shtikl broyt,
Oy, vu nemt men a rubl oyf shabes?

אוי, שבת, שבת, שבת,
ס׳איז שוין באַלד אַוועק דער שבת,
און ס׳איז ביטער ווי דער טויט,
אָן אַ שטיקל ברויט,
אוי, וווּ נעמט מען אַ רובל אויף שבת?

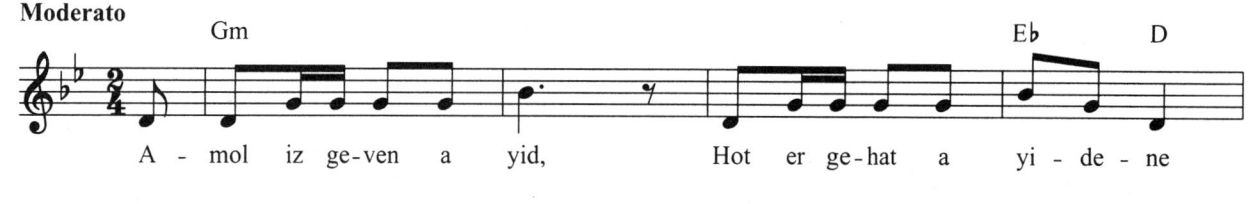
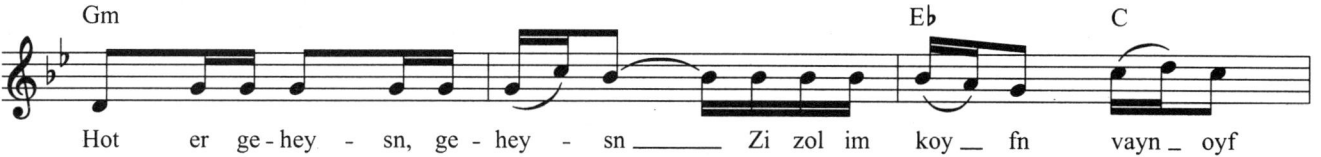

There once was a Jew who had a wife. And he asked her to buy him wine for the Sabbath.

Oh, shabes, shabes. Where do you get wine for the Sabbath? When there is no salt, and there is no fat—Where can you find wine for the Sabbath?

There once was a Jew who had a wife. And he asked her to bake him *khale* for the Sabbath.

There once was a Jew who had a wife. And he asked her to cook him meat for the Sabbath.

There once was a Jew who had a wife. And he told her: At least, make me *tsimmes* for the Sabbath.

Oh, shabes, shabes is almost over. And it's bitter as death to be without a piece of bread. Oh, where can you find a ruble for the Sabbath?

DER EYBERSHTER IZ DER MEKHUTN   דער אייבערשטער איז דער מחותּן

The Almighty Was the Bride's Father

    The allegorical song refers to the marriage between the Torah and the people of Israel which took place on Mount Sinai, with Moses officiating as matchmaker. It is folklorized from a poem "Der yikhes-shidekh" by Abraham Goldfaden (1840–1908) published in 1866. The words and music were published by S. Kisselgof in 1911. The song was in the repertory of singers Sidor Belarsky and Mascha Benya Matz, who sang it together on the recording *Amol iz geven a mayse,* compiled and narrated by Joseph Mlotek.

Der eybershter iz der mekhutn,	דער אײבערשטער איז דער מחותּן,
Di toyre iz di kale,	די תּורה איז די כּלה,
Moyshe Rabeynu iz der shadkhn geven.	משה רבינו איז דער שדכן געווען,
Der oremer yisrolik	דער אָרעמער ישׂראליק
Iz der khosn der fayner,	איז דער חתן דער פֿײַנער,
Oyf dem heylikn barg sinay	אױף דעם הײליקן באַרג סיני
Zaynen di tnoim geven.	זענען די תּנאים געווען.
Refrain:	**רעפֿרײן:**
Es flien yidelekh	עס פֿליִען ייִדעלעך
Un zingen lidelekh,	און זינגען לידעלעך,
Yederer shrayt bazunder:	יעדערער שרײַט באַזונדער,
Khosns tsad, kales tsad:	חתנס צד, כּלהס צד:
Mazl-tov!	מזל-טובֿ!
Mazl-tov, mazl-tov!	מזל-טובֿ! מזל-טובֿ!
Khosns tsad, kales tsad:	חתנס צד, כּלהס צד:
Mazl-tov, mazl-tov!	מזל-טובֿ! מזל-טובֿ!
A kale a reyne,	אַ כּלה אַ ריינע,
Zi iz tayer un sheyn,	זי איז טײַער און שײן,
Orntlekh un fayn,	אָרנטלעך און פֿײַן,
Zi iz beser fun alts;	זי איז בעסער פֿון אַלץ;
Perl bay ir shit zikh funem moyl,	פּערל בײַ איר שיט זיך פֿונעם מויל,
A gilderne keyt trogt zi oyfn haldz.	אַ גילדערנע קייט טראָגט זי אױפֿן האַלדז.
Dek op dayn dektukh,	דעק אָפּ דײַן דעקטוך,
Du tayere kale!	דו טײַערע כּלה!
Bavayz undz dayn ponem,	באַװײַז אונדז דײַן פּנים,
Mir viln dikh zen;	מיר װילן דיך זען;
Zet nor, ir yidn,	זעט נאָר, איר ייִדן,
Un kukt oyf ir ale,	און קוקט אױף איר אַלע,
Dos iz di amune,	דאָס איז די אמונה,
Di kale geven.	די כּלה געווען.

The Almighty was the bride's father, the Torah was the bride. Moses, our teacher, was the matchmaker. Poor little Israel was the fine bridegroom. The betrothal was announced on the holy Mount Sinai.

Jews are flying and singing little songs. Each one cries out one by one: From the bride's family, the groom's family: Congratulations!

The chaste bride is dear and beautiful, honorable and refined. She surpasses everything. Pearls drip from her mouth and she wears a golden chain around her neck.

Lift up your veil, dear bride—reveal your face. We want to see you. Just look, people, all of you gaze upon her. The bride was our faith.

ROYZ, ROYZ, VI VAYT BISTU

רויז, רויז, ווי ווײַט ביסטו

Rose, Rose, How Far Away You Are

    This Hassidic song describes how a secular song of foreign provenance evolved into one with a religious Hassidic concept of the Divine Presence and the Diaspora. According to Menakhem Kipnis, who published the song in 1925, the Rabbi Isaac Taub of Kaliv, Hungary, was strolling in the fields when he heard a shepherd singing a song "Ruzha, ruzha, yak ti daleka!" (Rose, Rose, how far away you are). The rabbi altered the words to make the song expressive of longing for the Divine Presence.

    In his column "Shprakhvinkl" in the Jewish Forward (August 30, 1976) Wolf Younin brought the Hungarian original together with a Yiddish-Hebrew version: "Erdo, erdo de magas vagy,/ Rozsam, rozsam de mesze vagy/ Ha az erdot levaghatnam/ Tied volnek edes babam/ Ha az erdot levaghatnam/ Tied volnek edes babam." /"Goles, goles, vi groys bistu/ Shkhine, shkhine, vi vayt bistu/ Ilu min hagolis hoytsienu/ Hoinu shninu yakhad oz." Menasha Unger wrote a story about the song entitled "How the Rabbi of Kalev Freed a Song" where he has an additional stanza. On September 27, 1976 Mascha Benya Matz cited a version that Zalman Shazar, former president of Israel, sang: "Vald, vald, vi groys bistu,/ Kale, kale vi vayt bistu,/ Az der vald volt vern avekgenumen,/ Volt ikh mit der kale tsuzamengekumen."

Royz, royz, vi vayt bistu,	רויז, רויז, ווי ווײַט ביסטו?
Vald, vald, vi groys bistu.	וואַלד, וואַלד, ווי גרויס ביסטו.
Volt di royz nisht azoy vayt geven,	וואָלט די רויז נישט אַזוי ווײַט געווען,
Volt der vald nisht azoy groys geven.	וואָלט דער וואַלד נישט אַזוי גרויס געווען.
Shkhine, shkhine, vi vayt bistu.	שכינה, שכינה, ווי ווײַט ביסטו,
Goles, goles, vi lang bistu.	גלות, גלות, ווי לאַנג ביסטו.
Volt di shkhine nisht azoy vayt geven,	וואָלט די שכינה נישט אַזוי ווײַט געווען,
Volt der goles nisht azoy lang geven.	וואָלט דער גלות נישט אַזוי לאַנג געווען.

    Rose, how far away you are. Forest, how big you are. If the rose were not so far away, the forest would not be so big.

    Holy spirit, how far away you are. Exile, how long you are. If the holy spirit were not so far away, the exile would not be so long.

DOS FREYLEKHE KHOSIDL

דאָס פֿרײלעכע חסידל

The Happy Hassid

Words and music by Abraham Goldfaden (1840–1908). The words were published in Goldfaden's first collection of Yiddish poems, *Dos yidele,* in 1866; the music was published by Chaim Kotylansky in 1944. This song was cited in the story of the founding of the Yiddish theater. When Goldfaden appeared in Jassy in the garden of Shimen Marks, in 1876, he recited his serious and very long poems *Dos pintele yid and Der malekh.* The audience, expecting lively entertainment and singing, grew increasingly bored and began to boo angrily. Goldfaden was rushed off the stage and one of the Broder Singers, Yisroel Grodner, quickly donned a robe, grabbed his wig of sidecurls and a Hassidic hat and jumped on the stage to sing "Dos freylekhe khosidl." The audience soon recovered from their angry mood. Goldfaden notes in his autobiography that although he was disappointed by this "debacle," it led him to the idea of creating a Yiddish theater to raise the level of taste and culture of Jewish audiences. Goldfaden's song is partly derivative of the song "Dos khsidishe mizinke" (The Hassidic Youngest Daughter) by his forerunner, folk poet Velvl Zbarzher-Ehrenkranz (1826(?)–1883) which itself is the prototype of the song "In rod arayn" (Into the Circle). It was a popular number in the repertory of actor-singer Ben Bonus.

A dank dir, gotenyu, libhartsiker, getrayer,
Far dayne groyse vinder*,
Kh'hob khasene gemakht mit mayn vayb
Ale mayne kinder.
Oy, mayn vayb, tants mit mir,
Nem dem eydem un ikh di shnir**.

    Refrain:
    Ale veysn umetum
    Az mayne kinder zaynen frum.
    Ay-ay-ay, gevald!
    Ay, ay, tate ziser!

A dank dir, gotenyu, libhartsiker, getrayer,
Mit mayn gantsn khayes,
Farvos ikh bin bay dir take azoy tayer,
Mer fun di ale hultayes.
Un mayne kinder, dos zestu aleyn dokh tsi***
Firn zikh ale, borukh hashem, oyf mayn stri.

Di apikorsim, az okh un vey iz tsu zey,
Tsi veln zey den hobn oylem-habe,
Az "mayo potshtyenye" iz bay zey
Gor der shenster borekh habe.
Bay zey heyst es epes "adye, bonzhur,"
Bay undz heyst es "skotsl kimt, gut morgn, gut yor."

אַ דאַנק דיר, גאָטעניו, ליבהאַרציקער, געטרײַער,
פֿאַר דײַנע גרויסע ווינדער (וווּנדער),
כ׳האָב חתונה געמאַכט מיט מײַן ווײַב
אַלע מײַנע קינדער.
אוי, מײַן ווײַב, טאַנץ מיט מיר,
נעם דעם איידעם און איך די שניר.

    רעפֿרײן:
    אַלע ווייסן אומעטום,
    אַז מײַנע קינדער זײַנען פֿרום.
    אײַ־אײַ־אײַ, געוואַלד!
    אײַ, אײַ, טאַטע זיסער!

אַ דאַנק דיר, גאָטעניו, ליבהאַרציקער, געטרײַער,
מיט מײַן גאַנצן חיות,
פֿאַר וואָס איך בין בײַ דיר טאַקע אַזוי טײַער,
מער פֿון די אַלע הולטײַעס.
און מײַנע קינדער, דאָס זעסטו אַליין דאָך צי (צו),
פֿירן זיך אַלע, ברוך השם, אויף מײַן סטרי.

די אַפּיקורסים, אַז אָך און ווײ איז צו זײ,
צי וועלן זײ דען האָבן עולם־הבא,
אַז „מאַיאַ פּאַטשטיעניע" איז בײַ זײ
גאָר דער שענסטער ברוך־הבא.
בײַ זײ הייסט עס עפּעס „אַדיע, באָנזשור,"
בײַ אונדז הייסט עס „סקאָצל קומט, גוט מאָרגן, גוט יאָר."

---

* vunder
** shnur
*** tsu

Allegretto

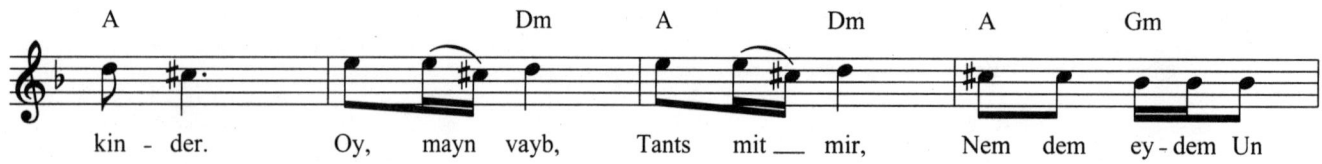

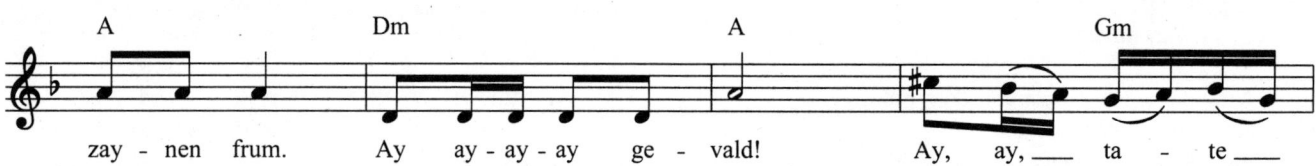

Thank you, dear God, so generous and faithful, for your great wonders. I and my wife have married off all my children. Oh, my wife, dance with me—You with the son-in-law and I with the daughter-in-law.

Everyone everywhere knows that my children are pious. Oh God! Oh dear Father!

Thank you, dear God, so generous and faithful, with all my heart for holding me so dear to You, more than all the heretics. And my children, You can see for yourself, behave, thank God, according to my ways.

The heretics, woe to them! will they have the world to come when "My greatest respect" is for them the best way to bless God. With them it's "adieu," "bonjour," while we say "skotsl kumt" (look who's here!), hello, how are you?

Two Letters to the Rabbi of Liady

TSVEY BRIV TSUM LYADER REBN

צוויי בריוו צום ליאדער רבין

This humorous macaronic song consists of two almost identical stanzas with contrasting moods, which are expressed by different interpretations of the vocables "ay-ay-ay." In the first stanza, the letter writer deplores the sad state of his affairs by singing "ay-ay-ay" with a melancholy sigh. In the second stanza, time has passed and his prayers have been answered—conditions have improved and the syllables are now expressed with resoluteness and joy. The song was published by Menakhem Kipnis in 1925 and later by Chaim Kotylansky and others. It was parodied in the theater song *Mayn tayer Jekele, shik mir a tshekele!* (My Dear Jackie, Send Me a Check!) words by Jacob Jacobs.

V'myestyetshku lyadinyu,—
A pintele.
Mogilyovskoy gubernyu,—
A pintele.
Dukhovnomu Rabinu Shneyersonu—
A pintele.

Oy-vey, hiney zay visn, du heyliker rebenyu,
Az di parnose iz bay mir nisht azoy
    ay-ay-ay-ay-ay-ay-ay;
Un mayn vayb iz bekav-habries oykh nisht azoy
    ay-ay-ay-ay-ay-ay-ay;
Un du bist dokh der groyser
    ay-ay-ay-ay-ay-ay-ay!
To helf zhe mir!

Refrain:
V'myestyetshku lyadinyu,
Mogilyovskoy gubernyu,
Dukhovnomu Rabinu Shneyersonu.

V'myestyetshku lyadinyu.
A pintele.
Mogilyovskoy gubernyu.
A pintele.
Dukhovnomu Rabinu Shneyersonu.
A pintele.

Oy-vey, hiney zay visn, du heyliker rebenyu,
Az di parnose iz bay mir shoyn
    ay-ay-ay-ay-ay-ay-ay!
Un mayn vayb iz bekav habries oykh
    shoyn ay-ay-ay-ay-ay-ay-ay!
Bistu dokh take der groyser
    ay-ay-ay-ay-ay-ay-ay!
To dank ikh dir!

To the little town of Liady—a period. In the province of Mogilev—a period. To our holy Rabbi Schneerson—a period.

Oh know herewith, O holy rabbi, that my income is not so ay-ay-ay, nor my wife's health is so ay-ay-ay. And you, after all, are the great ay-ay-ay! So—help me!

To the little town of Liady, in the province of Mogilev—to our holy Rabbi Schneerson.

To the little town of Liady—a period. In the province of Mogilev—a period. To our holy Rabbi Schneerson—a period.

Oh know herewith, O holy rabbi, that my income is now ay-ay-ay, and my wife's health is also ay-ay-ay. You, after all, are the great ay-ay-ay! So—I thank you!

TSION

ציון, ציון

Zion

Text and music by Abraham Goldfaden (1840–1908). The words were first published in *Dos heylike land*, Zhitomir, 1891, entitled "Knaan" (Canaan); the music was published by Israel and Samuel E. Goldfarb in 1929.

Akh tsion, tsion, du heylik land,	אַך, ציון, ציון, דו הייליק לאַנד,
Vi heylik bistu bay mir,	ווי הייליק ביסטו בײַ מיר,
Fargesn zol ikh in mayn rekhter hant,	פֿאַרגעסן זאָל איך אין מײַן רעכטער האַנט,
Oyb ikh vel fargesn in dir.	אויב איך וועל פֿאַרגעסן אין דיר.
Heylik iz dokh in dir yeder shpan,	הייליק איז דאָך אין דיר יעדער שפּאַן,
Bavizn in dir hot zikh got,	באַוויזן אין דיר האָט זיך גאָט,
Ven er hot durkh Moyshe, dem getlekhn man,	ווען ער האָט דורך משה, דעם געטלעכן מאַן,
Geshikt far undz di tsen gebot.	געשיקט פֿאַר אונדז די צען געבאָט.
Di heylike oves shlofn in dayn shoys:	די הייליקע אָבֿות שלאָפֿן אין דײַן שויס:
Avrom, Yitskhok, Yankev un Dovid;	אַבֿרהם, יצחק, יעקבֿ און דוד;
Dort ruen zikh undzere heldn oys	דאָרט רוען זיך אונדזערע העלדן אויס
Mit zeyere shverdn bekoved!	מיט זייערע שווערדן בכּבֿוד!

Refrain: רעפֿרײן:

Oy, oy, oy, vi benk ikh azoy,	אוי, אוי, אוי, ווי בענק איך אַזוי,
Nokh dir, heylik land,	נאָך דיר, הייליק לאַנד,
Oy, oy, oy, vi benk ikh azoy,	אוי, אוי, אוי, ווי בענק איך אַזוי,
Oyshaltn bin ikh nit umstand.	אויסהאַלטן בין איך ניט אומשטאַנד.

Oyf di shteynerne vegn, vos keyn beys-lekhem geyt,	אויף די שטיינערנע וועגן, וואָס קיין בית-לחם גייט,
Zet men a keyver dort shteyn,	זעט מען אַ קבֿר דאָרט שטיין,
Un punkt halbe nakht, ver dortn shteyt,	און פּונקט האַלבע נאַכט, ווער דאָרטן שטייט,
Hert men a shreklekh geveyn.	הערט מען אַ שרעקלעך געוויין.
Men krekhtst, men ziftst, oy-vey, oy-vey,	מען קרעכצט, מען זיפֿצט, אוי-וויי, אוי-וויי,
Dos iz undzer muters kol,	דאָס איז אונדזער מוטערס קול,
Veynt Rokhl tsu got mit a geshrey,	וויינט רחל צו גאָט מיט אַ געשריי,
Ire kinder, er helfn zol.	אירע קינדער ער העלפֿן זאָל.
Zi geyt nit tsurik in ir ru arayn	זי גייט ניט צוריק אין איר רו אַרײַן
Biz zi hert nit a treyst fun dem himl,	ביז זי הערט ניט אַ טרייסט פֿון דעם הימל,
Biz got aleyn shlefert zi nit ayn,	ביז גאָט אַליין שלעפֿערט זי ניט אײַן,
In ir zisn, heylikn driml.	אין איר זיסן, הייליקן דרימל.

Oh Zion, you holy land—how holy you are to me! May I forget my right hand, if I forget you. For every step in you is holy. God revealed Himself in you when, through Moses, our teacher, that godly man, He sent the Ten Commandments for us. Our holy ancestors sleep in your bosom: Abraham, Isaac, Jacob and David. There our heroes are resting honorably with their swords.

Oh, how I long for you, holy land. Oh, how I long—I cannot bear it.

On the rocky road that leads to Bethlehem, you can see a tomb standing there, and, exactly at midnight, whoever stands there can hear terrible weeping. There's groaning and sighing, oh woe! It's our mother's voice—

Rachel is crying out to God that He should help her children. She won't return to her rest till she hears some comfort from Heaven, till God Himself puts her to sleep in her sweet, holy slumber.

IN MITN VEG SHTEYT A BOYM

אין מיטן וועג שטייט אַ בוים

A Tree Stands Halfway Down the Road

    Folksong. Text published by S. Ginzburg and P. Marek in 1901; words and music published in *90 geklibene yidishe folkslider,* 1926. The text sometimes begins "Oyfn veg shteyt a boym." Israeli musicologist Issachar Fater suggests that the song derives from the end of the '70s of the 18th century, when Rabbi Menakhem Mendl of Vitebsk and Rabbi Israel of Polotsk led a few hundred Hassidim to Palestine.

    A children's parody was published in the *Mitteilungen zur judischen Volkskunde* 22 (1907). Yiddish poet Itsik Manger used the first two lines in his popular song "Oyfn veg shteyt a boym" (On the Road a Tree Stands) expressing the love of a mother for her fledgling. Chava Lapin recalls a parody that the Halutsim (Pioneers) sang: "Oyfn veg shteyt a boym, shteyt er ayngeboygn/ Fort a yid keyn erets-yisroel/ Mit tserisene hoyzn/ Got, got, groyser got,/ Du bist dokh a tate,/ Az mir veln mertse shem onkumen in erets-yisroel/ Vet men leygn a late." (On the road a tree is bent, a Jew goes to Palestine in torn pants. - God, great God, You are a father. When we will, with luck, arrive in Palestine, we will put on a patch). Other Yiddish poets like Aaron Zeitlin and Zalman Schneour used these lines to portray strong images in their Holocaust poems. Schneour writes in "Lebn kloyster": "Lebn kloyster shteyt a boym, / Shteyt er ayngeboygn, / Hengt oyf im der rov fun shtetl / Mit oysgepikte oygn" (Near the church a bent tree stands. On it the rabbi of the town hangs, with gouged out eyes).

In mitn veg shteyt a boym,
Shteyt er ayngeboygn;
Fort a yid keyn erets-yisroel
Mit farveynte oygn.

Got, got, groyser got!
Lomir davnen minkhe,
Az yidn veln forn keyn erets-yisrol
Vet zayn sosn-vesimkhe! simkhe!

אין מיטן וועג שטייט אַ בוים,
שטייט ער אײַנגעבױגן,
פֿאָרט אַ ייִד קײן אֶרֶץ־יִשְׂרָאֵל
מיט פֿאַרװײנטע אױגן.

גאָט, גאָט, גרויסער גאָט!
לאָמיר דאַװנען מִנחָה, -
אַז ייִדן װעלן פֿאָרן קײן אֶרֶץ־יִשְׂרָאֵל,
װעט זײַן שָׂשׂוֹן־וְשִׂמְחָה שִׂימחה!

A tree stands halfway down the road, stands bent over. A Jew is traveling to Palestine with eyes full of tears.

God, dear God! Let's say the afternoon prayer. When Jews will come to Palestine, there will be great rejoicing.

SHNIRELE PERELE GILDERNE FON

שנירעלע-פערעלע, גילדערנע פֿאָן

Little String, Little Pearl

Folksong, text published by S. Ginzburg and P. Marek in St. Petersburg, 1901; music was published by Joel Engel in 1909, also in the children's compilation *Di gilderne pave*, 1949. The lines of the advent of the Messiah appear in numerous Sabbath "God of Abraham" prayers. The melody was used for a Hebrew song "Na-aleh L'artsenu" (On to Our Land). Zalmen Mlotek also submitted an English hymn "Praise Ye the Lord" which Herbert Fromm set to this melody. This song, rendered by Lorin Sklamburg, is one of the most popular songs in the Klezkamp Folk Arts Program.

Shnirele perele, gilderne fon,	שנירעלע-פערעלע, גילדערנע פֿאָן,
Moshiekh ben Dovid zitst oybn on.	משיח בן דוד זיצט אויבן אָן.
Halt a bekher in der rekhter hant,	האַלט אַ בעכער אין דער רעכטער האַנט,
Makht a brokhe oyfn gantsn land.	מאַכט אַ ברכה אויפֿן גאַנצן לאַנד.
Oy, omeyn veomeyn, dos iz vor,	אוי, אָמן ואָמן - דאָס איז װאָר,
Meshiekh vet kumen hayntiks yor!	משיח װעט קומען הײַנטיקס יאָר.
Vet er kumen tsu forn—	װעט ער קומען צו פֿאָרן -
Veln zayn gute yorn.	װעלן זײַן גוטע יאָרן.
Vet er kumen tsu raytn—	װעט ער קומען צו רײַטן -
Veln zayn gute tsaytn.	װעלן זײַן גוטע צײַטן.
Vet er kumen tsu geyn—	װעט ער קומען צו גײן -
Veln di yidn in erets-yisroel aynshteyn!	װעלן די ייִדן אין ארץ-ישׂראל אײַנשטײן.

Little string, little pearl, golden banner—the Messiah, the son of David, is sitting on his throne. He holds a goblet in his right hand and says a blessing for the entire land.

Oh amen and amen—this is true: The Messiah will come this year.

If he comes riding in a wagon, there will be good years. If he comes riding on a horse, there will be good times. If he comes walking, the Jews will dwell in Erets Israel.

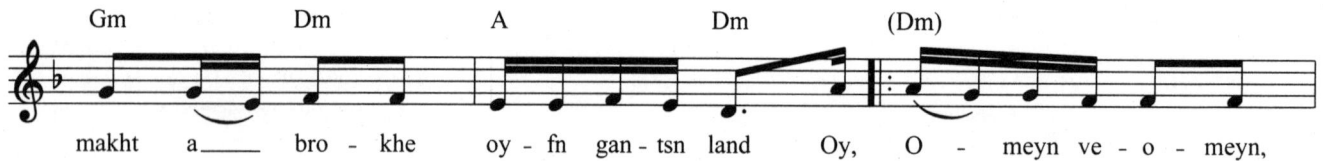

TSI KENSTU DOS LAND?

צי קענסטו דאָס לאַנד?

Do You Know the Land?

Words by Simon S. Frug (1860–1916), printed in Sholem Aleichem's *Di yidishe folks-biblyotek*, 1891; published with the music in A. Bulkin and L. Efron, 1917. The song echoes the opening lines of the famous poem *Mignon* by Johann Wolfgang von Goethe "Kennst du das Land, wo die Zitronen bluhn?" Musicologist Jack Gottlieb informs that Goethe's poem was set to music by numerous composers like Beethoven, Schubert, Schumann, Hugo Wolf, Tschaikovsky, Rubinstein, Liszt and others, but the Yiddish song does not resemble any of them.

Mendele Moykher Sforim also quotes a parody of Goethe's song about Cherson in his story "Di alte mayse": "Hot ir gehert dos land kherson,/ Nit vayt funem feter Ishmoel" (Did you hear of the land Cherson, not far from Uncle Ishmael?).

Tsi kenstu dos land vu esroygimlekh blien,
Vu tsign esn bokser anshtot groz, anshtot groz;
Gebrotene gendzelekh, katshkelekh flien,
Tsemukim-vayn tut flisn on a mos, on a mos.

Mit lulovim, mit lulovim tut men dekher dekn,
Un mandlen, un mandlen vaksn oyf yeder shtekn.

Refrain:
Oy ahin, ahin, ahin!
Oy, rebenyu, gevald, gevald!
Volt ikh mir avek, avek, avek!
Oy, take bald!

Tsi kenstu dos land vu Meshiekh tsidkeynu
Vet kumen oyf a vaysn, vaysn ferd,
Un vet blozn a tkiye gdule,
Un oyfvekn di meysim fun der erd!

Un vet firn, un vet firn undzer folk Yisroel
In undzer land, in undzer land, tsum feter Yishmoel!

צי קענסטו דאָס לאַנד וװ אתרוגימלעך בליִען,
וװ ציגן עסן באָקסער אַנשטאָט גראָז, אַנשטאָט גראָז,
געבראָטענע גענדזעלעך, קאַטשקעלעך פֿליִען,
צמוקים־װײַן טוט פֿליסן אָן אַ מאָס, אָן אַ מאָס.

מיט לולבֿים, מיט לולבֿים טוט מען דעכער דעקן,
און מאַנדלען, און מאַנדלען װאַקסן אױף יעדער שטעקן.

רעפֿרײן:
אױ אַהין, אַהין, אַהין!
אױ, רביניו, געװאַלד, געװאַלד!
װאָלט איך מיר אַװעק, אַװעק, אַװעק!
אױ, טאַקע באַלד!

צי קענסטו דאָס לאַנד, וװ משיח צידקנו
װעט קומען אױף אַ װײַסן, װײַסן פֿערד,
און װעט בלאָזן אַ תּקיעה גדולה,
און אױפֿװעקן די מתים פֿון דער ערד!

און װעט פֿירן, און װעט פֿירן פֿאָלק ישׂראל,
אין אונדזער לאַנד, אין אונדזער לאַנד, צום פֿעטער ישמעאל!

Do you know the land where citrons bloom, where goats eat carob instead of grass? Roast geese, ducks are flying, raisin wine flows endlessly.

They hatch the roofs with palm trees, and almonds grow on every stick.

Oh—to go there! Oh rabbi dear, help! I would love to go—and right now!

Do you know the land where the Messiah, our righteous one, will come riding on a white horse? And blow a great resurrecting breath to wake the dead from out of the earth. And will lead, will lead our people, Israel, to our land, to our uncle Ishmael.

KHALUTSIM GIKHER!

חלוצים גיכער!

Pioneers, Faster!

Folksong entitled "Ematay" about colonists of Palestine was published by S. E. Goldfarb and A. W. Binder in 1929 and 1933 respectively. The tune of "Ematay" was also published in the Metro *Album of Selected Palestinian Hebrew, Chassidic and Jewish Dances and Songs* compiled by Henry Lefkowitch, in 1939. In recent years the song, in the arrangement by Zalmen Mlotek, was revived by the Workmen's Circle Chorus during its tour of Israel in 1988. Compiler recalls that in the 1930s the Russian refrain was sung in English: "Good-bye America,/ Good-bye Yankee fashion,/ We're off to Palestine/ To heck with the depression!"

Ve-im lo akhshav ematay?

ואם לא עכשו אימתי?

Khalutsim, gikher,
Khalutsim, zikher,
Nit aropgelozt di kep.
Pakt ayn di peklekh,
Farneyt di zeklekh,
Vayl der poyezd fort avek.

חלוצים, גיכער,
חלוצים זיכער,
ניט אַראָפּגעלאָזט די קעפּ.
פּאַקט אײַן די פּעקלעך,
פֿאַרנייט די זעקלעך,
װײַל דער פּױעזד פֿאָרט אַװעק.

Proshtshaytye, vse druzya,
Proshtshay, korova,
Yedyem, yedyem navsegda
Artsa yisrael.

פּראָשטשײַטיע װסע דרוזיאַ,
פּראָשטשײַ קאָראָװאַ,
יעדיעם, יעדיעם נאַװסעגדאַ
ארצה ישׂראל!

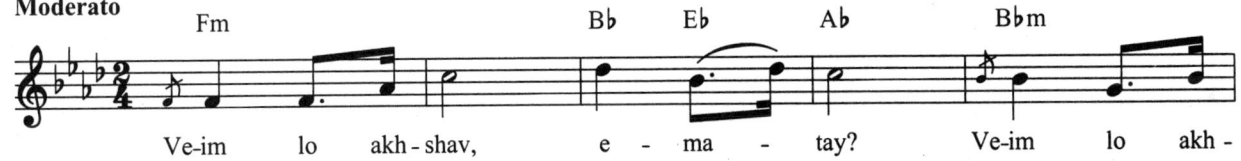

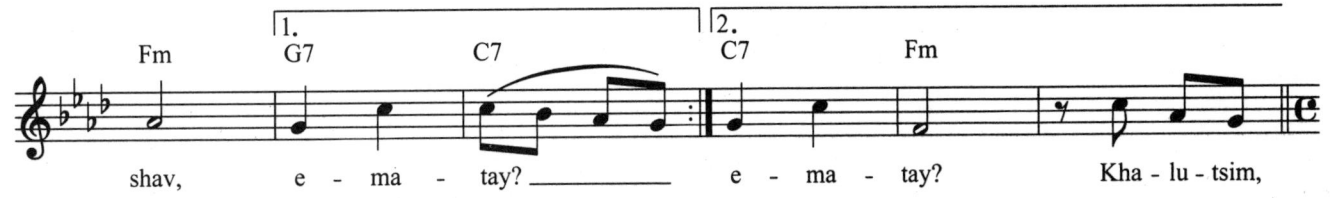

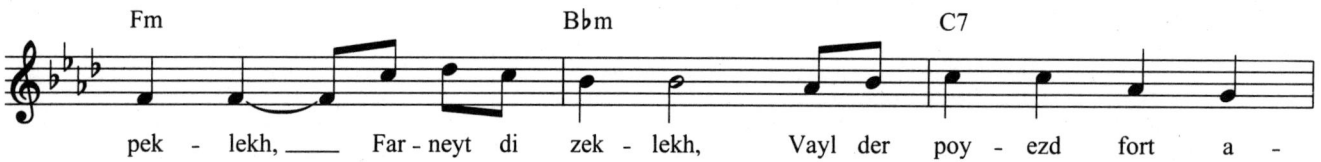

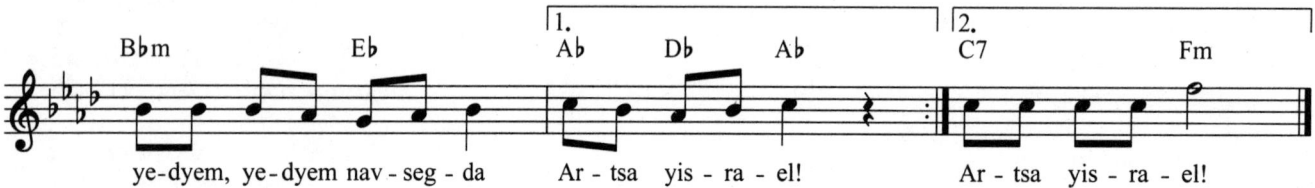

If not now, when?

Pioneers, faster! Pioneers, with certainty! Don't hang your heads—Pack your knapsacks, darn your socks, for the train is departing.

Goodbye, all my friends, goodbye, cows! We are going forever to the land of Israel.

YIDDISH REDT ZIKH AZOY SHEYN

ייִדיש רעדט זיך אַזוי שיין

Yiddish Sounds So Nice

Words by Isidor Lillian (1882–1960); music by Maurice Rauch (1910–1994).

Yidn redn yidish,	ייִדן רעדן ייִדיש,
Iz vos iz do der khidesh—	איז וואָס איז דאָ דער חידוש -
A yid hot lib a yidish vort in moyl.	אַ ייִד האָט ליב אַ ייִדיש וואָרט אין מויל.
A yid fregt:—Ma shemeykhem?	אַ ייִד פֿרעגט: - מה שמיכם?
Git op sholem-aleykhem,	גיט אָפּ שלום עליכם
Un zogt: Hamavdl ben koydesh l'khoyl.	און זאָגט: - המבֿדיל בין קודש לחול.
Redn yidn yidish,	רעדן ייִדן ייִדיש,
Klingt es dokh negidish,	קלינגט עס דאָך נגידיש,
Vayl yidn redn yidish azoy sheyn;	ווײַל ייִדן רעדן ייִדיש אַזוי שיין;
Un vil er makhn kidesh,	און וויל ער מאַכן קידוש,
Makht er es oyf yidish,	מאַכט ער עס אויף ייִדיש,
Voden, oyf goyish? ver vet im farshteyn?	וואָדען אויף גויִש? ווער וועט אים פֿאַרשטיין?
Yidish redt zikh azoy gring,	ייִדיש רעדט זיך אַזוי גרינג,
Yidish leygt zikh oyf der tsing,	ייִדיש לייגט זיך אויף דער צינג,
Yidish redn mames,	ייִדיש רעדן מאַמעס,
Tates, zeydes, babes.	טאַטעס, זיידעס, באָבעס.
Aderabe pruvt oyf goyish	אדרבא פרוווט אויף גויִיש,
Zogt: gut-shabes.	זאָגט: - גוט שבת.
Yidish redt zikh azoy sheyn,	ייִדיש רעדט זיך אַזוי שיין,
Yidish iz dokh mole-kheyn.	ייִדיש איז דאָך מלא חן.
Moykhl avoynes	מוחל עוונות
Di andere leshoynes,	די אַנדערע לשונות
Az yidish redt zikh azoy sheyn!	אַז ייִדיש רעדט זיך אַזוי שיין!

Jews speak Yiddish—what's so remarkable about that? A Jew likes a Yiddish word in his mouth. A Jew asks: How are things with you? He says: "Sholem-aleykhem." When Jews speak Yiddish, it sounds rich, for Jews speak Yiddish so beautifully.

Yiddish sounds so nice. Yiddish rolls off the tongue. Yiddish is spoken by mothers, fathers, grandmothers, and grandfathers. By all means try to say "Good Sabbath" in a foreign tongue. Yiddish sounds so nice, for Yiddish is full of charm. No, thank you, to other languages, since Yiddish sounds so nice!

LID FUN MAYN DOR

לִיד פֿון מײַן דור

Song of My Generation

Poem by Wolf Younin (1908–1984); music by Eli Rubinstein. Received from Sylvia Younin and Mina Bern. Music transcribed by Zalmen Mlotek. The song was in the repertoire of Ben Bonus.

Vos zhe makht ir, gute fraynd, \
Nokh azoy fil yor? \
Oysgehungert bin ikh haynt \
Nokh a varem vort. \
Shikert mikh der nign ayn, \
Der nign fun mayn dor, \
Azoy vi alter, guter vayn \
Un fartraybt di zorg.

וואָס זשע מאַכט איר, גוטע פֿרײַנד, \
נאָך אַזוי פֿיל יאָר? \
אויסגעהונגערט בין איך הײַנט \
נאָך אַ וואַרעם וואָרט. \
שיכּורט מיך דער ניגון אײַן, \
דער ניגון פֿון מײַן דור. \
אַזוי ווי אַלטער, גוטער ווײַן \
און פֿאַרטרײַבט די זאָרג.

Toyznt yor shveb ikh arum \
Tsvishn tog un nakht \
Un zi bagleyt mikh umetum, \
Zi—mayn mames shprakh; \
Oyf yidish zing ikh un ikh shtum, \
Un ikh veyn un lakh, \
Afile ven a shturem kumt \
Un rayst arop mayn dakh.

טויזנט יאָר שוועב איך אַרום \
צווישן טאָג און נאַכט \
און זי באַגלייט מיך אומעטום, \
זי - מײַן מאַמעס שפּראַך; \
אויף ייִדיש זינג איך און איך שטום, \
און איך וויין און לאַך, \
אַפֿילו ווען אַ שטורעם קומט \
און רײַסט אַראָפּ מײַן דאַך.

    Refrain: \
    To—shpil, shpil, Shime-Elye, \
    Shpil mit dayn kapelye, \
    Klezmer getraye, \
    Shpilt zhe biz kayor! \
    Nokh heyser un shneler \
    Fun a tarantele, \
    Shpilt oyf mit fayer \
    Dos lid fun mayn dor!

רעפֿרײַן: \
טאָ - שפּיל, שפּיל שימע-עליע, \
שפּיל מיט דײַן קאַפּעליע, \
קלעזמער געטרײַע, \
שפּילט זשע ביז קאַיאָר! \
נאָך הייסער און שנעלער \
פֿון אַ טאַראַנטעלע, \
שפּילט אויף מיט פֿײַער \
דאָס ליד פֿון מײַן דור!

Flien feygl zalbedrit, \
Royshn shtil vi zayd; \
Feygl, feygl—nemt mikh mit \
In der vayter vayt. \
Vel ikh flien vi ir flit \
Mit volkns bay mayn zayt \
Un zingen oybn dort mayn lid— \
Dos lid fun undzer tsayt.

פֿליִען פֿייגל זאַלבעדריט, \
רוישן שטיל ווי זײַד; \
פֿייגל, פֿייגל - נעמט מיך מיט \
אין דער ווײַטער ווײַט. \
וועל איך פֿליִען ווי איר פֿליט \
מיט וואָלקנס בײַ מײַן זײַט - \
און זינגען אויבן דאָרט מײַן ליד – \
דאָס ליד פֿון אונדזער צײַט.

Mit a finger oyf der shoyb \
Shrayb ikh shtume reyd: \
"Guter bruder—hof un gloyb, \
Fun gold iz undzer keyt!"

מיט אַ פֿינגער אויף דער שויב \
שרײַב איך שטומע רייד: \
"גוטער ברודער - האָף און גלויב, \
פֿון גאָלד איז אונדזער קייט!"

Ze dem zeydns alte boyd
Dort in orbit flit
Mit alts vos er hot ayngekoyft
Far undz oyf dem yarid.

זע דעם זיידנס אַלטע בויד
דאָרט אין אָרביט פֿליט
מיט אַלץ וואָס ער האָט אײַנגעקויפֿט
פֿאַר אונדז אויף דעם יאַריד.

How in the world are you, good friends, after so many years? I'm hungering today for a friendly word. The melody makes me drunk, the melody of my generation, like good old wine, and drives my worries away.

I've been floating around for a thousand years between day and night, and it accompanies me everywhere—it, my mother tongue. I sing in Yiddish and I'm quiet in Yiddish, and I laugh and cry in Yiddish, even when a storm comes and rips off my roof.

So—play, play, Shime Elye, play with your band of faithful musicians. Play till dawn. Even more heated and faster than a a tarantella, play the song of my generation with fire!

Birds fly in groups of three, make quiet sounds like the rustling of silk. Birds, birds, take me along on your distant journey. I'll fly as you do, with clouds at my side, and I'll sing there, up above—the song of my generation.

With a finger on the windowpane, I write silent words: "Good brother, hope and believe. Our chain is made of gold!" See how grandfather's covered wagon is flying there in orbit, with everything he bought for us at the market.

ZING SHTIL!
SONGS IN A QUIET AND REFLECTIVE MOOD

זינג שטיל!

LEYG DAYN KOP   לייג דײַן קאָפּ

Lay Your Head

Words by H. Leivick (1888–1962). The melody by L. Birnov, which was recorded by cantor Misha Alexandrovich, was transcribed by compilers. Another melody to the poem was written by American Yiddish composer Solomon Golub.

Leyg dayn kop oyf mayne kni, Gut azoy tsu lign; Kinder shlofn ayn aleyn, Groyse darf men vign.	לייג דײַן קאָפּ אויף מײַנע קני, גוט אַזוי צו ליגן; קינדער שלאָפֿן אײַן אַליין, גרויסע דאַרף מען וויגן.
Kinder hobn shpilekhlekh,— Shpiln ven zey viln; Groyse shpiln nor mit zikh, Muzn eybik shpiln.	קינדער האָבן שפּילעכלעך, - שפּילן ווען זיי ווילן: גרויסע שפּילן נאָר מיט זיך, מוזן אייביק שפּילן.
Hob nit moyre—ikh bin do, Kh'vel dir nit farshtoysn; Host genug geveynt shoyn haynt, Vi es past a groysn.	האָב ניט מורא - איך בין דאָ כ׳וועל דיר ניט פֿאַרשטויסן; האָסט גענוג געוויינט שוין הײַנט, ווי עס פּאַסט אַ גרויסן.
Ongeveynt un ongeklogt— Kh'vel dir itst farvign; Leyg dayn kop oyf mayne kni, Gut azoy tsu lign.	אָנגעוויינט און אָנגעקלאָגט - כ׳וועל דיר איצט פֿאַרוויגן; לייג דײַן קאָפּ אויף מײַנע קני, גוט אַזוי צו ליגן.

Lay your head upon my knees, it's good to lie that way. Children fall asleep themselves, grown-ups must be rocked.

Children have their little toys, and play whenever they will. Grown-ups play by themselves, and must always play.

Have no fear, for I am here. I won't push you away. You have wept enough today, as a grown-up must.

You have wept and cried, now I will rock you. Lay your head upon my knees, it's good to lie that way.

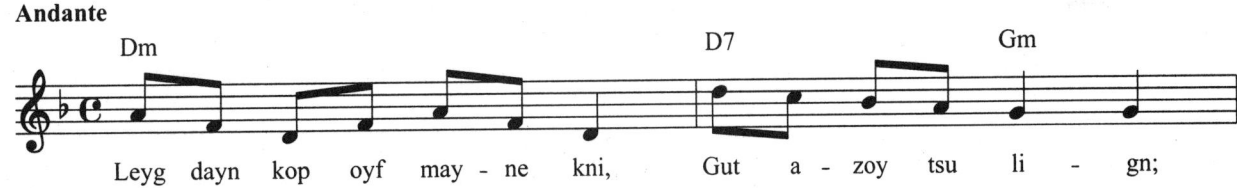

MIT FARMAKHTE OYGN   מיט פֿאַרמאַכטע אויגן

When Your Eyes Are Closed

Words by Itsik Manger (1901–1969); music by N. Hirsh. Transcribed by the compilers from a recording of Khave Alberstein on the record "Poems and Songs by Itzik Manger," CBS 52568.

Mit farmakhte oygn
Herstu nenter dem yam.
Mit fiberndike finger
Filstu gringer dem gram.

Di goldene pave
Derkenstu in fli.
Un a benkshaft vert shener
Ven zi iz fun nisht-hi.

Di midkeyt vert mider
Bay der shvel fun a hoyz,
Ven du knist, filstu sharfer
Az got iz groys.

Got kavikhol iz groys,
Haynt punkt vi a mol.
Nisht vayl er dunert in himl,
Nor vayl er khlipet in tol.

Az voyl iz tsu dem
Vos hot dos khlipen derhert,
Dir iz aza herung
Gevezn bashert.

Un a trer iz gefaln
In dayn gemit,
Un mit vund un mit vunder
Zikh tseblit in dayn lid.

מיט פֿאַרמאַכטע אויגן
הערסטו נענטער דעם ים.
מיט פֿיבערנדיקע פֿינגער
פֿילסטו גרינגער דעם גראַם.

די גאָלדענע פֿאַווע
דערקענסטו אין פֿלי.
און אַ בענקשאַפֿט ווערט שענער
ווען זי איז פֿון נישט-הי.

די מידקייט ווערט מידער
בײַ דער שוועל פֿון אַ הויז,
ווען דו קניסט פֿילסטו שאַרפֿער
אַז גאָט איז גרויס.

גאָט כּבֿיכול איז גרויס,
הײַנט פּונקט ווי אַ מאָל.
נישט ווײַל ער דונערט אין הימל,
נאָר ווײַל ער כליפּעט אין טאָל.

אַז וווֹיל איז צו דעם
וואָס האָט דאָס כליפּען דערהערט,
דיר איז אַזאַ הערונג
געוועזן באַשערט.

און אַ טרער איז געפֿאַלן
אין דײַן געמיט,
און מיט וווּנד און מיט ווונדער
זיך צעבליט אין דײַן ליד.

When your eyes are closed, you hear the sea is closer. With agitated fingers you feel the rhythm more clearly.

The golden peacock you recognize in its flight, And a longing becomes dearer when it comes from an absent one.

The weariness grows more weary at the threshold of a house. When you kneel, you feel more strongly the greatness of God.

The God of the Universe is great, today just as in the past, not for His thunder in the sky, but for His sobbing in the dale.

For blessed is the man who heard this sobbing. You were destined to hear it.

And a tear fell in your spirit, and you nursed it well and long. And with wounds and wonder it blossomed into song.

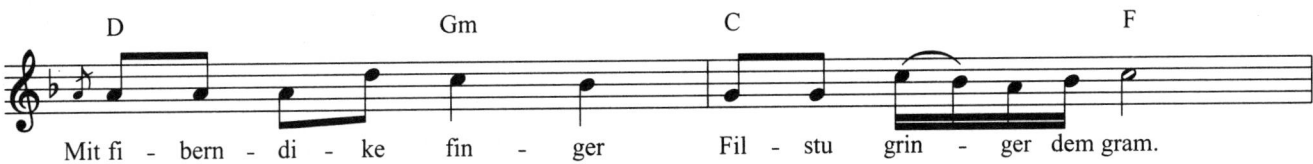

DI BERYOZKELE

די בעריאָזקעלע

The Birch Tree

Words by David Einhorn (1886–1973); published by M. Kipnis in 1918. The song was popular in Poland in the 1930's. It is a favorite in the repertoire of Soviet Yiddish singer Emil Gorovets.

Ruik, ruik, shoklt ir gelokte, grine kepl
Mayn vaysinke beryozkele un davnt on a shir,
Yedes, yedes bletele irs sheptshet shtil a tfile...
Zay shoyn, kleyn beryozkele, mispalel oykh far mir!.

Ikh bin do an elnter gekumen fun der vaytn,
Fremd iz mir der got fun dan un fremd iz mir zayn shprakh,
Nisht er vet mayn troyer zen un nisht farshteyn mayn tfile,
Khotsh ikh vel mispalel zayn, mispalel zayn a sakh.

Fun dem vaytn mayrev hot zikh troyerik farganvet
In di dine tsvaygelekh a rozer, tsarter shtral
Un a laykhtn kush geton di bletlekh, di kleyne,
Velkhe hobn, dremlendik, gehorkht dem nakhtigal.

Fun di breyte felder iz a vintele gekumen
Un dertseylt di bletlekh legendn on a shir...
Epes hot in hartsn tif bay mir genumen benken:
Zay shoyn, kleyn beryozkele, mispalel oykh far mir!...

רויִק, רויִק, שאָקלט איר געלאָקטע, גרינע קעפל
מײַן ווײַסינקע בעריאָזקעלע און דאַוונט אָן אַ שיעור,
יעדעס, יעדעס בלעטעלע אירס שעפטשעט שטיל אַ תּפילה
זײַ שוין, קליין בעריאָזקעלע, מתפּלל אויך פֿאַר מיר!...

איך בין דאָ אַן עלנטער געקומען פֿון דער ווײַטן,
פֿרעמד איז מיר דער גאָט פֿון דאַן און פֿרעמד איז מיר זײַן שפּראַך,
נישט ער וועט מײַן טרויער זען און נישט פֿאַרשטיין מײַן תּפילה,
כאָטש איך וועל מתפּלל זײַן, מתפּלל זײַן אַ סך.

פֿון דעם ווײַטן מערבֿ האָט זיך טרויעריק פֿאַרגנבֿעט
אין די דינע צווײַגעלעך אַ ראָזער, צאַרטער שטראַל,
און אַ לײַכטן קוש געטאָן די בלעטלעך, די קליינע,
וועלכע האָבן, דרעמלענדיק, געהאָרכט דעם נאַכטיגאַל.

פֿון די ברייטע פֿעלדער איז אַ ווינטעלע געקומען
און דערציילט די בלעטלעך לעגענדן אָן אַ שיעור,
עפּעס האָט אין האַרצן טיף בײַ מיר גענומען בענקען:
זײַ שוין, קליין בעריאָזקעלע, מתפּלל אויך פֿאַר מיר!...

Softly, softly my little white birch tree shakes her curly green head, praying without end. Her every leaf whispers a prayer. Pray, little birch tree, pray too for me. I've come here alone, from far away. Strange to me your God from here, and strange His tongue. He will not see my sorrow, nor understand my words, even though I'll pray so much to Him.

From the distant West, a soft red ray of sun has stolen sadly into your thin branches, and lightly kissed your little leaves—dreamily listening to the nightingale. From the broad fields came a breeze that told countless legends to the tree. Something deep in my heart began to yearn. Pray, little birch tree, pray too for me.

Ru - ik, ru - ik sho - klt ir ge - lok - te gri - ne

ke - pl, Mayn vay - sin - ke ber - yoz - ke - le un da - vnt on a shir.

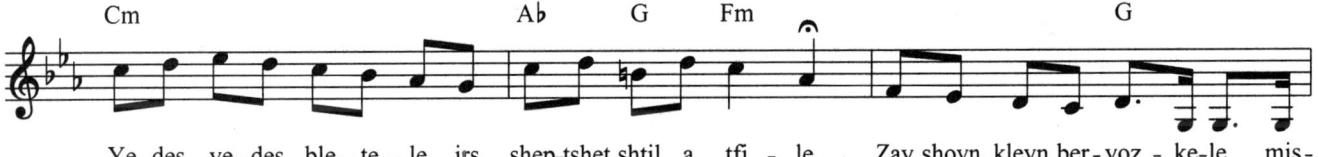
Ye - des, ye - des, ble - te - le irs shep-tshet shtil a tfi - le, Zay shoyn, kleyn ber - yoz - ke - le, mis-

pa - lel oykh far mir, Zay shoyn, kleyn ber - yoz - ke - le, mis - pa - lel oykh far mir.

IKH UN DI VELT

איך און די וועלט

The World and I

Poem by Abraham Reisen (1875–1953); melodies by Maurice Rauch (1910–1944) and Sidor Belarsky (1900–1975) are both presented.

Ven di gantse velt volt laydn,	ווען די גאַנצע וועלט וואָלט לײַדן,
Mir aleyn zol gut zayn bloyz,	מיר אַליין זאָל גוט זײַן בלויז,
Volt ikh dan di velt di gantse	וואָלט איך דאַן די וועלט די גאַנצע
Ayngeladn in mayn hoyz.	אײַנגעלאַדן אין מײַן הויז.
Ikh volt treystn zi un tsertlen	איך וואָלט טרייסטן זי און צערטלען
Un gezogt: Nit zorg zikh, velt!	און געזאָגט: – ניט זאָרג זיך, וועלט!
Biz zi volt tsu zikh gekumen	ביז זי וואָלט צו זיך געקומען
Un zikh oyf di fis geshtelt.	און זיך אויף די פֿיס געשטעלט.
Ven di velt geven volt gliklekh,	ווען די וועלט געווען וואָלט גליקלעך,
Ikh aleyn bloyz ful mit leyd,	איך אַליין בלויז פֿול מיט לייד,
Volt ikh dan tsu ir gekumen	וואָלט איך דאַן צו איר געקומען
Un gefodert: Gib mir freyd!	און געפֿאָדערט: – גיב מיר פֿרייד!
Ober az mir laydn beyde,	אָבער אַז מיר לײַדן ביידע,
I di velt i ikh aleyn,	אי די וועלט אי איך אַליין,
Hot di velt nit vu tsu kumen	האָט די וועלט ניט ווו צו קומען
Un ikh hob nit vu tsu geyn.	און איך האָב ניט ווו צו גיין.

If the whole world were suffering and things were good only for me, I would invite the whole world to my house. I would comfort and caress it, and say: Don't worry, world! Till it recovered and got back on its feet. If the world were happy and only I were suffering, I would go to it and demand: Give me happiness! But since both of us are suffering, the world and I, the world has no one to go to and neither do I.

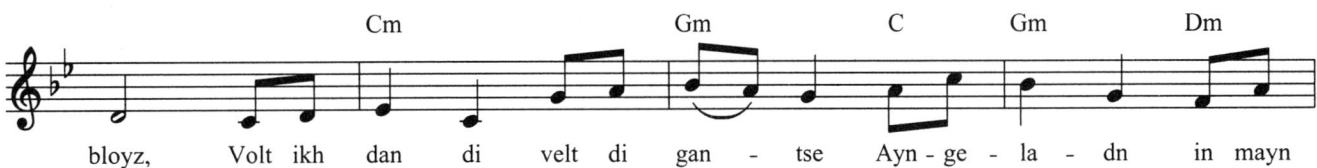

ALEYN IN VEG / אַליין אין וועג

I Walk Out Alone Onto the Road

Poem by M. Lermontov (1814–1841): "Vikhazhu odin ya na dorogu" was translated by Abraham Reisen (1875–1953), music by E. Sashin. Published in sheet music by Joseph P. Katz in 1915. Numerous Yiddish translations of the Russian poem were printed in the *Perl*. The song was parodied by D. Apotheker in *Di yidishe bine*, N. Y., 1897: "Di shlekhte tsaytn" (The Hard Times) about the depression. Also Abraham Goldfaden's song "Shtil un fintster iz di nakht in droysn" was contrafacted to the melody of *Vikhazhu* (printed in Sholem Aleichem's *Di yidishe folks-biblyotek*, 1891).

Kh'gey aroys aleyn in veg in breytn,   כ׳גיי אַרויס אַליין אין וועג אין ברייטן,
S'glantst der veg durkh dinem nepl-shtoyb,   ס׳גלאַנצט דער וועג דורך דינעם נעפּל-שטויב,
Shtil di nakht, der midber hert got reydn,   שטיל די נאַכט, דער מידבר הערט גאָט ריידן,
Un di shtern zingen got a loyb.   און די שטערן זינגען גאָט אַ לויב.

Oyfn himl—vunderlekh un herlekh...   אויפֿן הימל - וווּנדערלעך און הערלעך...
S'rut di erd in bloen shayn gehilt.   ס׳רוט די ערד אין בלויען שײַן געהילט.
Vos zhe iz mir azoy bang un shverlekh?   וואָס זשע איז מיר אַזוי באַנג און שווערלעך?
Vart ikh, vos? Tsi hob ikh vos farshpilt?   וואַרט איך, וואָס? צי האָב איך וואָס פֿאַרשפּילט?

Neyn! Ikh vart fun lebn gornisht vayter,   ניין! איך וואַרט פֿון לעבן גאָרנישט ווײַטער,
Un der nekhtn art mikh oykh nisht fil—   און דער נעכטן אַרט מיך אויך נישט פֿיל -
Kh'zukh nor ru, vern a bafrayter   כ׳זוך נאָר רו, ווערן אַ באַפֿרײַטער
Lozn alts, antshlosn vern shtil...   לאָזן אַלץ, אַנטשלאָסן ווערן שטיל...

Nit mit yenem kaltn shlof fun keyver—   ניט מיט יענעם קאַלטן שלאָף פֿון קבֿר -
Eybik shlofn volt ikh hobn lust,   אייביק שלאָפֿן וואָלט איך האָבן לוסט,
Shlogn zol mit lebn yeder eyver,   שלאָגן זאָל מיט לעבן יעדער אבֿר,
Otemdik zikh heybn zol di brust.   אָטעמדיק זיך הייבן זאָל די ברוסט.

Tog un nakht ikh hern zol zikh tsien   טאָג און נאַכט איך הערן זאָל זיך ציִען
A gezang fun libe on a shir;   אַ געזאַנג פֿון ליבע אָן אַ שיעור;
Un a demb zol eybik grinen, blien,   און אַ דעמב זאָל אייביק גרינען, בליִען,
Beygn zikh un royshn iber mir...   בייגן זיך און רוישן איבער מיר...

I walk out alone onto the broad road. The road shines with a thin fog. The night is still, the desert hears God talking, and the stars sing a paean to God.

In the sky, wonderful and lofty, the earth rests, enveloped in the blue glow. Why, then, do I feel so sad and heavy of heart? Am I waiting perhaps? Have I wasted some opportunity?

No! I expect nothing further from life, and yesterday doesn't bother me much either. I seek only rest when I shall be free to leave everything behind and finally grow still.

Not with that cold sleep of the grave—I would gladly sleep forever. Let every limb pulsate with life, let my breast heave with breath.

Day and night let me hear them singing an endless love song, and let an oak tree grow green and bloom forever, and bend low and rustle over me.

FREGT DI VELT AN ALTE KASHE

פֿרעגט די וועלט אַן אַלטע קשיא

The World Asks an Ancient Question

    Folksong. Published by the St. Petersburg Society for Jewish Folk Music in 1909, in the arrangement of Ephraim Shkliar; also by Henry Lefkowitch in this country in 1915. The interpretation of the vocables expresses the meaning of the question and reply. The song entitled "L'enigme eternelle" was treated to an artistic setting for voice and orchestra by Maurice Ravel in: "Deux melodies hebraiques." In her book *Vagabond Stars* Nahma Sandrow cites the singing of the motif by the famous Soviet Jewish actor and director Solomon Michoels: "In the last month of 1939, in the face of [this] oncoming destruction and in symbolic resistance to it, Mikhoels played perhaps his greatest role, in a play commemorating Sholem Aleichem's eightieth birthday. . . A motif for the production was the folk melody that Tevye hummed as he left the town: 'Fregt di velt an alte kashe'. . ."

Fregt di velt an alte kashe:
Trala-tradi-ri-di-rom?
Entfert men: tradi-ridi-reylom,
Oy, oy, tradi-ridi-rom!
Un az me vil, ken men dokh zogn: tray-dim!
Blaybt dokh vider di alte kashe:
Trala-tradi-ri-di-rom?

פֿרעגט די וועלט אַן אַלטע קשיא:
טראַלאַ־טראַדי־רי־די־ראָם?
ענטפֿערט מען: טראַדי־רידי־רײלאָם,
אױ, אױ, טראַדי־רידי־ראָם!
און אַז מע װיל, קען מען דאָך זאָגן: טרײ־דים!
בלײבט דאָך װידער די אַלטע קשיא:
טראַלאַ־טראַדי־רי־די־ראָם?

    The world asks an ancient question: Trala-tradi-ridi-rom? The answer is: tradi-ridi-reylom, oy, oy, tradi-ridi-rom.

    And if you want, you can even say: tray-dim! Still the ancient question remains: Trala-tradi-ridi-rom?

DOS GOLDENE LAND
THE GOLDEN LAND

דאָס גאָלדענע לאַנד

LOZT ARAYN!

Let Us In!

Words by M. Jaffee, music by Joseph Rumshinsky (1881–1956). Transcribed by the compilers from a recording of Aaron Lebedeff, 1928. The song was revived in the musical *The Golden Land*.

A yunger tate ayngeboygn,
In elis-ayland, vind un vey,
Tsvey kinder kleyne hot er dertsoygn,
Yesoymim beyde zaynen zey.

Di mame hobn zey farloyrn,
Un ahergekumen mit groys mi;
Farshlosn iz far zey di toyern,
Dem tatn lozt men tsu zey nit tsi (tsu).

Tsebrokhn, tserisn,
On gevisn
Vern hertser do far der tir;
Oy, yidn, trern,
Shoyn tsayt zolst hern—
Di gantse velt shrayt yetst tsu dir:

Lozt arayn, lozt arayn!
Hot nit keyn hertser fun shteyn.
Efnt di toyern fun dem goldn land,
Ir zet mentshn faln, shtrekt oys zey a hant!
Lozt arayn, lozt arayn!
Tsebrekht nit keyn hertser, o neyn.
Di gantse velt mentshn
Vet aykh derfar bentshn,
Di toyern makht oyf
Un lozt undz arayn!

A young father, bent over, on Ellis Island, woeful and sad—two little children he raised, both of them orphans. They've lost their mother and have come here with great effort. The gates are closed to them—their father is not allowed to go to them.

Broken, torn apart, without conscience—that's what hearts become here at the door. Oh Jews, in tears cry out: It's time you heard. The whole world cries out to you:

Let us in, let us in! Don't have hearts of stone. Open the gates of the golden land. You see people falling—stretch out your hand. Let us in, let us in! Don't break our hearts, oh no! The whole world will bless you for it. Open the gates and let us in!

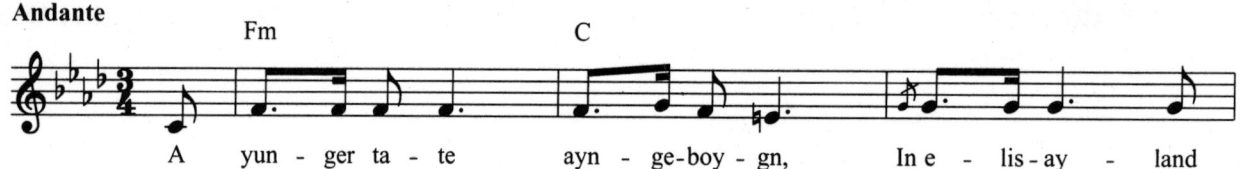

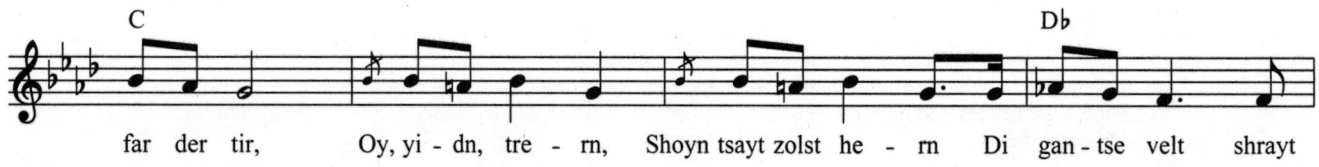
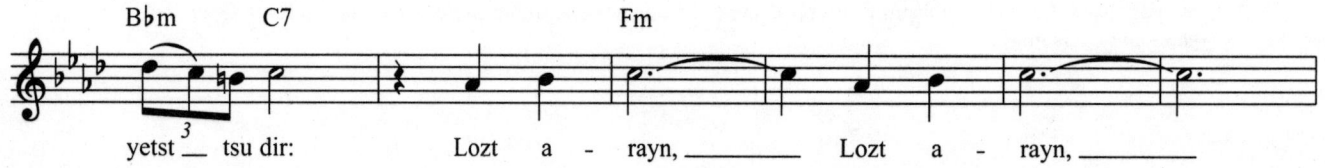

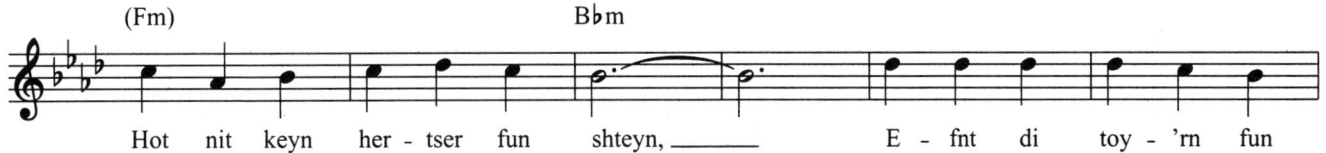

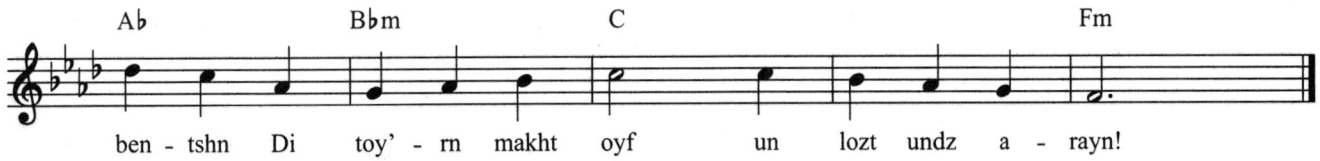

TUNKL BRENT A FAYER

טונקל ברענט אַ פֿײַער

A Fire Burns Dimly

Song of an *agune* (deserted wife) was submitted to the *Perl* by Jacob Gorelik. The music of the song is found among the manuscripts of YIVO's pre-war Ethnographic Committee in Vilna. Another version by Sara Benjamin was also cited in which the wife is told that her husband in America has married another woman. Other *agune* songs were treated by compiler in her paper, "America in East European Yiddish Folksong," 1954.

Tunkl brent a fayer
In shtiln tsorn, blas,
An umet oyf der hayzl,
An umet oyfn gas.

Der vint, der vint, der beyzer,
Er rayst mit beyz gefil;
Do klapt imer shtarker,
Do klapt imer shtil.

- Gut-ovnt, shvester Dvoyre,
Mayn kumen iz nit gut.
Dayn man fun amerike
Shikt dir op a get.

Er vil dikh nit kenen,
Er vil dikh nit visn;
Dayn man fun amerike
Shikt dir op a get.

טונקל ברענט אַ פֿײַער
אין שטילן צאָרן, בלאַס,
אַן אומעט אויף דער הײַזל,
אַן אומעט אויפֿן גאַס.

דער ווינט, דער ווינט, דער בייזער,
ער רײַסט מיט בייז געפֿיל;
דאָ קלאַפּט אימער שטאַרקער,
דאָ קלאַפּט אימער שטיל.

- גוט אָוונט, שוועסטער דבֿורה,
מײַן קומען איז ניט גוט,
דײַן מאַן פֿון אַמעריקע
שיקט דיר אָפּ אַ גט.

ער וויל דיך ניט קענען,
ער וויל דיך ניט וויסן;
דײַן מאַן פֿון אַמעריקע
שיקט דיר אָפּ אַ גט.

Andante

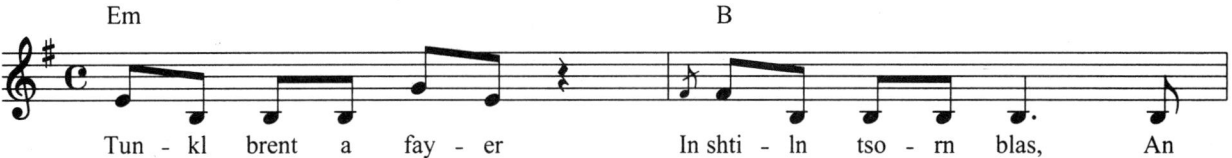
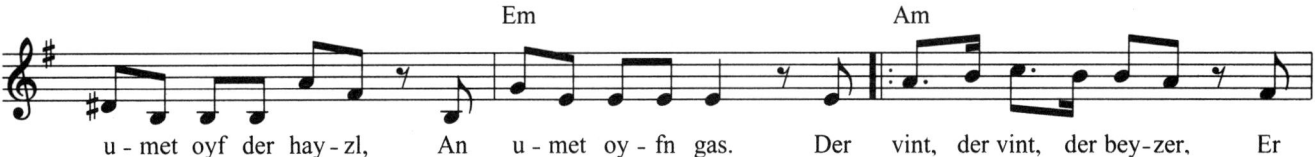

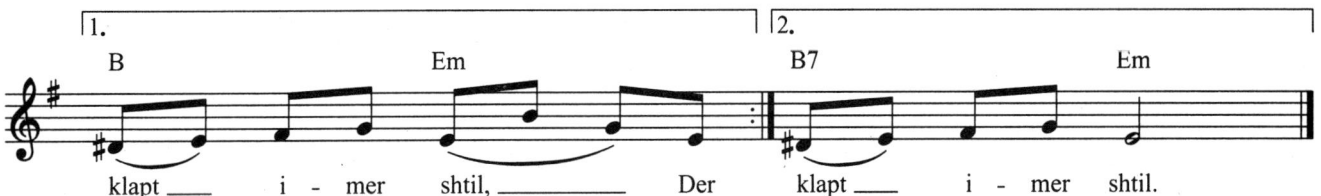

A fire burns dimly, in silent rage, white. Sorrow lies upon the house and there is sorrow in the street. The wind, the angry wind—it tears at us with angry feeling. Here it blows strongly, here it blows quietly.

Good evening, sister Deborah—my coming is not good. Your husband sends from America a divorce for you. He doesn't want to know you, he doesn't want to see you. Your husband from America is sending you a divorce.

VU NEMT MEN PARNOSE? ווו נעמט מען פרנסה?

How Can I Make a Living?

Words and music by David Meyerowitz (1867–1943), published in 1934. In her book about the Lodz Ghetto, Gila Flam cites a song "It's Shackles and Chains" with the opening melody of this song. A parody by Ruvn Lipshitz about the DP camp appears in his book *Lebedik amkho* (Bergen Belsen, 1946). The song was revived in the musical *The Golden Land* by Joanne Borts.

Mentshn, git an eytse mir,
Un ratevet oyf gikh!
Danken vel ikh aykh dafir,
Ikh ken nit helfn zikh.
Di tsayt iz biter, zeyer shlekht,
Dos lebn geyt nit ayn,
S'iz yoysherdik, nit mer vi rekht,
Ir zolt bahilfik zayn.

Refrain:
Vu nemt men parnose?
Vu nemt men parnose?
S'iz shver tsu zukhn un gefinen,
Keyner git nit tsu fardinen.
Vu nemt men parnose?
Nit nor ikh, kemat vi ale
Fregn yetst di zelbe shayle:
Vu, vu nemt men, oy,
Vu nemt men parnose?

Ikh veys as di "en-ar-ey" *
Zogt mir: hof un vart,
Do hungert mikh az ikh dergey,
Der mogn vert fardart.
Men zogt az der "depreshon
Vet batsoln mit protsent.
Nor dem bloyen foygl ken ikh nit esn,
Un der lendlord mont nokh rent.

---

* NRA

People, give me some advice, and rescue me quickly! I'll thank you for it—I can't help myself. The times are bitter, very bad; life's not going well. It's only just, no more than right, that you should be helpful.

How can I make a living? It's hard to seek and find. No one gives me a job.

How can I make a living? Not just I—almost everyone now asks the same question: How can I make a living?

I know the NRA tells me: Hope and wait—Here I'm starving to death, my belly is getting thin. They say the depression will repay us with interest, but I can't eat the blue bird and the landlord still demands rent.

A GRUS FUN DI "TRENTSHES"

אַ גרוס פֿון די "טרענטשעס"

Regards from the Trenches

Song about the first World War, words and music by Isidor Lillian (1882–1960), published in 1918. The second stanza speaks of fighting for a Jewish homeland. The song was revived in the musical *The Golden Land*.

Ikh halt in hant a briv,	איך האַלט אין האַנט אַ בריוו,
Ikh hob dem briv gekrign haynt,	איך האָב דעם בריוו געקריגן הײַנט,
Der briv iz zeyer vikhtik	דער בריוו איז זייער וויכטיק
Un oykh zeyer interesant.	און אויך זייער אינטערעסאַנט.
In dem briv gelezn hob ikh	אין דעם בריוו געלעזן האָב איך
Gute nays a sakh,	גוטע נײַס אַ סך,
Un take in dem zelbn briv	און טאַקע אין דעם זעלבן בריוו
Iz do a grus far aykh.	איז דאָ אַ גרוס פֿאַר אײַך.

Refrain: / **רעפֿרײן:**

Ikh breng aykh a grus fun di "trentshes"*	איך ברענג אײַך אַ גרוס פֿון די "טרענטשעס,"
Ikh breng aykh a grus fun di "boys,"	איך ברענג אײַך אַ גרוס פֿון די "בויס,"
Zey kemfn mit mut,	זיי קעמפֿן מיט מוט,
Mit kurazh un mit blut,	מיט קוראַזש און מיט בלוט
Un fun di daytshn lakhn zey zikh oys.	און פֿון די דײַטשן לאַכן זיי זיך אויס.
Ikh breng aykh a grus fun di "Sammys,"—	איך ברענג אײַך אַ גרוס פֿון די "סעמיס,"
Dos iz der grus, dos zogn zey:	דאָס איז דער גרוס, דאָס זאָגן זיי:
Oyb mir zenen shoyn derinen,	אויב מיר זענען שוין דערינען,
Muzn mir di shlakht gevinen	מוזן מיר די שלאַכט געווינען
Iz der grus fun "Uncle Sam's" armey.	איז דער גרוס פֿון "אָנקל סעמס" אַרמיי.

S'iz do a shtikl hofnung,	ס'איז דאָ אַ שטיקל האָפֿנונג,
Es shaynt a shtral fun glik,	עס שײַנט אַ שטראַל פֿון גליק,
Es halt derbay, mir zoln krign	עס האַלט דערבײַ, מיר זאָלן קריגן
Undzer land tsurik.	אונדזער לאַנד צוריק,
Es grindet zikh in yedn land	עס גרינדעט זיך אין יעדן לאַנד
A yidishe legyon,	אַ ייִדישע לעגיאָן,
Zey geyen un kemfn far der heym	זיי גייען און קעמפֿן פֿאַר דער היים
Fun undzer natsyon.	פֿון אונדזער נאַציאָן.

Refrain: / **רעפֿרײן:**

Ikh breng aykh a grus fun di "trentshes,"	איך ברענג אײַך אַ גרוס פֿון די "טרענטשעס,"
Ikh breng aykh a grus fun di "boys,"	איך ברענג אײַך אַ גרוס פֿון די "בויס,"
Dos yidishe blit**	דאָס ייִדישע בליט (בלוט)
Un dos pintele yid,	און דאָס פּינטעלע ייִד,
Es flakert nokh atsind,	עס פֿלאַקערט נאָך אַצינד,
Es lesht nit oys.	עס לעשט ניט אויס.
A grus fun di yidishe heldn,	אַ גרוס פֿון די ייִדישע העלדן,
Dos iz der grus, dos zogn zey:	דאָס איז דער גרוס, דאָס זאָגן זיי:
Undzer alte heym banayen,	אונדזער אַלטע היים באַנײַען,
Undzer heylik land bafrayen,	אונדזער הייליק לאַנד באַפֿרײַען,
Lebn zol di yidishe armey!	לעבן זאָל די ייִדישע אַרמיי!

---

* trenches
** blut

I hold in my hand a letter—I received it today. The letter is very important and also very interesting. In the letter I read a lot of good news, and in the same letter there are regards for you.

I bring you regards from the trenches, I bring you regards from the boys. They're fighting bravely, with courage and with blood, and they laugh at the Germans. I bring you regards from the G.I.'s. This is their greeting, here's what they say: As long as we're in it, we must win the battle. That's the greeting from Uncle Sam's army.

There is some hope—a ray of happiness is shining. We're at the point of getting our country back. In every country they're establishing a Jewish Legion. They going to fight for the homeland of our nation.

I bring you regards from the trenches, I bring you regards from the boys. The Jewish blood and the core of Jewishness—it's still flaring up now, it's not being extinguished. Regards from the Jewish heroes. This is their greeting, here's what they say: To renew our ancient home, to free our holy land—long live the Jewish army!

Hu-Tsa-Tsa

Words and music by Fishl Kanapoff, printed in 1924. The song was adapted in the musical *The Golden Land* where it was sung by actor Bruce Adler.

Ikh zing far aykh yetst a lid,	איך זינג פֿאַר אײַך יעצט אַ ליד,
Hu-tsa-tsa, hu-tsa-tsa,	הו צאַ צאַ, הו צאַ צאַ.
Ikh gleyb dos lidl iz zeyer git*,	איך גלייב דאָס לידל איז זייער גיט (גוט),
Hu-tsa-tsa, hu-tsa-tsa.	הו צאַ צאַ, הו צאַ צאַ.
Oyb dos lid vet aykh gefeln,	אויב דאָס ליד וועט אײַך געפֿעלן,
Hu-tsa-tsa, hu-tsa-tsa,	הו צאַ־צאַ, הו צאַ צאַ.
Vel ikh aykh tsufridn shteln.	וועל איך אײַך צופֿרידן שטעלן,
Hu-tsa-tsa, hu-tsa-tsa.	הו צאַ־צאַ, הו צאַ צאַ.
A griner kumt in land arayn,	אַ גרינער קומט אין לאַנד אַרײַן,
Vert er bald a "singlman"—	ווערט ער באַלד אַ ,,סינגלמאַן;''
Koym krigt er nor a shtikl "dzhab,"**	קוים קריגט ער נאָר אַ שטיקל ,,דזשאַב,''
Fargest er in der heym dos vayb.	פֿאַרגעסט ער אין דער היים דאָס ווײַב.
In a restoran bin ikh arayn,	אין אַ רעסטאָראַן בין איך אַרײַן,
Ikh hob gegesn zeyer fayn.	איך האָב געגעסן זייער פֿײַן;
Dos esn hot mir gut geshmekt,	דאָס עסן האָט מיר גוט געשמעקט,
Bay nakht hot dos mikh oyfgevekt.	בײַ נאַכט האָט דאָס מיך אויפֿגעוועקט.
Mayn shkheyne zogt zi hot mir lib,	מײַן שכנה זאָגט זי האָט מיר ליב,
Ikh kum arayn tsu ir in shtib***,	איך קום אַרײַן צו איר אין שטיב (שטוב);
Zi hot mikh fayn oyfgenumen,	זי האָט מיך פֿײַן אויפֿגענומען,
Iz der man in mitn ongekumen.	איז דער מאַן אין מיטן אָנגעקומען.
"Prohibishon" iz yetst shtark in kraft,	,,פּראָהיבישאָן'' איז יעצט שטאַרק אין קראַפֿט,
Dos trinken hot men opgeshaft,	דאָס טרינקען האָט מען אָפּגעשאַפֿט;
Shpor ikh mir fil gelt ayn,	שפּאָר איך מיר פֿיל געלט אײַן,
Ikh makh mir bronfn, ikh makh mir vayn.	איך מאַך מיר בראָנפֿן, איך מאַך מיר ווײַן.
Oyf a khasene bin ikh geven,	אויף אַ חתונה בין איך געווען,
Amuzirt zikh zeyer sheyn,	אַמוזירט זיך זייער שיין;
A mitsve-tentsl tantsn ale,	אַ מיצווה-טענצל טאַנצן אַלע,
Un ikh tants mit der kale.	און איך טאַנץ מיט דער כּלה.

---
* gut
** job
*** shtub

Dos "smukn" kost do zeyer tayer,	דאָס "סמוקן" קאָסט דאָ זייער טײַער,
Farbren ikh nit di gelt in fayer,	פֿאַרברען איך ניט די געלט אין פֿײַער;
Ikh zits mir oyf dem "ruf" gants hoykh	איך זיץ מיר אויף דעם "רוף" גאַנץ הויך,
Un tsi fun dem koymen umzist dem roykh.	און צי פֿון דעם קוימען אומזיסט דעם רויך.

Geendikt hob ikh shoyn mayn lid,	געענדיקט האָב איך שוין מײַן ליד,
Un oyb es makht aykh apetit,	און אויב עס מאַכט אײַך אַפּעטיט,
Oyb dos lidl iz mir gelingen,	אויב דאָס לידל איז מיר געלינגען (געלונגען),
Kent ir ale mit mir mitzingen.	קענט איר אַלע מיט מיר מיטזינגען.

I'll sing a song for you now—Hu-tsa-tsa, Hu-tsa-tsa. I think the song is very good—Hu-tsa-tsa, Hu-tsa-tsa. If the song pleases you, Hu-tsa-tsa, Hu-tsa-tsa, I will be satisfied. Hu-tsa-tsa, Hu-tsa-tsa.

A new immigrant enters the land. Right away he becomes a "single" man. No sooner has he gotten some sort of job, than he forgets his wife in the old country.

I went into a restaurant and ate very well. The food tasted good to me—at night it woke me up...

My neighbor says she loves me—I go into her house. She receives me very well, but her husband arrives in the middle of things.

Prohibition is now in force—drinking has been abolished. It saves me a lot of money—I make my own whiskey and wine.

I went to a wedding and had a very good time. Everyone danced a *mitsve* dance, and I danced with the bride.

Smoking is very expensive here, so I don't burn up my money in fire. I sit on the roof, way up high, and inhale the smoke from the chimney for nothing.

Now my song is finished, and if it gave you an appetite; if the song was successful, you may all sing with me.

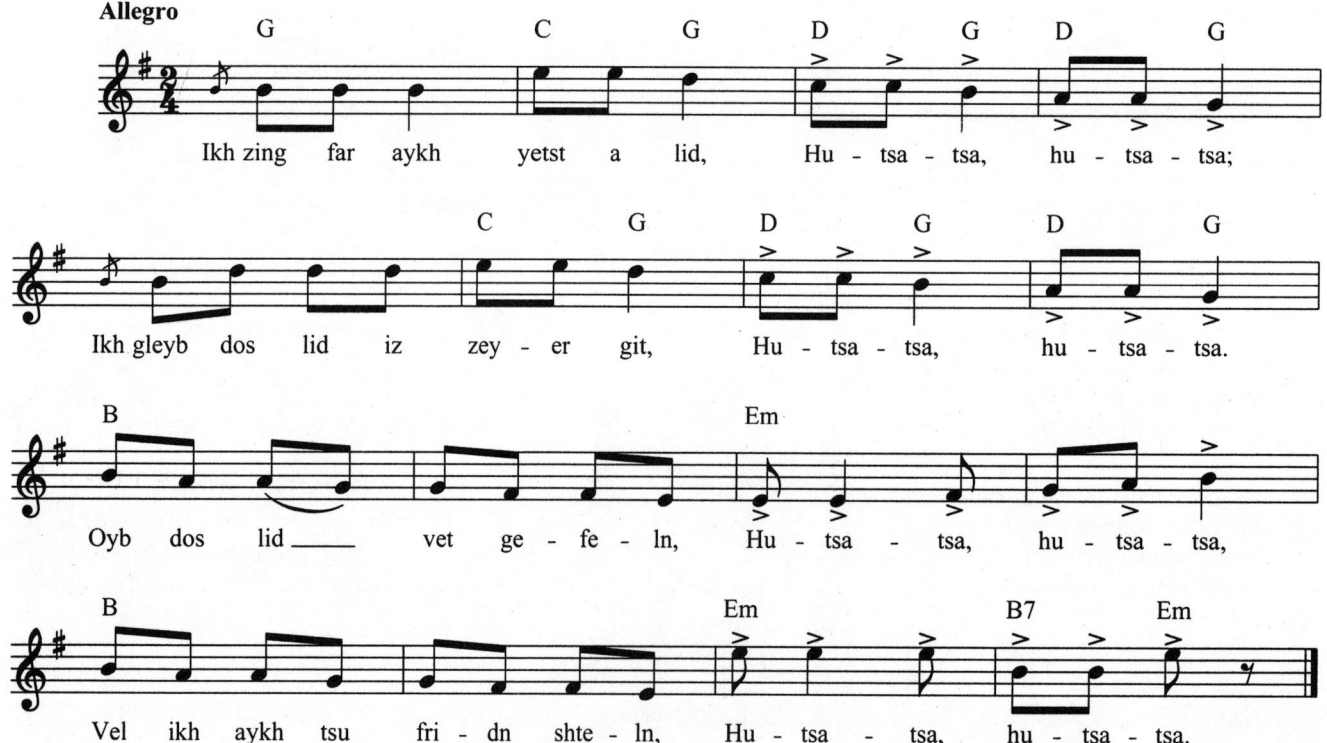

Levine and His Flying Machine

LEVIN MIT ZAYN "FLYING" MASHIN

לעווין מיט זײַן "פֿלײַינג מאַשין"

In 1927 Charles A. Levine, an American Jew, flew with pilot Clarence Chamberlin across the Atlantic to land outside Berlin, thus beating Charles Lindbergh's distance record. A number of songs acknowledging this feat were published, at least two in Yiddish.

This song is in Yiddish and English. Yiddish words by Joseph Tanzman, English words by Saul Bernie, music by Sam Coslow. Published in sheet music by Spier and Coslow, Inc., 1927. The English words of the refrain are:

"Levine! Levine!/ You're the hero of your race,/ Levine, Levine,/ You're the greatest Hebrew ace./ We got a thrill when Chamberlin flew,/ But you were right there too,/ We're proud of you!/ Levine, Levine,/ Just an ordinary name,/ But you brought it everlasting fame,/ We welcome you home!/ From over the foam,/ Levine with your Flying Machine!" Words of the song appear in Mark Slobin's *Tenement Songs*. It was introduced by Henry Saposnik on the *Kapelye* record. The song was revived in the musical *The Golden Land*.

Es flien heldn iber groyse yamen,
Un men zingt fun zey gor umetim*,
Nor eyn yidn darf men nit farzamen
Zingen loyb-gezangen vegn im.

Azoy iz oykh in ale visnshaftn,
Vu an oyftu, dortn iz a yid,
Say in khokhme, say in groyse kreftn,
Iberal iz er bald in der mit.

Refrain:
Levin! Levin!
Bist der held yetst fun yisrol!
Levin! Levin!
Vi di oves fun amol!
Ven Tshemberlin iz ongekumen dort,
Bistu geven mit im
Bald oyfn ort.
Levin! Levin!
Nit geklert un nit getrakht,
Hostu dayn nomen groys gemakht.
Un brokhes on tsol
Vintsht dir dayn yisrol,
Levin mit dayn "flaying mashin"**

---

* umetum
** flying machine

Heroes fly over great oceans and people sing about them everywhere, but we shouldn't delay singing songs of praise to a certain Jew. That's how it is in all sciences: Wherever there's an accomplishment, there there is a Jew. Both in wisdom and in great strength, everywhere he is right in the middle.

Levine, Levine! You are now the hero of Israel. Levine, Levine! Like our ancestors of long ago. When Chamberlin arrived there, you were with him right there. Levine, Levine! You didn't think about it—you made your name famous. And countless blessings are wished you by your Israel—Levine with your flying machine.

ZUMER BAY NAKHT OYF DI DEKHER

זומער בײַ נאַכט אױף די דעכער

Summer at Night on the Rooftops

    Words by Louis Gilrod (1879–1930) set to an English song "On a Good Old Trolley Ride," published in the *Lidermagazin*, no. 19, Hebrew Publishing Co., 1908. The song was adapted during the Holocaust to become a song about forgetting for a while about ghetto and concentration camp life. It was submitted by Sonia Tencer, Montreal, who recounts that after the war, she met a girl in Stuthof, Germany, with whom she had lived through the liquidation of the Vilna Ghetto. The girl told Sonia that the following song was sung in the Camp in Kloge, Estonia:
    "Zuntik bay nakht oyfn boydem/ Iz dokh a vunderlekhe tsayt / Fargest on dem geto un lager/ Verst fun kloge bafrayt, / Dort kumt nit der saniteter / Me ken dortn ton vos men vil, / Me hot nit gelebt / Ver es iz nit geven / Zuntik bay nakht oyfn boydem" (Sunday night on the garret is such a wonderful time. You forget about the ghetto and camp, you become free of Kloge. There the inspector of the sick house doesn't come. You can do whatever you want there. You haven't lived, whoever has not been on the garret on Sunday night).

Fun kristi biz kenen
Ir zolt zen di stsenen
In a heyser zumer nakht.
Fun brum-strit un hekher
Bay nakht oyf di dekher,
Es lebt zikh, es roysht zikh, a prakht.
Me tantst un me kusht zikh,
Me shvitst un me visht zikh,
Me trinkt sode-vaser a sakh.
Far boyes un meydn
Iz a varer gan-eydn
Zumer bay nakht oyf a dakh.

Refrain:
Zumer bay nakht oyf di dekher,
Dan iz a goldene tsayt,
Me loyft fun di rumkes, di lekher,
Me vert vi fun "prizn" bafrayt.
Ahin kumen nit keyn polislayt,
Dort meg men ton yede zakh!
Ir hot keyn sheyns nit gezen,
Oyb ir zayt nit geven
Zumer bay nakht oyf a dakh.

Koym zukht ir ver kales,
Mit alerley mayles,
Dan zolt ir nit trakhtn keyn sakh,
Fregt nit keyn eytses,
Nem di fis oyf di pleytses,
Un marsht bald aroyf oyf a dakh.
Ir vet shoyn dertapn
A moyd vi a lapn,
Klepn vet zi shoyn tsu'n aykh,
Zi lozt zikh a khap ton,
A kush un a glet ton
Zumer bay nakht oyf a dakh.

From Chrystie Street to Cannon, you should see the scenes on a hot summer night. From Broome Street and above, at night on the rooftops, there's life and noise—it's wonderful! People dance and kiss one another; they sweat and wipe themselves off. They drink a lot of soda. For boys and girls it's a real Paradise—summer at night on the rooftops.

Summer at night on the rooftops, that is a golden time. They run from the tiny rooms, the holes-in-the wall—they're freed from "prison." No policemen go there—there you can do anything. You haven't seen anything really nice if you haven't been on the rooftops in summer at night.

If you are looking for suitable brides, waste no time, get yourself up on a roof. You'll find a sturdy gal who'll yield to your endearments, summer at night on the rooftops.

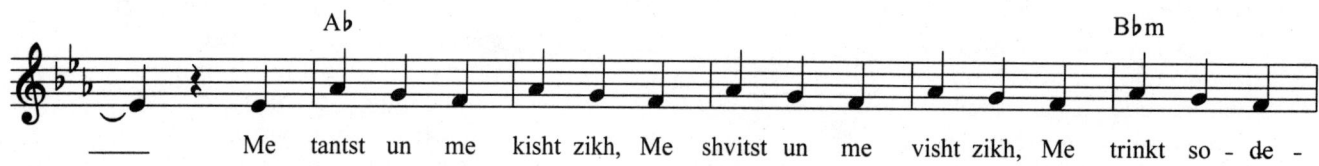

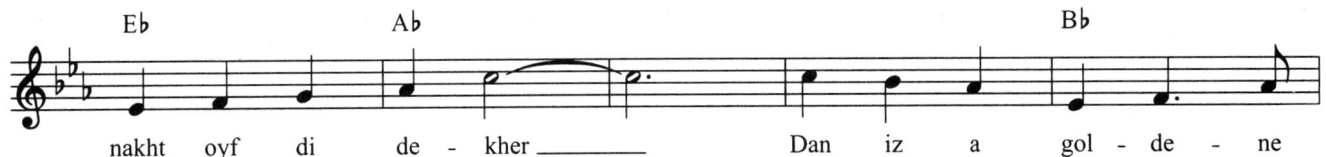
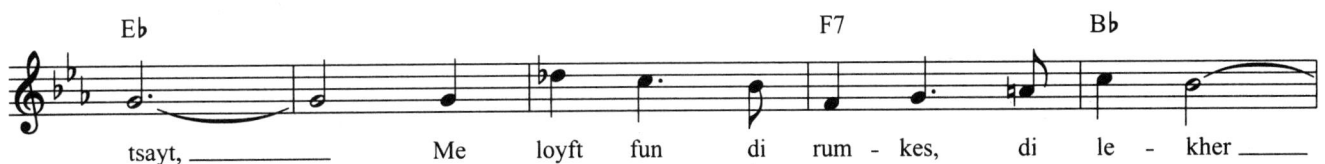

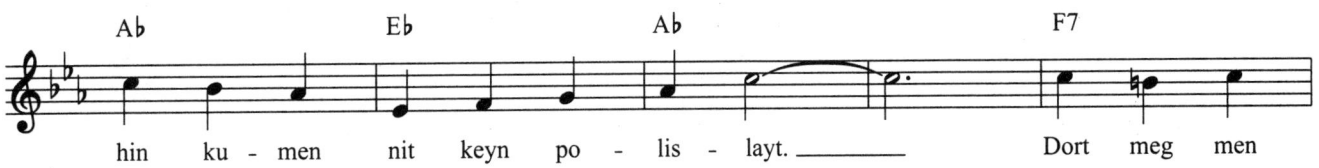

IKH BIN A YID!
SONGS OF THE FORMER SOVIET UNION

איך בין אַ ייִד!

Dzhankoye

Folksong of Jewish farmers in the Crimea in the middle '20s, published by Moishe Beregovski-Itsik Fefer in 1938. In the YIVO Archives there is a ghetto song of Transnistria which is an adaptation of Dzhankoye (sent in by Itsik Schwartz, Baku, 1948), about an old man who collects corpses from the concentration camp to bring them to the cemetery for burial. The first stanza is:

"Az me geyt keyn obadivke, / Iz nit vayt keyn balanivke. / Dortn iz a lagerl faran, / Mentshn lign op mes-lesn / Nish' getrunken, nish' gegesn / Fritsl zogt:—azoy darf es zayn! (When you go to Obadivka, it's not far from Balanivke, there is a concentration camp. People lie there for days, without drink, without food. Fritz says: that's how it should be!). A variant collected by Moishe Beregovski and Reuven Lerner was published in *Sovetish heymland*, 1968:4. Also Chava Lapin recalls that in Israel in the 50s, the melody was sung to the words of "Daroma leElat."

In recent times the melody of "Dzhankoye" was used in a Purim song by Dmitri Yakirevitch, printed in the bulletin *Mame-loshn* no. 2, 1989, issued by the Initiative Group of the Yiddish Culture Association in Moscow.

Az men fort keyn sevastopol,
Iz nit vayt fun simferopol,
Dortn iz a stantsiye faran.
Ver darf zukhn naye glikn?
S'iz a stantsye an antikl,
In dzhankoye, dzhan, dzhan, dzhan.

    Refrain:
    Hey, dzhan, hey, dzhankoye,
    Hey, dzhanvili, hey, dzhankoye,
    Hey, dzhankoye, dzhan, dzhan, dzhan.

Entfert, yidn, oyf mayn kashe,
Vu'z mayn bruder, vu'z Abrashe?—
S'geyt bay im der trakter vi a ban.
Di mume Leye bay der kosilke,
Beyle bay der molotilke,
In dzhankoye, dzhan, dzhan, dzhan.

Ver zogt, az yidn konen nor handlen,
Esn fete yoykh mit mandlen,
Nor nit zayn keyn arbets-man?
Dos konen zogn nor di sonim,—
Yidn, shpayt zey on in ponem,
Tut a kuk oyf dzhan, dzhan, dzhan!

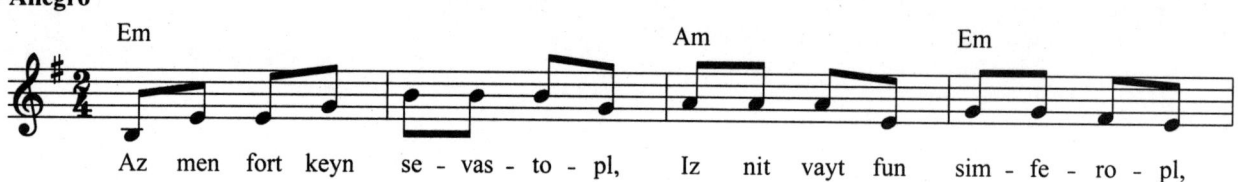

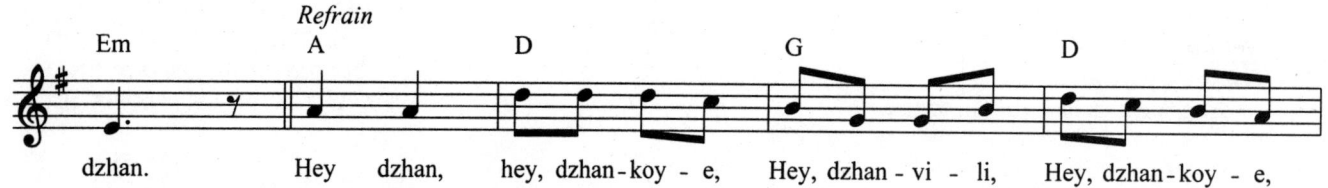
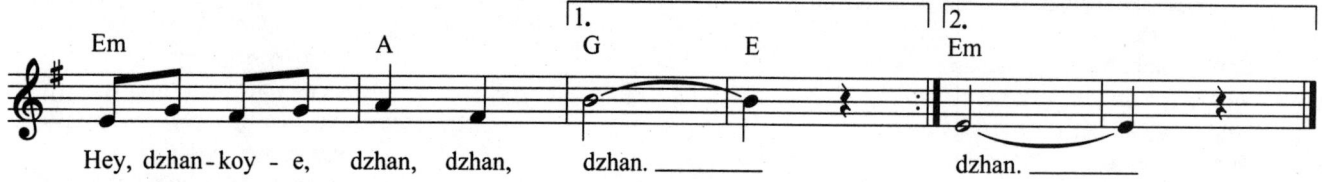

If you travel to Sevastopol, not far from Simferopol there's a railroad station. Who needs to look for new good things? It's a very special station, in Dzhankoye, Dzhan, dzhan, dzhan.

Hey dzhan, hey Dzhankoye, Hey Dzhanvili, hey Dzhankoye, Hey Dzhankoye, dzhan, dzhan dzan.

Answer my question, people—where's my brother, where's Abrasha? His tractor is running like a train. With my aunt Leah at the reaper and Beyle at the thresher, in Dzhankoye, dzhan, dzhan, dzhan.

Who says that Jews know only about trade and how to eat fat soup with almonds, but not how to be workingmen? Only our enemies can say that. People, spit in their faces—Take a look at dzhan, dzhan, dzhan.

KEGN GOLD FUN ZUN

קעגן גאָלד פֿון זון

Toward the Golden Sunrise

Words by Soviet Yiddish poet Shloyme Lopatin (1902–1943). The melody is similar to the Bialystok ghetto song "Rifkele di shabesdiker" (Rifkele the Sabbath widow) by Peysakh Kaplan.

Kegn gold fun zun geyt oyf mayn gold fun veytsn,
Kegn gold fun zun geyt oyf mayn goldn glik.
Naye horizontn rufn mikh un reytsn,
Naye lider zing ikh, yidisher muzhik.

Geyt di arbet freylekh fun gants fri biz ovnt,
Zun iz mayn hudok, un feld iz mayn fabrik,
Nekhtn shkheynim vayte—haynt shoyn azoy noent,
Ukrayiner poyer, yidisher muzhik.

קעגן גאָלד פֿון זון גייט אויף מײַן גאָלד פֿון ווייצן,
קעגן גאָלד פֿון זון גייט אויף מײַן גאָלדן גליק.
נײַע האָריזאָנטן רופֿן מיך און רייצן,
נײַע לידער זינג איך, ייִדישער מוזשיק.

גייט די אַרבעט פֿריילעך פֿון גאַנץ פֿרי ביז אָוונט,
זון איז מײַן הודאָק, און פֿעלד איז מײַן פֿאַבריק,
נעכטן שכנים ווײַטע – הײַנט שוין אַזוי נאָענט,
אוקראַיִנער פּויער, ייִדישער מוזשיק.

Toward the golden sunrise, my golden wheat is rising. Toward the golden sunrise, my golden happiness is rising. New horizons call me and excite me. I sing new songs—Jewish farm owner.

The work goes joyfully, from quite early till evening. The sun is my time signal and the field my factory. Yesterday they were distant neighbors, today they're so near. Ukrainian peasants, Jewish farm owners.

229

S'IZ DER STEP

סיאיז דער סטעפ

These Are the Steppes

Words by Soviet Yiddish poet Mendl Abarbanel (1888–1957); music by Ben Yomen (1901–1970). Published in the composer's collection *Zing, mayn folk*, 1946.

S'iz der step shoyn opgeshorn,
Un shoyn alts tsunoyfgenumen.
Libster mayner, kum tsu forn,
Ikh vel vartn oyf dayn kumen, hey!

Di arbuzn zaynen tsaytik,
S'geyt di zaft fun zey ariber,
Ful mit ziskeyt ongegosn,
Vi mayn harts iz ful mit libe.

Un di karshn, libster mayner,
Zaynen shvarts vi dayne oygn.
Ongeshotn oyf di beymer
Un di tsvaygn zikh azh boygn.

Kum tsu forn, libster mayner,
Un genug shoyn undz tsu troymen,
Rayf un tsaytik iz mayn libe,
Vi s'iz tsaytik mayne floymen.

סיאיז דער סטעפ שוין אָפּגעשאָרן,
און שוין אַלץ צונויפֿגענומען.
ליבסטער מײַנער, קום צו פֿאָרן,
איך וועל וואַרטן אויף דײַן קומען, היי!

די אַרבוזן זײַנען צײַטיק,
סיגייט די זאַפֿט פֿון זיי אַריבער,
פֿול מיט זיסקייט אָנגעגאָסן,
ווי מײַן האַרץ איז פֿול מיט ליבע.

און די קאַרשן, ליבסטער מײַנער,
זײַנען שוואַרץ ווי דײַנע אויגן.
אָנגעשאָטן אויף די ביימער
און די צווײַגן זיך אַזש בויגן.

קום צו פֿאָרן, ליבסטער מײַנער,
און גענוג שוין אונדז צו טרוימען,
רײַף און צײַטיק איז מײַן ליבע,
ווי סיאיז צײַטיק מײַנע פֿלוימען.

The steppes have been mowed already and everything has been gathered.

Dearest mine, come visit me—I'll wait for your arrival. The watermelons are ripe, their juice is overflowing; they're full of sweetness, as my heart is full of love.

And the cherries, dearest mine, are black like your eyes. The trees are loaded and the branches are bending. Come visit me, dearest mine, and enough for us of dreaming. My love is ripe just like my plums.

MASHINEN HUDYEN BINEN   מאַשינען הודיען בינען

Machines Drone Like Bees

Words by Z. Smolyanski; music by S. Polonski (b. 1910). Published in the composer's collection, 1931. The song was popular in the U. S. in the 1930s–1940s.

Mashinen hudyen binen,	מאַשינען הודיען בינען,
S'tsitern di vent,	ס׳ציטערן די ווענט,
Kh'shtey do bay mashinen	כ׳שטיי דאָ בײַ מאַשינען
Mit tseglite hent.	מיט צעגליטע הענט.
Vern do geshafn	ווערן דאָ געשאַפֿן
Toyznter por shikh,	טויזנטער פּאָר שיך,
Redelekh un pasn	רעדעלאַך און פּאַסן
Loyfn azoy gikh.	לויפֿן אַזוי גיך.
Hudyet der baginen,	הודיעט דער באַגינען,
Hudyet der hudok,	הודיעט דער הודאָק,
Shtiler zayt, mashinen,	שטילער זײַט, מאַשינען,
Rut a bisl op.	רוט אַ ביסל אָפּ.
Mashinen hudyen binen,	מאַשינען הודיען בינען,
S'tsitern di vent,	ס׳ציטערן די ווענט,
Kh'shtey do bay mashinen	כ׳שטיי דאָ בײַ מאַשינען
Mit tseglite hent.	מיט צעגליטע הענט.

Machines drone like bees, the walls shake. I stand here by the machines with glowing hands. Here they make thousands of pairs of shoes. Wheels and belts run so fast!

You drone when the workday begins, you're droning when it ends. Be quieter, machines—rest up a bit!

DOS FREYLEKHE SHNAYDERL

דאָס פֿריילעכע שניידערל

The Happy Tailor

Words by Joseph Kerler (born 1918); composer unknown. Popularized by Joanne Borts and Judy Bressler.

Oy, hob ikh haynt, khevre-layt	אוי, האָב איך הײַנט, חבֿרה־לײַט,
A nigndl gehert,	אַ ניגונדל געהערט,
Darf men poshet oyslekn di finger.	דאַרף מען פּשוט אויסלעקן די פֿינגער.
Baym neyen un fastrigeven,	בײַם נייען און פֿאַסטריגעווען,
Baym klingen mit der sher,	בײַם קלינגען מיט דער שער,
Ale mayne beyndelekh zey zingen.	אַלע מײַנע ביינדעלעך, זיי זינגען.
Hert—	הערט -
Oy, daray, daray-ram, ay!	אוי, דאַרײַ, דאַרײַ־ראַם, אײַ!
Ver bin ikh un vos hob ikh den	ווער בין איך און וואָס האָב איך דען
Oyf gor der groyser velt,	אויף גאָר דער גרויסער וועלט,
Saydn nor mayn bidne sher un ayzn;	סײַדן נאָר מײַן בידנע שער און אײַזן,
A lyadne dribne kremerl,	אַ ליאַדנע דריבנע קרעמערל,
Ven kh'kum nor oyf zayn shvel,	ווען כ׳קום נאָר אויף זײַן שוועל,
Ken dokh mir di hinter tir bavayzn.	קען דאָך מיר די הינטער־טיר באַווײַזן.
Nor—	נאָר -
Oy, daray, daray-ram, ay!	אוי, דאַרײַ, דאַרײַ־ראַם, אײַ!
S'iz epes nit mit alemen	ס׳איז עפּעס ניט מיט אַלעמען,
Mayn sheyner balebos,	מײַן שיינער באַלעבאָס,
Er hert nit oyf tsu shelten un tsu shrayen,	ער הערט ניט אויף צו שעלטן און צו שרײַען,
A gantsn tog er mordevet	אַ גאַנצן טאָג ער מאָרדעוועט,
Un shnoret mit der noz,	און שנאָרעט מיט דער נאָז,
Nor ikh her im dafke far a drayer.	נאָר איך הער אים דווקא פֿאַר אַ דרײַער.
Vayl—	ווײַל -
Oy, daray, daray-ram, ay!	אוי, דאַרײַ, דאַרײַ־ראַם, אײַ!
Oy iz mir haynt, khevre-layt,	אוי, איז מיר הײַנט, חבֿרה־לײַט,
Nishkoshedik un voyl,	נישקשהדיק און וווילל,
Un zat bin ikh, oy zat—a fargenign,	און זאַט בין איך, אוי זאַט - אַ פֿאַרגעניגן,
Vos hob ikh den a gantsn tog	וואָס האָב איך דען אַ גאַנצן טאָג
Gehat haynt in mayn moyl?	געהאַט הײַנט אין מײַן מויל?
Khuts dem tam gan-eydndikn nign.	חוץ דעם טעם גן־עדנדיקן ניגון.
Hert—	הערט -
Oy, daray, daray-ram, ay!	אוי, דאַרײַ, דאַרײַ־ראַם, אײַ!

Oh fellows, did I hear today a wonderful tune! It was so sweet! While I was sewing and basting and clanging with my scissors, all my little bones were singing. Listen—Oh, daray, daray-ram!

Who am I and what do I have in all the wide world, but just my wretched scissors and iron? A mere little storekeeper, if I come to his door, can show me the backdoor. But—Oy, daray, daray-ram!

He doesn't seem all there, my fancy boss; he never stops cursing and yelling. All day long he thrashes and sniffles with his nose. But I listen to him for just three groschen's pay, because—Oy, daray, daray-ram!

Oh, fellows, do I feel good today! And I feel full, really full—it's a pleasure! But what did I have all day in my mouth besides the heavenly-tasting tune? Listen—Oy, daray, daray-ram!

DEM ZEYDNS NIGNDL

דעם זיידנס ניגונדל

Grandfather's Little Tune

Words by Shike Driz (1908–1971); music by Saul Berezovsky (1908–1975) and Josh Waletzky are presented.
Joseph Schrogin also wrote music to the poem.

Gehert hob ikh dertseyln, Az in dem vayn dem altn Hot aleyn der zeydenyu A nigndl bahaltn.	געהערט האָב איך דערציילן, אַז אין דעם וויַן דעם אַלטן האָט אַליין דער זיידעניו אַ ניגונדל באַהאַלטן.
Gis mir on, mayn tayere, A bekherl mit vayn— Lekhayim vel ikh trinken, Gezunt zolstu mir zayn!	גיס מיר אָן, מיַן טיַערע, אַ בעכערל מיט וויַן - לחיים וועל איך טרינקען, געזונט זאָלסטו מיר זיַן!
Gehert hob ikh dertseyln— Un s'iz mistam keyn lign, Az in der tsveyter koyse Ligt dem zeydns nign.	געהערט האָב איך דערציילן -- און ס'איז מסתּם קיין ליגן, אַז אין דער צווייטער כּוסע ליגט דעם זיידנס ניגון.
Gis mir on, mayn tayere, A glezele mit yayin! Far ale mayn libe Vel ikh oystrinken lekhayim!	גיס מיר אָן, מיַן טיַערע, אַ גלעזעלע מיט יין! פאַר אַלע מיַנע ליבע וועל איך אויסטרינקען לחיים!
Gehert hob ikh dertseyln, Az dortn muz er lign— Az oyfn dno fun dritn kos— Der nign-she-benign.	געהערט האָב איך דערציילן, אַז דאָרטן מוז ער ליגן - אַז אויפן דנאָ פון דריטן כּוס - דער ניגון שבניגון.
Gis mir on, mayn tayere, Dem same bestn yayin, Lomir take far dem nign Oystrinken lekhayim!	גיס מיר אָן, מיַן טיַערע, דעם סאַמע בעסטן יין, לאָמיר טאַקע פאַר דעם ניגון אויסטרינקען לחיים!

I've heard people say that my grandfather himself hid a little tune in the old wine. Pour me a goblet of wine, my dear. I'll drink a toast to your good health.

I've heard people say, and it's probably true, that grandfather's tune is to be found in the second cup. Pour me, my dear, a glass of wine. I'll drink a toast to all my dear ones.

I've heard people say that it must be there, at the bottom of the third cup, the tune to end all tunes. Pour me, my dear, from the very best wine. Let's drink a toast to that tune.

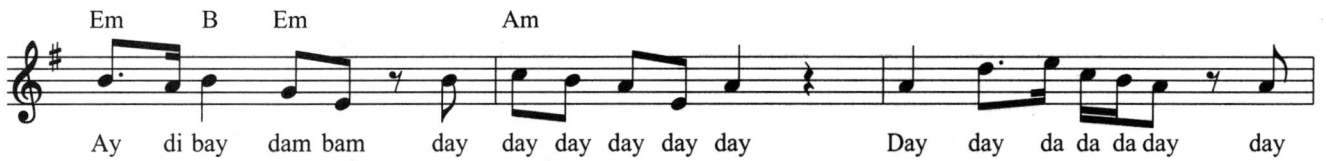
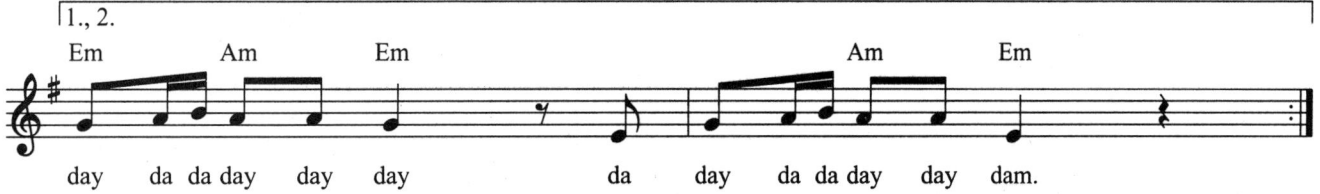
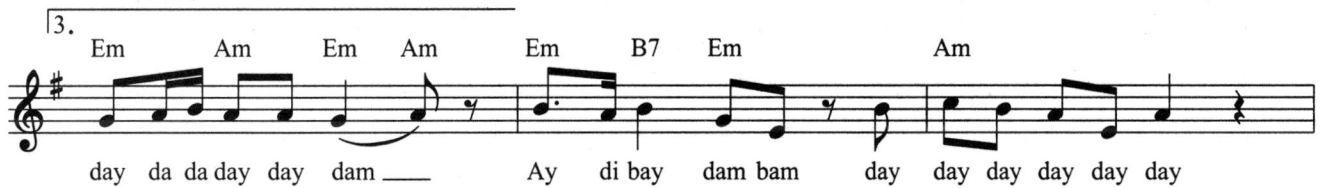

Copyright © 1975 Joshua Waletzsky

A GLEZELE LEKHAYIM

אַ גלעזעלע לחיים

Let's Raise a Glass of Cheer Now

Words by Soviet Yiddish poet B. Bergholtz. Published in the *Anthology of Yiddish Folksongs*, compiled by Aharon Vinkovetzky, Abba Kovner and Sinai Leichter, where it was transcribed from a 1963 recording of Misha Alexandrovich. Compilers found that the music originally derives from a song with the same title but different words by Joseph Rumshinsky (1881–1956), published in sheet music by the Hebrew Publishing Company in 1913. (see *Perl*, October 17, 1986, for a note-by-note comparison of the melodies.)

A glezele lekhayim es shadt nit nemen haynt,
Ven me zitst bay a yomtevdikn tish;
A glezele lekhayim—far frayndshaft un far fraynd,
Me zol shtendik nor munter zayn un frish!

אַ גלעזעלע לחיים עס שאַדט ניט נעמען הײַנט,
ווען מען זיצט בײַ אַ יום-טובֿדיקן טיש;
אַ גלעזעלע לחיים - פֿאַר פֿרײַנדשאַפֿט און פֿאַר פֿרײַנד,
מע זאָל שטענדיק נאָר מונטער זײַן און פֿריש!

A glezele lekhayim far alt un yung vos zitsn do,
Un far yedern bazunder,
vos zaynen haynt mit undz nito!
A glezele lekhayim—der bekher ful mit vayn —
Far der zun, zi zol shtendik mit undz zayn!

אַ גלעזעלע לחיים פֿאַר אַלט און יונג וואָס זיצן דאָ,
און פֿאַר יעדערן באַזונדער,
וואָס זײַנען הײַנט מיט אונדז ניטאָ!
אַ גלעזעלע לחיים - דער בעכער פֿול מיט ווײַן -
פֿאַר דער זון, זי זאָל שטענדיק מיט אונדז זײַן!

A glezele lekhayim trinken mir atsind,
Nor oyf simkhes bay yedern fun aykh!
A glezele lekhayim far muter un far kind,
Az mit nakhes di mame zol zayn raykh!

אַ גלעזעלע לחיים טרינקען מיר אַצינד,
נאָר אויף שׂימחות בײַ יעדערן פֿון אײַך!
אַ גלעזעלע לחיים פֿאַר מוטער און פֿאַר קינד,
אַז מיט נחת די מאַמע זאָל זײַן רײַך!

A glezele lekhayim—nit opshteyn zol fun aykh di shayn,
Keyn shvartser tog in lebn
in der mishpokhe zol nit zayn!
A glezele lekhayim iz oystrinken keday,
Ven me zet zikh mit fraynd oyf dos nay!

אַ גלעזעלע לחיים - ניט אָפּשטיין זאָל פֿון אײַך די שײַן,
קיין שוואַרצער טאָג אין לעבן
אין דער מישפּחה זאָל ניט זײַן!
אַ גלעזעלע לחיים איז אויסטרינקען כּדאַי,
ווען מע זעט זיך מיט פֿרײַנד אויף דאָס נײַ!

A glezele lekhayim far undzer groysn land,
Iber undz zol der himl heln reyn!
A glezele lekhayim—ikh vintsh aykh nor, zol zayn,
Mit a shmeykhl oyf di lipn zolt ir geyn!

אַ גלעזעלע לחיים פֿאַר אונדזער גרויסן לאַנד,
איבער אונדז זאָל דער הימל העלן רײן!
אַ גלעזעלע לחיים - איך ווינטש אײַך נאָר, זאָל זײַן,
מיט אַ שמייכל אויף די ליפּן זאָלט איר גיין!

A glezele lekhayim bagleytn zol undz shtendik greyt!
Mit layblekhe un noente me
zol keyn mol nit zayn tsesheydt!
A glezele lekhayim—far alts, vos undz bahelt!
Un far sholem oyf der gantser velt!

אַ גלעזעלע לחיים באַגלייטן זאָל אונדז שטענדיק גרייט!
מיט לײַבלעכע און נאָענטע מע
זאָל קיין מאָל ניט זײַן צעשיידט!
אַ גלעזעלע לחיים - פֿאַר אַלץ, וואָס אונדז באַהעלט!
און פֿאַר שלום אויף דער גאַנצער וועלט!

Let's raise a glass of cheer now—it doesn't hurt to drink as we sit here at the festive meal. Let's raise a glass of cheer for friendship and for friends. May we always feel cheerful and fresh!

Let's raise a glass of cheer for old and young who are here, and for all of our friends who aren't here today. Let's raise a glass of cheer and let the goblet be full of wine—for the sun, may it always be with us!

Let's raise a glass of cheer now for celebrations of every one of you. Let's raise a glass of cheer for mother and her child. May the mother be rich in pride.

Let's raise a glass of cheer, may the light never depart from you. May dark times never come to your family. Let's raise a glass of cheer—it's good to drink it down when you meet old friends again.

Let's raise a glass of cheer now for our great land. Over us may the sky be bright and clear. Let's raise a glass of cheer now—I wish you may have a smile of joy on your lips.

Let's raise a glass of cheer, may it always stand ready for us. May we never be separated from our kinfolk and our loved ones. Let's raise a glass of cheer for everything that brightens our life and for peace in the whole world!

SHPIL ZHE MIR A LIDELE IN YIDISH

שפיל זשע מיר אַ לידעלע אין ייִדיש

Play Me a Little Song in Yiddish

Words by Soviet Yiddish poet Yoysef Kotliar (1908–1962). It is also sung as "Zing zhe mir a lidele in yidish." The music by Henech Kon (1898–1972) was written before World War II.

Moishe Elbaum, columnist, wrote in the Jewish Forward on June 26, 1968 how he co-authored the words to Henech Kon's melody for the film "Di freylekhe kabtsonim," in Warsaw, 1938, starring the actors Zhigan and Shumacher. Later the song was excised from the film, but the original words were: "Shpil a tango mir oyf yidish, / Er zol zayn khsidish un negidish, / Az di bobeshi aleyn / Zol kenen oykh farshteyn / Un take oykh a mitsve-tentsl geyn. / Shpilt, shpilt, klezmerlekh, shpilt, / Vi a yidish harts benkt un filt; / Klapt, klapt, paykelekh geshvind, / Fargesn zol men tsores atsind." (Play me a tango in Yiddish; it should be Hassidic and rich, that grandma herself should understand it and dance a wedding dance to it. Play, play, musicians, play how a Jewish heart yearns and feels. Bang, bang quickly, drums, let us forget our troubles now).

When he was in Vladivostok during the war, Elbaum gave the song to a Jewish singer from Russia. Years later, at a reception for the chief rabbi of Moscow, Rabbi Judah Leib Lewin in New York in 1968, he was surprised to hear Cantor Stiskin from Russia sing the following version: "Shpilt, shpilt, klezmerlekh, shpilt, / Vi nor a bafrayter mentsh filt;/ Zingt mir dos flamik-groyse lid, / Vi s'zingt bloyz a sovetisher yid" (Play, play, musicians, play. As only a freed man feels. Sing me the great fiery song as only a Soviet Jew sings).

The song was also adapted during the Holocaust: "Shpil zhe mir a tango oys fun pleytim / Fun dem folk tsezeytn un tseshpreytn, / Az kinder, groys un kleyn, / Zoln kenen dos farshteyn/ Un take a tentsele geyn" (Play me a tango about refugees, of a people scattered and dispersed, that children, large and small, should be able to understand and really dance). This song was sung in the Broadway play *The Wall*. Another ghetto song "In krayuvke" (In Hiding) was also adapted from this song. Ethnomusicologist Michael Alpert informed compilers that he heard the tune (without the refrain) as a Hassidic piece "Yismekhu bemalkhuskho" from Bukovina, recorded on a 78 rpm disc by klezmer Shloymke Bekerman in the '20s. He also heard the tune played by violinist Leon Schwartz and clarinetist Andy Statman.

Shpil zhe mir a lidele in yidish,	שפיל זשע מיר אַ לידעלע אין ייִדיש,
Dervekn zol es freyd un nisht keyn khidesh,	דערוועקן זאָל עס פֿרייד און ניט קיין חידוש,
Az ale, groys un kleyn,	אַז אַלע, גרויס און קליין,
Zoln kenen dos farshteyn,	זאָלן קענען דאָס פֿאַרשטיין,
Fun moyl tsu moyl dos lidele zol geyn!	פֿון מויל צו מויל דאָס לידעלע זאָל גיין!

Refrain: רעפֿריין:
Shpil, shpil, klezmerl, shpil.	שפיל, שפיל, קלעזמערל, שפיל,
Veyst dokh vos ikh meyn un vos ikh vil—	ווייסט דאָך וואָס איך מיין און וואָס איך וויל -
Shpil, shpil, shpil a lidele far mir,	שפיל, שפיל, שפיל אַ לידעלע פֿאַר מיר,
Shpil a lidele mit harts un mit gefil!	שפיל אַ לידעלע מיט האַרץ און מיט געפֿיל!

A lidele on ziftsn un on trern,	אַ לידעלע אָן זיפֿצן און אָן טרערן,
Shpil azoy az ale zoln hern,	שפיל אַזוי אַז אַלע זאָלן הערן,
Az ale zoln zen	אַז אַלע זאָלן זען
Ikh leb un zingen ken	איך לעב און זינגען קען,
Shener nokh un beser vi geven.	שענער נאָך און בעסער ווי געווען.

Shpil zhe mir a lidele fun sholem!	שפיל זשע מיר אַ לידל פֿון שלום!
Zol shoyn zayn sholem, nit keyn kholem!	זאָל שוין זײַן שלום, ניט קיין חלום!
Az felker, groys un kleyn,	אַז פֿעלקער, גרויס און קליין,
Zoln kenen dos farshteyn,	זאָלן קענען דאָס פֿאַרשטיין,
On krig un on milkhomes zikh bageyn.	אָן קריג און אָן מילחמות זיך באַגיין.

Lomir zingen s'lidele tsuzamen
Vi gute fraynd, vi kinder fun eyn mamen!
Mayn eyntsiker farlang,
S'zol klingen fray un frank
In alemens gezang, oykh mayn gezang!

לאָמיר זינגען ס'לידעלע צוזאַמען,
ווי גוטע פֿרײַנד, ווי קינדער פֿון איין מאַמען!
מײַן איינציקער פֿאַרלאַנג,
ס'זאָל קלינגען פֿרײַ און פֿראַנק,
אין אַלעמענס געזאַנג, אויך מײַן געזאַנג!

Play me a little song in Yiddish—may it wake joy and no surprises, so everyone, young and old, can understand it. Let the song go from mouth to mouth.

Play, musicians, play—you know what I have in mind and what I want. Play a little song for me—play a little song with heart and feeling.

A song without sighs and without tears—play so everyone can hear it, so everyone can see I'm alive and I can sing even better and more beautifully than before.

Play me a little song about peace—let there be peace already, let it not be a dream, so nations great and small can understand it and not engage in battles and wars.

Let's sing the little song together like good friends, like children of one mother. My only request is that it ring out freely and honestly—in everyone's song, my song too.

S'YIDISHE MEYDELE

דאָס ייִדישע מיידעלע

The Jewish Girl

Words by Soviet Yiddish poet Rokhl Boimwol (born 1914); music by Soviet Yiddish singer-composer Emil Gorovets.

Dos yidishe meydele Do fun antkegn — Oygn vi karshn, A kind — a farmegn!	דאָס ייִדישע מיידעלע דאָ פֿון אַנטקעגן - אויגן ווי קאַרשן, אַ קינד - אַ פֿאַרמעגן!
S'yidishe meydele — Heyst zi gor Nastye! Zog ikh "Gut-morgn" ir, Entfert zi: "Zdrastye!"	ס'ייִדישע מיידעלע - הייסט זי גאָר נאַסטיע! זאָג איך ,,גוט-מאָרגן'' איר, ענטפֿערט זי - ,,דראַסטיע''.
Zog ikh ir: — meydele, Veyst, haynt iz peysakh! — Entfert zi: Peysakh vet Zayn, morgn, veys ikh.	זאָג איך איר - מיידעלע, ווייסט, הײַנט איז פּסח! - ענטפֿערט זי: - פּסח וועט זײַן מאָרגן, ווייס איך.
Kh'ze oyf ir shterndl Leygn zikh karbn, - Peysakh-tsayt veln mir Eyelekh farbn. . .	כ'זע אויף איר שטערנדל לייגן זיך קאַרבן, - פּסח-צײַט וועלן מיר אייעלעך פֿאַרבן . . .
Ze ikh, dos meydele Aylt nit in droysn, Shteyn lebn mir Oyf di trep iz zi oysn.	זע איך, דאָס מיידעלע אײַלט ניט אין דרויסן, שטיין לעבן מיר אויף די טרעפּ איז זי אויסן.
Freg ikh zi: Vilst mit di kinder nit shpiln, Oder dikh shrekt, Vos a hunt tut dort biln?	פֿרעג איך זי: - ווילסט מיט די קינדער ניט שפּילן, אָדער דיך שרעקט, וואָס אַ הונט טוט דאָרט בילן?
Shtamlt zi: - S'yogt mikh der langer Andreyka, Drot mit a shtekn Un shrayt mir "yevreyka!"	שטאַמלט זי: - ס'יאָגט מיך דער לאַנגער אַנדרייקאַ, דראָט מיט אַ שטעקן און שרײַט אויף מיר ,,יעוורייקאַ!''

The Jewish girl who lives across the street—with eyes like black cherries, a child, a treasure! The Jewish girl, her name is Nastye.

I say "good-morning" to her and she answers "hello"* I say to her: girl, do you know today is Passover? She answers: Passover comes, that I know. She wrinkles her little forehead: On Passover we'll color little eggs.

I see that the girl is not hurrying outside. Standing next to me on the stairs is she. I ask her: Don't you want to play with the children? Or does it frighten you that a dog is howling there? She murmurs: Tall Andreyka is chasing me. He's threatening me with a stick and yells at me: "Jewess."

She stammers: Tall Andreyka is chasing me. He's threatening me with a stick and yells at me: "Jewess!"

IKH BIN A YID!

אִיךְ בִּין אַ ייִד

I Am a Jew

Words by Itsik Fefer, born 1900—murdered on August 12, 1952 during the Stalin era together with other prominent Yiddish writers and cultural leaders. Music by Emil Gorovets, Soviet Yiddish singer, who immigrated to this country in 1974. He performed this song at the annual Workmen's Circle August 12th commemorations of the Liquidation of Yiddish Writers in Soviet Russia which took place at City Hall.

Der vayn fun doyresdikn doyer
Hot mir geshtarkt in vanderveg,
Di beyze shverd fun payn un troyer
Hot nit farnikhtet mayn farmeg.

Mayn folk, mayn gloybn un mayn blien,
Zi hot mayn frayheyt nit geshmidt.
Fun unter shverd hob ikh geshrien:
Ikh bin a yid!

Der kluger kneytsh fun Reb Akive,
Di khokhme fun Yeshayes vort
Hobn genert mayn dursht, mayn libe
Un zi mit has tsunoyfgeport.

Der shvung fun makabeyer heldn,
Bar Kokhbas blut in maynem zidt,
Fun ale shayters fleg ikh meldn:
Ikh bin a yid!

Un oyf tsepikenish di sonim,
Vos greytn kvorim shoyn far mir,
Vel ikh unter di fraye fonen
Nokh hobn nakhes on a shir.

Kh'vel mayne vayngertner farflantsn
Un fun mayn goyrl zayn der shmid,
Kh'vel nokh oyf di sonims keyver tantsn!
Ikh bin a yid!

דער װײַן פֿון דורותדיקן דויער
האָט מיר געשטאַרקט אין װאַנדערװעג,
די בייזע שווערד פֿון פּײַן און טרויער
האָט ניט פֿאַרניכטעט מײַן פֿאַרמעג.

מײַן פֿאָלק, מײַן גלויבן און מײַן בליִען,
זי האָט מײַן פֿרײַהייט ניט געשמידט.
פֿון אונטער שווערד האָב איך געשריִען:
איך בין אַ ייִד!

דער קלוגער קנייטש פֿון רב עקיבֿא,
די חכמה פֿון ישעיהס וואָרט
האָבן גענערט מײַן דורשט, מײַן ליבע
און זי מיט האַס צונויפֿגעפּאָרט.

דער שוווּנג פֿון מכּבּיער העלדן,
בר כּוכבאס בלוט אין מײַנעם זידט,
פֿון אַלע שײַטערס פֿלעג איך מעלדן:
איך בין אַ ייִד!

און אויף צעפּיקעניש די שׂונאים,
וואָס גרייטן קבֿרים שוין פֿאַר מיר,
וועל איך אונטער די פֿרײַע פֿאָנען
נאָך האָבן נחת אָן אַ שיעור.

כ'װעל מײַנע װײַנגערטנער פֿאַרפֿלאַנצן
און פֿון מײַן גורל זײַן דער שמיד,
כ'וועל נאָך אויף די שׂונאימס קבֿר טאַנצן!
איך בין אַ ייִד!

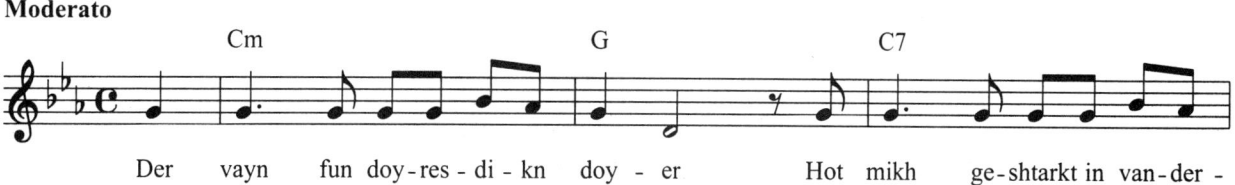

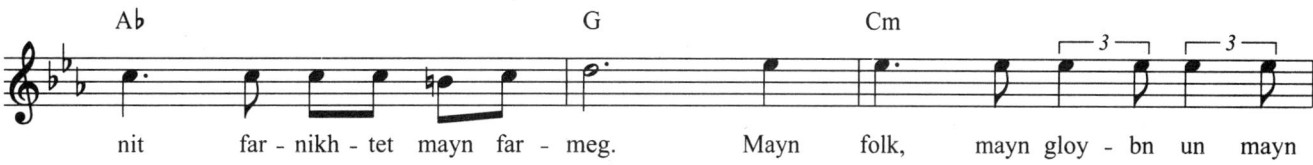

The generations-old wine has strengthened me in my wanderings. The angry sword of pain and sorrow has not destroyed my treasure. My people, my faith and my flowering—it has not chained my freedom. From under the sword I've cried out: I am a Jew!

The clever twists of Rabbi Akiva, the wisdom of Isaiah's words nourished my thirst and my love, and fought against hate. The zest of the Maccabbean heroes and Bar Kokhba's blood boils in mine. From all the burnings at the stake I've cried out: I am a Jew!

And may my enemies be pierced by spears, those who are preparing a grave for me. Beneath the flag of freedom I'll yet have no end of pleasure. I'll plant my vineyards and be the architect of my fate. I'll yet dance on my enemies' graves! I am a Jew!

AM YISROEL KHAY!

עם ישראל חי!

The People of Israel Live!

Words by Soviet Jewish poet Joseph Kerler (born 1918), who emigrated to Israel in 1971. The song was published in the *Anthology of Yiddish Folksongs,* IV (1987). The accompanying footnote states that "the song was created in the circles of new immigrants from Soviet Russia, which they call 'gazlen-land' (the land of bandits)." Actor-singer Theodore Bikel sings: "Khay, khay, zoln zey geyn in dr'erd arayn" (Live, live, let them go to hell!).

Oyf tselokhes ale sonim	אויף צו להכעיס אלע שונאים
Lomir frank un fray,	לאָמיר פֿראַנק און פֿרײַ,
Lomir zingen mit kavone:	לאָמיר זינגען מיט כּוונה:
Undzer lidl "khay!"	אונדזער לידל ,,חי!''
Refrain:	רעפֿרײן:
Khay, khay!	חי, חי!
Lebn zol di zunenshayn,	לעבן זאָל די זונענשײַן,
Khay, khay!	חי, חי!
Freylekh zol bay yidn zayn!	פֿריילעך זאָל בײַ ייִדן זײַן!
Oyf tselokhes ale sonim—	אויף צו להכעיס אלע שונאים -
Am yisroel khay!	עם ישראל חי!
Alts mir veln iberkumen,	אַלץ מיר וועלן איבערקומען,
Alts iz dokh keday;	אַלץ איז דאָך כּדאַי;
Un in erets veln mir kumen,	און אין ארץ וועלן מיר קומען,
Kumen say vi say!	קומען סײַ ווי סײַ!
Undzer sheyner vayter shtern	אונדזער שיינער ווײַטער שטערן
Shaynt undz fun der fray;	שײַנט אונדז פֿון דער פֿרײַ;
Zol di gantse velt derhern,	זאָל די גאַנצע וועלט דערהערן,
Vi mir zingen "khay!"	ווי מיר זינגען ,,חי!''

Resoluto

The Devil take all our enemies! Let us, openly and freely, sing out deliberately our little song: Live!

Live! Long live the sunshine! Live! Let all Jews be happy! The Devil take all our enemies. The people of Israel still live!

We will overcome everything. Everything is worth it, and we'll get to Israel—We'll get there anyway. Our beautiful, distant star shines to us from the free land. Let the whole world hear how we sing: Live!

SHULDIKE UMSHULDIKE

שולדיקע אומשולדיקע

Guilty Innocents

One of the Forbidden Songs (Farbotene lider) which were sung clandestinely in Soviet Russia in the '60s. Transcribed by the compilers from a record by David Eshet, Israel.

Der urteyl iz shoyn lang geven a farshtendlekhe zakh,
Nor ordenung iz ordenung, a mishpet vert gemakht.
Der prokuror iz fun forshung fil gevorn nebekh shvakh,
Der shuldiker hot ale mol tsufil getrakht.

    Un di mame iz eynzam oyf a veg,
    Zi vandert gantse nekht un gantse teg,
    Es redt far ir a tsiterdike trer,
    Keyn verter hot di mame shoyn nisht mer.
    Nor keyner fregt nisht vos do iz geshen,
    Vayl yeder zorgt far zayn shtikl broyt,
    Men geyt farbay un keyner vil nisht zen,
    Vayl yeder eyner tsitert far zayn hoyt.

Der mishpet hot geendikt zikh dort ergets in sibir,
Der zun hot in a vinternakht dertrunken zikh fun tsar,
Der rikhter hot bakumen nokhn mishpet a papir,
Tsu forn glaykh keyn krim un zikh dort opruen derfar.

    Un di mame iz eynzam oyf a veg,
    Vi gro un fintster zaynen ire teg.
    Zi hot shoyn mer keyn moyre nisht, o neyn,
    Zi geyt un geyt, abi nisht blaybn ergets shteyn.
    Zi trakht fun zun un fregt far velkhe zind,
    Tsi iz nokh do faran a groyser got,
    Nor di mentshn zaynen toyb un zaynen blind,
    Ir goyrl makhn zey tsu shand un shpot.

Un plutsling iz gekumen a tsayt, an ander tsayt.
Dem rikhters zibn gute yor zaynen oykh farbay,
Di mame hot bakumen
a briv in sibir dortn vayt—
Az der zun geven iz umshuldik un zi iz fray.

    Geyt zi a mide oyf a veg,
    Zet nisht mer di friling-bloye teg.
    Di velt kumt ir antkegn mit a loyb,
    Nor zi zitst far ale shtum un toyb.
    Zi zet far zikh di lagern fun dort,
    Vi mentshn shtarbn oys fun payn un noyt,
    Zi zet di mosrim vos urteyln mit a vort
    Di ale shuldike umshuldike tsum toyt.

דער אורטייל איז שוין לאַנג געווען אַ פֿאַרשטענדלעכע זאַך,
נאָר אָרדענונג איז אָרדענונג, אַ מישפּט ווערט געמאַכט.
דער פּראָקוראָר איז פֿון פֿאָרשונג פֿיל געוואָרן נעבעך שוואַך,
דער שולדיקער האָט אַלע מאָל צו פֿיל געטראַכט.

    און די מאַמע איז איינזאַם אויף אַ וועג.
    זי וואַנדערט גאַנצע נעכט און גאַנצע טעג.
    עס רעדט פֿאַר איר אַ ציטערדיקע טרער.
    קיין ווערטער האָט די מאַמע שוין נישט מער.
    נאָר קיינער פֿרעגט נישט וואָס דאָ איז געשען.
    ווײַל יעדער זאָרגט פֿאַר זײַן שטיקל ברויט.
    מען גייט פֿאַרבײַ און קיינער וויל נישט זען.
    ווײַל יעדער איינער ציטערט פֿאַר זײַן הויט.

דער מישפּט האָט געענדיקט זיך דאָרט ערגעץ אין סיביר.
דער זון האָט אין אַ ווינטערנאַכט דערטרונקען זיך פֿון צער,
דער ריכטער האָט באַקומען נאָכן מישפּט אַ פּאַפּיר,
צו פֿאָרן גלײַך קיין קרים און זיך דאָרט אָפֿרוען דערפֿאַר.

    און די מאַמע איז איינזאַם אויף אַ וועג.
    ווי גרא און פֿינצטער זענען אירע טעג.
    זי האָט שוין מער קיין מורא נישט, אַ ניין,
    זי גייט און גייט, אַבי נישט בלײַבן ערגעץ שטיין.
    זי טראַכט פֿון זון און פֿרעגט פֿאַר וועלכע זינד,
    צי איז נאָך דאָ פֿאַראַן אַ גרויסער גאָט,
    נאָר די מענטשן זענען טויב און זענען בלינד,
    איר גורל מאַכן זיי צו שאַנד און שפּאָט.

און פּלוצלינג איז געקומען אַ צײַט, אַן אַנדער צײַט.
דעם ריכטערס זיבן גוטע יאָר זענען אויך פֿאַרבײַ.
די מאַמע האָט באַקומען
אַ בריוו אין סיביר דאָרטן ווײַט. . .
אַז דער זון געווען איז אומשולדיק און זי איז פֿרײַ.

    גייט זי אַ מידע אויף אַ וועג,
    זעט נישט מער די פֿרילינג־בלויע טעג.
    די וועלט קומט איר אַנטקעגן מיט אַ לויב,
    נאָר זי זיצט פֿאַר אַלע שטום און טויב.
    זי זעט פֿאַר זיך די לאַגערן פֿון דאָרט,
    ווי מענטשן שטאַרבן אויס פֿון פּײַן און נויט,
    זי זעט די מוסרים וואָס אורטיילן מיט אַ וואָרט
    די אַלע שולדיקע אומשולדיקע צום טויט.

The sentence was already a foregone conclusion, but order is order—a trial is under way. The prosecutor, poor fellow, grew weak from much investigation. The guilty man always thought too much.

And his mother is alone on the road. She wanders night and day. A trembling tear speaks for her—the mother no longer hears any words. But no one asks what happened here, for everyone worries about himself. People pass by and no one wants to see, for everyone is afraid for his own skin.

The sentence ended somewhere in Siberia. The son, in a winter night, drowned himself from sorrow. The judge received a directive to go immediately to the Crimea and take a vacation.

And the mother is alone on the road. How gray and dark her days are! She is no longer afraid, oh no! She walks and walks so as not to stay in one place. She thinks about her son and asks what sin he was guilty of, whether there is still a great God. But people are deaf and blind. They mock her fate.

Suddenly there came a time, a different time. The judge's seven good years were past. The mother received a letter from distant Siberia: that her son was innocent and she is free.

She walks wearily on a road, no longer sees the spring-like days. The world comes to meet her with praise. But she sits mute and deaf before everyone. She pictures the prison camps there, how people die of pain and deprivation. She sees the informers who, with one word, sentence all the guilty innocents to death.

ANTSHULDIKT! אַנטשולדיקט!

Excuse Me!

One of the "Farbotene lider" (Forbidden Songs) which were sung clandestinely in Soviet Russia in the 1960s. Transcribed by the compilers from a recording by David Eshet, Israel.

Vinter, vi tif der shney un shtark der frost,
Ikh bin dokh oyf der fray un fil mikh vi a knekht.
Ikh vil shoyn mer nit zayn bay aykh oyf kest,
Ikh dank aykh far di ale teg un nekht.

Nit fregt far vos a shvalb vil nit zayn nest,
Un zukht a shtikl heym dort in a vaytn hek,
A dank vos ir mayn opshtam nisht fargest,
Antshuldikt, ikh zog dem emes on shum shrek.

Ikh veys ir ale shteyt arum un lakht
Un trakht az mayn gedank iz nor a zind,
Dort shaynt far mir yisroel mit prakht,
Un ruft mikh: kum aheym, du bist mayn kind.

Gleybt mir, ikh bin nit mer vos kh'bin geven,
Un mayne brider lozn zikh nisht shekhtn mer.
Ikh vil nokh bay mayn lebn mayn land derzen,
Antshuldikt mir—dos iz mayn bager.

Genug geven shoyn eyn mol babi-yar,
Ikh hob kemat fargesn yene shvartse teg,
Dermont mikh un ikh dank aykh zeyer derfar,
Ikh veys shoyn gut vu s'firt mayn lange veg.

Winter, how deep the snow and dense the frost. I am, after all, free but I feel like a slave. I don't want to be your non-paying guest anymore—I thank you for all the days and nights.

Don't ask why a swallow doesn't want his nest, and looks for some kind of home far away. Thanks for not forgetting who I'm descended from. Excuse me, I tell the truth fearlessly.

I know you all stand around and laugh, and think that my ideas are simply sinful. Over there, Israel shines gloriously for me, and calls me: come home, you are my child.

Believe me, I am no longer what I was, and my brothers no longer allow themselves to be slaughtered. I want to see my land while I am still alive. Excuse me—that is my desire today.

One Babi Yar was enough—I'd almost forgotten those black days. Remind me, and I thank you very much for that. I know very well where my long road leads to.

FUN YIDISHN TEATER
THEATER SONGS

פֿון ייִדישן טעאַטער

A Year After the Wedding

אַ יאָר נאָך דער חתונה

Words by Isaac Reingold (1873–1903), popular song-writer of Chicago; the song was published in sheet music by S. Schenker and Son in 1913. It was also entitled *Beser iz tsu blaybn a moyd* (It Is Better to Remain a Maid) with lyrics by Reingold and music attributed to J. Rumshinsky. According to the published song in the *Selected Songs and Poems of Reingold*, 1952, the tune is called "Der rebes nigele" from the operetta *Khokhmas noshim*. The song spread to Eastern Europe and was included in the Soviet collection of Z. Skuditsky, 1936, as an anonymous song. S. Z. Pipe, Dov and Meir Noy, and other folklorists surmised that the song came from the theatre, without identifying the author or play. The melody appears as a "Frailach" in the *Kammen International Dance Folio*, no. I, and as a "nign" in M. Beregovski, 1962 (no. 115).

A yor ersht nokh mayn khasene
Un zet vi kuk ikh oys,
Taynet a yung vaybele un khlipet shtark,
Oy gute, libe shvesterlekh,
Dem sod zog ikh aykh oys,
Az a man iz nor a tsore oyfn kark.
Geven bin ikh a meydele,
A freylekhe, gor moyredik,
Geshtift mit yunge laytelekh hob ikh dan,
Haynt bin ikh a yidene,
Shvakh un more-shkhoyredik,
Un ales vayl ikh hob gevolt a man.

Er darf a lebn makhn bloyz,
Un ikh, oy, vos bin ikh nit in hoyz?
Oy, a vayb un a damele,
A dinst un oykh a mamele,
Ales, ales kumt dokh on mit shverer noyt,
Oy, es iz keyn kleynikeyt,
Ikh shver aykh bay a reynikeyt,
Az beser iz tsu blaybn gor a moyd.

Vu zenen mayne glikn,
Vos hob ikh mikh geyogt?
Getroymt fun 'nokh der khasene',
Gehoft oyf glik!
A man hob ikh gekrogn
Oyf sonim nor gezogt,
A shod vos khapn ken ikh nit tsurik!
Gemeynt hob ikh avade
Lib hot mikh mayn tayerer,
Ikh hob dokh im azoy fil mi gekost,
Kh'vel lebn nokh der khasene gliklekher, frayerer,
Tsum sof hot zikh a boydem oysgelozt!

אַ יאָר ערשט נאָך מײַן חתונה
און זעט ווי קוק איך אויס,
טענהט אַ יונג ווײַבעלע און כליפעט שטאַרק,
אוי גוטע, ליבע שוועסטערלעך,
דעם סוד זאָג איך אײַך אויס,
אַז אַ מאַן איז נאָר אַ צרה אויפֿן קאַרק.
געווען בין איך אַ מיידעלע,
אַ פֿריילעכע, גאָר מוראדיק,
געשטיפֿט מיט יונגע לײַטעלעך האָב איך דאַן,
הײַנט בין איך אַ ייִדענע,
שוואַך און מרה-שחורהדיק,
און אַלעס ווײַל איך האָב געוואָלט אַ מאַן.

ער דאַרף אַ לעבן מאַכן בלויז,
און איך, אוי, וואָס בין איך ניט אין הויז?
אוי, אַ ווײַב און אַ דאַמעלע,
אַ דינסט און אויך אַ מאַמעלע,
אַלעס, אַלעס קומט דאָך אָן מיט שווערער נויט,
אוי, עס איז קיין קלייניקייט,
איך שווער אײַך בײַ אַ ריינקייט,
אַז בעסער איז צו בלײַבן גאָר אַ מויד.

ווו זענען מײַנע גליקן,
וואָס האָב איך מיך געיאָגט?
געטרוימט פֿון 'נאָך דער חתונה,'
געהאָפֿט אויף גליק,
אַ מאַן האָב איך געקראָגן
אויף שונאים נאָר געזאָגט,
אַ שאָד וואָס כאַפּן קען איך ניט צוריק!
געמיינט האָב איך אַוודאי
ליב האָט מיך מײַן טײַערער,
איך האָב דאָך אים אַזוי פֿיל מי געקאָסט,
כ'וועל לעבן נאָך דער חתונה גליקלעכער, פֿרײַערער,
צום סוף האָט זיך אַ בוידעם אויסגעלאָזט!

Nokh eyder kh'hob mikh arumgezen,	נאָך איידער כ'האָב מיך אַרומגעזען,
Ikh ken dokh shoyn mer in gas nit geyn!	איך קען דאָך שוין מער אין גאַס ניט גיין,
Bashert fun got a zibele,	באַשערט פֿון גאָט אַ זיבעלע,
A kind groys vi a tsibele,	אַ קינד גרויס ווי אַ ציבעלע,
Fun dem kleynem nefeshl hob ikh dem toyt,	פֿון דעם קליינעם נפֿשל האָב איך דעם טויט,
A katerl, a hustele,	אַ קאַטערל, אַ הוסטעלע,
Es veynt un tsit dos brustele,	עס וויינט און ציט דאָס ברוסטעלע,
Az liber iz tsu blaybn gor a moyd!	אַז ליבער איז צו בלײַבן גאָר אַ מויד!
Der man kumt zikh tsum greytn,	דער מאַן קומט זיך צום גרייטן,
Vos veys er vi ikh layd,	וואָס ווייס ער ווי איך לײַד,
Er est zikh op di vetshere	ער עסט זיך אָפּ די וועטשערע
Un dreyt zikh oys,	און דרייט זיך אויס,
Ikh dertseyl im mayne tsores,	איך דערצייל אים מײַנע צרות,
Nor khotsh mit meser shnayd,	נאָר כאָטש מיט מעסער שנײַד,
Dos kind vil er nit nemen oyfn shoys!	דאָס קינד וויל ער ניט נעמען אויפֿן שויס!
Geyt shtendik in teater	גייט שטענדיק אין טעאַטער
Un nemt a 'sit' a tayern,	און נעמט אַ 'סיט' אַ טײַערן,
Dokh mikh mit zikh mitnemen vil er nish'	דאָך מיך מיט זיך מיטנעמען וויל ער נישׁ',
Kh'bin, zogt er, nor bashafn	כ'בין, זאָגט ער, נאָר באַשאַפֿן
Tsum vashn un tsum shayern,	צום וואַשן און צום שײַערן,
Tsum kokhn un derlangen alts tsum tish.	צום קאָכן און דערלאַנגען אַלץ צום טיש!
Koym shray ikh, er zol on mir nit geyn,	קוים שרײַ איך, ער זאָל אָן מיר ניט גיין,
Nu, heyst er mir shrayen oyf di tseyn.	נו, הייסט ער מיר שרײַען אויף די צײן,
Er khapt zayn hut, zayn shtekele,	ער כאַפּט זײַן הוט, זײַן שטעקעלע,
Un lozt mikh mit dem brekele,	און לאָזט מיך מיט דעם ברעקעלע,
Ikh zing a troyer nigele fun heler hoyt.	איך זינג אַ טרויער ניגעלע פֿון העלער הויט,
Es veynt un shrayt dos pitsele,	עס וויינט און שרײַט דאָס פּיצעלע,
Do helft keyn vort, keyn shmitsele,	דאָ העלפֿט קיין וואָרט, קיין שמיצעלע,
Oy, liber iz tsu blaybn gor a moyd!	אוי, ליבער איז צו בלײַבן גאָר אַ מויד!

It's just a year after my wedding and see how I look! complains a young wife, sobbing loudly.—O good and dear sisters of mine, I'll tell you the secret: A man is just a pain in the neck. I was once a happy girl, lively and flamboyant, I flirted with young men then. Today I am an old married wife, weak and quite depressed, and all because I wanted a husband.

He only has to make a living. And I, what don't I do in the house? A wife and a lady, a servant and also a mother. Everything is so hard for me. It's not just a little thing, I swear it by the Holy Book. Better to have stayed unmarried.

Where are my joys? Why did I rush into it so fast? I dreamed of the time after the wedding, and hoped for joy. The husband I got I wouldn't wish on my enemies. Too bad I can't go back into the past! I thought that surely my dear one loved me well. After all, I cost him so much effort, that after the wedding I'd live more freely and happily. But all my hopes came to naught.

Before I even looked around, I could no longer go outside the house. God soon gave me a little one, a baby as big as an onion. The little creature is the death of me. A cold, a cough, he cries and tugs my breast. It's far better to stay a single girl! My husband comes home when the meal's all prepared. What does he know of how I suffer? He eats his supper and turns away. I tell him my troubles but it's like talking to the wall. He won't take the baby onto his lap.

He always goes to the theater.and buys an expensive ticket. But he doesn't want to take me too, oh no! I was, he says, created just for washing and scouring, for cooking and serving things to the table. If I start to yell: Don't go without me! he tells me to yell all I want—he won't pay any attention. He grabs his hat and walking cane and leaves me with the infant. I sing a sad tune from the bottom of my heart. The little one cries and screams. Neither words nor spanking helps. Oh! Better to stay a single girl!

ZE DOS KLEYDL, TATESHI

זע דאָס קלײדל, טאַטעשי

See the Dress, Daddy Dear

Words by Itsik Manger (1901–1969); music by Henech Kon (1898–1972) from Manger's play *Hotsmakhs tekhter* (Hotsmakh's Daughters). The play is based on Abraham Goldfaden's operetta *Di kishef-makherin* (The Sorceress).

Ze dos kleydl, tateshi,
Di same letste mode!
Azoyns farmogt nisht, tateshi,
Di froy fun voyevode;
Azoyns farmogt nisht, tateshi,
Di froy fun voyevode.

Oy vi sheyn, oy vi sheyn,
Mole tam un mole kheyn!
In a kleydl, aza kleydl,—
Ken men khlebn tantsn geyn!

Ze di shikhlekh, tateshi,
Fun same bestn leder,
Azoyne shikhlekh, tateshi,
Hot dokh nisht ayeder;
Azoyne shikhlekh, tateshi,
Hot dokh nisht ayeder.

Oy vi sheyn, oy vi sheyn,
Mole tam un mole kheyn!
In azoyne sheyne shikhlekh,
Ken men khlebn tantsn geyn!

Ze dem khosn, tateshi,
Vos ikh hob bakumen;
Mir hobn zikh baym fotograf
Shoyn aropgenumen;
Mir hobn zikh baym fotograf
Shoyn aropgenumen.

Oy vi sheyn, oy vi sheyn,
Mole tam un mole kheyn!
Mit a khosn, aza khosn—
Ken men khlebn tantsn geyn!

זע דאָס קלײדל, טאַטעשי,
די סאַמע לעצטע מאָדע!
אַזױנס פֿאַרמאָגט נישט, טאַטעשי,
די פֿרױ פֿון װאָיעװאָדע;
אַזױנס פֿאַרמאָגט נישט, טאַטעשי,
די פֿרױ פֿון װאָיעװאָדע.

אױ װי שײן, אױ װי שײן,
מלא טעם און מלא חן!
אין אַ קלײדל, אַזאַ קלײדל, -
קען מען כ׳לעבן טאַנצן גײן!

זע די שיכלעך, טאַטעשי,
פֿון סאַמע בעסטן לעדער,
אַזױנע שיכלעך, טאַטעשי,
האָט דאָך נישט אײדער;
אַזױנע שיכלעך, טאַטעשי,
האָט דאָך נישט אײדער.

אױ װי שײן, אױ װי שײן,
מלא טעם און מלא חן!
אין אַזױנע שײנע שיכלעך
קען מען כ׳לעבן טאַנצן גײן!

זע דעם חתן, טאַטעש,
װאָס איך האָב באַקומען;
מיר האָבן זיך בײַם פֿאָטאָגראַף
שױן אַראָפּגענומען;
מיר האָבן זיך בײַם פֿאָטאָגראַף
שױן אַראָפּגענומען.

אױ װי שײן, אױ װי שײן,
מלא טעם און מלא חן!
מיט אַ חתן, אַזאַ חתן,–
קען מען כ׳לעבן טאַנצן גײן!

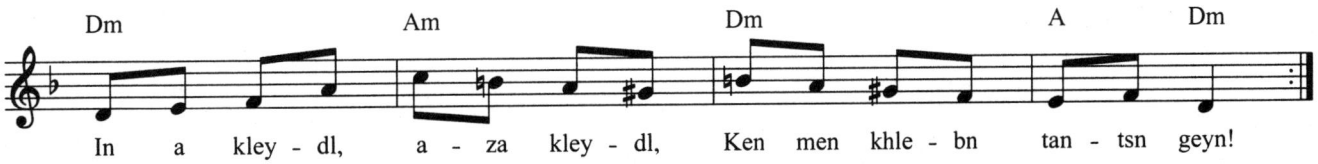

See the dress, daddy dear, it's the latest style. No one has the like, daddy dear, not even the governor's wife. Oh how nice, oh how nice! Full of charm and full of grace! In such a lovely dress, you can really dance.

See the slippers, daddy dear, of the finest leather. Such good slippers, daddy dear, not everyone has. Oh how nice, oh how nice! Full of charm and full of grace! In a pair of such lovely slippers you can really dance.

See my bridegroom, daddy dear, that I just received. We already had our photograph taken at the photographer's. Oh how nice, oh how nice! Full of charm and full of grace! With such a bridegroom you can really dance.

KH'VIL NISHT KEYN SAKH NOR A BISELE   כ׳וויל נישט קיין סך, נאָר אַ ביסעלע

I Don't Want Much, Just a Little

Words and music by Max Perlman for the play "A Honeymoon in Israel." Published in 1962.

Shoyn fun eybik on, zint di velt eksistirt,
Hot zikh der mentsh a farlang ayngefirt,
Raykhtum, ashires, dos iz zayn bager,
Un vifl er hot, vil er hobn alts mer.
Un vi lang halt on di gantse shpil,
Iz tsu vos darf a mentsh azoy fil?

   Refrain:
   Kh'vil nisht keyn sakh, nisht keyn sakh,
   Nor a bisele,
   Ver darf aynraysn di velt?
   Kh'vil nisht keyn sakh, nisht keyn sakh,
   Nor a bisele,
   Kh'zukh keyn koved, nisht keyn gelt.
   Yo, vayl dos lebn fargeyt,
   S'iz dokh nor a kinder-shpil,
   Zol es geyn vi es geyt,
   Ver darf hobn azoy fil?
   Kh'vil nisht keyn sakh, nisht keyn sakh,
   Nor a bisele, oy!
   Lebn ruik oyf der velt.

Es viln haynt felker bahershn di velt,
M'greyt tsu milkhomes tsu makhn nor gelt.
Moykhl di toyves un moykhl dos glik,
Far mir iz mayn kleyntshinke land oykh genig*.
Kh'vil nit zayn mekhtik durkh blit,**
Nor lebn bekoved als yid.

---

* genug
** blut

For uncounted eons since the world began, man has made a demand. Riches, wealth—that's his desire. No matter how much he has, he wants more. And no matter how long the game goes on. Why does a man need so much?

I don't want much, not much, just a little. Who needs to flaunt one's wealth? I don't want much, not much, just a little. I seek no honors, no money. For life passes away—it's just a child's game. Let things go as they will—who needs to worry so much. I don't want much, not much, just a little, Oh! To live peacefully in the world.

Nations these days want to rule the world. They plan wars just to make money. For me, my tiny country is sufficient. I don't want to be mighty by shedding blood—just to live honorably as a Jew.

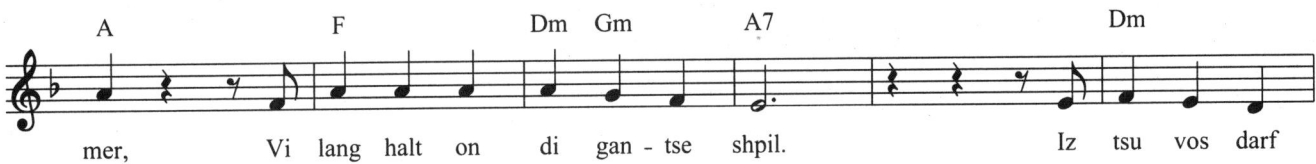

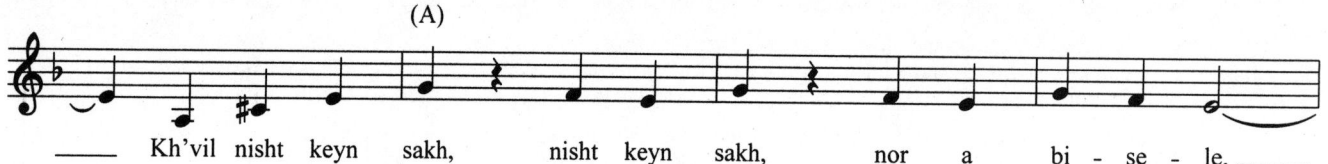

BLIMELEKH TSVEY

בלימעלעך צוויי

Two Little Flowers

Music by Peretz Sandler (1881–1926), from the play *Mendl in yapan* (Mendel in Japan). Published in 1924. The song was one of the favorites of compiler Chana Mlotek's father Leo Gordon, of blessed memory.

- Zorg nit, zol dir nit ton bang, Du vest nit laydn lang, Vayl dort vel ikh Nit fargesn dir, Gleyb es mir. Ales, ales vel ikh ton Dikh nemen dort ahin. Megst zikher zayn. Eybik blayb ikh dayn, Ikh shver es dir.	- זאָרג ניט, זאָל דיר ניט טאָן באַנג, דו וועסט ניט לײַדן לאַנג, ווײַל דאָרט וועל איך ניט פֿאַרגעסן דיר, גלייב עס מיר; אַלעס, אַלעס וועל איך טאָן דיך נעמען דאָרט אַהין, מעגסט זיכער זײַן, אייביק בלײַב איך דײַן, איך שווער עס דיר.
- Oy, du forst avek, Oy, du forst avek. Oyf vemen lozstu mikh iber? Oyf yamen vel ikh shvimen, Nor tsu dir tsu kimen,* Fun ales bistu mir liber.	- אוי, דו פֿאָרסט אַוועק, אוי, דו פֿאָרסט אַוועק. אויף וועמען לאָזסטו מיך איבער? אויף ימען וועל איך שווימען, נאָר צו דיר צו קימען (קומען). פֿון אַלעס ביסטו מיר ליבער!
- S'iz mir erger nokh fun dir, Du megst es gleybn mir, Mayn harts vet laydn, Benken on a shir.	-- ס'איז מיר ערגער נאָך פֿון דיר, דו מעגסט עס גלייבן מיר; מײַן האַרץ וועט לײַדן, בענקען אָן אַ שיעור.
Refrain: Blimelekh tsvey Geblit tif in vald. Tsesheydt hot men zey, Tserisn mit gvald. Eyns muz in ek velt geyn, Dos tsveyte elnt aleyn, Ver ken dem veytik fun Di blimelekh farshteyn?	**רעפֿריין:** בלימעלעך צוויי געבליט טיף אין וואַלד, צעשיידט האָט מען זיי, צעריסן מיט געוואַלד. איינס מוז אין עק וועלט גיין, דאָס צווייטע עלנט אַליין, ווער קען דעם ווייטיק פֿון די בלימעלעך פֿאַרשטיין?
Blimelekh tsvey Farvelkt far der tsayt, Tsesheydt hot men zey Iber yamen vayt. Dos lebn vet farflien, Zey kenen mer nit blien, Di blimelekh tsvey, Zey veln zikh shoyn mer nit zen.	בלימעלעך צוויי פֿאַרוועלקט פֿאַר דער צײַט, צעשיידט האָט מען זיי איבער ימען ווײַט; דאָס לעבן וועט פֿאַרפֿליִען, זיי קענען מער ניט בליִען, די בלימעלעך צוויי, זיי וועלן זיך שוין מער ניט זען.

---

* kumen

Nokh a regn, libster mayn,
Kumt dos glik un zunenshayn,
Lyube mayn,
Mir veln nokh gliklekh zayn.

Dayne sheyne oygn tsvey
Lindern mayn tifn vey,
Lyube mayn,
Du heylst mayn shmerts un payn.

Mir veln vider hobn freyd,
Mer nit zayn tsesheydt.
Lebn ruik shtil, solid,
Zingen sheyn dos lid:

Blimelekh tsvey. . .

נאָך אַ רעגן, ליבסטער מײַן,
קומט דאָך גליק און זונענשײַן,
ליובע מײַן -
מיר וועלן נאָך גליקלעך זײַן.

דײַנע שיינע אויגן צוויי,
לינדערן מײַן טיפֿן וויי,
ליובע מײַן,
דו היילסט מײַן שמערץ און פּײַן.

מיר וועלן ווידער האָבן פֿרייד,
מער ניט זײַן צעשיידט;
לעבן רויִק שטיל, סאָליד
זינגען שיין דאָס ליד:

בלימעלעך צוויי. . .

Don't worry, don't let it upset you. You won't suffer very long. For when I'm there, I won't forget you, believe me. Everything I'll do to bring you there. You may be sure that you'll always be mine, I swear to you.

Oh, you're going away! For whom are you leaving me? I'll swim across the oceans just to get to you—I love you more than anything. It's even worse for me than for you, you may believe me. My heart will suffer and yearn for you endlessly.

Two little flowers bloomed deep in the woods. Someone separated them, tore them apart by force. One must go to the far corners of the earth, while the other stays alone and lonely. Who can feel the pain of the little flowers?

Two little flowers withered before their time, Someone separated them by broad oceans. Life will fly past and they'll bloom no longer. The two little flowers, they won't be seen anymore.

After a rain, my dearest, come happiness and sunshine, after all. My darling—we will yet be happy. Your beautiful eyes lighten my deep pain. My darling—you heal my pain. We'll be happy again and no longer be separated. We'll live quietly again, for always, and sing the song with joy.

KHAVE חוה

Eve

Words by Solomon Smulewitz-Small (1868–1943); music by Louis Friedsell (1863–1923), from the play *Der antlofener soldat* (The Deserter). The song was published in sheet music by A. Goldberg in 1905. Joseph Rumshinsky writes in his autobiography *Klangen fun mayn lebn* that the famous Russian basso Feodor Chaliapin often sang the song in Russian translation at his concerts. In a German song "Ghetto, Lied und Shimmy" about a Polish-Jewish fiddler, words and music by Ralph Benatzky (published in 1923 by Edition Bristol A. G. Vienna-Berlin), the melody of "Khave" appears as the refrain. The footnote on the songsheet refers to the melody as a Russian-Jewish folksong.

Zint got hot fun Odems beyn	זינט גאָט האָט פֿון אָדמס ביין
A Khave im gemakht,	אַ חוה אים געמאַכט,
Oy, hot er zikh oystsushteyn	אוי, האָט ער זיך אויסצושטיין
Fun ir say tog, say nakht.	פֿון איר סײַ טאָג, סײַ נאַכט.
Oy, esn breng ir khotsh in bet,	אוי, עסןברענג איר כאָטש אין בעט,
Zi est a gantsn tog.	זי עסט אַ גאַנצן טאָג;
Pruv nit gebn ir oyf a "het"	פּרוּװ ניט געבן איר אויף אַ ״העט,״
A yomer un a klog.	אַ יאָמער און אַ קלאָג.
Ot geveynt un shoyn a shmeykhl,	אָט געװײנט און שוין אַ שמייכל,
Lange hor un kurtser seykhl.	לאַנגע האָר און קורצער שׂכל,
Bald fargest zi vemen zi hot lib.	באַלד פֿאַרגעסט זי װעמען זי האָט ליב.
Ven es kumen on di tsaytn,	װען עס קומען אָן די צײַטן,
Az es shtekht ir in di zaytn,	אַז עס שטעכט איר אין די זײַטן,
Nem khotsh hent un fis	נעם כאָטש הענט און פֿיס
Un loyf aroys fun shtib.	און לויף אַרויס פֿון שטיב. (שטוב)
Eyn zakh, in shlof	איין זאַך, אין שלאָף
Iz zi gut on a sof.	איז זי גוט אָן אַ סוף.
Khave, oy, oy, oy,	חוה, אוי, אוי, אוי,
Khave, vi kumt es?	חוה, װי קומט עס?
Khave,	חוה,
Mikh vundert gor on a shir;	מיך װוּנדערט גאָר אָן אַ שיעור;
Khave, oy, oy, oy,	חוה, אוי, אוי, אוי,
Khave,	חוה,
Ikh volt geven tshikave	איך װאָלט געװען טשיקאַװע
Zen vos vet aroyskumen fun dir.	זען װאָס װעט אַרויסקומען פֿון דיר.

Since God, from Adam's bone, made an Eve for him, oh, does he have to put up with a lot from her, both day and night! Oh, she expects him to bring her meals in bed, she eats all day long. Try not giving her money to buy a hat! She whines and complains.

She was just now crying, and now she smiles. Long of hair, but short of common sense. Right away she forgets whom she loves. When she has a pain in her side, you might as well pick yourself up and run out of the house. One thing: when she sleeps, she is very, very good.

Eve, oh, oh, Eve, how come? Eve, it's an endless wonderment to me. Eve, oh, oh, Eve, I'd be curious to see what will become of you.

VU NEMT MEN A BISELE MAZL?

ווו נעמט מען אַ ביסעלע מזל?

Where Do We Find a Little Luck?

Song attributed to Ben Zion Wittler (1907–1961). Popularized by Mike Burstyn.

A mentsh vos hot nor mazl,
Iz dos festgeshtelt,
Az du host a bisl mazl,
Gehert dir di gantse velt.

Refrain:
Vu nemt men a bisele mazl?
Vu nemt men a bisele glik?
Dos redele zol zikh shoyn dreyen
Un brengen mayn mazl tsurik.
Di velt, zi iz dokh bashafn
Far ale mentshn glaykh.
Vu nemt men a bisele,
Khotsh oyf a bisele,
Vu nemt men a bisele glik?

Mentshn, zey shtrebn bay tog un bay nakht,
Vi azoy tsu makhn vos mer gelt,
Yeder eyner trakht;
Men loyft un men yogt zikh
Ahin un aher,
Vayl vifl men farmogt,
Vil men alts mer.
Men iz nor mekane
Vos a tsveyter hot,
Ikh ober freg nor eyn zakh bay got:

Vu nemt men a bisele mazl?

Everyone knows that the person who has luck owns the world.

Where do we find a little luck? Where do we find some happiness? I wish the wheel would turn around and bring my luck back to me. The world, it was just created for everyone equally. Where do we find a little, at least a little—where do we find some happiness?

People, they try hard by day and by night. To make just as much as they can, each one of them thinks. They run and they run all around and about. No matter what they have- It's never enough. People are jealous of everyone else, but I ask just one thing from God: where do we find a little luck?

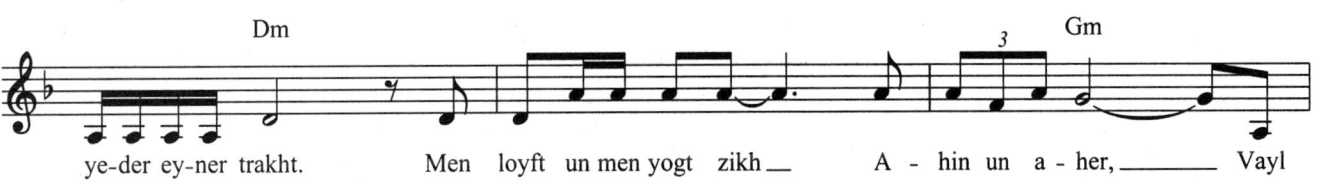

GETO!
SONGS OF THE HOLOCAUST

געטאָ!

HER, MAYN KIND, VI VINTN BRUMEN

הער, מײַן קינד, ווי ווינטן ברומען

Listen to the Wind Roar, My Child

Published in S. Kaczerginsky's collection *Lider fun di getos un lagern*. The song was sung in the ghetto of Oszmiana (a town near Vilna). The words were sung to a popular Polish melody. According to Aleksander Kulisiewicz in Polskie Piesni Obozowe 1939–1945, 1975 (unpublished), one song with this melody was the Polish ghetto song *Elzunia* (There once was a little girl Elzunia. She is dying alone, for her father was in Maidanek and her mother in Auschwitz). The words, written by a nine-year old girl, were found sewn in her shirt. Below the text was written with crooked letters: "I sang it to the tune of the lullaby. 'Na Wojtusia z popielnika iskiereczka mruga (From the oven little sparks blink). I am grateful to Dr. Bret Werb of the U.S. Holocaust Memorial Museum for this information. The melody was also used for two other Yiddish songs: one of the many melodies of Sholem Aleichem's famous lullaby *Shlof, mayn kind* (Sleep, My Child) and *Dos kranke yingl* (The Sick Boy), both published in Bine Shteinberg's *Undzer gezang*.

Her, mayn kind, vi vintn brumen,	הער מײַן קינד, ווי ווינטן ברומען,
Makh di oygn tsu,	מאַך די אויגן צו,
Dayn tatn hot men tsugenumen,	דײַן טאַטן האָט מען צוגענומען,
Kh'veys aleyn nit vu.	כ׳ווייס אליין ניט ווּ.
Ikh aleyn mit dir geblibn,	איך אליין מיט דיר געבליבן,
Vey un vind iz mir,	ווײ און ווינד איז מיר,
Geven zaynen mir nefashes zibn—	געווען זײַנען מיר נפֿשות זיבן—
Itst nor ikh mit dir.	איצט נאָר איך מיט דיר.
Oysgebitn dayne zakhn,	אויסגעביטן דײַנע זאַכן,
S'tut mir vey dos harts,	ס׳טוט מיר ווײ דאָס האַרץ,
Ver vet dir itst naye makhn,	ווער וועט דיר איצט נײַע מאַכן,
Di nakht iz lang un shvarts	די נאַכט איז לאַנג און שוואַרץ.
Nito in shtub keyn zup, keyn bisl,	ניטאָ אין שטוב קיין זופּ, קיין ביסל,
Nito keyn shtikl broyt,	ניטאָ קיין שטיקל ברויט,
Dayne shikh zaynen tserisn,	דײַנע שיך זײַנען צעריסן,
Shlof, mayn kind, in noyt.	שלאָף, מײַן קינד, אין נויט.
Her, mayn kind, men tor nit veynen,	הער, מײַן קינד, מען טאָר ניט וויינען,
Der postn geyt do um,	דער פּאָסטן גייט דאָ אום,
Shisn ken er, ven er t'meynen,	שיסן קען ער, ווען ער ט׳מיינען,
Az men geyt arum.	אַז מען גייט אַרום.

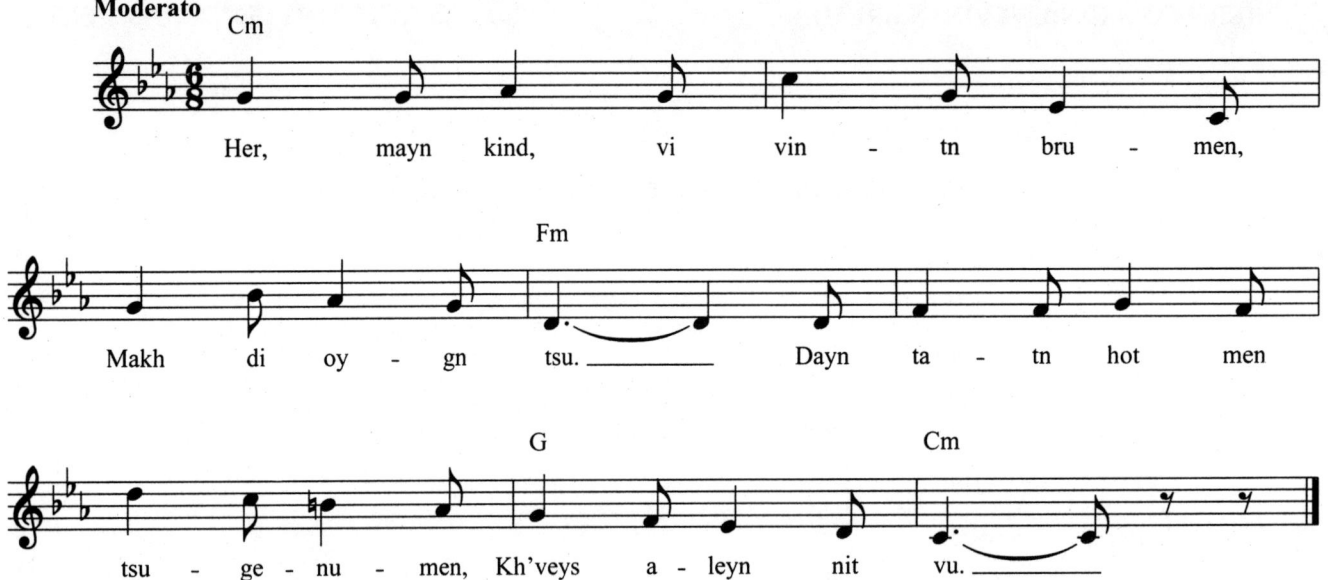

Listen to the wind roar, my child. Close your eyes. They've taken your father away, I have no idea where. Only I remain with you, woe is me. There were seven of us, now there's only you and me. I've pawned your things, my heart aches. Who will make new clothes for you now? The night is long and dark. There's no soup in the house, not a bit; there's not a piece of bread. Your shoes are all torn. Sleep, my child, in poverty. Listen to me, my child, we must not cry. The guard walks around and will shoot us if he thinks someone is here.

SHVAYG, KINDELE, SHVAYG, SHVELBELE

שווײַג, קינדעלע, שווײַג, שוועלבעלע

Be Quiet, Little Child; Be Still, Little Swallow

Recorded by Pinkhes Guter (Toronto), submitted by Dr. Sidney and Lorna Katz (Great Neck) as a song of the Warsaw Ghetto and transcribed by the compilers. Also titled *Treblinke*. Other versions of the song were published in Shoshana Kalisch's *Yes, We Sang!* and without the melody in S. Kaczerginsky's *Lider fun di getos un lagern* and Moyshe Prager's *Min Hametsar Koroti*. Albert Veisbrut, Margate, Fla., writes that the song was sung in the Skarzysko Camp in 1942-1944.

Dort nisht vayt,	דאָרט נישט ווײַט,
Dort vu der umshlag-plats dort shteyt,	דאָרט וווּ דער אומשלאַג-פּלאַץ דאָרט שטייט,
Dort vu men shtupt zikh in der breyt	דאָרט וווּ מען שטופּט זיך אין דער ברייט
In di vagonen.	אין די וואַגאָנען.
Dort, vu a kind shrayt tsu der mamen:	דאָרט, וווּ אַ קינד שרײַט צו דער מאַמען:
Oy, Mame, loz mikh nit aleyn,	אוי, מאַמע, לאָז מיך ניט אַליין,
Ikh vil geyn mit dir tsuzamen.	איך וויל גיין מיט דיר צוזאַמען.
Shvayg, kindele, shvayg, shvelbele,	שווײַג, קינדעלע, שווײַג, שוועלבעלע,
Zog nisht oys, az du bist a yid,	זאָג נישט אויס, אַז דו ביסט אַ ייִד,
Vayl brider, shvester, tate-mame	ווײַל ברידער, שוועסטער, טאַטע-מאַמע
Forn ale tsuzamen	פֿאָרן אַלע צוזאַמען,
Forn ale tsum farsamen.	פֿאָרן אַלע צום פֿאַרסמען.
Shvayg, kindele, shvayg, hertsele,	שווײַג, קינדעלע, שווײַג, הערצעלע,
Zog nit oys, az du bist a yid.	זאָג ניט אויס, אַז דו ביסט אַ ייִד.
Di politsey,	די פּאָליציי,
Zi hot geheysn shneler geyn,	זי האָט געהייסן שנעלער גיין,
Ir vet nit visn fun keyn noyt,	איר וועט ניט וויסן פֿון קיין נויט,
Bakumen dray kilo broyt.	באַקומען דרײַ קילאָ ברויט,
Un mit dem broyt hot men zey	און מיט דעם ברויט
Geshikt tsum toyt,	האָט מען זיי געשיקט צום טויט,
Zey veln mer nit tsurikkumen.	זיי וועלן מער ניט צוריקקומען.
Treblinke dort,	טרעבלינקע דאָרט,
Dos iz dos yidishe gute ort,	דאָס איז דאָס ייִדישע גוטע אָרט,
Ver kumt ahin farblaybt shoyn dort,	ווער קומט אַהין פֿאַרבלײַבט שוין דאָרט.
Vet mer nit tsurikkumen.	וועט מער ניט צוריקקומען.
Dort vu a kind shrayt tsu der mamen:	דאָרט וווּ אַ קינד שרײַט צו דער מאַמען:
Oy, mame, loz mikh nit aleyn,	אוי, מאַמע, לאָז מיך ניט אַליין,
Ikh vil geyn mit dir tsuzamen.	איך וויל גיין מיט דיר צוזאַמען.

Over there not far away, at the loading platform, where they push and shove in the railroad car; over there where a child cries out to his mother: I want to go with you!

Be quiet, little child; be still, little swallow. Don't tell anyone you're a Jew! For your brothers, sisters and parents are all going away to be killed. Be quiet, little child; be still, dear heart. Don't tell anyone you're a Jew!

The police ordered everyone to walk faster: "You will know no want, you'll get three killos of bread." And with that bread, they sent them to their deaths. They will return no more.

Treblinka over there—that's the Jewish cemetery. Whoever goes there stays there and returns no more. There where a child cries out to his mother: O mother, don't leave me alone. I want to go with you!

Song of the Bialystok Ghetto

LID FUN BYALISTOKER GETO

לידֿ פֿון ביאַליסטאָקער געטאָ

Song published in *Songs and Scenes of Bialystok Ghetto*. (N.Y., Feb. 7, 1948). The text was also published by S. Kaczerginsky who attributes the words to I. Zukerman or H. Goldstein of the Bialystok Ghetto. Markovtshizne is a village, 10 kilometers from Bialystok, where Jews were led for forced labor. The Bialystok Jews called the German officer Aletsky from Posen "Mesh" (Copper) because he had red hair. At first they called him "Meshener kop"(Copper Head), later they shortened the name to "Meshl."

A markovtshizner bin ikh, dos fil ikh gut.
Naket un borves di fis—ikh farkil mayn blut.
"Farflukhter"—shrayt men oyf mir un s'harts tut mir vey,
Geyogt mikh, getribn, bay gornisht geblibn, nor klep un geshrey.

Refrain:
Arbet flaysik, ober shneler makh es bald,
Fun Meshlen dem geln bakumstu dayn gehalt.
A hintish lebn on inhalt, on tsil—
Markovtshizne, a troyerike shpil.

Ikh hob gehat a tatn, a mamen, oy-vey,
Shvester-brider oykh derbay.
Geblibn bin ikh elnt vi a shteyn,
Haynt zits ikh bay der arbet un krits di tseyn.

Ikh hob gehat a froy, vi a mamenyu getray,
Kinderlekh mayne—vi brilyantn tsvey.
Tsesheydt azoy plutslung, tsesheydt mit gevald,
Ikh vel keyn mol nit fargesn ayer likhtik geshtalt.

Di mame fun engshaft oyfn feld zikh dershtikt,
Di iberike nonte oyf yener velt geshikt.
Derfar muz ikh horeven bay tsigl un leym,
Fun shtub mikh fartribn, di tfise mayn heym.

Di tfise mayn heym, a shreklekhe nest.
Klep un geshreyen un khazershe kest.
Gants fri bay der arbet un shpet tsurik aheym,
Un eyner fregt dem tsveytn: vos vet fun undz zayn?

Far ale eyn goyrl, far ale eyn shtrebn,
Azoy vi brider darfn mir lebn,
Ober ven es hungert eyn bruder—dayn gevisn iz vu?
Troyerik iz markovtshizne nokh dertsu.

275

I'm from Markovtshizne, indeed I am. Naked and barefoot—my blood is chilled. "Accursed one!" they scream at me and my heart aches. They've chased me, driven me, and left me with nothing but blows and shouts.

Work hard, but finish quickly and right away. You get your pay from red-haired "Copper." A dog's life without meaning or purpose. O Markovtshizne, it's a sad little game.

I had a father and mother, oh woe, and brothers and sisters too. I've been left lonely as a stone—now I sit at my work and grind my teeth. I had a wife, faithful like a dear mother. My little children were like two diamonds. We were separated so suddenly, forcibly separated. I'll never forget their radiant faces. Their mother choked from the crowding in the field. My other nearest and dearest have been sent to the next world. That's why I have to work hard on bricks and clay. They've driven me from my house, and prison is my home. Prison is my home, a horrible nest; blows and shouts and food fit for a pig. Early to work and back home late, and each asks the others: what will become of us?

EYKHO? איכה?

How?

The song appears twice in S. Kaczerginsky's collection of ghetto and concentration camp songs (pp. 14 and 246) without the melody. It was sung in the Bialystok region, Borki-Kamionka. It was also sung in Transnistria (between the Dnieper and Bug Rivers) where Jews from Rumania, especially from Bessarabia and Bukovina were deported. The ghetto song was based on an earlier song that was sung during the Petlura pogroms in Bessarabia. That text was published in the *YIVO Bleter* in 1932. Clara Krasner, mother of Molly Freedman, recorded the song in response to our request, which her son-in-law Robert Freedman then submitted to us. The melody was transcribed by the compilers and thus is printed for the first time.

Farvolknt der himl,
Keyn shtraln zet men nisht;
Es royshn ale gasn—
S'kapet mit blut.

Di botey-medroshim,
Ongevorn zeyer vert;
Men makht fun zey shtaln,
M'shtelt in zey arayn ferd.

Refrain:
Eykho—vi azoy?
Far vos shvaygstu dem goy?
Vu iz, tate, dayn rakhmones?
Re'ey ad'!

Fun dem himl gib a kik (kuk),
Un oyf di yidn gib a blik,
Lesh shoyn op dos fayer
Un loz shoyn zayn genig! (genug)

Di heylike sforim—
Zey zaynen tsuker-zis;
M'rayst fun zey shtiker
Un m'varft oyf dem mist.

Di kleyntshinke kinderlekh
Fun der mames brist;
M'rayst fun zey shtiker
Un m'varft oyf dem mist.

Mir shteyen un betn
In kamyanker lager dort:
Got, hob rakhmones,
Un loz undz aroys fun dem ort!

Es iz beser tsu esn
A trukn shtikl broyt,
Vi eyder tsu shtarbn
Fun lagershn toyt.

How? The sky is cloudy, no rays are seen. All the streets are stirring—blood is flowing. The synogogues have been desecrated; they make stables of them and put horses in them.

How? Why are You silent to the Gentile? Where is Your compasion, Father? Look, O Lord!

Look down from Heaven and cast a glance at the Jews. Extinguish the fire already, and let it be enough! The Holy Books so precious, they tear pieces from them and throw them in the garbage. The littlest children, still at their mothers' breasts, they tear them away and throw them in the garbage. We stand and plead in the Kamyank concentration camp: God, have mercy and let us out of this place!

HABEYT MISHOMAYIM UREEY

הבט משמים וראה

Look Down from Heaven!

The words and music were published in S. Kaczerginsky's *Lider fun di getos un lagern*. Kaczerginsky surmises that the song was written in the Lublin region, where many Jews of Poland and other occupied countries were herded together. He notes that the text of the song is unique in the subject matter of ghetto and concentration camp songs. The song was also published in English translation in Lucy S. Dawidowicz' *A Holocaust Reader*, N.Y., 1976.

Oy, habeyt mishomayim ureey—
Kuk arop fun himl un ze
Ki hoyinu lalaag vokeles,
Lalaag vokeles bagoyim,
Mir zaynen dokh a gelekhter bay zey.
Nekhshavnu katsoyn latevakh:
Oy, bashefer, vi kenstu tsukukn aza zakh?

Mir zaynen dokh keyn mol keyn barite (barute),
Nor tomid tsu der shkhite.

Refrain:
Deriber betn mir dikh ale mol:
Helf shoyn undz, shoymer Yisroel,
Un farnem shoyn undzere trern,
Vayl keyner vil zey nit hern.
Mir shrayen dokh "shma Yisroel!"
Oy, farnem shoyn, shoymer goy ekhod,
Bavayz ake felker az du bist undzer got,
Mir hobn dokh keynem, nor dikh eynem,
Vos dayn nomen is Adoyshem Ekhod.

Zorim oymrim: eyn toykheles vesikvo,
Di felker zogn, az far undz iz
Keyn hofenung nito.
Men meg undz yogn,
Men meg undz plogn,
Mir hobn zikh far keynem
Nit tsu farklogn;
Ober mir veysn dokh,
Az in himl bistu do!
Oyf dir iz der posek faran:
"Hiney loy yonum veloy yishon"
Du muzst dokh hitn
Dayne kinder.
Deriber veysn mir
Az in himl bistu do!
Mit mofsim, mit vinder (vunder)

Khuso Ad' oleynu	חוסה ד' עלינו
Veal titnenu beyedey—	ואל תתננו בידי—
Hob rakhmones, gib undz nit iber	האָב רחמנות, גיב אונדז ניט איבער
In di hent fun zey;	אין די הענט פֿון זיי.
Lomo yoymru hagoyim	למה יאמרו הגוים
Aye eloheyhem,	איה אלהיהם.
Dos iz dokh shtendik zeyer geshrey.	דאָס איז דאָך שטענדיק זייער געשריי.
Oy, yidele, yidele, vos hostu do tsu ton,	אוי ייִדעלע, ייִדעלע, וואָס האָסטו דאָ צו טאָן.
Nem dir dayn pekele un gey dir keyn Tsiyon.	נעם דיר דײַן פּעקעלע און גיי דיר קיין ציאָן (ציון)
Mir voltn antlofn	מיר וואָלטן אַנטלאָפֿן
Nor der veg iz nit ofn,	נאָר דער וועג איז ניט אָפֿן,
Farvos lozstu mit undz azoy ton?!	פֿאַר וואָס לאָזסטו מיט אונדז אַזוי טאָן?

Oh, look down from Heaven, look down from Heaven and see how we have become a laughing stock. We are a laughing stock to them, we are considered sheep for the slaughter. O, Creator, how can You just watch such things? We have never been able to rest—we have always been sent to slaughter.

Therefore we constantly plead to You: Help us now, O, Guardian of Israel, and pay heed to our laments, for no one wants to listen to them though we cry out: "Hear, O, Israel!" Oh, take notice, Guardian of this nation. Show all the nations that You are our God, for we have no one, only You, whose name is The One God.

Strangers say there is no salvation. The nations say there is no hope for us. They are allowed to chase us, torment us. We have no one to complain to, but we know that You are there in Heaven! There is a passage in the Bible about You: "He neither sleeps nor slumbers," for You must protect Your children. Therefore we know that You are there, in Heaven, with miracles and wonders.

Spare us, O, Lord, give us not into their hands. Why should people ask: "Where is their God?" For this is always their cry: O Jew, Jew—what business do you have here? Take your packs and go to Zion! We would flee, but the way is not open. Why do You let them treat us this way?

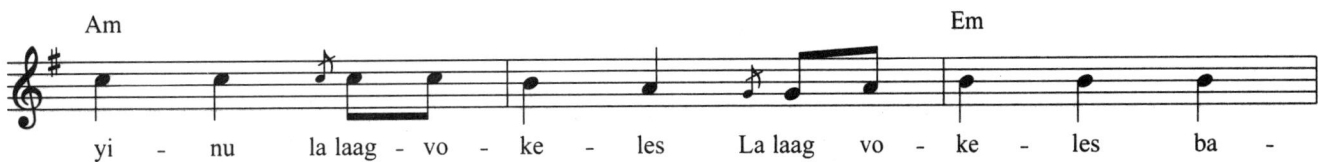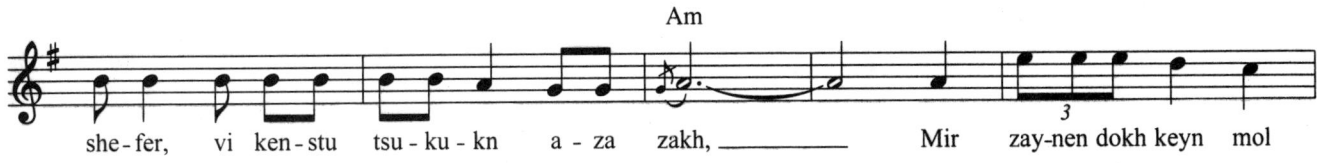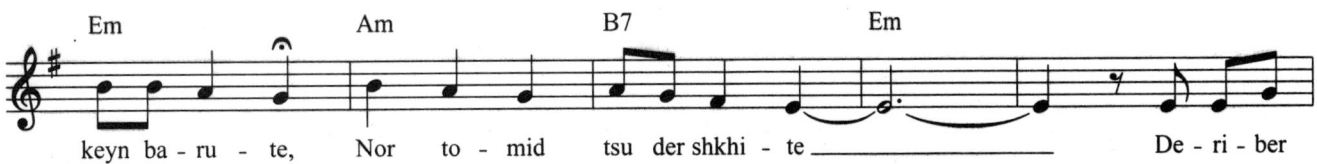

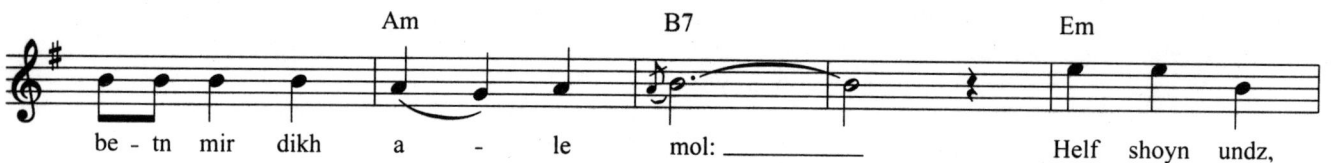

UN A YINGELE VET ZEY FIRN

אוּן אַ ייִנגעלע וועט זיי פֿירן

And a Little Child Shall Lead Them

Poem by H. Leivick, based on the End-of-Days prophecies of Isaiah. Melody based on the refrain of a Yiddish folksong *Shmerl mit dem fidl, Tevye mitn bas*. The song was transcribed by compilers from a record-cassette of Sarah Gorby, *Songs of the Ghetto*. A few of Leivick's lines were adjusted to fit the melody. According to the informant who submitted it to the *Perl,* the song was sung at a Ghetto Memorial in Paris.

Dayn kholem groyser novi, kholem vider,
Bavayz zikh vider iber khorevdike vent,
Nit kuk vos der vos ruft dikh zitst a mider
Dos klogt er oyfn yingele vos ligt farbrent.

A volf darf voynen mit a sheps tsuzamen,
Dos yingele darf firn zey mit zayne hent,—
Dervayl kum, novi, brengen treyst der mamen,
Vos klogt-baklogt ir yingele vos ligt
farbrent.

Tsum lempert darf a tsigele zikh tulyen—
Zey zoln hobn beyde zikh derkent;
Di mame vigt a puste vig, tut lulyen, lulyen,
Dos yingele ligt toyt, oyf ash farbrent.

A ku darf shprayzn mit a ber oyf fiter,
Mit gutskeyt tsu a kind zol zayn a shlang genent,
Nor mir zaynen geven biz itster shlekhte hiter—
Dos yingele ligt toyt, oyf ash farbrent.

Di mame shtaygt aroyf fun bunker-t'homen
Mit ire vigndike hent tsu dir gevendt;
O novi, novi, breng dem akhris hayomim
Makh lebedik dos yingele vos ligt farbrent.

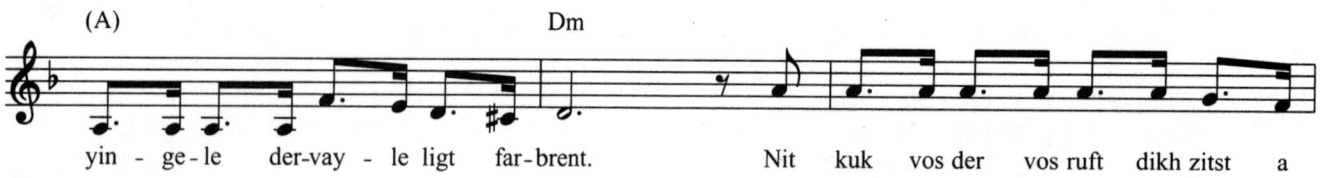

Dream your dream again, great prophet! Show yourself again over destroyed walls. Pay no mind that he who calls you sits wearily—he is mourning his little boy who was cremated.

A wolf is to dwell with a sheep; the little boy is to lead them by the hand. Meanwhile come, prophet, and bring comfort to his mother who mourns her little boy who was cremated.

A lamb is to lie down with a leopard when they meet. The mother rocks an empty cradle and croons lullabys. Her little boy lies dead, burned to ashes.

A cow is to feed with a bear. A snake is to play with a child. But we have been poor guardians so far. The little boy lies dead, burned to ashes.

The mother climbs up out of the bunker depths and turns to you, wringing her hands. O prophet, prophet, bring the End of Days! Resurrect the little boy who was cremated!

SELECTED BIBLIOGRAPHY

Altman, Shalom. *The Judaean Songster.* N.Y.: 1934

Anthology of Yiddish Folksongs, see Vinkovetsky, Aharon et alia.

Bastomski, S. *Unter di grininke beymelekh.* Vilna: 1931

Belarsky, Sidor. *My Favorite Songs.* New York: 1951

Sidor Belarsky Songbook. N.Y.: 1970

Ben Yomen. *Oneg Shabbat Songs.* Miami Beach, Fla.: 1962
— *Zing, mayn folk.* Philadelphia: 1946

Beregovski, M. *Evreiskaya narodnye instrumentalnaya muzika.* Moscow: 1987
—*Evreiskie narodnye pesni.* Moscow: 1962

Beregovski, M. and I. Fefer. *Yidishe folkslider.* Kiev: 1938

Binder, A. W. *New Palestinean Folk Songs.* Book II. N.Y.: 1933

Binishe lider. Vilna: 1932

Bitter, Albert. *Zing-a-lid, 60 arbeter un folkslider.* N.Y.: 1940
—*Zing-a-lid, 50 arbeter un folks-lider.* N.Y.: 1941

Bloch-Lederer, Leye. *Di shenste geklibene yidishe lider... :* 1992

Bugatch, Samuel. *Doyres zingen.* N.Y.: 1951

Bulkin, A. and L. Efron. *Zamlbukh far kinder—lider un shpiln mit gezang.* Vilna: 1917

Cahan, Yehude-Leyb. *Shtudyes vegn yidisher folksshafung.* ed. M. Weinreich. N.Y.: 1952
—*Yidishe folkslider mit melodyes oys dem folksmoyl.* N.Y.: 1912
—"*Yidishe folkslider, naye zamlungen,*" *Pinkes.* N.Y.: 1927–28.
Both collections reprinted in: *Yidishe folkslider mit melodyes,* ed. M. Weinreich. N.Y.: 1957 [Collected Works]

Engel, Joel. *Judische Volkslieder.* Moscow: 1909

Fater, Issachar. *Yidishe muzik un ire problemen.* Tel Aviv: 1985

Flam, Gila. *Singing for Survival, Songs of the Lodz Ghetto, 1940–45.* Urbana and Chicago: 1992

Frankel, Hai and Topsy. *Jiddische Lieder.* Frankfurt: 1981

Di fraye muze, see Glatstein, I.

Gebirtig, Mordecai. *Mayne lider.* Cracow: 1936

Gelbart, Michel. *Lomir zingen.* N.Y.: 1938–39
—*Mir zingen.* N.Y.: 1951
—*Zing mit mir.* N.Y.: 1945

Gershteyn, I. *Lider far a gemishtn khor, 2.* Vilna: 1939

Gezang un kamf, 3, ed. Jacob Schaefer. N.Y.: 1935

Di gildene pave, comp. I. Goichberg. N.Y.: 1949

Ginzburg, Saul M. and Peysakh S. Marek. *Evreiskiya narodniya pesni v Rossii.* St. Petersburg: 1901

Glatstein [Glatshteyn], I. *Di fraye muze.* Warsaw: 1918

Goldfaden, Abraham. *Dos yidele.* 1866
—*Di yidene.* Odessa: 1872

Goldfarb, Israel and S. E. Goldfarb. *The Jewish Songster, Part II,* 1929

Goldin, M. *Evreiskie narodnia pesni.* Moscow: 1972

Dos heylike land, comp. Bertha Flekser and Israel Noroditsky. Zhitomir: 1891

Jasnogorodski, N. *[Lider].* Kiev: circa 1910

Kalisch, Shoshana. *Yes, We Sang! Songs of the Ghettos and Concentration Camps.* N.Y.: 1985

Kaczerginski / Kaczerginsky, Shmerke, *Lider fun di getos un lagern.* New York, 1948

Shmerke Katsherginski-ondenk-bukh. Buenos Aires: 1955

Kinder-fraynd (Muzikalishe biblyotek) no. 6 (Warsaw, November 1937)

Kipnis, Menakhem. *60 folks-lider.* Warsaw: [1918]
—*80 folks-lider.* Warsaw: [1925]

Kipnis, M. and Z. Zeligfeld. *Populerste folks-lider fun Z. Zeligfeld un M. Kipnises repertuar.* Warsaw: n.d.

Kisselgof, Sussman. *Lider-zamlbukh far der yidisher shul un familye.* St. Petersburg: 1911

Klezkamp Songbook. [Songbook of the Klezkamp Yiddish Folk Arts Program]. 1989

Kotylansky, Chaim. *Folks-gezangen.* 1944

Kremer, Isa. *Album of Jewish Folk-Songs.* London/N.Y. and Sydney: 1930

Lamkoff, Paul. *Ten Hebrew Song Classics.* Los Angeles: 1929

Landau, Alfred, "*Bamerkungen tsum yidishn folklor*" *Filologishe shriftn fun YIVO,* I: 1926
—*Mitteilungen der Gesellschaft fur judische Volkskunde,* XI, 1 (1903)

Lehman, Shmuel. *Arbet un frayhayt.* Warsaw: 1921
—*Ganovim-lider mit melodyes.* Warsaw: 1928

Liptzin, Sam. *Zingen mir.* Bronx, N.Y.: 1949

Manger, Itsik. *Shtern un shtoyb.* N.Y.: 1967

Mir zingen, Zamlung fun arbeter un folkslider far kinder, yugnt un dervaksene. Paris: 1946

Mlotek, Eleanor Gordon. "America in East European

Yiddish Folk Song," *The Field of Yiddish*, ed. Uriel Weinreich. N.Y.: 1954
—"International Motifs in the Yiddish Ballad," For Max Weinreich on His Seventieth Birthday. The Hague: 1964
—*Mir trogn a gezang.* N.Y.: 1972

Mlotek, Joseph. *Yidishe kinder, alef.* N.Y.: 1971

Mlotek, Joseph and Chana Mlotek. *Perl fun der yidisher poezye.* Tel Aviv: 1974
—"*Perl fun der yidisher poezye*" The Jewish Forward. N.Y.: 1970–

Mlotek, Eleanor Gordon and Joseph Mlotek. *Pearls of Yiddish Song.* N.Y.: 1988

90 geklibene yidishe folkslider. Warsaw: 1926

Noy, Dov and Meir Noy. *Yidishe folkslider fun galitsye.* Jerusalem: 1971

Ost und West, 1905

Perlmutter, Sholem. *Yidishe dramaturgn un teater-kompozitors.* N.Y.: 1952

Polonski, S. *Far yugnt, lider-zamlung.* Moscow/Kharkov/Minsk: 1931

Prilutski (Prylucki), Noyekh. *Yidishe folkslider, 2.* Warsaw: I, 1911; II, 1913

Pups, Rute. *Dos lid fun geto.* Warsaw: 1962

Raley. *Zingendik, lider far yugnt.* Vilna: 1936

Ran, Leyzer. "*Tsu der biografye fun a folkslid*" *Di goldene keyt,* 110–111 (1983)

Reingold, Isaac. *Selected Songs and Poems of Reingold.* Chicago: 1952

Rosenfeld, Lulla. *Bright Star of Exile, Jacob Adler and the Yiddish Theater.* N.Y.: 1977

Rubin, Ruth. *A Treasury of Jewish Folksong.* N.Y.: 1950
—*Voices of a People.* New York/London: 1963

Sandrow, Nahma. *Vagabond Stars, A World History of Yiddish Theater.* N.Y., Hagerstown, San Francisco, London: 1977

Schack, Sarah Pitkowsky and E. S. Cohen. *Yiddish Folk Songs.* N.Y.: 1924

Schwartz, Julian. *15 Cantece Idis Popularizate.* Bucharest: 1946

Shakhnovski, Nokhem. *Lider gezungen funem folk.* Paris: 1958

Silbermintz, Seymour. *Songs of Israel.* N.Y.: 1949

Silverman, Jerry. *The Yiddish Song Book.* Briarcliff Manor, N.Y.

Singer, Mendel and Moshe Bik. *Al haahava.* Haifa: 1951

Skuditski, Z. *Folklor-lider, 2,* ed. M. Viner. Moscow: 1936

Slobin, Mark. *Old Jewish Folk Music: The Collections and Writings of Moshe Beregovski.* Philadelphia: 1982

Shteinberg, Bine, *Undzer gezang,* Tel Aviv: 1984

Sutzkever, Abraham. *Vilner geto, 1941–1944.* Buenos Aires: 1947

Tsaytshrift far yidisher geshikhte, demografye un ekonomik, literatur-forshung, shprakh-visnshaft un etnografye, II–III. Minsk: 1927–28

Tsions harfe. Warsaw: 1917

Undzer gezang. Warsaw: 1947

Unter di grininke beymelekh. Vilna: 1935

Vayner, Abrasha. *Undzer gezang.* Warsaw: 1930

Vinkovetzky, Aharon, Abba Kovner, Sinai Leichter, *Anthology of Yiddish Folksongs. Vol. I–IV.* Jerusalem: 1984–87

Warshavsky, Mark. *Yidishe folkslider.* 1901

Wellers, Georges. *De Drancy a Auschwitz.* Paris: 1946

Wilno, ed. Ephim H. Jeshurin. N.Y.: 1935

Wohlberg, Max. "The Music of the Synagogue as a Source of the Yiddish Folk Song," *Musica Judaica,* vol. II, no. 1 (1977–78)

Di yidishe bine. N.Y.: 1897

Yidisher folklor, nos. 1–3 (1954–1962)

Yidisher folklor, Filologishe shriftn fun YIVO, V. Vilna: 1938

INDEX OF TITLES AND FIRST LINES

A dank dir, gotenyu, libhartsiker, getrayer, see *Dos freylekhe khosidl*
A glezele lekhayim / 238
A glezele lekhayim es shadt nit nemen haynt / 238
A grus fun di "trentshes" / 216
A gut-morgn dir. Hirsh Dovid, see *Hirsh Dovid*
A gut-morgn, Feyge Soshe / 117
Akh, mayn libe Sore Dvoshe, see *Yosl un Sore Dvoshe*
Akh, troyert, badoyert, see *Khurbn titanik*
Akh, tsion, tsion, du heylik land, see *Tsion*
Alef—indikes / 67
Alef—indikes est der nogid
Aleyn in veg / 205
A mame hot a tekhterl, see *Der kashtnboym*
A markovtshizner bin ikh, see *Lid fun byalistoker geto*
A mentsh vos hot nor mazl, see *Vu nemt men a bisele mazl?*
Amol iz geven a yid / 172
Am yisrol khay! / 246
Antshuldikt! / 250
A sheyner tog / 11
A sheyner tog, a frilings tog / 11
Ay-li, lyu-li, ay-li, lyu-li, see *Nor a mame*
A yingele, a meydele / 16
A yomtev makht oyf ale merk, see *Mir kumen on*
A yor ersht nokh mayn khasene / 253
A yor nokh der khasene / 253
A yunger tate ayngeboygn, see *Lozt arayn*
Az ikh bin gekumen keyn rakhmestrivke, see *Sore un Rifke*
Az me fort keyn sevastopol, see *Dzhankoye*
Barikadn / 84
Beylis, see *Mendl Beylis*
Bay mir iz an oytser faran, see *Der oytser*
Blimelekh tsvey / 261
Breytbard, see *Zishe Breytbard*
Brontshele / 21
Dayn kholem, groyser novi, kholem vider, see *Un a yingele vet zey firn*
Dem zeydns nigndl / 235
Der eybershter iz der mekhutn / 174
Der kashtnboym / 51
Der kremer / 74
Der oytser / 124
Der rebe tut vunder, see *Nisim venifloes*
Der urteyl iz shoyn geven a farshtendlekhe zakh, see *Shuldike umshuldike*
Der vayn fun doyresdikn doyer, see *Ikh bin a yid!*
Der yold iz mikh mekane / 160
Di beryozkele / 200
Di khasene iz geven in der kazarme / 146
Di lena / 83
Di mame hot mikh fun der heym aroysgetribn, see *Koyft a tsaytung!*
Di sapozhkelekh / 30
Di svet-shap / 78
Di tsukunft / 86

Dort nit vayt, see *Shvayg, kindele, shvayg, shvelbele*
Dos freylekhe khosidl / 77
Dos freylekhe shnayderl / 233
Dos kleyne tsigaynerl / 165
Dos naye lid / 93
Du meydele, du fayns / 37
Dzhankoye / 227
Er hot mir tsugezogt / 49
Es flien heldn iber groyse yamen, see *Levin mit zayn "flying" mashin*
Es iz nokh faran aza blum / 59
Es royshn in shap azoy vild di mashinen, see *Di svet-shap*
Eyder ikh leyg mikh shlofn / 62
Eykho / 277
Farkoyfn di sapozhkelekh, see *Di sapozhkelekh*
Farvolknt der himl, see *Eykho*
Fintster in tfise, keytn klingen, see *Lid fun Leo Frenk*
Fraytik oyf der nakht / 170
Fregt di velt an alte kashe / 207
Funem sheynem vortsl aroys / 102
Fun kristi biz kenen, see *Zumer bay nakht oyf di dekher*
Gehert hob ikh dertseyln, see *Dem zeydns nigndl*
Gevald, vu nemt men? see *Varnitshkes*
Habeyt mishomayim ureey / 279
Her, mayn kind, vi vintn brumen / 271
Heyda, nu, tsurik in kheyder / 8
Hirsh Dovid / 108
Hob ikh mir a mantl / 106
Hob ikh mir a mantl fun fartsaytikn tukh / 106
Hu-tsa-tsa / 219
Ikh bin a yid! / 244
Ikh bin shoyn a meydl in di yorn / 24
Ikh ganve in der nakht / 162
Ikh hob dikh lib vi a peysakhdikn rosl / 23
Ikh halt in hant a briv, see *A grus fun di "trentshes"*
Ikh un di velt / 202
Ikh zing far aykh yetst a lid, see *Hu-tsa-tsa*
Ikh zits mir bay der arbet / 36
Ikh zits mir bay der arbet un ikh arbet / 28
In a kleynem engn shtibl, see *Zishe Breytbard*
In a shtetele pitshepoy / 113
In dem shmoln gesele, see *Sorele*
In der fintster / 56
In der fintster zaynen dayne oygn shener / 56
In land, vu es kaylt zikh di lena, see *Di lena*
In mayn gortn / 57
In mayn gortn hot a brunem / 57
In mitn veg shteyt a boym / 183
In prisutsvye hot men mikh gebrakht, see *Di khasene iz geven in der kazarme*
Itsik shpitsik / 115
Itsik shpitsik, got-mit-dir / 115
Kegn gold fun zun / 229
Kegn gold fun zun geyt oyf mayn gold fun veytsn / 229
Khalutsim gikher! / 189

Khatskele / 97
Khatskele, Khatskele, shpil mir a kazatskele /
Khave / 266
Kh'bin a tsigaynerl a kleyner, see *Dos kleyne tsigaynerl*
Kh'gey aroys aleyn in veg in breytn, see *Aleyn in veg*
Kh'hob gelibt a meydl fun akhtsn yor / 41
Khurbn titanik / 141
Kh'vel zikher, Avreml, der ershter nisht lakhn, see *Ver der ershter vet lakhn*
Kh'vil nisht keyn sakh, nor a bisele / 258
Kishenever pogrom / 144
Kol mekadesh shevii / 110
Kol mekadesh shevii koroui loy /
Koyft a tsaytung! / 71
Krokhmalne gas / 56
Krokhmalne gas, ikh ken zi gut /
Lekhayim / 95
Lekhayim, a shnepsl lomir makhn /
Leo Frenk, see *Lid fun Leo Frenk*
Levin mit zayn "flying" mashin / 221
Leyg dayn kop / 197
Leyg dayn kop oyf mayne kni / 197
Lid fun byalistoker geto / 275
Lid fun Leo Frenk / 138
Lid fun mayn dor / 193
Lid fun Yendl Beylis / 135
Lomir onheybn tsu derklern / 99
Lomir zingen, kinderlekh, see *Tshiribim*
Lozt arayn! / 209
Mashinen hudyen binen / 231
Mayne khaveyrim / 90
Mayne khaveyrim - bloyz arbeter-yatn /
Mendl Beylis, see *Lid fun Mendl Beylis* /
Mentshn, git an eytse mir, see *Vu nemt men parnose?*
Mentshn, zey shtrebn bay tog un bay nakht, see *Vu nemt men a bisele mazl?*
Mir kumen on / 18
Mit farmakhte oygn / 198
Nem mir aroys a ber fun vald / 39
Nisim nisim / 127
Nisim venifloes / 130
Nor a mame / 6
O, di velt vet vern yinger, see *Di tsukunft*
Oyf tselokhes ale sonim, see *Am yisroel khay!*
Oh, habeyt mishomayim ureey, see *Habeyt mishomayim ureey*
Oy, hob ikh haynt, khevre-layt, see *Dos freylekhe shnayderl*
Oy, vet mir der rebe shmaysn /
Royz, royz, vi vayt bistu / 176
Ruik, ruik, shoklt ir gelokte, grine kepl, see *Di beryozkele*
S'falt a shney / 64
Shlof, mayn feygele / 4
Shlof, mayn kind, shlof keseyder /
Shnel loyfn di reder / 80
Shnel loyfn di reder, vild klapn mashinen /
Shnirele, perele, gilderne fon /
Shoyn fun eybik on zayt di velt eksistirt, see *Kh'vil nisht keyn sakh, nor a bisele*

Shoyn haynt dray yor az ikh stradaye / 32
Shoyn tsvey-dray yor az mir firn a libe / 26
Shpil, gitar! / 167
Shpil, gitar, biz mayn tsar vet oyfhern / 167
Shpil zhe mir a lidele in yidish / 240
Shteyt in feld a beymele / 2
Shtromen blut un taykhn trern, see *Kishenever pogrom*
Shvayg, kindele, shvayg, shvelbele / 271
S'iz der step / 230
S'iz der step shoyn opgeshorn / 230
Sorele / 53
Sore un Rifke / 153
S'yidishe meydele / 242
Tates, mames, kinderlekh, see *Barikadn*
Tonu rabonen / 104
Tshiribim / 132
Tsi kenstu dos land? / 187
Tsi kenstu dos land vu esroygimlekh blien / 187
Tsion / 181
Tsvey briv tsum lyader reb /
Tsvey taybelekh / 34
Tsvey taybelekh zenen ibern vaser gefloygn /
Tunkl brent a fayer / 212
Un a yingele vet zey firn / 283
Un zol vi vayt nokh zayn di tsayt, see *Dos naye lid*
Varnitshkes / 102
Veim lo akhshav ematay? see *Khalutsim gikher*
Ven di gantse velt volt laydn, see *Ikh un di velt*
Ven di goldn zun fargeyt, see *Es iz nokh faran aza blum*
Ver der ershter vet lakhn / 13
Ver klapt dos azoy shpet bay nakht? see *Brontshele*
Vi halt men dos oys? see *Mendl Beylis*
Vilne / 151
Vilne, shtot fun gayst un tmimes /
Vinter, vi tif der shney un shtark der frost, see *Antshuldikt!*
V'myestyetshku lyadinyu, see *Tsvey briv tsum lyader rebn*
Vos dreystu zikh arum bay mayne fentsterlekh? / 45
Vos zhe makht ir, gute fraynd? see *Lid fun mayn dor*
Vu bistu geven? / 43
Vu iz dos gesele? / 47
Vu iz dos gesele, vu iz di shtib? /
Vu nemt men a bisele mazl? / 267
Vu nemt men parnose? / 214
Yidish redt zikh azoy sheyn / 191
Yidn redn yidish, see *Yidish redt zikh azoy sheyn*
Yidn shmidn / 76
Yidn shmidn, zingen /
Yosl un Sore Dvoshe / 119
Zayt Got hot fun Odems beyn, see *Khave*
Ze dos kleydl, tateshi / 256
Zingendik / 88
Zishe Breytbard / 147
Zitst zikh der kremer in kreml, see *Der kremer*
Zorg nit, zol dir nit ton bang, see *Blimelekh tsvey*
Zumer bay nakht oyf di dekher / 223
Zuntik bin ikh nit geven in kheyder, see *Oy, vet mir der rebe shmaysn*

LIST OF AUTHORS AND COMPOSERS

Abarbanel, M. (d. 1957)
S'iz der step

Adler, Jacob (1873–1973)
A sheyner tog

Beigelman, David (C) (1887–1944)
Hirsh Dovid
Ikh ganve in der nakht
Nisim, nisim
Yidn shmidn

Belarsky, Sidor (C) 1900–1975
Ikh un di velt

Ben Yomen (C) (1901–1970)
Amol iz geven a yid *
S'iz der step

Berezovsky, Saul (C) (1908–1975)
Dem zeydns nigndl

Bergoltz, B.
A glezele lekhayim

Bernstein, Abraham M. (C) (1865–1932)
Kishenever pogrom

Bialik, Chaim Nachmen (1873–1934)
In mayn gortn

Birnov, L. (C)
Leyg dayn kop

Boimwol, Rokhl (b. 1914)
S'yidishe meydele

Broderson, Moishe (1890–1956)
Hirsh Dovid
Ikh ganve in der nakht
In a shtetele pitshepoy (?)
Nisim, nisim
Yidn shmidn

Broydo, Kasriel (1907–1943)
Yosl un Sore Dvoshe

Coslow, Sam (C)*
Levin mit zayn "flying" mashin

Driz, Shike (1908–1971)
Dem zeydns nigndl

Edelshtat, David (1866–1892)
Shnel loyfn di reder

Einhorn, David (1886–1973)
Di beryozkele
Nor a mame

Fefer, Itsik (1900–1952)
Ikh bin a yid

Folman, Lola (C) (1908–1979)
Der kashtnboym

Friedsell, Louis (C) (1863–1923)
Khave

Frug, Simon S. (1860–1916)
Kishenever pogrom
Tsi kenstu dos land vu di esroygim blien?

(C) composer
* author and composer

Gebirtig, Mordecai* (1877–1942)
Ver der ershter vet lakhn

Gelbart, Michel (C) (1889–1966)
Shteyt in feld a beymele

Gilrod, Louis (1879–1930)
Zumer bay nakht oyf di dekher

Glatstein, Jacob (C)
Mayne khaveyrim

Goldfaden, Abraham* (1840–1908)
Der eybershter iz der mekhutn
Der freylekher khosidl
Shlof, mayn feygele
Tsion

Gorovets, Emil (C) (b. 1926)
Ikh bin a yid
S'yidishe meydele

Hirsh, N. (C)
Itsik shpitsik
Mit farmakhte oygn

Jaffee, M.
Lozt arayn!

Jassinowsky, Pinchos (C) (1886–1954)
Der kremer

Kaczerginsky, Shmerke (1908–1954)
Barikadn

Kanapoff, Fishl*
Hu-tsa-tsa

Kerler, Joseph (b. 1918)
Am yisroel khay!
Dos freylekhe shnayderl

Kogan, Lev (C)
Der oytser

Kon, Henech (C) (1898–1972)
Shpil zhe mir a lidele oyf yidish
Ze dos kleydl, tateshi

Kotliar, Joseph
Shpil zhe mir a lidele oyf yidish

Krakovski, Yankev*
Leo Frenk

Lamkoff, Paul (C)
Zingendik

Landau, Zishe (1889–1937)
In der fintster

Leivick, H. (1888–1962)
A yingele vet zey firn
Leyg dayn kop

Lermontov, M. (1814–1841)
Aleyn in veg

Liessin, Abraham (1872–1938)
Der kremer
Di lena

Lillian, Isidor (1880–1960)
A grus fun di "trentshes" *
Yidish redt zikh azoy sheyn

289

Liptzin, Sam (1893–1980)
Lekhayim

Lopatin, Sloyme
Kegn gold fun zun

Manger, Itsik (1901–1969)
Dos kleyne tsigaynerl
Itsik shpitsik
Mit farmakhte oygn
Ze dos kleydl, tateshi

Meyerowitz, David * (1867–1943)
Vu nemt men parnose?

Mlotek, Joseph (b. 1918)
Mayne khaveyrim

Olshanetsky, Alexander (C) (1892–1946)
Vilne

Peretz, Y. L. (1852–1915)
Shteyt in feld a beymele

Perlman, Max*
Kh'vil nit keyn sakh nor a bisele

Perlov, Yitskhok (1911–1980)
Der kashtnboym

Pirozhnikoff, Isaac (C) (1859–1933)
Heyda nu, tsurik in kheyder

Pokrass, Samuil I. (1894–1939)
Shpil gitar

Polonski, S. (C)
Mashinen hudyen

Rauch, Maurice (C) (1910–1994)
Ikh un di velt
Yidish redt zikh azoy sheyn

Reingold, Isaac (1873–1903)
A yor nokh der khasene

Reisen, Abraham (1875–1953)
Aleyn in veg
Dos naye lid
Ikh un di velt

Roisenblatt, H. (1878–1956)
Heyda nu, tsurik in kheyder

Rosenfeld, Morris (1862–1923)
Di svetshap

Rubin, Herts (C) (1911–1958)
Dos kleyne tsigaynerl

Rubinstein, Eli (C)
Dos lid fun mayn dor

Rumshinsky, Joseph (C) (1881–1956)
A glezele lekhayim
Lozt arayn!

Russotto, Henry A. (C)
Khurbn titanik

Sandler, Peretz (C)
Blimelekh tsvey

Schaefer, Jacob (C) (1888–1936)
Shnel loyfn di reder

Schwartz, Simche* (1900–1974)
Koyft a tsaytung

Shrogin, Joseph (C) (1902–1974)
Lekhayim

Smolyanski, Z.
Mashinen hudyen

Smulewitz-Small, Solomon (1868–1943)
Khave
Khurbn titanik

Sternheim, Nokhem* (1879–1942)
Sorele

Tanzman, Joseph
Levin mit zayn "flying" mashin

Telesin, Z. (1905–1996)
Der oytser

Troupianski, Yankl (C) (1909–1944)
Mir kumen on

Waletzky, Josh (C)
Dem zeydns nigndl

Warshavsky, Mark (1840–1907)
Sore un Rifke

Weiner, Lazar (C) (1897–1982)
Shnel loyfn di reder

Weinper, Zishe (1893–1957)
Zingendik

Winchefsky, Morris (1856–1932)
Di tsukunft

Wittler, Ben Zion* (1907–1961)
Krokhmalne gas
Vu nemt men a bisele mazl?

Wolfson, A. L. (1867–1946)
Vilne

Wolfsthal, Khone (C) (1851–1924)
Fraytik oyf der nakht

Younin, Wolf (1908–1984)
Dos lid fun mayn dor

Yud, Nokhem (1888–1966)
Mir kumen on

COMBINED INDEX OF THREE BOOKS
MTAG = MIR TROGN A GEZANG
POYS = PEARLS OF YIDDISH SONG
SOG = SONGS OF GENERATIONS

A brivele der mamen, MTAG / 144
A dank dir, gotenyu, libhartsiker, getrayer, *see Dos freylekhe khosidl*
A glezele lekhayim, SOG / 238
A glezele lekhayim, es shadt nit nemen haynt, SOG /
A glezele yash, MTAG / 68
A grus fun di "trentshes," SOG / 216
A gut-morgn dir, Hirsh-Dovid, *see Hirsh Dovid*
A gut-morgn Feyge Soshe, SOG / 117
A kalte nakht, a nepldike, fintster umetum, *see Papirosn*
A khazndl oyf shabes, MTAG / 108
Akh, mayn libe Sore-Dvoshe, *see Yosl un Sore-Dvoshe*
A kholem, MTAG / 24
Akh, troyert, badoyert, *see Khurbn titanik*
Akhtsik er un zibetsik zi, MTAG / 62
Akh, tsion, tsion, du heylik land, *see Tsion*
A kind a goldene, POYS / 16
A kind iz dos a goldene, POYS / 16
A kind nokh in kheyder bin ikh dokh atsind, *see Ot geyt Yankele*
Ale brider, MTAG / 160
Alef—indikes, SOG / 67
Alef—indikes est der nogid, SOG / 67
Aleyn in veg, SOG / 205
A malekh veynt, POYS / 38
A mame hot a tekhterl, *see Der kashtnboym*
A markovtshizner bin ikh, dos fil ikh gut, *see Lid fun byalistoker geto*
A mentsh vos hot nor mazl, *see Vu nemt men a bisele mazl?*
Amol iz geven a mayse, MTAG / 104
Amol iz geven a yid, SOG / 172
Am yisroel khay, MTAG / 194
Am yisroel khay, SOG / 246
A nign, POYS / 112
Ani holakhti beyar veshomati bas kol, *see Katarina moloditsa*
Antshuldikt, SOG / 250
A pastekhl, MTAG / 130
A pastekhl iz geven amol, MTAG / 130
Arbeter-froyen, POYS / 68
Arbeter-froyen, laydnde froyen! POYS / 68
Arbeter-ring-himen, MTAG / 100
Aroyskumen zolstu mayn meydl, MTAG / 46
Arum dem fayer, MTAG / 176
A sheyner tog, SOG / 11
A sheyner tog, a frilings tog, SOG /
A shtetl iz amerike, *see Lebn zol amerike*
Avek di yunge yorn, MTAG / 132
Avremele, gib nor a kuk, *see Avremele un Yosele*
Avremele un Yosele, MTAG / 198
Avreml der marvikher, MTAG / 200
A yingele, a meydele, SOG / 16

Ay-li, lyu-li, ay-li, lyu-li, *see Nor a mame*
A yomtev makht oyf ale merk, *see Mir kumen on*
A yor ersht nokh mayn khasene, SOG / 253
A yor nokh der khasene, SOG / 253
A yunger tate ayngeboygn, *see Lozt arayn!*
Az der Rebe Elimeylekh, *see Der Rebe Elimeylekh*
Az der rebe tantst, POYS / 127
Az ikh bin gekumen keyn rakhmestrivke, *see Sore un Rifke*
Az ikh vel zogn "lekho doydi," POYS / 157
Az ikh volt gehat dem keysers oytsres, POYS / 2
Az me fort keyn sevastopol, *see Dzhankoye*
Az Tshipe-Trayne iz in shtub arayngekumen, *see Di bord*
Barikadn, SOG / 84
Batrakht dem mentsh ven er iz raykh, *see Mit keyn gelt tor men nit shtoltsirn*
Bay dem shtetl, POYS / 14
Bay dem shtetl shteyt a shtibl, POYS / 14
Bay mir iz an oytser faran, *see Der oytser*
Bayt zhe mir oys a finfuntsvantsiker, MTAG / 60
Belz, POYS / 260
Berele, mayn libinker, *see Nokh a glezele tey*
Beshas der shadkhn iz gekumen tsu mayn zeydn, *see Di mashke*
Bin ikh mir a khosidl, POYS / 129
Bin ikh mir a khosidl, a freylekhe brie, POYS / 129
Blimelekh tsvey, SOG / 261
Blond bistu vi a zangl, *see Dos zangl*
Brengt der shadkhn mir a shidekh, *see Kh'vil nisht aza khosn*
Brider un shvester fun arbet un noyt, *see Di shvue*
Brontshele, SOG / 21
Bulbes, MTAG / 74
Dayn kholem, groyser novi, kholem vider, *see Un a yingele vet zey firn*
Dem Bal-shem-tovs zemerl, POYS / 133
Dem ershtn tog peysakh, *see Kishenever pogrom*
Dem milners trern, MTAG / 120
Dem pedlers brivele, POYS / 242
Dem zeydns brokhe, POYS / 100
Dem zeydns nigndl, SOG / 235
Der eybershter iz der mekhutn, SOG / 174
Der filosof, MTAG / 124
Der fodem, POYS / 72
Der kashtnboym, SOG / 51
Der kranker shnayder, POYS / 76
Der kremer, SOG / 74
Der oytser, SOG / 124
Der Rebe Elimeylekh, MTAG / 168
Der rebe hot geheysn freylekh zayn, POYS / 136
Der rebe shtelt zikh oyf baym tish, *see Khasidimlekh*
Der rebe tut vunder, *see Nisim venifloes*

Dertseyl mir, alter, *see* Belz
Der urteyl iz shoyn geven a farshtendlekher zakh, *see* Shuldike umshuldike
Der vayn fun doyresdikn doyer, *see* Ikh bin a yid!
Der yid der shmid, POYS / 90
Der yid hot in zayn lebn, *see* Got un zayn mishpet iz gerekht
Der yid, nebekh, loyft vi fun fayer, *see* Elis-ayland
Der yold iz mir mekane, SOG / 160
Der yunginker shnayderl, POYS / 39
Di beryozkele, SOG / 200
Di bord, MTAG / 128
Di dray neytorins, POYS / 70
Di goldene pave, MTAG / 106
Di grine kuzine, MTAG / 142
Di khasene iz geven in der kazarme, SOG / 146
Di krenetse, POYS / 196
Di lena, SOG / 83
Di mame dertseylt, POYS / 96
Di mame hot mikh fun der heym aroysgetribn, *see* Koyft a tsaytung!
Di mashke, POYS / 163
Di mekhutonim geyen, MTAG / 56
Di mizinke oysgegebn, MTAG / 54
Di oygn royt, di lipn blo, *see* Di dray neytorins
Dire-gelt, MTAG / 76
Dire-gelt un oy-oy-oy, MTAG / 76
Di sapozhkelekh, SOG / 30
Di shtub iz kleyn, di shtub iz alt, *see* Der kranker shnayder
Di shvue, MTAG / 98
Di sokhe, MTAG / 96
Di svetshap, SOG / 78
Di tsukunft, SOG / 86
Di velt nemt mikh arum mit shtekhike hent, *see* Eybik
Di verbe, POYS / 42
Di zun hot zikh bahaltn, *see* Der fodem
Di zun iz fargangen, MTAG / 204
Di zun iz fargangen, shoyn triblekh gevorn, MTAG / 204
Di zun vet aruntergeyn, MTAG / 180
Di zun vet aruntergeyn untern barg, MTAG / 180
Dona, dona, POYS / 175
Don un Donye, POYS / 58
Don hot tsvey peyelekh shvartse, *see* Don un Donye
Dort nisht vayt, *see* Shvayg, kindele, shvayg shvelbele
Dort, vu grozn zaynen naser, *see* Di krenetse
Dos alte porfolk, MTAG / 206
Dos baytshl kreln, POYS / 60
Dos fertsnte yor, MTAG / 136
Dos fertsnte yor iz ongekumen, vey, oy vey! MTAG / 136
Dos freylekhe khosidl, SOG / 177
Dos freylekhe shnayderl, SOG / 233
Dos kleyne tsigaynerl, SOG / 165
Dos lid fun ayznban, MTAG / 126
Dos lid fun broyt, MTAG / 102
Dos lidl fun goldenem land, MTAG / 208
Dos naye lid, SOG / 93
Dos pintele yid, POYS / 231
Dos zangl, POYS / 63

Dray tekhterlekh, MTAG / 210
Du, du, POYS / 32
Du meydele du fayns, SOG / 37
Du vest zayn a gvir, mayn Zhamele, *see* Zhamele
Dzhankoye, SOG / 227
Efnt tir un efnt toyer, *see* Am yisroel khay
Elis-ayland, POYS / 244
Ergets vayt, POYS / 84
Er hot mir tsugezogt, SOG / 49
Erloybt lozt zikh dinen, *see* Vos geven iz geven un nito
Es flien heldn iber groyse yamen, *see* Levin mit zayn "flying" mashin
Es hot mir mayn mame dertseylt, az a mol, *see* Di mame dertseylt
Es iz nokh faran aza blum, SOG / 59
Es iz tsu mir gekumen a kuzine, *see* Di grine kuzine
Es kumt tsu flien di goldene pave, *see* Di goldene pave
Es rayst dos harts fun der shreklekher plog, *see* Lid fun trayengl-fayer
Es royshn in shap azoy vild di mashinen, *see* Di svetshap
Es shaynt di levone, es glantsn di shtern, *see* Zamd un shtern
Eybik, POYS / 199
Eyder ikh leyg mikh shlofn, SOG / 62
Eykho, SOG / 277
Eyli, Eyli, POYS / 220
Eyli, Eyli, lomo azavtoni? POYS / 220
Eynzam, MTAG / 162
Far aykh, mentshn, muz ikh mikh baklogn, *see* Vu zaynen mayne zibn gute yor?
Farkoyfn di sapozhkelekh, *see* Di sapozhkelekh
Farvolknt der himl, *see* Eykho
Far vos, MTAG / 184
Far vos iz dos likhtele farloshn? MTAG / 184
Faryomert, farklogt, POYS / 223
Fintster in tfise, keytn klingen, *see* Lid fun Leo Frenk
Fisherlid, POYS / 34
Fonye ganev, MTAG / 134
Fort a fisher oyfn yam, *see* Fisherlid
Forverts, brider, in di reyen, *see* Makhnes geyen
Fraytik oyf der nakht, MTAG / 110
Fraytik oyf der nakht, SOG / 170
Fregt di velt an alte kashe, SOG / 207
Fun dem himl tsugeshikt, *see* Ver hot aza yingele?
Funem sheynem vortsl aroys, SOG / 102
Fun kosev biz kitev, POYS / 131
Fun kristi biz kenen, *see* Zumer bay nakht oyf di dekher
Fun vanen heybt zikh on a libe, MTAG / 16
Gedenkt ir yene zise tsaytn, *see* Zmires
Gehert hob ikh dertseyln, *see* Dem zeydns nigndl
Gevald, vu nemt men? *see* Varnitshkes
Geven amol a yid mit a yidene, POYS / 98
Gey ikh mir shpatsirn, MTAG / 37
Got un zayn mishpet iz gerekht, POYS / 234
Groyser Got, mir zingen lider, *see* Dos lid fun broyt
Habeyt mishomayim ureey, SOG / 279
Harshl, POYS / 179
Harshl iz geven eyner fun di groyse, POYS / 179
Hekher! beser! *see* Di mizinke oysgegebn

Hemerl, *see Tsum hemerl*
Her, mayn kind, vi vintn brumen, SOG / 271
Her nor, du sheyn meydele, MTAG / 32
Hershele, POYS / 53
Hershele, du lebst in mayn zikorn, POYS / 53
Heyda nu, tsurik in kheyder, SOG / 8
Heysn, heys ikh Yosl Ber, *see Yosl-Ber*
Hey, tsigelekh, MTAG / 213
Hey, tsigelekh, kumt aher tsu mir geshvind, MTAG / 213
Hirsh Dovid, SOG / 108
Hirsh Lekert, MTAG / 94
Hob ikh mir a mantl, SOG / 106
Hob ikh mir a mantl fun fartsaytikn tukh, SOG /
Hob ikh mir an altn daym, MTAG / 66
Hobn mir a nigndl, *see Undzer nigndl*
Hof, hof, hof, *see Hof un gleyb*
Hof un gleyb, POYS / 86
Hulyet, hulyet, beyze vintn, POYS / 66
Hulyet, hulyet, kinderlekh, MTAG / 214
Hu-tsa-tsa, SOG / 219
Iber ale grenetsn, SOG /
Iber felder, vegn, *see Yidl mitn fidl*
Ikh bin a "border" bay mayn vayb, POYS / 254
Ikh bin a yid, SOG / 244
Ikh bin oyf felder, velder fraye, *see Laptshes*
Ikh bin shoyn a meydl in di yorn, SOG / 24
Ikh bin shoyn vider "singl," *see Ikh bin a border bay mayn vayb*
Ikh derman zikh in dem fraytik oyf der nakht, *see Fraytik oyf der nakht*
Ikh ganve in der nakht, SOG / 162
Ikh gey aroys oyfn ganikl, *see Oyfn ganikl*
Ikh halt in hant a briv, *see A grus fun di "trentshes"*
Ikh hob a kleynem yingele, *see Mayn yingele*
Ikh hob dikh lib vi a peysakhdikn rosl, SOG / 23
Ikh ken a meydl, MTAG / 45
Ikh un di velt, SOG / 202
Ikh vel a zemerl dir zingen, gotenyu! *see Dem Bal-shem-tovs zemerl*
Ikh vil nit geyn in kheyder, MTAG / 12
Ikh vil nit keyn ayzerne keytn, MTAG / 86
Ikh zing far aykh yetst a lid, *see Hu-tsa-tsa*
Ikh zits mir bay der arbet, SOG / 37
Ikh zits mir bay der arbet un ikh arbet, SOG / 28
In a groysn dorf, freylekh iz atsind, *see Yaneks khasene*
In a kleynem engn shtibl, *see Zishe Breytbard*
In an orem shtibele, POYS / 9
In a shtetele pitshepoy, SOG / 113
In dem beys-hamikdesh, in a vinkl kheyder, *see Rozhinkes mit mandlen*
In dem shmoln gesele, *see Sorele*
In der fintster, SOG / 56
In der fintster zaynen dayne oygn shener, SOG / 56
In der kuznye, MTAG / 82
In der kuznye bay dem fayer, MTAG / 82
In der tifkeyt fun der nakht, *see Kholemen khaloymes*
In droysn geyt a regn, *see Fonye ganev*
In kamf, MTAG / 80
In land, vu es kayklt zikh di lena, *see Di lena*

In mayn gortn, SOG / 57
In mayn gortn hot a brunem, SOG / 57
In mitn veg shteyt a boym, SOG / 183
In prisutsvye hot men mikh gebrakht, *see Di khasene iz geven in der kazarme*
In rod arayn, POYS / 153
In sahara, vu men vandert, *see S'iz a lign*
In sokhe, *see Di sokhe*
In veldl, baym taykhl, dort zenen gevaksn, *see Margaritkelekh*
In yedn land, oyf yedn ort, *see Dos pintele yid*
Ir hot gevis, libe mentshn, gehert, *see Lid fun titanik*
Itsik hot khasene gehat, POYS / 165
Itsik shpitsik, SOG / 115
Itsik shpitsik, Got-mit-dir, SOG / 115
Iz a kabtsn amol gevezn, *see A nign*
Iz gekumen a khazn in a kleyn shtetl, *see A khazndl oyf shabes*
Kartofl-zup mit shvomen, MTAG / 216
Katarina moloditsa poydi syuda, POYS / 167
Kegn gold fun zun, SOG / 229
Kegn gold fun zun geyt oyf mayn gold fun veytsn, SOG / 229
Keyner veys nit vos ikh zog, *see Eynzam*
Keyn kotsk fort men nisht, *see Kotsk*
Khalutsim gikher, SOG / 189
Khane, mayn vaybl, du shlofst? *see Dos alte porfolk*
Khasidimlekh, MTAG / 112
Khatskele, SOG / 97
Khatskele, Khatskele, shpil mir a kazatskele, SOG / 97
Khave, SOG / 266
Kh'bin a tsigaynerl a kleyner, *see Dos kleyne tsigaynerl*
Kh'bin geven a kleyner yat, *see Kh'vel shoyn mer nit ganvenen*
Kh'gey aroys aleyn in veg in breytn, *see Aleyn in veg*
Kh'gey arum baym breg fun yam, *see Du, du*
Kh'hob far dir, mayn held, keyn moyre, *see Mayn tate a koyen*
Kh'hob fargesn ale libste, *see Yam-lid*
Kh'hob gehat a mamenyu, *see Regndl*
Kh'hob gelibt a meydl fun akhtsn yor, SOG / 41
Kh'hob zikh gekoyft a baytshl kreln, *see Dos baytshl kreln*
Kholemen khaloymes, POYS / 184
Khurbn titanik, SOG / 141
Kh'vel shoyn mer nit ganvenen, POYS / 177
Kh'vel zikher, Avreml, der ershter nisht lakhn, *see Ver der ershter vet lakhn*
Kh'vil nisht aza khosn, MTAG / 220
Kh'vil nisht keyn sakh, nor a bisele, SOG / 258
Kinder-yorn, MTAG / 222
Kinder-yorn, zise kinder-yorn, MTAG / 222
Kishenever pogrom, MTAG / 137
Kishenever pogrom, *see Lid fun kishenever pogrom*
Kol mekadesh, SOG / 110
Kol mekadesh shevii koroui loy, SOG / 110
Kotsk, POYS / 138
Koyf mir nit keyn lokenes, *see Yoshke fort avek*
Koyft a tsaytung, SOG / 71
Krokhmalne gas, SOG / 156

Krokhmalne gas, ikh ken zi gut, SOG / 156
Kum aher, du filosof, see Der filosof
Kum, Leybke, tantsn, MTAG / 228
Laptshes, POYS / 46
Lebn zol Kolombus, MTAG / 140
Lekhayim, MTAG / 53
Lekhayim, SOG / 95
Lekhayim, a shnepsl lomir makhn, SOG / 95
Leo Frenk, see Lid fun Leo Frenk
Levin mit zayn "flying" mashin, SOG / 221
Leybke, mayn liber, dos vet keyn guts nisht gebn, see Kum, Leybke, tantsn
Leyg dayn kop, SOG / 97
Leyg dayn kop oyf mayne kni, SOG / 197
Leyg ikh mir in bet arayn, POYS / 48
Leyg ikh mir mayn kepele, POYS / 114
Lid fun byalistoker geto, SOG / 275
Lid fun kishenever pogrom, SOG / 144
Lid fun Leo Frenk, SOG / 138
Lid fun mayn dor, SOG /
Lid fun Mendl Beylis, SOG / 135
Lid fun titanik, POYS / 104
Lid fun trayengl-fayer, POYS / 251
Lomir ale zingen a zemerl, MTAG / 156
Lomir ale zingen, lomir ale zingen, MTAG / 156
Lomir beyde a libe shpiln, MTAG / 18
Lomir, lomir, lomir, lomir, see Der yid der shmid
Lomir onheybn tsu derklern, SOG / 99
Lomir zikh iberbetn, POYS / 26
Lomir zikh iberbetn, ovinu shebashomayim, POYS / 214
Lomir zingen dos sheyne lid, see Rabeynu Tam
Lomir zingen, kinderlekh, see Tshiribim
Lozt arayn, SOG / 209
Makhnes geyen, MTAG / 84
Mamenyu, lyubenyu, POYS / 28
Mamenyu, lyubenyu, kroynele, hartsele, POYS / 28
Mamenyu mayne, POYS / 119
Mamenyu mayne, mamenyu harts, POYS / 119
Margaritkelekh, MTAG / 40
Mashinen hudyen binen, SOG / 231
May-ko mash-me-lon, POYS / 116
May-ko mash-me-lon der regn? POYS / 116
May-lid, POYS / 82
Mayne khaveyrim, SOG / 190
Mayne khaveyrim, bloyz arbeter-yatn, SOG / 190
Mayn kind, mayn treyst, du forst avek, see A brivele der mamen
Mayn rue-plats, MTAG / 150
Mayn tate a koyen, MTAG / 219
Mayn tsavoe, MTAG /d 92
Mayn yingele, MTAG / 148
Mekhuteneste mayne, MTAG / 58
Mekhuteneste mayne, mekhuteneste getraye, MTAG / 58
Melokhe-melukhe, POYS / 92
Mendl Beylis, see Lid fun Mendl Beylis
Mentshn, git an eytse mir, see Vu nemt men parnose?
Mir hobn di heymishe flamen, see Arbeter-ring-himen
Mir kumen on, SOG / 18
Mir vern gehast un getribn, see In kamf

Mit farmakhte oygn, SOG / 198
Mit keyn gelt tor men nit shtoltsirn, POYS / 271
Motele, MTAG / 224
Motl der apreyter, POYS / 248
Moyshele, mayn fraynd, MTAG / 122
Nem mir aroys a ber fun vald, SOG / 39
Nisim, nisim, SOG / 127
Nisim venifloes, SOG / 130
Nit bay tog un nit bay nakht, see Di verbe
Nit zukh mikh, vu di mirtn grinen, see Mayn rue-plats
Nokh a glezele tey, MTAG / 226
Nokh der sude, far kol-nidre, see Dem zeydns brokhe
Nokhemke, mayn zun, POYS / 161
Nor a mame, SOG / 6
O, di velt vet vern yinger, see Di tsukunft
O gute fraynd, ven ikh vel shtarbn, see Mayn tsavoe
O hemerl, hemerl, klap, see Tsum hemerl
O kum shoyn shtiler ovnt, MTAG / 178
O liber, mir hobn geshlosn, POYS / 75
On a heym bin ikh yung geblibn, see Avreml der marvikher
Ongezolyet oyfn hartsn, makht men a lekhayim, see Zol shoyn kumen di geule
O, tayere mame, du fregst mikh vos makh ikh, see Dem pedlers brivele
Ot geyt Yankele, POYS / 18
Ovnt-lid, POYS / 194
Oy, Abram, POYS / 24
Oy, Abram, ikh ken on dir nisht zayn! POYS / 24
Oy, a nakht a sheyne, POYS / 22
Oy, bobenyu, zog nokh nit "Got fun Avrom," see Zol nokh zayn shabes
Oy, dortn, dortn, MTAG / 26
Oy, dortn, dortn, ibern vaserl, MTAG / 26
Oyfn barg, ibern barg, see Avek di yunge yorn
Oyfn boydem shloft der dakh, POYS / 80
Oyfn furl ligt dos kelbl, see Dona, dona
Oyfn ganikl, MTAG / 38
Oyfn oyvn zitst a meydl, see Tumba
Oyfn pripetshik, MTAG / 2
Oyfn pripetshik brent a fayerl, MTAG / 2
Oyfn veg shteyt a boym, MTAG / 164
Oyf tselokhes ale sonim, see Am yisroel khay!
Oy, habeyt mishomayim ureey, see Habeyt mishomayim ureey
Oy, hob ikh haynt, khevre-layt, see Dos freylekhe shnayderl
Oy, lomir zikh tsekushn, see Itsik hot khasene gehat
Oy, mamenyu, tayere, mamenyu lib, see Der yunginker shnayderl
Oy, nem guter klezmer, dayn fidl in hant, see Dos lidl fun goldenem land
Oy, vet mir der rebe shmaysn, SOG / 19
Oy-vey, rebenyu, POYS / 140
Oy vifl yorn, see Dem milners trern
O, zayt gezunterheyt, mayne libe eltern, see Zayt gezunterheyt!
Papir iz dokh vays, MTAG / 20
Papir iz dokh vays un tint iz dokh hvarts, MTAG / 20
Papirosn, POYS / 267
Partizaner-himen, see Zog nit keyn mol

Patshe kikhelekh, MTAG / 7
Patshe, patshe, kikhelekh, MTAG / 7
Pozharne komande, MTAG / 120
Rabeynu Tam, MTAG / 170
Reb Motenyu, POYS / 142
Regndl, POYS / 110
Reyzele, MTAG / 48
Royz, royz, SOG / 176
Royz, royz, vi vayt bistu, SOG / 176
Rozhinkes mit mandlen, MTAG / 4
Ruik, ruik, shoklt ir gelokte, grine kepl, see Di beryozkele
S'brent! briderlekh, s'brent! see Undzer shtetl brent
S'falt a shney, SOG / 64
Sha-sha, es zol zayn shtil, POYS / 148
Sha, shtil, makht nisht keyn gerider, POYS / 144
Sha, shtil, un nit gezorgt, POYS / 146
Shivas tsion, POYS / 217
Shlekhte kumen un farbaytn, see Ikh vil nit geyn in kheyder
Shlof, mayn feygele, SOG / 4
Shlof, mayn kind, MTAG / 152
Shlof, mayn kind, mayn treyst, mayn sheyner, MTAG / 152
Shlof mayn kind, shlof keseyder, SOG / 69
Shlof zhe mir shoyn, Yankele, mayn sheyner, *see Yankele*
Shmilik, Gavrilik, MTAG / 146
Shmilik, Gavrilik, khaveyrimlekh tsvey, MTAG / 146
Shnel loyfn di reder, SOG / 80
Shnel loyfn di reder, vild klapn mashinen, SOG / 80
Shnirele perele gilderne fon, SOG / 185
Sholem-aleykhem, MTAG / 64
S'hot mir mayn tate nokh kindvayz gezogt, *see Zing shtil*
Shoyn fun eybik on, zayt di velt eksistirt, *see Kh'vil nisht keyn sakh, nor a bisele*
Shoyn haynt dray yor az ikh stradaye, SOG / 32
Shoyn tsvey-dray yor vi mir firn a libe, SOG / 26
Shpil gitar, SOG / 167
Shpil, gitar, biz mayn tsar vet oyfhern, SOG / 167
Shpil mir, tsigayner, *see Vaylu*
Shpilt aykh, libe kinderlekh, *see Hulyet, hulyet, kinderlekh*
Shpil zhe mir a lidele in yidish, SOG / 240
Shprayz ikh mir, MTAG / 70
Shprayz ikh mir mit gikhe, mit gikhe trit, MTAG / 70
Shterndl, MTAG / 116
Shterndl, shterndl, bloyer shtafetele, MTAG / 116
Shteyt a bokher un er trakht, *see Tum-balalayke*
Shteyt in feld a beymele, SOG / 2
Shteyt zikh dort in gesele, *see Reyzele*
Shtiler ovnt, tunkl-gold, *see Ovnt-lid*
Shtromen blut un taykhn trern, *see Lid fun kishenever pogrom*
Shuldike umshuldike, SOG / 248
Shvartse karshelekh, MTAG / 78
Shvartse karshelekh rayst men, MTAG / 78
Shvartse oygn hobn fayer, POYS / 56
Shvayg, kindele, shvayg, shvelbele, SOG / 271
S'iz a lign, MTAG / 182

S'iz der step, SOG / 230
S'iz der step shoyn opgeshorn, SOG / 230
S'iz haynt akurat gevorn fuftsik yor, *see Akhtsik er un zibetsik zi*
S'iz nito keyn nekhtn, POYS / 159
S'loyfn, s'yogn shvartse volkn, POYS / 78
Sorele, SOG / 53
Sore un Rifke, SOG /153
S'yidishe meydele, SOG / 242
Tates, mames, kinderlekh, *see Barikadn*
Tayere Malke, POYS / 202
Tayere Malkele, POYS / 50
Tonu rabonen, SOG / 104
Tonu rabonen, hobn undzere khakhomim gelernt, SOG / 104
Toybn, POYS / 192
Toybn shteyen bay mayn fentster, POYS / 192
Tsen brider, POYS / 121
Tsen brider zaynen mir geven, POYS / 121
Tsen kopikes, MTAG / 42
Tsen kopikes hob ikh, MTAG / 42
Tshiribim, SOG / 132
Tsi kenstu dos land? SOG / 187
Tsi kenstu dos land vu esroygimlekh blien? SOG / 7
Tsion, SOG / 181
Tsi zol ikh zikh farshraybn, *see Pozharne komande*
Tsum hemerl, MTAG / 78
Tsvey briv tsum lyader rebn, SOG / 179
Tsvey taybelekh, SOG / 34
Tsvey taybelekh zenen ibern vaser gefloygn, SOG / 34
Tumba, MTAG / 44
Tum-balalayke, MTAG / 30
Tunkl brent a fayer, SOG / 212
Umru mayne, POYS / 62
Un a yingele vet zey firn, SOG / 283
Un az es kumt der liber peysakh, *see Sha, shtil, un nit gezorgt!*
Un du akerst, MTAG / 90
Un du akerst un du zeyst, MTAG / 90
Undzer nigndl, MTAG / 158
Undzer rebenyu, POYS / 125
Undzer shtetl brent, MTAG / 231
Un mir zaynen ale brider, *see Ale brider*
Unter a kleyn beymele, POYS / 36
Unter beymer, POYS / 4
Unter di grininke beymelekh, POYS / 6
Unter di khurves fun poyln, MTAG / 192
Un zol vi vayt nokh zayn di tsayt, *see Dos naye lid*
Vakht oyf, MTAG / 88
Varnitshkes, SOG / 102
Vaylu, POYS / 190
Veim lo akhshav ematay? *see Khalutsim gikher!*
Vemes shtime her ikh klingen? *see May-lid*
Ven di gantse velt volt laydn, *see Ikh un di velt*
Ven di goldn zun fargeyt, *see Es iz nokh faran aza blum*
Ven es dremlt dos shtetl, POYS / 44
Ven ikh nem a bisele yash, oy-oy, *see A glezele yash*
Ven mit mazl, gezunt un lebn, *see Dray tekhterlekh*
Ver der ershter vet lakhn, SOG / 13
Ver hot aza yingele? POYS / 12
Ver hot dos gezen, *see Dos lid fun ayznban*

Ver ken di sheynkeyt fun a yam farshteyn? *see Umru mayne*
Ver klapt dos azoy shpet bay nakht? *see Brontshele*
Ver se veyst nisht, ver se veyst nisht, *see Melokhe-melukhe*
Ver s'iz nit geven, *see Tayere Malkele Ver zingt es dort?* POYS / 188
Ver zingt es dort oyf yenem breg, POYS / 188
Vi halt men dos oys? *see Lid fun Mendl Beylis*
Vi lang, o vi lang vet ir blaybn nokh shklafn, *see Vakht oyf*
Vilne, SOG / 151
Vilne, shtot fun gayst un tmimes, SOG / 151
Vinter, vi tif der shney un shtark der frost, *see Antshuldikt*
Vi shlekht un vi biter, POYS / 108
Vi shlekht un vi biter s'iz tsu dinen bay yenemen, POYS / 108
V'myestyetshku lyadinyu, *see Tsvey briv tsum lyader rebn*
Vos dergeystu mir di yorn? MTAG / 34
Vos dergeystu mir di yorn, mayne yunge, yunge yorn? MTAG / 34
Vos dreystu zikh arum bay mayne fentsterlekh? SOG / 145
Vos geven iz geven un nito, POYS / 274
Vos hobn mir tsu mitog haynt? *see Kartofl-zup mit shvomen*
Vos makhstu epes, Moyshele, *see Moyshele, mayn fraynd*
Vos toyg mir der sheyner vayngortn? POYS / 30
Vos vet der sof zayn, Motl, zog zhe mir? *see Motele*
Vos vet zayn az Meshiakh vet kumen, POYS / 170
Vos ze ikh durkh di shoybn? *see Shivas tsion*
Vos zhe makht ir, gute fraynd? *see Lid fun mayn dor*
Voyl iz dem rebn un di khsidim, *see Der rebe hot geheysn freylekh zayn*
Vu bistu geven? SOG / 43
Vu iz dos gesele? SOG / 47
Vu iz dos gesele, vu iz di shtib? SOG / 47
Vu nemt men a bisele mazl? SOG / 267
Vu nemt men parnose? SOG / 214
Vu zaynen mayne zibn gute yor? POYS / 268
Yam-lid, POYS / 212
Yaneks khasene, POYS / 155
Yankele, MTAG / 8

Yidish redt zikh azoy sheyn, SOG / 191
Yidl mitn fidl, POYS / 258
Yidn redn yidish, *see Yidish redt zikh azoy sheyn*
Yidn shmidn, SOG / 76
Yidn shmidn, zingen, SOG / 76
Yisrolik, kum aheym, POYS / 227
Yome, Yome, MTAG / 22
Yome, Yome, shpil mir a lidele, MTAG / 22
Yoshke fort avek, POYS / 106
Yosl Ber, POYS / 173
Yosl un Sore Dvoshe, SOG / 119
Zamd un shtern, POYS / 210
Zayt gezunterheyt, POYS / 102
Zayt got hot fun Odems beyn, *see Khave*
Ze dos kleydl, tateshi, SOG / 256
Zhamele, POYS / 88
Zingendik, SOG / 88
Zingendik, treyst zikh di velt di farvundete, SOG / 88
Zing shtil, POYS / 182
Zishe Breytbard, SOG / 147
Zitst zikh der kremer in kreml, *see Der kremer*
Zmires, POYS / 237
Zog, maran, POYS / 205
Zog maran, du bruder mayner, POYS / 205
Zog mir, yidl, bruder mayner, *see Yisrolik, kum aheym*
Zog nit keyn mol, MTAG / 190
Zog nit keyn mol az du geyst dem letstn vet, MTAG / 190
Zogt der rebe Reb Motenyu, *see Reb Motenyu*
Zog zhe, rebenyu! *see Vos vet zayn az Meshiakh vet kumen?*
Zol nokh zayn shabes, POYS / 207
Zol shoyn kumen di geule, MTAG / 172
Zolst azoy lebn, MTAG / 10
Zolst azoy lebn un zayn gezunt, MTAG / 10
Zol zayn, MTAG / 186
Zol zayn, az ikh boy in der luft mayne shleser, MTAG / 186
Zorg nit, zol dir nit ton bang, *see Blimelekh tsvey*
Zumer bay nakht oyf di dekher, SOG / 223
Zuntik bin ikh nit geven in kheyder, *see Oy, vet mikh der rebe shmaysn*
Zuntik bulbes, *see Bulbes*
Zun in mayrev, POYS / 186

באשולדיקט געוואָרן אין רוסלאַנד אין יאָר 1911, אַז ער האָט דערמאָרדעט אַ קריסטלעך קינד און ייִדן און אויך ניט־ייִדן אין דער וועלט זענען אויפֿגעטרייסלט געוואָרן פֿון דעם שרעקלעכן בילבול. מיר דרוקן אויך אַ ליד וועגן לעאָ פֿראַנק, וואָס איז אומשולדיק געמישפּט געוואָרן פֿאַר אַן ענלעכן בילבול אין אַמעריקע און איז נאָך דעם ווי דער טויט־אורטייל איז דורכן גאָווערנאָר פֿאַרביטן געוואָרן אויף אייביקער תּפֿיסה, געלינטשט געוואָרן אין 1915 פֿון אַן אויפֿגערייצטן המון אַנטיסעמיטן. מיר האָפֿן אַז די נייע דורות וועלן מיט די לידער באַקאַנט ווערן, און פּונקט ווי דאָס ליד פֿון אונדזערע פֿריִערדיקע ביכער וועגן דעם טרייענגל־פֿײַער פֿון יאָר 1912, וואָס איז געזונגען געוואָרן אין דער ייִדיש־ענגלישער שפּיל „דאָס גאָלדענע לאַנד" און ווערט איצט געזונגען פֿון יונגע קינסטלער אויף זייערע קאָנצערטן, וועלן אויך די היסטאָרישע לידער אין דעם בוך וועלן אַ טייל פֿון זייער רעפּערטואַר.

כּדי צו קענען אַרויסגעבן אַזאַ בוך דאַרף מען קענען שאַפֿן די נייטיקע פֿאָנדן. פּונקט ווי בײַ די פֿריִערדיקע ביכער האָבן זיך אויך איצט אָפּגערופֿן ליִענערס און פֿרײַנד וואָס האָבן צוגעטראָגן ברייטהאַרציקע בײַשטײַערונגען כּדי דאָס בוך זאָל קענען דערשײַנען. אויף אַן אַנדער אָרט דערמאָנען מיר זייערע נעמען מיט אונדזער האַרציקסטן דאַנק צו יעדן איינעם פֿון זיי.

**

צוצוגרייטן דאָס בוך מיט אַלע די ייִדישע טעקסטן, די ענגלישע טראַנסליטעראַציע און איבערזעצונגען, די מוזיק מיט די אַקאָרדן און אילוסטראַציעס און דער עיקר – די אַלע הערות וועו און פֿון וועמען די לידער זענען געשאַפֿן געוואָרן, האָט בײַ אונדז גענומען פֿינעף יאָר אַרבעט. מיר ווילן דאָ האַרציק דאַנקען ד״ר בערל זומאָף, וועלכער האָט שוין איבערגעזעצט די לידער פֿון יעקבֿ גלאַטשטיין און אַבֿרהם סוצקעווער, פֿאַר זײַנע ענגלישע איבערזעצונגען אין דעם בוך, דעם מוזיקער זלמן מלאָטעק פֿאַר זײַנע גוטע עצות בײַם פּלאַנירן דאָס בוך און די מוזיק־אַקאָרדן וואָס ער האָט געשאַפֿן צו די לידער, דער קינסטלערין צירל װאָלעצקי פֿאַר דער אילוסטראַציע אויפֿן שער־בלאַט און די אילוסטראַציעס צו יעדן קאַפּיטל אינעם בוך און חנן קיאל און פּעגי דייווויס פֿאַר דער ייִדישער און ענגלישער שריפֿט אויפֿן שער־בלאַט. אַ דאַנק קומט אויך פּערל קרופּיט, עלענאַ לייקינד און הערבערט לאַזאַרוס פֿאַר זייער טעכנישער הילף בײַם צוגרייטן דעם מאַנוסקריפּט, חוה לאַפֿין, ראָבערט קאַפּלאַן און סטיווען דאָלינג פֿאַר זייער זאָרג, אַז דאָס בוך זאָל קענען דערשײַנען.

מיר האָפֿן אַז אונדזער נײַ בוך „לידער פֿון דור צו דור" וועט, ווי אונדזערע פֿריִערדיקע ביכער, ווידער אַ מאָל דערגרייכן צו די נײַע ייִדישע דורות, וועלכע וועלן די לידער מיט דער זעלביקער פֿרייד און הנאה, מיט וועלכע עס האָבן די לידער געזונגען און זינגען די אונדזערע נאָך איצט, באָבעס און זיידעס און טאַטעס און מאַמעס. מיר האָפֿן אויך ווײַטער צו קענען ממשיך זײַן אונדזער רובריק „פּערל פֿון דער ייִדישער פּאָעזיע" אין „פֿאָרווערטס" און צו געפֿינען נײַע פּערל פֿון אונדזערע פֿאָלקס־אוצרות און זיי קענען ברענגען צו נײַע דורות ייִדישע ליִענערס און זינגערס.

מיר ווידמען דאָס בוך צו אונדזערע אייניקלעך לייזער־בנימין, אַבֿרהם־יצחק, באַשע־מלכּה, און אלישע־מענדל, אין וועמענס מײַלער עס לעבט דאָס ייִדישע וואָרט און ליד.

חנה און יאָסל מלאָטעק

אין אויגוסט פון יאר 1995 האבן מיר געדרוקט אין "פֿאַרווערטס" אַ וואַריאַנט פון מיכל גאָרדאָנס ליד "די באָרד" וואָס גאָרדאָן האָט געדרוקט אין יאר 1868 (אפשר געשאַפֿן נאָך פֿריִער). עטלעכע וואָכן שפּעטער האָבן מיר דערהאַלטן בריוו מיט וואַריאַנטן פון דעם ליד, וואָס עס האָבן צוגעשיקט לייענערס פון סווענציאַן, ליטע, און פון נתניה, מדינת-ישראל. זיי האָבן געשריבן אַז דאָס ליד ווערט איצט נאָך אַלץ געזונגען אויף היימישע שמחות אָבער אַ ביסל אַנדערש ווי עס איז געווען אָריגינעל געשריבן.

מ.מ. וואַרשאַווסקיס "אויפֿן פּריפּעטשיק", וואָס איז צום ערשטן מאָל געדרוקט געוואָרן אין דער צײַטונג "דער ייִד" און איז אַרײַן אין וואַרשאַווסקיס בוך, וואָס איז אַרויס אין קיִעוו אין 1901 איז געשפּילט געוואָרן אין דעם פֿילם "שינדלערס ליסטע", וואָס האָט עס שוין געזען מיליאָנען מענטשן, און ווען מען האָט געפֿרעגט יצחק פּערלמאַנען וואָס מע זאָל שפּילן בײַם פֿאַרשטעלן אים אויף אַ קאָנצערט לכבֿוד זײַן 50סטן געבוירן-טאָג אין טאַנגלווּד, דער זומער-רעזאָרט, וווּ עס קומען צו יעדן סימפֿאָנישן קאָנצערט מיט די באַרימטסטע אַמעריקאַנער דיריגענטן, טויזנטער מוזיק-ליבהאבערס, האָט ער געבעטן מע זאָל שפּילן ניט קיין אַנדער ליד ווי "אויפֿן פּריפּעטשיק" און אַ גרויסער טייל פֿונעם עולם האָט מיטגעזונגען דאָס ליד, וואָס איז נאָך הײַנט ניט ווייניקער פּאָפּולער ווי מיט הונדערט יאָר צוריק, ווען עס איז געשאַפֿן געוואָרן.

וועגן דעם פֿענאָמענאַלן דערפֿאָלג פון די ייִדישע פֿאָלקסלידער פון די אַנאָנימע פֿאָלקסזינגערס און פון אונדזערע פּאָעטן און קאָמפּאָזיטאָרן זאָגן אויך עדות די פֿאַקטן, אַז זינט 1972, ווען עס איז אַרויס אונדזער בוך "מיר טראָגן אַ געזאַנג", זענען שוין אַרויס זעקס עדיציעס מיט צוואַנציק טויזנט קאָפּיעס, פֿונעם בוך "פּערל פון ייִדישן ליד", וואָס איז געדרוקט געוואָרן אין פֿינף טויזנט קאָפּיעס אין דרײַ טויזנט עקזעמפּלאַרן אין יאר 1988 און איז איבערגעדרוקט געוואָרן אין פֿינף טויזנט קאָפּיעס אין 1992, איז איצט, ווען מיר גייען צום דרוק מיט אונדזער נײַ בוך, געבליבן ווייניקער ווי צוויי טויזנט ביכער. אויך די טאַשמעס מיט אַ צאָל פון די לידער, זענען שוין לאַנג אויספֿאַרקויפֿט און עס דאַרפֿן איצט געדרוקט ווערן נײַע. אויך די ביכער "פּערל פון דער ייִדישער פּאָעזיע" (פּרץ-פֿאַרלאַג, תל-אָבֿיבֿ, 1974) און די געטאָ-לידער "מיר קומען אָן" זענען שוין לאַנג אויספֿאַרקויפֿט און מיר זוכן פֿאַנדן זיי אויף סינײַ אַרויסצוגעבן.

***

אין דעם איצטיקן נײַעס בוך לידער, וואָס וועגן די מערסטע פון זיי האָבן זיך אָנגעפֿרעגט אונדזערע לייענערס פון "פֿאָרווערטס", האָבן מיר אַרײַנגענומען נאָר אַזעלכע וואָס זענען אין די פֿריִערדיקע ביכער ניט געוואָרן געדרוקט. ווידער האָבן מיר צווישן זיי לידער פון די קינדער-יאָרן, לידער פון ליבע און חתונות, פון אַרבעט, נויט און פּראָטעסט און נאַציאָנאַלע מאָטיוון, און אויך מאָטיוון פון ייִדישן טעאַטער און געטאָ-לידער. מיר ווילן באַזונדערס אַרויסהייבן די אָפּטיילן פון לידער וואָס זענען געשאַפֿן געוואָרן אין סאָוועטן-פֿאַרבאַנד און די היסטאָרישע לידער. מיר האָבן די לעצטע יאָרן צוגעקראָגן אַ צאָל נײַע לייענערס פון דער לענדער פון געוועזענעם סאָוועטן-פֿאַרבאַנד און אויך פון נײַע אימיגראַנטן פון די דאָזיקע לענדער. לייענערס פון אוקראַיִנע און ווײַסרוסלאַנד שרײַבן אונדז, אַז זיי נוצן אונדזערע ביכער אין זייערע ייִדישע שולן און זיי שיקן אונדז אויך צו לידער וואָס מע האָט דאָרט געשאַפֿן. מיר האָבן אַ סך יאָרן אויף אונדזערע פּראָטעסט- און אָנדענק-פֿאַרזאַמלונגען דעם 12טן אויגוסט געפֿאָדערט און געהאָפֿט, אַז עס וועלן זיך עפֿענען די אַרכיוורנע טירן פֿון דער אימפּעריע וואָס האָט געהאַלטן אָפּגעשלאָסן מיליאָנען פון אונדזערע קולטור-אוצרות. זינט 1990 האָט זיך אונדז אײַנגעגעבן אײַנצושטעלן אַ ברידערלעכע פֿאַרבינדונג מיט די דאָרטיקע ייִדן און מיר ברענגען אין דעם בוך אַ צאָל לידער וואָס עס האָבן געשאַפֿן סאָוועטיש-ייִדישע קאָמפּאָזיטאָרן און שרײַבערס. מיר דרוקן אויך צוויי פון די "פֿאַרבאָטענע לידער" וואָס זענען דאָרט געזונגען געוואָרן געהיים.

מיט די היסטאָרישע לידער וואָס מיר דרוקן אין דעם בוך וועלן געעפֿנט ווערן פֿאַר די נײַע דורות קאַפּיטלעך פון אונדזער ייִדישער געשיכטע מיט וועלכער זיי זענען ווייניק באַקאַנט: וועגן קישענעווער פּאָגראָם אין 1903, ווען ייִדן פון אַמעריקע, הערנדיק דאָס ליד "שענקט די טויטע אויף תּכריכים און די לעבעדיקע בּרויט", האָבן געזאַמלט און געשיקט הילף צו די געליטענע; וועגן מענדל בייליס, וועלכער איז

הקדמה פֿון די צונויפֿשטעלערס

ווען מיר האָבן אין אָקטאָבער פֿון יאָר 1995 אויסגעשיקט צום דרוק דעם מאַנוסקריפּט פֿון אונדזער נײַ בוך „לידער פֿון דור צו דור", איז געוואָרן פֿינף און צוואַנציק יאָר, ווי מיר האָבן דעם 25סטן אָקטאָבער פֿון יאָר 1970 אָנגעהויבן דרוקן אונדזער ווענטלעכע רובריק „פּערל פֿון דער ייִדישער פּאָעזיע" אין „פֿאָרווערטס". אין משך פֿון די פֿינף און צוואַנציק יאָר האָבן מיר אידענטיפֿיצירט און געדרוקט טויזנטער לידער פֿון וועלכע אונד- זערע לייענערס פֿון צפֿון- און דרום-אַמעריקע, מדינת-ישׂראל, אייראָפּע און אויסטראַליע האָבן געדענקט נאָר שורות, און זיי האָבן אונדז געבעטן אויסצוגעפֿינען ווער עס זענען די מחברים, און מיר זאָלן אויך דרוקן דעם פֿולן טעקסט פֿון די לידער. מיר האָבן דאָס געטאָן און מיר האָבן אויך געדרוקט וואַריאַנטן פֿון לידער, וואָס אַ צאָל פֿון זיי זענען געשאַפֿן געוואָרן מיט מער ווי הונדערט יאָר צוריק פֿון מחברים, וועמענס נעמען נעמען נישט נאָר די לייענערס געדענקען נישט, נאָר אויך פּראָפֿעסיאָנעלע זינגערס ווייסן וועגן זיי ניט און זיי שרײַבן אויף די פּלאַטעס און טאַשמעס וואָס זיי גיבן אַרויס, אַז דאָס זענען פֿאָלקסלידער פֿון אומבאַקאַנטע מחברים. דאָ נישט לאַנג איז אין דײַטשלאַנד אַרויס אַ פּלאַטע מיט ייִדישע לידער און אַהרן צײַטלינס ליד „אויפֿן פּויל ליגט אַ קעלבל" צו וועלכן שלום סעקונדאַ האָט געשריבן די מוזיק. איז עס דאָרט פֿאַרגעשטעלט געוואָרן ווי אַ ליד וואָס איז געשאַפֿן געוואָרן אין דער וואַרשעווער געטאָ.

דאָס ליד, אַגבֿ, ווערט אויך געזונגען אין קאָרעאַניש און יאַפּאַניש און איז רעקאָרדירט אויף דעם דיסקן, אָבער אָן אַ נעמען פֿון דעם מחבר און קאָמפּאָזיטאָר. מיט אַ צײַט צוריק האָט די אַלמנה פֿון דעם דיכטער לייב מלאך זיך באַקלאָגט אין דער פּרעסע, אַז דער יוגנט-הימען פֿון דער פּועלי ציון, וואָס מאַן איר לייב מלאך האָט געשאַפֿן, ווערט צוגעשריבן צו עמעצן אַנדערש. אַזעלכע אומפֿינקטלעכקייטן זענען צום באַדויערן דאָ אַ סך. אין דעם בוך, ווי אין די פֿריִערדיקע צוויי, האָבן מיר זיך באַמיט צוריק אויפֿצולעבן די נעמען פֿון די פּאעטן און קאָמפּאָזיטאָרן, וועמענס לידער זענען עס ווערן געזונגען ווי אַנאָנימע פֿאָלקסלידער.

***

מיר האָבן באַשלאָסן אַנצורופֿן אונדזער נײַ בוך „לידער פֿון דור צו דור", ווײַל אַ גרויסע צאָל פֿון די לידער, וואָס זענען געשאַפֿן געוואָרן און געוואָרן פּאָפּולער מיט אַ סך יאָרן צוריק, ווערן נאָך הײַנט געזונגען, אָדער ווערן אויפֿגעלעבט פֿון די קינדער און אייניקלעך פֿון די אימיגראַנטישע באָבע-זיידע און פֿון יונגע מוזיקערס איבער גאָר דער וועלט און זיי ווערן איצט ווידער באַקאַנט און פּאָפּולער. אָט זענען נאָר עטלעכע פֿאַקטן.

אין יאָר 1975 האָט אַ גרופּע יוגנטלעכע אַרויסגעגעבן אַ פּלאַטע מיט ייִדישע לידער, וואָס זיי האָבן זיך אויסגעלערנט און געזונגען אין דעם ייִדישן זומער-קעמפּ „המשך", וואָס איז געבויט געוואָרן פֿון זייערע עלטערן, וואָס זענען געקומען קיין ניו-יאָרק נאָך דער צווייטער וועלט-מלחמה. איינע פֿון די לידער אויף דער פּלאַטע איז געווען „די וועלט ווערט ייִנגער" („די צוקונפֿט") פֿון מאַריס ווינטשעווסקי, וואָס איז געווען פּאָפּולער אין פֿאַרמלחמהדיקן פּוילן. ווינטשעווסקי (1856-1932) האָט דאָס ליד געשריבן אין די סוף-יאָרן פֿון 19טן י״ה. איצט ווערט דאָס ייִדישע ליד געזונגען אין אַן ענגלישער פּיעסע „אַ שיינע מיידל", וואָס ווערט די לעצטע יאָרן געשפּילט אין צענדליקער אַמעריקאַנער אוניווערסיטעטן און עס גייט כּמעט ניט אַוועק קיין וואָך, אַז דער אַרבעטער-רינג זאָל נישט קריגן קיין בריוו עמעצן צוצושיקן די פּלאַטע און געבן די דערלויבעניש צו זינגען דאָס ליד אין דער פּיעסע. איבעריק צו זאָגן, אַז דער אַרבעטער-רינג גיט די דערלויבעניש און דאָס ליד, וואָס איז געשאַפֿן געוואָרן מיט מער ווי הונדערט יאָר צוריק, ווערט איצט געזונגען און געהערט פֿון אַ סך טויזנטער אַמעריקאַנער ייִדן און אויך ניט-ייִדן.

***

אין חודש יולי פֿון הײַנטיקן יאָר האָבן מיר צען טויזנט ייִדן פֿון אַלע דורות אויף אַן אַרבעטער-רינג פֿעסטיוואַל מיטגעזונגען מיט זעקס קלעזמער-אַנסאַמבלען און דעם פֿידל-ווירטואָז יצחק פּערלמאַן מ. ווינטשעווסקיס ליד „און מיר זענען אַלע ברידער", משה נאַדירס „דער רבי אלימלך" און אַנדערע ייִדישע לידער, וואָס זענען געשאַפֿן געוואָרן מיט אַ סך יאָרן צוריק.

אַרײַנפיר פֿון דבֿ נוי

די צוויי ערשטע זאַמלונגען פֿון חנה און יוסף מלאָטעק – מיר טראָגן אַ געזאַנג (ערשטער אַרויסלאָז – 1972) און פּערל פֿון ייִדישן ליד (1988) פֿאַרנעמען דעם אויבנאָן צווישן די ייִדישע פֿאָלקסלידער-אָפּקלײַבן און זאַמלונגען, פּובליקירט אין די נאָך-מלחמה-יאָרן.

דערויף זאָגט עדות ניט נאָר דאָס כמות פֿון די פּובליקירטע אויפֿלאַגעס און פֿאַרקויפֿטע קאָפּיעס. דאָס כמות איז דאָך ניט תמיד דער סימן מובֿהק פֿון דעם איכות. אָבער ס'איז קלאָר, אַז דער נײַער דור פֿון ייִדיש-זינגערס און פֿון ליבהאָבערס פֿונעם ייִדישן פֿאָלקסליד און פֿון דער ייִדישער פֿאָלקסמוזיק איז אַנדערש פֿון די פֿאַרמלחמהדיקע דורות. הײַנטצײַטיקע אַנטײלנעמערס אין ייִדיש-זינגקרײַזן און אין ייִדישע קלעזמער-קעמפּן האָבן על-פּי-רובֿ אַן אַקאַדעמישע בילדונג און זענען פֿאַראינטערעסירט ניט נאָר אין זינגען צוזאַמען און אַפֿילו ניט נאָר אין די ווערטער און אין די מעלאָדיעס. זיי אינטערעסירט אויך די ביאָגראַפֿיע פֿונעם ליד, זײַן אָפּשטאַם, זײַן פֿאַרשפּרייטונג, זײַנע וואַריאַנטן און פּאַראַלעלן, זײַנע מקורות און השפעות. אין דער ייִדישער עסטעטישער ליטעראַטור זענען מיר ניט געוווינט צו אַזאַ וויסנשאַפֿטלעכן צוגאַנג, אָבער דער וויסנשאַפֿטלעכער אינטערעס פֿון די צוזאַמענשטעלערס איז קענטיק אין זייערע אָפּקלײַבן און פּובליקאַציעס און דאָס האָט בלי ספק אַ צוציִונגס-כוח פֿאַר די הײַנטצײַטיקע סטודענטן וואָס זענען מעטאָדאָלאָגיש אויפֿגעוואַקסן אויף אינטעלעקטועלער נײַגעריקייט.

די 125 לידער פֿונעם נײַעם דריטן באַנד דערגאַנצט דעם אָפּקלײַב און זיי רעפּרעזענטירן אויך סײַ לידער וואָס דער נאָמען פֿון זייער מחבר איז פֿאַרגעסן געוואָרן און סײַ לידער וואָס זייער מחבר איז גוט באַקאַנט, אָבער זיי האָבן זוכה געווען צו אַ פֿאָלקלאָריזאַציע-פּראָצעס וועלכער האָט אָפֿט געענדערט די ווערטער און די מוזיק פֿונעם זינגליד, כאָטשע דער עיקר, דאָס רעמל, איז געבליבן. אין דער ייִדישער טראַדיציע שאַפֿט „דאָס דריטע מאָל" אַ „חזקה", וואָס איר שורש שטאַמט פֿונעם עבֿרישן „חזק" - שטאַרק. די דריטע זאַמלונג פֿאַרפֿעסטיקט טאַקע אירע צוויי עלטערע שוועסטער.

עס דוכט מיר אַז די הויפּט-סיבה פֿון דער אויבן-דערמאָנטער הצלחה ליגט בעיקרשט אין דעם וואָס די צוזאַמענשטעלערס האָבן באַוויזן צו פֿאַראייניקן אין זייערע זאַמלונגען, און אין זייערע אַקטיוויטעטן בכלל, צוויי טענדענצן וואָס בדרך כלל עקזיסטירט אַ קאָנפֿראָנטאַציע צווישן זיי. דער סינטעז פֿאַרבינדט די ליבע צום זינגענדיקן פֿאָלק, מיט וועלכן עס איז פֿאַראַן אַ שטענדיקער קאָנטאַקט, מיט דער ליבע צום זינגליד ווי אַן אויסדרוק פֿון ייִדישער פֿאָלקס-שעפֿערישקייט. די צוויי ליבעס זענען בײַ דעם מלאָטעק-פּאָרל געקניפּט און געבונדן, און ביידע פֿאַרנעמען אויך אין דער הינזיכט אַן איינציקן און באַזונדערן פּלאַץ אין דער געשיכטע פֿון אונדזער פּרעסע, פֿאָלקלאָריסטיק און עטנאָמוזיקאָלאָגיע.

זינט 1970, מער ווי אַ דור, פֿירן חנה און יאָסל מלאָטעק אין פֿאָרווערטס אַן אָפּטייל אונטערן נאָמען „פּערל פֿון דער ייִדישער פּאָעזיע", וואָס זײַן עיקרדיקער טייל איז געוואידמעט דעם לייענער און וואָס הייסט טאַקע „לייענער דערמאָנען זיך לידער". אַ דאַנק דעם דאָזיקן קאָנטאַקט, ווערן אָפֿט די לייענערס פֿאַרוואַנדלט אין מאַטיוויורטע זאַמלערס און אינפֿאָרמאַנטן, און ווערן אַ טייל פֿון דעם נישטערן און פֿאָרשן - אַן אָפּקלײַב פֿון די מאַטעריאַלן געדרוקט אין דעם ערשטן אַנדערטהאַלבן יאָר פֿון דעם אָפּטיילס קיום איז אַרוים אין תל-אָבֿיבֿ אין 1974 אונטערן נאָמען פּערל פֿון דער ייִדישער פּאָעזיע און באַוויזט באַשעמפּערלעך אַז אַזאַ מיטאַרבעט צווישן פֿאָרשערס (די מלאָטעקס האָבן זיך טאַקע באַניצט מיטן פּסעוודאָנים „א. פֿאָרשער") און לייענערס איז מעגלעך און קען צוטראָגן גאָר אַ סך צו לידער-ביאָגראַפֿיעס.

קומט טאַקע אַ האַרציקן יישר-כוח פֿאַר די צונויפֿשטעלערס פֿאַר זייער דערגאַנצונגס-אָפּקלײַב. לאָמיר זיי ווינטשן לאַנגע און געזונטע יאָרן פֿון שעפֿערישקייט און פֿון קעגנזײַטיקע קאָנטאַקטן מיט אַ וואַקסנדיקן עולם פֿון לייענערס, זינגערס, פֿאָרשערס.

פֿאָרװאָרט פֿון אליעזר װיזעל

ייִדישע לידער גייען, װי אייביקע תּפֿילות, פֿון דור צו דור, פֿון האַרץ צו מוח, פֿון מוח צו נשמה.

גייענדיק אָט־אַזױ, ברענגען זײ טרײסט צו פֿאַרמאַטערטע זקנים און פֿאַרחלומטע קינדער.

און נישט בלױז טרײסט ברענגען זײ, נאָר אױך פֿרײד און ליבשאַפֿט.

װער האָט דער ערשטער אױסגעזונגען אונדזערס אַ ליד?

די מאַמע, די טײַערע, װאָס האָט געװאַלט איר קינד אײַנשלעפֿערן?.

אָדער דער װאַנדערער װאָס האָט, אין שקיעה־שעהען, זײַן חלום פּרובירט באַלײַכטן מיט שטראַלן פֿון אַמאָל?

אפֿשר גאָר דער חסיד װאָס האָט מיט זײַן ניגון דעם שבת, בײַ שלש סעודות, מיט אַלע כּוחות באַגערט צוריקצוהאַלטן?

זאָגט ,,ייִדיש ליד" און איר דערמאָנט זיך אָן אײַערע קינדער־יאָרן.

זאָגט ,,ייִדיש ליד" און סיװילט זיך מיט אײַך מיטזינגען ־ נאָסטאַלגישע לידער: ,,אױפֿן פּריפּעטשיק", ,,ראָזשינקעס מיט מאַנדלען", ,,מאַטעלע" און טאַקע מרדכי געבירטיגס ,,עס ברענט, אױ, ברידערלעך, עס ברענט".

דבֿקות־ניגונים, נשמה־לידער, אַרבעטער־לידער: ס'איז אַ גאָרטן מיט פֿיל בײמער, אַ בוך מיט פֿיל קאַפּיטלען, אַ פּאַלאַץ מיט אַ סך צימערן.

פֿון װאַנען שטאַמט מײַן ליבשאַפֿט צום ייִדישן ליד? ס'איז עלטער װי מײַן ליבשאַפֿט צו מוזיק ־ ס'איז װי אַן אוצר װאָס מע געפֿינט די סטרונעס פֿון אַ צעטלאָזן פֿידל.

דאָס ייִדישע ליד איז דער יום־טובֿ פֿון דער ייִדישער שפּראַך און די עקשנותדיקע אַנטשלאָסנקייט גובר צו זײַן ייִאוש און רעזיגנאַציע.

301

דאָס בוך איז ארויסגעגעבן
אַ דאַנק דער ברייטהאַרציקער מתנה פֿון
וויליאַם ווערניק אין אָנדענק פֿון
זײַן באַליבטער פֿרוי
רות ווערניק

און גרעסערע בײַשטײַערונגען פֿון:

פֿיליפּ איידעלמאַן, ניו־יאָרק

אַרבעטער־רינג דרום־ראַיאָן קולטור־פֿונדאַציע, פֿלאָרידע

אסתּר בורשטיין, ברוקלין, ניו־יאָרק

סענדער, ע״ה, און מינדל וויסמאַן, נאָרט מיאַמי־ביטש, פֿלאָרידע

וויקטאָר זאַלצמאַן, מאַרגייט, פֿלאָרידע
אין אָנדענק פֿון זײַן באַליבטן ברודער שלמה און שװעגערין בערניס

אַרנאָלד זיסק, האָלאַנדייל, פֿלאָרידע
אין אָנדענק פֿון זײַן באַליבטער פֿרוי ראָז

מאָטל און ד״ר עמא זעלמאַנאָוויטש, בראָנקס, ניו־יאָרק

אַבֿרהם און יצחק לוסקי און משפּחות, שאַרלאָט, נאָרט קאַראָלײַנאַ
אין אָנדענק פֿון זייערע באַליבטע עלטערן ישׂראל און פֿייגל לוסקי

נאָע לעווין, מיאַמי־ביטש, פֿלאָרידע

אַבֿרהם פֿײַמאַן, עליזאַבעט, נ.דזש.

שׂרה פֿרידמאַן, דעטרויט, מישיגען
אין אָנדענק פֿון איר באַליבטן מאַן משה

הערי און מאַרעלין קייגין, קליוולאַנד, אָהײַאָ

שעלבי שאַפּיראָ, וואַשינגטאָן, ד.ק.

משה שיוועק, מאָנטרעאַל, קוויבעק
אין אָנדענק פֿון זײַן באַליבטער מוטער מילדרעד

Joseph Mlotek

Yiddish author, poet and pedagogue. Presently Managing Editor of the Yiddish *Forverts*, author of its column "In the World of Yiddish" and co-author of column "Pearls of Yiddish Poetry" since 1970. Educational Director Emeritus of the Workmen's Circle; author of Yiddish textbooks and records, co-editor of Yiddish song and poetry anthologies *Pearls of Yiddish Song; Perl fun der yidisher poezye;* editor of *Kultur un Lebn*. Director of the Committee for the Revitalization of Yiddish Culture in the former Soviet Union, member of the Editorial Staff, *Di Tsukunft*.

Eleanor Chana Mlotek

Ethnomusicologist and folklorist. Music Archivist of the YIVO Institute for Jewish Research. Co-Editor with Joseph Mlotek of column "Pearls of Yiddish Poetry" in the Yiddish *Forverts*. Co-compiler of six anthologies of Yiddish song and poetry, including *Mir Trogn A Gezang, Pearls of Yiddish Song* and *Perl fun der yidisher poezye*. Author of a number of research papers on Yiddish folksongs.

Both compilers have been the recipients of a number of awards: from the National Foundation for Jewish Culture, Atran Foundation of the Congress for Jewish Culture, Folk Arts Institute of the YIVO Institute for Jewish Research. Joseph Mlotek, moreover, has received the Manger Prize for Yiddish Literature, Tel-Aviv, the Beth Sholem Aleichem Prize, Tel-Aviv, and the Dr. Hirsh Rosenfeld Prize, Montreal.

לידער פֿון דור צו דור:
נײַע פּערל פֿון ייִדישן ליד

מיט טעקסטן, מוזיק, טראַנסליטעראַציע, ענגלישע איבערזעצונגען,
באַמערקונגען און גיטאַר-אַקאָרדן

חנה און יוסף מלאָטעק

איבערזעצונגען	בערל זומאָף
מוזיק-רעדאַקטאָר	זלמן מלאָטעק
אילוסטראַציעס	צירל וואַלעצקי

אַרויסגעגעבן פֿון אַרבעטער-רינג
ניו-יאָרק